A General List of Neat[?]
Park Estate Mak 1 Jan[?]

No.	Names	Age	No.	Names	Age	No.	Names
	Needham	13	39	Nelson	6	77	Sajeant
	James	14	40	Royal	6		Thomas
	Monday	14		Frank	6		Namby
	Roger	17		Pitts	6	88	Morgan
5	Phillip	11		Ebony	6		Needham
	Lloyd	11		Johnston	6		Caesar
	Jackson	10	45	Redman	6		Toby
	Soldier	10		Garrison	9		Lomas
	Mumbay	10		Broad	5	85	Chuckey
10	Cole	10		Powers	5		Toney
	Saturday	10		Major	5		Gold
	Matcham	10	50	Sinclair	5		Nago
	Whynot	13		Pinnock			Robbin
	Billy	11		Joe	9	90	Jamaica
15	Cremen	9		Anthony	5		Marshall
	Dawkins	9		Blackwall	5		Billy
	Coward	9	55	Stephen			Traveller
	Nature	9		Cricket	5		Spaniard
	Saltpond	9		Pizarro	5	95	Duke
20	Walter	9		Spider	5		Ned
	Portland	9		Blood	5		Madcap
	Hazard	9	60	Rabbit	5		George
	William	8		Robin			Davis
	Ring	8		Freeman	5	100	Harry
25	Fairbairn	8		Driver	5		Warwick
	Doctor	8		Dice	5		Cornwall
	John	8	65	Sampson	5		Cambridge
	Hector	8		Tom	5		Hampshire
	Sam	7		Harvey	5	105	Cooper
30	Leaving	7		Darby	5		Lanthorn
	Dover	7		Blackman	5		Nero
	Bash	7	70	Morrice	5		Brindle
	Wine	7		John	5		Whynot
	Baldy	7		Hannah	5	110	Sam
35	Camel	7		Golburn	8		Monday
	Hart	7		Peter			Silvar
	Sly	6	75	Sampson			Boatman
38	Rodney	6	76	Wanting		114	Ring

A JAMAICAN PLANTATION

The History of
Worthy Park
1670–1970

Lluidas Vale, looking south during crop time. Worthy Park factory is in the upper centre, Lluidas Vale village beyond. In the foreground is the site of Swansea Estate; to the right, Tydixon; in the left background, Thetford. The road in the centre of the picture leads from St. Ann's and Camperdown to Point Hill, Guanaboa, and Spanish Town; the Ewarton road is to the left, the Croft's Hill road to the right background. The 1,250-foot contour completely encloses the valley.

A JAMAICAN PLANTATION

The History of
Worthy Park
– 1670–1970

MICHAEL CRATON

AND

JAMES WALVIN

University of Toronto Press

© Michael Craton & James Walvin, 1970

First published in Canada and the United States
by University of Toronto Press,
Toronto and Buffalo

ISBN 0 8020 1727 4

Printed in Great Britain

Contents

List of Illustrations

Preface

Few institutions and fewer individuals have a sense of being part of history: generally we build for our sons and grandsons, not for three hundred years. Yet on 28 November 1970, Worthy Park celebrates its tercentenary, the publication of this book being designed to coincide with the event. Rare is the West Indian sugar estate with a continuous history half as long and, even more remarkably, no existing estate has hitherto had its full history written.[1] For a description and explanation of the unique continuity of Worthy Park we offer the book which follows; yet how the book itself came about also requires some explanation.

The Jamaican climate is inimical to paper records. Patents, wills, and deeds the Government kept, and these have narrowly survived the ravages of heat, damp, insects, earthquakes, and periodic neglect. Records kept on estates have been less fortunate. The planters were notoriously unlettered, writing—or paying someone to write—only what they had to. Business records, in any case, begin to die as the transactions they record are completed. With the collapse of the business itself, they become corpses without mourners, thrown into a corner and then shovelled out as garbage like deconsecrated bones.[2] Worthy Park has been exceptional in this as in other respects, though in the preservation of its business records chance has played as large a part as calculation.

The earliest owners of Worthy Park were no better than the majority of their peers in keeping for posterity records of their estate management and business transactions. But in the fifth generation, Rose Price of Penzance set a standard which has been followed for most of the subsequent seven generations. On 9 April 1795, on leaving Jamaica to become an absentee, he wrote the following for the benefit of his Attorney and Overseer at Worthy Park:

There are always five separate books to be kept on Worthy Park viz: a great Plantation Book, a store book, a Boiling House Book, a still House Book, and a Daily labour Book. I have left five compleat Books on the Estate & I request that when they are filled with writing that five more may be purchased or written home for, and that the old ones may be carefully laid up, as the Books of the Estates are the only Records by which future generations can inform themselves of the management of the Plantations.[3]

Rose Price wrote in an age of optimism; but Worthy Park went out of the Price family in 1863, changed hands again in 1899, and was sold for a third and final time in 1918. For much of this period, conditions in the sugar industry were so depressed that the plantations seemed doomed to extinction and there was little purpose in informing future generations of their management. Records of wages, purchases, plantings, and production continued to be kept, but the ancient records disappeared from sight, to be rediscovered by accident many years later. In 1919, two boys were playing hide-and-seek in the loft of the book-keepers' barracks at Worthy Park when they stumbled over piles of grimy leather-covered tomes. Dragged into the sunlight and roughly brushed, they disclosed reams of copperplate; listing slaves and their conditions in the same terms as working steers, white men 'to save the deficiency' (whatever that might be), supplies from distant London, Bristol, Cork, and produce computed in archaic hogsheads, 'potts', and puncheons.

The two boys were Owen and George Clarke, destined in the fullness of time to be the owner-managers of Worthy Park, and in the 'great Plantation Books' they had uncovered material for a far more intriguing game of hide-and-seek. For nearly fifty years the notion that these books might become the basis for a history of the estate lay maturing in their minds. At last, in 1967, with the three-hundredth anniversary of the first grant only three years away, the present authors were introduced to the records and invited to do what they could. Fascinated as much by the closed society of Lluidas Vale and its roots as by the records themselves, they began their labours as soon as possible, working to the deadline of 28 November 1970. The rest was merely expenditure: vulgar things like money, and priceless commodities such as time and people's help.

At first the book was conceived as no more than a fattish pamphlet; and indeed a study, however elaborate, strictly limited to a single estate would amount to little more than an extended footnote to Jamaican history. Yet the project grew as research spread outwards, disclosing neglected, underworked, or misunderstood areas for which Worthy Park provided an excellent case study or corrective. Humbly, the authors suggest that the completed book is at least a sequence of footnotes. It may help to illuminate the foundation of West Indian sugar plantations, and their 'slave society', which consisted of both the politicking plantocracy and the imported Africans whom they owned but did not understand. It may also say something valuable of the management of estates and their Negro work-forces, and the persistent ways in which attitudes and methods survived nominal emancipation and the onset of modern technology; of the impact of what the 'imperialists' called colonial independence, and something even of what the future may hold in store. If this book has succeeded, it is not just the story of a single Jamaican plantation and its people over three hundred years; it is a history, from the inside out, of Jamaica, of the British West Indies, and of the sugar industry which dominated the economy so long and has done so much, for good or evil, to shape West Indian society.

Research, begun at Worthy Park, quickly led on to Spanish Town, Kingston, and then to Washington, D.C., London, Cornwall, and even (by proxy) to Sydney, Australia. This scattering of materials between colony, metropolis, and elsewhere has always been the bugbear of West Indian scholarship: it was complicated in this instance by the fact that the co-authors lived in Canada and England respectively. The book therefore became something of an exercise in triangulation.

The Canada Council gave two invaluable grants to aid research and publication. Mr. Clinton Black and his assistants in the Jamaican Archives, the whole staff of the Institute of Jamaica, and Mr. Whittingham of the Jamaican Island Record Office went beyond the call of duty to render assistance. The staffs of the Library of Congress in Washington, the Public Record Office, Historical Manuscripts Commission, and Public Record Office in London, the Public Library in Penzance, and the Mitchell Library in Sydney demonstrated the efficiency and courtesy they habitually show all serious researchers. Mrs. Ann Diebel and Miss Heather McLeod of Waterloo undertook some of the typing, and Mr. Pat Henriques some of the tedious transcription of deeds and wills in the Jamaican Island Record Office. Besides these, many individuals offered material, comments and advice, particularly Mr. J. F. A. Mason of Christ Church, Oxford, Lieutenant-Colonel Robin Rose Price of Ascot, Berkshire, Professors D. G. Hall of the University of the West Indies, Richard B. Sheridan of Kansas and Richard S. Dunn of Pennsylvania and several colleagues and senior students of the authors in the Universities of Waterloo, Ontario, and York, England.

The completion of *A Jamaican Plantation*, however, would not have been possible without the help and encouragement of the management of Worthy Park, particularly that of George F. Clarke, the Chairman and Managing Director of Worthy Park Farms, who gave every possible aid, withheld nothing, and quarrelled with nothing but errors of fact. When such a work as this is eventually finished, some feeling of dissatisfaction is normal, and salutary; but it is a rare history project in which the authors find so much peripheral pleasure in research and writing that they are sorry when the time is up and the book is irreversibly committed to print. For the defects of the work the authors must be wholly responsible; for any merits which it may possess, a large share of the credit must go to the Clarkes and the other people of Worthy Park—of all sorts and conditions—to whom the book is sincerely dedicated.

NOTES

[1] The masterly *A West India Fortune*, by Richard Pares (London, Longmans, 1950), is the nearest equivalent to the present book, and has been a constant *beau ideal*. It deals, however, with the fortunes of the Pinney family as planters in Nevis and merchants in England from the seventeenth to the middle of the nineteenth centuries, not with their estates as such.

[2] Any eighteenth-century materials still left on West Indian estates are rare indeed, but there are a scattered few transferred into safer keeping. The Dawkins Papers, for example, consigned to the Institute of Jamaica by the Sugar Manufacturers' Association, would provide an excellent basis for a monograph.

[3] *Worthy Park Plantation Book*, 1791–1811, Library of Congress, Washington, D.C.

Introduction

J amaica is a land of wood and water but mountainous too. In crossing the island most of the roads are forced to climb thousands of feet to negotiate the central ranges of igneous rock and limestone. 'The ideas people in Great Britain entertain of Jamaica having chiefly taken their rise from the information of those who have only visited the low lands, are in general very ill founded,' wrote Dr. John Quier in 1768. 'The internal part of the island is very high, broken land, and in some places, the mountains rise to a prodigious height: between the hills are interspersed large beautiful vallies, generally well cultivated, and laid out in rich farms and plantations.'[1]

Driving over to the north coast of Jamaica from Kingston and Spanish Town, the present and former capitals, one quickly plunges into the vertiginous gorge of the Rio Cobre, emerging into the wide vale of Linstead, before beginning the laborious ascent of Mount Diablo, the highest point of the road. Nestling under the wild Diablo massif is the village of Ewarton, from which a second-class road branches westward towards the geographical centre of the island. For five miles this little-frequented road climbs sinuously over the forested mountain, before pausing dramatically on a final ridge. Below is spread out a flat valley several square miles in extent, its lush green oval totally surrounded by blue-green mountains. This is the Vale of

1

Lluidas, which is dominated by the factory and estate of Worthy Park, the subject of this history.

The egregious Dr. Quier, who lived in Lluidas Vale for more than fifty years, described the view to be seen from the road entering the valley with typical eighteenth-century enthusiasm: '. . . which ever way the eye is turned, it is regaled with an endless variety of pleasing prospects: below, the plain delights it with the regularity of art; if directed upwards, it is never tired with viewing the romantic scenes which arise from so agreeable an assemblage of mountains, capped with clouds, shaggy woods crowned with perpetual verdure, steep precipices and hanging rocks.'[2]

The beauty of the view has not changed much in two hundred years, though with the development of Worthy Park, the 'regularity of art' must have increased considerably. The scene still changes with the passage of the clouds, the sun, and the seasons, from hour to hour and day to day; but today its constant focus is the incongruous brick spire of the Worthy Park chimney, which between January and May trails a permanent black plume of smoke as the mills devour the 125,000 tons of sugar cane produced in Lluidas Vale and its neighbouring areas. Clustered around the silvery slabs and gantries of the factory are the red zinc roofs of the estate offices and the old central buildings of Worthy Park and the satellite roofs of the bungalows of managerial and senior staff, painted pastel green. Farther away are the neat rows of workers' wooden cottages and the higgledy-piggledy huddle of Lluidas Vale village, with its Post Office, police station, church, and school.

Three thousand people live in Worthy Park's valley, but buildings, mostly sheltered by shade trees, do not obtrude on its peaceful landscape. The most distinctive feature of Lluidas Vale remains the quadrilateral pattern of the canefields, in such marked contrast to the unkempt wooded cloak of the mountains. Altogether there are 225 separate cane-'pieces' belonging to Worthy Park, divided up by neat 'intervals', or field roads, totalling 1,500 acres but varying in size from one to 25 acres. In crop time they present a multicoloured patchwork, ranging from the rich browns of fresh ploughed land to the dull bronze of dead cut trash, the tender green of young cane shoots, and the emerald tinged with gold of the ripened crop.

Worthy Park's canefields produce 7,000 tons of sugar in an average year, yet the estate does not prosper on sugar alone. Around the cane, on a thousand acres of smooth green pasture and on twice that area of tussocky guinea grass in the meadowy glades of the lower mountain slopes, roam 1,500 head of pedigree beef cattle, under the supervision of black cowboys. On chosen slopes and margins march neat lines of citrus—all kinds, including ortaniques, deliciously blended from sweet oranges and tangerines—providing a third major product for the great estate, 375 acres in all. Worthy Park is a model of diversification and land utilization; even its one touch of extravagance, 70 acres of golf course and playing fields, is ingeniously trimmed with 40 acres of burgeoning citrus trees. The nearby air-strip is no extravagance at all, for it is from this 125 × 2,000-foot greensward that chartered Cessna aircraft frequently spray and fertilize the fields.

The intrepid aerial cropdusters, flying round the valley's dangerous rim, would be the first to point out that Lluidas Vale is neither so flat nor so nearly oval as it seems at first glance. A fallen piece of Jamaica's limestone piecrust, it is only flat and smooth in contrast to the 'cockpits', scarps, and potholes of the harsh tropical karst topography that encircles it. Although the valley is rich in alluvial soils and the marls and clays that are the result of aeons of action by the elements on the natural rock, the naked limestone lies beneath, and breaks the surface in small outcrops on the valley's western side.[3] As in the surrounding mountains, there is little surface water, though the paths of underground drainage are traced by numerous gullies, which act as run-offs in the occasional periods of flood. The only permanent stream entering the valley, the Murmuring Brook from Juan de Bolas Mountain, is tapped by the Worthy Park aqueduct and, deprived of most of its water, peters out in the largest of the gullies. This dry watercourse, crossing the valley in a loop, acts as a confluence for all the other gullies, before plunging straight into Lluidas Blue Mountain by the Ewarton Road. The rock-filtered sinkhole where the great gully disappears, is the chief geological curiosity of Lluidas Vale. Cartographers confidently, and geographers more tentatively, have identified the Lluidas gullies as sources of the Rio Cobre, which emerges from the limestone strata at Riverhead, two miles away and 200 feet lower than the Worthy Park sinkhole.[4]

Because of its elevation—some 1,150 feet above sea level—Lluidas is cooler and moister than the Jamaican plains. As Dr. Quier pointed out so accurately in 1768:

Here an European may enjoy as cool a climate as he can reasonably wish for. The hottest part of the year is from May to October, when the wind is south-easterly, with smart showers about noon, though sometimes no rain falls for some weeks. The nights are foggy, or rather the air being loaded with vapours which the heat of the day has caused it to absorb; and as the heat abates, being unable to suspend them any longer in intimate union with itself, that moisture is thrown off in the form of clouds, which are still augmented in this woody region, by the copious exhalations of the earth and vegetables, which retain warmth longer than the circumambient air; and these clouds hang about the upper part of the mountains till they are again united by the sun with the rest of the atmosphere, or are swept away by the morning breeze. At this time of year [January] the thermometer commonly stands, at sun-rise, at about 70° and rises by noon to some degrees above 80; but very seldom so high as 85° or 86°. In the months of May and October, it sometimes rains incessantly, and the weather is so raw and cold as frequently to render a fire necessary. In November or December, the north wind sets in, and continues until May. As long as this wind blows, the nights are clear, and the days are cool and dry, except that, now and then, a transient shower falls. Indeed, when this wind blows strongly, the cold is quite intense for this latitude, and obliges us to keep a constant fire. On the 15th of this instant (January at 7 o'clock in the morning), the mercury in my thermometer was depressed to 51° at this place. . . . A prodigious quantity of rain falls in the course of a year, and the air is always so moist that metals will rust, however great the care taken of them: lixivial salts can scarcely be so closely corked in bottles, but they will dissolve; and wearing apparel, and whatever else that is in the least liable to grow mouldy, is kept in chests; and, where the air is confined, cannot be preserved from it but by frequently exposing them to the sun. In the low lands it rains but seldom, and when it does, it descends in torrents; but in the mountains, the rain falls oftener and more gradually. In the summer months it thunders and lightens often, though seldom violently. . . .[5]

Lluidas Vale, in other words, has one of the most fortunate climates to be found in the Caribbean, and rarely suffers those climatic extremes which make living in the tropics such an adventure and a trial. Worthy Park's mean average temperature is 73°, compared with Kingston's 78°, and its annual rainfall 60 inches, compared with 29 inches for downtown Kingston, and an extreme for the north-easterly slopes of the Blue Mountains of 252 inches. Sheltered by its mountain ramparts, Lluidas has not suffered a devastating hurricane in living memory, though notable floods occur about every fourth year, when the gullies course like giant brown snakes and a third of the valley round the over-taxed sinkhole is washed by waters up to 80 feet deep.[6]

Even in normal times, most of the gullies are easily traced by the groves of riverine trees and dense tropical undergrowth which flourish in the rich alluvium of these unworkable lands, and meander with apparent indecision across the precise rectangles of the sugar fields. Standing proudly above the rest are magnificent stands of bamboo up to 75 feet in height, planted since the eighteenth century to prevent soil erosion, and now one of the most arresting features of the landscape.

It is not just the feathery upsurges of bamboo that one would have to erase from the mind's eye in visualizing Lluidas Vale in its natural state, before the settlers came. Of the species of tree found in the valley, barely half are indigenous, and some of the original types have long since disappeared, axed for their valuable timbers. Over the past three centuries, the tropics have been scoured for trees and plants suitable for the West Indies which, finding an almost ideal habitat in Jamaica, have come to be regarded as native growths: timber, shade and ornamental trees such as logwood, cashew, casuarina, royal palm, imortelle; fruit trees such as coconut, citrus, mango, tamarind, breadfruit, banana, coffee, and the sugar-cane itself; and the flowering trees and shrubs that make parts of the valley a vivid green—bougainvillea, hibiscus, oleander, poinsettia, thunbergia. Even the pasture grasses were mostly imported: guinea grass from West Africa, and the bluish pangola from Natal.[7]

What then was Lluidas Vale like in 1670, when the first English settlers took out their patents for its valuable land? The mountains with their dense scrub and forest cannot have changed much, but the earliest plans show that the forest was originally much wider in extent. When they made the rough surveys sufficient for the 'plats' registered in the parish records under their names, the early settlers usually stated the character of their lands, and from the Plat Book of the Parish of St. John it seems that most of the acreage in Lluidas where sugar is now grown, and much of the pasture, too, was originally designated 'wood'. Only on the western side of the valley and in two patches to the north-east and south were found 'savannah', 'cutting grass', and 'ruinates'.[8]

The most fertile soils grew the richest woodland, and today it is only in remote pockets that such a luxuriant growth can be found as must once have almost covered the Vale of Lluidas: groves of wide-spreading guango, ba'cedar, budge gum, mahoe; timber trees prospering far from the woodman's axe, such as mahogany, cedar, braziletto; and towering above the rest, trees such as were used for boundary markers on the earliest plans, cotton trees, bullet trees, fiddle woods, santa marias. A hundred kinds of tropical shrub competed with the trees for space, and trunk, limb and branch were webbed together in an impenetrable tangle of epiphytes and parasites, choking grasses, hanging roots, and strangling vines. Everywhere were garish flowers and edible fruits unknown to Europeans in 1491.[9]

In the green twilight of the forests and out in the bright light of the savanna flew most of the 200 species of bird native to Jamaica, some of which the earliest travellers described as being tame as pets. Among the trees and around the rocks of the savanna scuttled the agouti, a tail-less rodent, and the iguana, a giant lizard, both prized as delicacies by the Indians but exterminated by the white men and their dogs. By the seventeenth century their place had been taken by the fierce wild hogs and the scrawny cattle that were the descendants of the animals re-leased by the Spaniards in the early days to provide fresh meat, which had multiplied hugely in the almost trackless wastes of the interior.

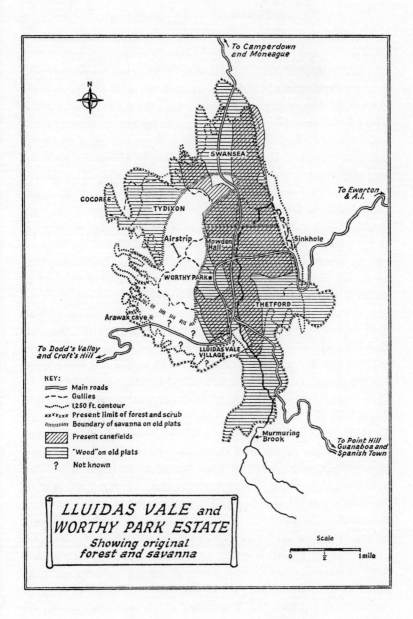

Only the hardiest of the Spanish 'cowkillers' ventured as far inland as Lluidas Vale, and none of them settled in the valley itself.

Indeed, it was the English, with their tireless quest for fertile lands, their axes and saws and slaves to wield them, who first proved the valley of Lluidas an ideal site for habitation. The Arawaks, who populated Jamaica several thousand years ago and probably numbered about 9,000 before Columbus came in 1494,[10] could not have found the valley an attractive place to live. These peaceful aboriginals knew no hard metals and had no way of felling timber save by fire. They needed running water, open spaces to provide protection from insects, and easily cultivated land; but above all they needed the sea. They were fearless seagoers, and travelled freely from place to place on the coasts in their cottonwood dugouts. They cultivated cassava and ate the guavas, sapodillas and other fruits that grew wild in profusion around them; but seafood provided most of their protein. Of the dozens of permanent Arawak sites identified in Jamaica, none has yet been found farther than five miles from the sea, and the 'kitchen middens' of all those explored have produced merely the remains of turtles, fish, and shell-fish and the occasional bones of agouti and iguana.[11]

The Arawaks from time to time did venture inland, following the valley bottoms and the ridges of the hills above the densest of the bush. Their remains have been found in twenty to thirty inland caves throughout Jamaica, nearly all more than 1,000 feet above sea level. The high interior of the island obviously held some special significance for the Jamaican Arawak, for the remains in the caves consist almost exclusively of crude graffiti, or 'petroglyphs', and carved black wooden 'zemis' connected with obscure Arawak rituals. Worthy Park, close to the heart of Jamaica, possesses such an arcane shrine, a shallow cave in a free-standing limestone hillock close to the Dodd's Valley road, where some petroglyphs in human shapes were recently found.[12]

It would be beguilingly easy to trace a connection between the Arawak migrations to Lluidas Vale and the tiny quantities of gold found in the igneous outcrops of the Point Hill region,[13] or even panned in specks from the Murmuring Brook; but unfortunately no evidence has come to light either in the early Spanish writings or the findings of archeologists that the Jamaican Arawaks even knew of the existence of gold. Another hypothesis that is most likely a myth is that which identifies remnants of Arawak blood in the veins of contemporary Jamaicans, particularly the proud Maroons of Trelawny and Portland. Las Casas—though prone to exaggeration—claimed as early as 1533 that only a hundred Jamaican Arawaks remained.[14] Few, if any, of these could have survived a further fifty years, and the chances of miscegenation with African Negroes imported as slaves by the Spaniards, were minimal.

Almost certainly, the ancestors of the present Maroons were two or three bands of Spanish Negroes, rough cowboys who roamed the interior with lances and bows, and who, though technically slaves, were as free and unmanageable as the wild beasts they hunted. One such band, under the almost legendary Juan Lubolo—alias Juan de Bolas—first populated the southern approaches of Lluidas Vale, around the time of the coming of the English in 1655. Juan Lubolo's squadron of irregular scouts, which never totalled more than 200 and gradually declined in numbers, established their *pelincos*,[15] or smallholdings, close to the fresh water of the Murmuring Brook. They farmed the open hillsides for cassava and maize, and rode out occasionally into the Lluidas savanna to round up the cattle and slaughter the hogs they had probably come to regard as their own. A rudimentary road—traceable today in the track from Juan de Bolas to Tydixon—was delineated on the earliest English grants, and this may have been the path first trodden by the followers of Juan Lubolo, or even by the Arawaks.

Lluidas Vale in 1655 was an almost perfect fastness, approachable only by the defiles of Point Hill in the south, Dodd's Valley in the west and Camperdown in the north. Yet Juan Lubolo's pitiful little band had neither the numbers nor the will to defend the valley after the Spaniards left Jamaica. Their few *pelincos* west of the Point Hill road were all that stood between the English settlers and the rich heartland of Lluidas Vale, once the settlers had defeated the Spaniards on the plains and began their relentless march into the Jamaican mountains.

NOTES

[1] J. Quier, J. Hume and others, *Letters and essays . . . on the West Indies by different practitioners*, London, J. Murray, 1778, xxvi.

[2] Ibid., xxvii. John Quier was born in England in 1738 or 1741 and educated at the University of Leyden. After a spell in the Army he went to Jamaica in 1767 and set up a practice based at Shady Grove, Lluidas, where he lived until his death in 1822. A widely-respected slave doctor and Member of the Assembly, he was a pioneer in inoculation for smallpox. See *Royal Gazette*, Jamaica, 21 September 1822; Heinz Goerke, 'The life and Scientific Works of Dr. John Quier, Practitioner of Physic and Surgery, Jamaica, 1738–1822', *West Indian Medical Journal*, V, xviii, 22–7.

[3] This type of interior valley in a predominantly karst topography is called a *polje*. Lluidas is such an outstanding example of the form that it has been used as an illustration in the forthcoming *International Geographical Atlas*.

[4] In fact, there is another small drainage basin at Old Woman's Savanna, three miles to the west of Worthy Park and three hundred feet higher, that may in turn provide Lluidas, and the Cobre, with some of its water. See R. M. Bent and E. L. Bent-Golding, *A Complete Geography of Jamaica*, London, Collins, 1966.

[5] Quier, op. cit., xvii–xxx. The reliability of Worthy Park's rainfall is still attributed to the surrounding forest cover, if not quite for the reason ascribed by Dr. Quier. On 9 February 1968, the temperature at Worthy Park at 5 a.m. was 45·3°, the lowest on record.

[6] Bent and Bent-Golding, op. cit.; Worthy Park Farms Meteorological Station Records; The Sugar Manufacturers of Jamaica Limited Research Department monthly rainfall reports; J. F. Brennan and others, *The Rainfall of Jamaica, 1870–1939*, Kingston, 1943. Records have been kept at Worthy Park continuously since 1877, and there are now eight sub-stations.

[7] A useful introduction is Dorothy P. Storer, *Familiar Trees and Cultivated Plants of Jamaica*, London, Macmillan, for the Institute of Jamaica, 1958.

[8] St. John's Parish Plat Book, 1665–1705: 1/72, 105, 128, 144, 147, 150, 151, 157, 160, 168, 170, 197, 200, 213. See below, II, 35. Since ruinates strictly are overgrown cultivations, areas so designated may well have been planted before.

[9] Sir Hans Sloane (1660–1753) gave the best early description of the animal and plant life of Jamaica: *A Voyage to the Islands Madera, Barbados, Nieves, S. Christophers and Jamaica, with the Natural History . . . of the last of those Islands*, etc., 2 vols., London, 1702, 1725, especially I, vii–cliv; *Catalogus plantarum quae in insula Jamaica sponte proveniunt*, etc., London, 1696. Another pioneer natural historian was Patrick Browne, *The Civil and Natural History of Jamaica*, etc., 3 vols., London, 1756.

[10] Ronald L. Vanderwal, 'Problems of Jamaican Pre-History', *Jamaica Journal*, XI, 3 September 1968, 10–13, dismisses earlier estimates of 60,000.

[11] Robert R. Howard, 'Introduction to the Archeology of Jamaica', *American Antiquity*, XXXI, 2, 1966; J. E. Duerden, 'Aboriginal Indian Remains in Jamaica', *Journal of the Institute of Jamaica*, II, 4 July 1897; Irving Rouse, 'The West Indies', in J. H. Steward (ed.) *Handbook of South American Indians*, V, Washington, Smithsonian Institution, 1948, 495–565; F. Morales Padrón, *Jamaica Española*, Seville, Escuela de Estudios Hispano-Americano, 1952, 25–6.

[12] A *zemi* found in an interior cave in 1757, and two others found in 1792 at

Spots in the Carpenter Mountains in the west of Jamaica, were discovered facing east, that is, towards the centre of the island. All three are now in the British Museum.

[13] H. R. Hose, *Geology and Mineral Resources of Jamaica*, Kingston, 1951; V. A. Zans, *Economic Geology of Jamaica*, Kingston, 1951; Geological Survey Department, *Synopsis of the Geology of Jamaica*, Kingston, 1962.

[14] Fr. B. de las Casas, *Historia de las Indias*, II, vi; *Brevissima relación de la destruyción de las Indias*, 10; Padrôn, op. cit., 259–62.

[15] Alias the Spanish spelling *palenques*, or the anglicization 'polincks'. At least as late as 1789 the word was used to describe smallholdings on marginal land growing provisions or raising small stock. *Pp 1731–1800, H. C., xxvi, 1789, 646 a, III.*

CHAPTER ONE

The Coming of the English

During the 161 years of Spanish rule the potential of Jamaica had hardly begun to be tapped. The island, soon to be the most valuable of all British colonies, was regarded by the Spaniards as of less worth than neighbouring Hispaniola and Cuba, which in turn were less desirable than the mainland colonies of Mexico and Peru. Visited irregularly for the smoked beef and pork, hides and tallow for which it was noted, Jamaica was not on the customary routes of the *flota* and *galeones* which served the more prosperous colonies. Its strategic importance and its vulnerability should have been recognized after the raids by English corsairs in 1597, 1603, and 1643,[1] but nothing effective had been done before the invasion of 1655.

At the end of the Spanish period the population of Jamaica was no more than 2,500, including women, children, and slaves,[2] a total that was outnumbered three-to-one by the invading forces under Admiral Penn and General Venables. Santiago de la Vega—the present Spanish Town—the only town, was said to contain 500 houses, but this was almost certainly an exaggeration. The remainder of the Spaniards lived within twenty miles of the capital, at Liguanea, Anaya (May Pen), Yama (Vere), and Guanaboa, or in *hatos*, ranches, scattered thinly over the southern plains, in the regions of Guatibacoa (Clarendon Plains),

Pereda (Pedro Plains), Ayala (Yallahs), or as far afield as the present Westmoreland and Morant Bay. The north shore of Jamaica was practically deserted, the first settlement at Sevilla la Nueva (St. Ann's Bay) having been abandoned in 1534. In 1611, the Abbot of Jamaica wrote:

... The whole of the rest of the island which is about 50 leagues long and little more than 15 wide is uncultivated and uninhabited, though there are many hunting grounds of horned stock in which the colonists have their shares in proportion to the ranches they formerly had stocked with tame cattle from which have sprung those that are now wild in these grounds. Nearly the whole year is taken up in killing cows and bulls only to get the hides and fat, leaving the meat wasted. There are also large herds of swine raised in the mountains, which are common to all who may wish to hunt them as is ordinarily done, obtaining therefrom a great quantity of lard and jerked pork. ...[3]

The chief deficiency from which Jamaica suffered under the Spaniards was that of a merchant marine.[4] Without even a handful of coasting vessels to carry products from place to place on the coasts or across the narrow reaches to Santo Domingo or Santiago de Cuba, Jamaica could not develop plantations and her rich resources of timber went untapped. Some pimento and cacao was grown, and a small surplus of cassava, which served as the local bread, but these were insufficient to encourage a flourishing export trade. Likewise, there were several sugar mills in the island when the English arrived, but their products were almost all consumed locally. The only benefit Jamaica gained from her obscurity was the cheapness of her provisions; an *arroba* of cassava seldom cost more than four reales, and as much as 52 pounds of the beef that was not wasted could be bought for a single *real*.[5]

The superb roadsteads of Kingston and Old Harbour in the populated south were seldom used by the Spaniards, and the inlets of the north shore were more often visited by foreign corsairs than by Spanish vessels. So destitute of shipping were the Jamaican Spaniards that they usually traversed the island overland on the infrequent occasions when it was necessary to visit the north shore. The common route is thought to have been a pathway up the valley of the Minho to

Old Woman's Savanna and then over to Moneague by way of the present Kellits and Bensonton, from which the harbours of Las Chorreras (Ocho Rios), Juracabesa (Oracabessa), and Sevilla could easily be reached.[6] There is, however, a possibility that the overland route used by the Spaniards went by Lluidas Vale. Once the terrain were known, the valley could easily have been reached from Santiago de la Vega, the Minho or Moneague, and certainly the Spaniards used it as a retreat and provision ground once the English had landed and taken their capital.

The Spaniards, with their militia of much less than a thousand men, were no match in the field for the 7,000 English soldiers who landed in Kingston Harbour on 10 May 1655. Despite the fact that the force under the command of Robert Venables was a motley mixture of discharged Cromwellian veterans and ill-disciplined adventurers from Barbados and the Leewards which had already failed ingloriously in an attempt to capture Hispaniola, the Spaniards did not offer any resistance at first. The Spanish Governor surrendered Santiago de la Vega and even sent supplies of cassava and beef to the English for some days; but this appears to have been a subterfuge to cover the flight of the non-combatants, while stouter souls retreated into the nearby hills to organize guerrilla resistance. In this the Negro cowcatchers were invaluable allies. Expert woodsmen, lancers, and archers, they proved to be as tenacious and dangerous foes as their descendants the Maroons were during the following century, and from their provision grounds at Lluidas they were able to succour the Spaniards hiding in the hills with cassava, maize, and smoked meat.

Having occupied the Spanish capital and sent out columns to ransack the *hatos* to the west, the English soon found that they were in a state far different from that of a victorious army. Poorly supplied from home, they were perpetually short of bread, not knowing how to prepare the growing cassava left behind by the Spaniards in their flight; and though they were surrounded by cattle they lacked the expertise to catch enough of the wily beasts. One of the disgruntled English officers even wrote home that they were 'starving in a cooks Shop'. Moreover, the Spaniards drove whatever cattle they could before

Driven cattle at Worthy Park. But for the breed of cow and the clothes of the 'cowboys' this scene might be of the estate in the seventeenth century, before the land was cleared and sugar grown. (*See Chapter One*)

1671 Map of Jamaica by John Seller. At that time the island was divided into only 14 parishes (precincts), of which two were as yet unnamed. Notice the cow being shot in the interior beyond St. John's

them, and their Negroes ambushed stragglers who went out hunting so that dozens were killed. Badly fed and intemperate, the soldiers had little resistance to disease and began to die in horrifying numbers, so that of the original 7,000 half were dead within six months, and barely 1,500 survived the first two years.[7]

Beleaguered, the English desperately turned to planting while the two commanders left for England to plead their cause.[8] Besides those unfortunate troops garrisoning unhealthy Santiago, regiments were sent out into the Liguanea Plain where Kingston now sprawls, to Angels at the entrance to the defile of the Rio Cobre, and to Guanaboa Vale, a small basin in the Red Hills to the north-west of the capital. Forays were organized and single soldiers or small parties were forbidden to go hunting for wild cattle, while the reluctant soldiery were set at the humiliating task of planting cassava. The best situated regiment was that at Guanaboa, first commanded by Colonel Anthony Buller and then in turn by Colonel Francis Barrington and Colonel Edward Tyson. Here, in a healthy angle of the Mountain River some 500 feet above sea level, were excellent soils which the Spaniards had long cultivated, and here the Guanaboa Regiment fought its lonely battle for survival against starvation, disease and the 'outlying Negroes' for five long years.

Eventually, planting prospered modestly in the Vale of Guanaboa and the survivors became 'seasoned' to the climate, the diet, and the disappointment of not becoming rich on plunder or veins of discovered gold. But the mountains and forests continued to belong to the Spaniards and their Negro allies who, after the death of Oliver Cromwell in 1658, redoubled their efforts to encourage the English invaders to forsake Jamaica. As late as 1660, small groups of Englishmen were ambushed by Spaniards around Guanaboa, and Colonel Barrington himself was killed by a jittery sentry. His successor, Colonel Tyson, determined to eradicate the Spanish threat for ever. The raids came mostly from the north, and ascending the Mountain River gorge with a large contingent of troops, Tyson came upon the Vale of Lluidas for the first time. There he discovered the 200 acres of cleared land from which Juan Lubolo and his followers were supplying the Spaniards.[9]

His *pelincos* captured and his faith in the Spaniards undermined, Juan Lubolo treated with the English. The price of his defection was formal confirmation of his leadership and a guarantee to his followers of their rights to their lands and of their rights as freemen.[10] These promises were incorporated into a proclamation by Deputy Governor Lyttleton three years later, which styled Lubolo Colonel of Black Militia and gave him the powers of a magistrate, and granted to all of his followers over 18 years of age, 30 acres of land.[11]

Reinforced and guided by 21 of Lubolo's Negroes, Edward Tyson led the fittest 80 of his men out of Lluidas over the mountains to the north coast. Travelling rapidly by way of the Camperdown valley and the basin of Moneague, the little band fell without warning on the Spanish camp near Las Chorreras. More than half the Spaniards were killed or captured and their commander, Don Cristobal de Ysassi, sued for a treaty to cover a Spanish evacuation. This, however, was rejected by Governor Doyley after the treacherous murder of an English emissary by a band of Negroes under Juan de Serras who remained faithful to the Spaniards, in their camp at Los Vermejales (Vera Ma Hollis). Ysassi and his pitiful remnant were forced to leave Jamaica as harried fugitives, setting sail in two large dugouts either from Oracabessa or Runaway Bay in April 1660.[12]

The indomitable Negroes from Vermejales continued to provide some resistance to the English occupation of Jamaica after the flight of the Spaniards. Intermittantly harassed by English columns, they never surrendered, spurning all overtures and falling back ever westward until they came to a refuge in the impenetrable Cockpit Country of Trelawny. They long remained a threat to the settlers of Guanaboa and their allies at Lluidas, ten miles farther north. Juan Lubolo himself was killed in an ambush by the followers of Juan de Serras, and as late as 1669 there were accounts of lightning raids on Guanaboa by bands of *cimarrones*.[13] By this time, however, the English occupation had become an irreversible fact.

In 1660, Charles II had been restored to the English throne, and with the change of allegiance and the defeat of the Spaniards the English garrison of Jamaica became dissatisfied with its status as a forgotten army of occupation, unreinforced, unsupplied and unpaid for almost three years. The Guanaboa Regiment, which contained a powerful element of Puritans reluctant to serve the King as faithfully as they had served the Cromwellian Protectorate,[14] in particular clamoured to be allowed to take out patents in land and realize the rich profits which they knew could be made from agriculture. Colonel Tyson himself was prevailed upon by a brother officer, Lieutenant-Colonel Raymond, to mutiny against the authority of Governor Doyley, who was so concerned with defence that he was thought to be unsympathetic towards planting, and so eager to be confirmed in his office that he was regarded as a turncoat by the stauncher Roundheads. As Governor Beeston later recounted, the Guanaboa faction began to 'set up for themselves, saying, they would live no more as an Army. And accordingly, August 2 [1660], they declared they would have the Island settled in Colonies, and make constables and civil officers.'[15]

With some difficulty, 'Raymond's Rebellion' was put down and both Raymond and Tyson were publicly shot after a court martial. But unrest continued in Guanaboa, and the protest of the two colonels was not entirely in vain. Governor Doyley officially disbanded the army in 1661, and in 1662 the first Royalist Governor, Lord Windsor, brought out with him generous provisions for the settlement of Jamaica. By a Royal Proclamation dated Whitehall, 14 December 1661, it was decreed that for the following two years 30 acres of land would be granted to any male or female over 12 years of age who would guarantee to plant them. The land was to be held in free tenure for ever, subject only to the payment of a nominal quit rent, the surrender of all gold and silver to the Crown and the payment of a 20 per cent duty on all fisheries and other mines. The only provisos were that the development of the lands must be begun within six months, and that the landholders were liable for militia service.[16]

With the sanction of Lord Windsor's Proclamation, the survivors of the Guanaboa and other Regiments turned more wholeheartedly to planting; and within a very few years the plantocratic basis of Jamaican society was laid. Although no direct connection can be proved, the parallels between the society developed in Jamaica after 1660 and that predicated in James Harrington's *Oceana* (published in 1656) are so close that it is tempting to call this new frontier society Harringtonian. *Oceana*, designed as a utopian model for post-revolutionary England, was even more applicable to an expanding imperial commonwealth in which land was the natural and original form of vested interest. Jamaica in particular was virgin territory, the result of a state-sponsored conquest, ripe for development by its 'conquerors'. In Harrington's utopia, primogeniture was no longer to be an inflexible rule of succession, so that younger sons had as much chance as the older; yet for the first time, property in land was to be directly geared to political power. Moreover, the militia was not only indispensable but directly tied to the degree of landowning and political power.

Whether we regard *Oceana* as a textbook or a commentary, it is worth remembering that Harrington wrote within a year of the conquest of Jamaica:

As he [Hobbes] said of the law, that without this sword it is but paper; so he might have thought of this sword, that without an hand it is but cold iron. The hand which holdeth this sword is the militia of a nation ... but an army is a beast that hath a great belly and must be fed; wherefore this will come into what pastures you have, and what pastures you have will come into the balance of propriety, without which the public sword is but a name or a mere spit-frog.[17]

The obligation of militia service was incorporated in royal decrees, and it was probably quite natural that the early settlers should retain some vestiges of their military origins; yet the identification of militia with social rank and political power seems to have gone far deeper in early Jamaica. As late as 1750, men were still given as titles the ranks they held in the local militia (the military capabilities of which were already laughable), and these ranks bore a direct relationship not only to their functions in the civil government but also, as a rule, to the size of their landholdings.

From the beginning it was obvious that neat parcels of 30 acres were impractical. Lands were uneven in quality and plantations as small as 30 acres could seldom be worked economically. Consolidation was

inevitable, and in this success went most readily to those planters with
the best resources of labour and capital. Consolidation was helped by
the tremendous mortality of the original holders, and by the number of
those with neither the capital nor will to work their holdings adequately. Having sold their lands to their rather more affluent seniors,
many disbanded soldiers either went off to serve as privateer crewmen,
or fell to the status of wage-earners or indentured servants. Since the
very first ventures in planting had been quasi-military operations in
which the private soldiers planted and reaped under the command of
their officers, it would have seemed quite natural that the 'other ranks',
once demobilized, should continue to work for their fomer military—
and present militia—officers.

Guanaboa Vale was typical of the early centres of English settlement
in Jamaica which, ordered to be close to the capital and to each other
for the purposes of defence, acted as nuclei for later expansion. The
Spaniards had used Guanaboa chiefly to grow cocoa, though the
valley had also produced indigo and provision crops. The English
adopted the Spanish cocoa 'walks', but seem to have lacked the expertise in the cultivation of the cacao tree which the Spaniards had acquired
from the Indians over the years, and gradually the cocoa walks at
Guanaboa fell victims to disease and neglect. Hans Sloane, writing of
the period around 1688, said that the only remaining cacao trees in the
valley were found on the margins of the plantations, grown through
lack of attention to a monstrous size.[18] The decline of cocoa at Guanaboa was probably speeded by the discovery of more suitable areas on
the north coast of Jamaica after 1670.[19] Likewise, indigo, a root producing a black dye that had an even more reliable sale in Engand than
cocoa, was found to grow much more easily around Vere in the
Clarendon Plains, which area soon gained almost a monopoly of
Jamaican indigo production.[20]

From the earliest years it was evident that sugar was potentially the
most profitable crop, at Guanaboa as in most parts of Jamaica. Sugar-
cane grew like a weed on cleared land, and the processes by which the
cane was made into molasses, muscovado and rum, while not simple,
were well known to the settlers from Barbados and the Leewards who

made up a large proportion of the early population. The British planters, moreover, were always served by a merchant fleet far more enterprising and flexible than that of the Spaniards.[21] Sugar, however, could only be worked economically on large plantations, and consequently needed far greater resources of land, labour, and capital than the production of cocoa, indigo, tobacco, pimento, and ginger, which were almost equally important in the early years.[22]

The almost inevitable progress towards consolidation and sugar monoculture which had already begun in Barbados was aided by the appointment of Sir Thomas Modyford as Governor of Jamaica in 1664.[23] Modyford was a wealthy Barbadian planter who had been agent for the Royal African Company for the supply of Negroes for Barbados, and he brought with him to Jamaica Instructions for the settlement of the island which he had evidently helped to frame. Modyford was authorized not only to ratify the original grants, but also to announce the throwing open of the huge areas reserved as Crown Lands to enterprising planters:

> The allotment of 400,000 acres of land for the Royal demesne to be suspended, for the better encouragement of the planters and those who will plant within five years, such grants to be under the broad seal of the island to the grantees and their heirs in free and common socage, reserving fit rents to the King; and a register theroff to be kept and sent home. . . .[24]

Settlers were to be exempt from English duties on their Jamaican produce until 1669, and spared the payment of any local duties on imports from England until 1685. To encourage the importation of white indentured labourers, each planter was to receive 30 acres for each 'servant' brought out, which allotment would devolve upon that fortunate individual if and when he completed four years' labour in Jamaica. The 'quit rent' to the Crown was fixed at a penny an acre per year, but even this moderate charge was only to be levied on land not merely 'planted' but also 'manured'. Thus, by the generous provisions of Modyford's Instructions, most of which were incorporated in an Act of the Jamaican Assembly in 1672,[25] the earliest settlers could take out patents for as much land as they could conceivably plant within the subsequent five years, and thereupon hold that land for ever on the most nominal payment. 'Planting', moreover, was never defined and always interpreted loosely, and so ineffectual were the means of checking which lands had been 'manured' that although within the first five years 209,000 acres were patented, only £150 had been collected in quit rents.[26]

Yet, though land was readily available to the early settlers—Mody-ford himself was the greatest of the patentees—labour and capital were so desperately short in Jamaica that sugar production did not dominate the economy until well after 1700. Although Bermuda and the Leewards (densely overpopulated), the workhouses of the English parishes, and even the prisons of Newgate and Bridewell were scoured for white indentured servants, disappointingly few went out to Jamaica, and even fewer lasted long on the Jamaican plantations.[27] In fact, after reaching a peak of 7,768 men, women, and children in 1673, the white population of Jamaica began an actual decline, falling as low as 1,400 after the French depredations of the 1690s, and not surpassing the 1673 total until the fourth decade of the eighteenth century. Although from about 1720 to the end of the eighteenth century the whites of Jamaica were outnumbered by slaves by ten to one, slaves were outnumbered by whites by three to one in 1660, only reached equal numbers around 1670, and by 1700 had scarcely achieved a numerical preponderance of five to one. In the early years of English settlement the supply of slaves to Jamaica fell chronically short of the demands of would-be planters.[28] Governor Modyford had been in-structed to persuade the Royal African Company to supply Jamaica with Negroes as it had supplied Barbados while he was agent there, but the Company was unwilling or unable to provide Jamaica with slaves at prices which the planters could afford, or to provide sufficient credit facilities. The real trouble was shortage of capital in Jamaica. In 1680, the Jamaican planters prevailed upon the British Government to order the Royal African Company to send up to 3,000 slaves a year to Jamaica for £18 each, at six months credit on good security; but the Company complained that the Jamaican planters already owed them £110,000.[29]

It was only after the Royal African Company lost its monopoly in 1698 and the private traders began to sell Negroes to Jamaica with credit extended up to a year and payment in sugar that the slave population soared and plantations spread like a forest fire.[30]

In 1670 the entire population of Jamaica was only about 13,700, of whom 1,500 were privateers, 1,200 women and children, and about 8,000 slaves and free Negroes.[31] The civil government of the island, however, was already well organized, in a form which James Harrington might have devised had he not been a republican and had he been considering a country but a fraction of the size of his Oceana. Jamaica was divided into twelve parishes, each with its *Custos Rotulorum* (a functionary equivalent to the Lord Lieutenant of an English county but with a seat in the Council), two Magistrates, constables, and two Members in the House of Assembly at Spanish Town. In the shortage of leadership, Magistrates and Members were often the same men.[32]

Guanaboa, with its church and vestry house, was the 'capital' of the Parish of St. John, which extended at that time from the vale of St. Thomas westwards to the Porus Mountains, and from the Red Hills outside Spanish Town northwards to Mount Diabolo.[33] Although it stretched into trackless 'waste', St. John's was among the most populous and prosperous parishes in the island in 1670, containing 83 white families and 996 persons in all. Of this total, there were altogether some 250 whites, 550 slaves, and 200 free Negroes in the Juan de Bolas *pelincos*.[34] In St. John's Parish more than 25,000 acres had already been patented—an eighth of the Jamaican total—with an average holding of approximately 300 acres.[35]

The parochial hierarchy of St. John's was already well established in 1670. Custos, Councillor, and Colonel of the Guanaboa Regiment of militia was John Cope, who held a large plantation in Guanaboa Vale; but close behind him in status were Major Thomas Ayscough, holder of 880 acres, J.P. and almost perennial Member of the Assembly, who commanded an independent troop of horse in the militia, Captain (later Colonel) Whitgift Aylmer, owner of 394 acres and also J.P. and M.H.A., and Lieutenant (later Captain and Major) Francis Price, sole owner of 175 acres at Guanaboa and partner in a holding of 150 acres in neighbouring St. Catherine's. All four of these rustic oligarchs were commissioned veterans of the Cromwellian army, seasoned survivors, and now modest planters growing a little cocoa and indigo and rather more sugar. Ayscough, Aylmer, and Price[36] were to be among the first to take advantage of Modyford's new patents and move from Guanaboa on to the Vale of Lluidas, and Francis Price was destined to be the founder of Worthy Park and of the Price dynasty that was to play a significant part in Jamaican history during the eighteenth and early nineteenth centuries.

NOTES

[1] Santiago was first captured and ransomed by Sir Anthony Shirley in 1597. In 1603, Captain Christopher Newport was repulsed by Melgarejo de Cordova, the Spanish Governor. In 1643, Santiago was captured and ransomed a second time, by Captain William Jackson, in reprisal for the Spanish sack of Old Providence in 1640. See Morales Padrón, op. cit., 245–50; Frank Cundall and Joseph L. Pietersz, *Jamaica Under the Spaniards*, Kingston, Institute of Jamaica, 1919, 19–20, 26–8; Vincent T. Harlow, 'The Voyages of Captain William Jackson, 1642–1645', *Camden Miscellany*, XIII (1923), 15–20.

[2] In 1611 the Abbot of Jamaica informed the King that the population was 1,500, made up of 523 Spanish adults, 173 Spanish children, 107 free Negroes, 74 Indians (probably from the Mosquito Coast), 558 slaves, and 75 foreigners (probably Portuguese Jews); Records of the Audiencia de Santo Domingo, 54-3-29, 79-4-6, Archivo General de Indias, Seville, quoted by Cundall and Pietersz, op. cit., 34.

[3] *Ibid.*, 35.

[4] Padrón, op. cit., 301–2, *Una riqueza sin flota.*

[5] Cundall and Pietersz, op. cit., 35. An *arroba* was approximately 25 pounds and a real was worth about six pence. This gives a value of less than a penny a pound for cassava and a halfpenny a pound for beef.

[6] This is the route traced, more by intuition than by documentation, by S. A. G. Taylor, *The Western Design, An Account of Cromwell's Expedition to the Caribbean*, Kingston, Institute of Jamaica for the Jamaica Historical Society, 1965, 193.

[7] C. H. Firth (ed.), *The Narrative of General Venables*, London, Longmans, for the Royal Historical Society, 1900, 39 and *passim*; S. A. G. Taylor, op. cit., 92.

[8] Admiral Penn left Jamaica on June 25, General Venables on July 4, 1655. Both were thrown into the Tower for desertion; *ibid.*, 73–4.

[9] E. Noel Sainsbury and others (eds.), *Calendar of State Papers, Colonial Series, America and the West Indies, 1574–1737*, 43 vols., London, Longmans and H.M.S.O., 1860–1963; Addenda, 1574–1670, 331, 132.

[10] Charles Leslie, *History of Jamaica*, London, 1740, relates the tradition that Juan Lubolo defected because his wife had been seduced by a Spaniard.

[11] Proclamation of 1 February 1663, Colonial Entry Books, 34, 75–9; 37, 27–8; *C.S.P. Col. A.W.I., 1661–8*, 412, p. 122.

[12] Cundall and Pietersz, op. cit., 94–103; S. A. G. Taylor, op. cit., 181–93.

[13] Information of John Stile to Secretary of State, *C.S.P. Col. A.W.I., 1669–74*, 181.

[14] As late as 1670, for example, the Council of Jamaica ordered the release from prison of two Quakers from Guanaboa; Minutes of Council, 26 January 1670, *C.S.P. Col. A.W.I., 1669–74*, 148.

[15] 'A Journal Kept by Col. William Beeston From His First Coming to Jamaica', *Interesting Tracts relating to the Island of Jamaica*, St. Jago de la Vega, 1800, 27 April 1660, 273.

[16] *C.S.P. Col. A.W.I., 1661–8*, 195.

[17] James Harrington, *Oceana*, edited by S. B. Liljegven, Heidelberg, 1924, 16.

[18] Sloane, op. cit., lxx–i.

[19] Cranefield, 'Observations on the Present State of Jamaica', C.O. 138/2 (1675).

[20] B.T. (Jamaica), 20 April 1700, *C.S.P. Col. A.W.I.*, XVIII, 347 (1700).

[21] Already, by 1670, 20 vessels over 80 tons visited Jamaica each year; Charles Modyford to Lord Arlington, 22 January 1670, *C.S.P. Col. A.W.I., 1669–74*. This total was to rise to over 250 a year by 1750, in response to increased sugar production.

[22] In Charles Modyford's report of 1670, cocoa, indigo and pimento were mentioned as Jamaica's chief products, ahead of sugar. After sugar came cotton, fustic, 'tortoise shell', braziletto, tobacco, ginger; *ibid.* By 1700, however, the value of the 13,000 hogsheads of sugar exported (£211,000) greatly exceeded the value of the second crop, indigo (£100,000). Pimento, ginger, cotton, annotto, and fustic together were valued at only £50,000, and cocoa was not even mentioned as an export crop; B. T. (Jamaica), 20 April 1700, *C.S.P. Col. A.W.I.*, XVIII, 347.

[23] Ironically, however, Modyford predicted an optimistic future for the smallholder in Jamaica, probably with the intention of attracting white servants and freemen to the island; 'A View of the Condition of Jamaica', *Journal of the House of Assembly* I, Appendix; Patterson, op. cit., 19.

[24] 18 February 1664, *C.S.P. Col. A.W.I., 1661–8*, 664. The original plat for Worthy Park (1670) was '. . . by Vertue of a Warrt from His Excellency Sᵣ Thomas Modyford Bᵗ etc. . . .'; St. John's Plat Book, 105/122. See below, II, 28.

[25] 'An Act for the better adjusting and more easy collecting of his majesty's quit rents &c. and taking out patents', May 1672, *Journal of Assembly*, I, 6. The procedure for taking out patents, however, was pretty well established already, the earliest dating from 1663.

[26] 'Survey of Jamaica', Charles Modyford to Arlington, 23 September 1670, *C.S.P. Col. A.W.I., 1669–74*, 99–103.

[27] White population of Jamaica: 1660, 4,400?; 1662, 3,653; 1664, 3,150; 1670, 4,200; 1673, 7,768; 1675, 5,500; 1695, 2,400; 1696, 1,390; 1740, c. 7–8,000; 1774, 20,500; H. Orlando Patterson, *Sociology of Slavery*, London, McGibbon and Kee, 1967, 17–18, 21, 23; *C.S.P. Col. A.W.I., 1574–1660*; Edward Long, *History of Jamaica*, London, 1774, I, 2, 2. Cf. G. W. Roberts, *Population of Jamaica*, Cambridge, 1957.

[28] Approximate Negro population of Jamaica: 1658, 1,400; 1664, 8,000?; 1673, 9,500; 1693, 40,000; 1740, 100,000; 1778, 205,000; Patterson, op. cit., 95.

29 Planters to Lords of Trade, 4 October; Journal of the Lords of Trade, 4 November 1680, *C.S.P. Col. A.W.I. 1677–80*, 1574.

30 Ironically, the price rose steadily. In 1700, the London merchants were accused of having destroyed the Royal African Company's monopoly by adopting the arguments of the planters, only to charge £34 a head for slaves on harsh credit terms; William Beeston to Committee of Trade, 5 January 1700, *C.S.P. Col. A.W.I.*, XVIII, 15.

31 Modyford's report of January 1670 almost certainly contains errors. It stated that the Negro population then was only 2,500; yet census figures for 1664 and 1673 gave 8,000 and 9,504 respectively; Patterson, op. cit., 95.

32 In fact, Jamaica was first divided into fifteen 'precincts or parishes' by the very first Act of the Jamaican Assembly in 1664; but only twelve were named, *Journal of the Assembly*, I. For the early constitutional history of Jamaica, see Agnes M. Whitson, *The Constitutional History of Jamaica*, London, 1929.

33 Kit S. Kapp, *The Printed Maps of Jamaica*, Kingston, Bolivar Press, 1958, VII–XXI. St. Thomas-ye-Vale was carved out of St. John's some time between 1675 and 1690. Two Members from St. Thomas-ye-Vale sat in the Assembly as early as 1675, but the new parish was not inscribed on maps before about 1700; *ibid.*, XXV. Around the same time, St. Dorothy Parish was carved out of St. Catherine's.

34 Modyford to Arlington, 23 September 1670, *C.S.P. Col. A.W.I., 1669–74*, 99–103. This merely gave the total population figure of 996, but the population in 1680 was said to be 199 whites and 751 blacks; *C.S.P. Col. A.W.I., 1677–80*, 1370. In 1670, there were said to be 717 families in Jamaica, and of the 209,000 acres patented, 25,197 were in St. John's.

35 *C.S.P. Col. A.W.I., 1669–74*, 102. The total given was 25,197, giving an average of about 304 acres, though the average acreage in Guanaboa itself was closer to the original 30 acres than to this figure, which was boosted by large speculative patents outside the Guanaboa basin.

36 Modyford to Arlington, loc. cit. (1670). Ayscough was Member for St. John's, 1664–71, 1679–86; Aylmer, 1701–2, 1706–7, 1708–11; Price, 1675–8, 1679–86.

CHAPTER TWO

Francis Price and the Foundation of Worthy Park

Unlike Barbados, where the records begin long after the land had been divided and developed, Jamaica provides an excellent opportunity to examine the very foundations of the sugar economy and planto-cratic society. Yet even in Jamaica the truth is shrouded in myths. Against the interpretation of 'imperialist' historians that Jamaica was the result of conscious policy and theory is now ranged that which sees the basis of the slave-owning sugar plantocracy as sheer opportunism by a fortunate riff-raff. The planters themselves, however, created a myth out of the right of conquest.[1]

Certainly Jamaica was as much an economic and social frontier—as virgin a territory—as Virginia half a century earlier. Here was a fertile island still cloaked with forest, more suitable even than Barbados for sugar if only capital could be generated; a social void offering political power as well as affluence to those who could penetrate and tame it. Although the guerrilla activities of the Maroons have probably been underestimated, the opposition to the Jamaican planters was much less severe than that provided by the Red Indian of the Virginia backwoods or the Carib of the Lesser Antilles. And yet after they had received the

Spanish-cultivated lands in strict relation to their military rank, after they had pre-emptively assumed far larger inland acreages than they could quickly develop, and after they had forged a political society designed to serve their own ends and had begun to move against imperial authority, the Jamaican planters claimed that the land and the power was theirs by right of conquest. As early as 1715, a Jamaican Governor wrote scathingly of his plantocratic opponents in the Assembly that they were the sons of 'old soldiers who called themselves the conquerors of the land'.[2]

In a study of the fortunes of the Price family and the earliest history of Worthy Park are excellent opportunities to demythologize early Jamaican history. The original records are scanty and fragmented, but they do exist. With them the historical detective can return to the obscure beginnings and estimate the role of Worthy Park's founder; and founder and estate can serve as models instructive of all Jamaica, all British sugar islands, or even all British plantation societies on the frontier of the infant empire.

On 13 March 1670 Lieutenant Francis Price filed a patent for '840 acres situate lying and being at Luidas in St. John's Parish called Worthy Park', the neat diagram of which, allegedly surveyed by one Francis Inians, was entered in the St. John's Plat Book on 28 November 1670.[3] Who was this Francis Price, and where, precisely, were the original 840 of Worthy Park's present 12,000 acres?

The proud descendants of the modest Lieutenant provided him with a lineage that was probably as fictitious as it was exalted. The idea that their progenitors had been nobodies was anathema to the eighteenth-century plantocracy. Though their forebears had obviously been less wealthy than themselves, they had come to Jamaica, it was maintained, not to make but to regain their fortunes. Legend, retailed uncritically by Burke's *Peerage* and by Fuertado, the tireless genealogist of Jamaica, claims that Francis Price was descended from 'Caradoc Vreichvras, Prince between the Wye and Severn', and that he 'came to Jamaica as a Captain in the Army under Penn and Venables in 1655 and settled here after the reduction of the island'.[4]

The princely descent of Francis Price is incapable of proof, one way

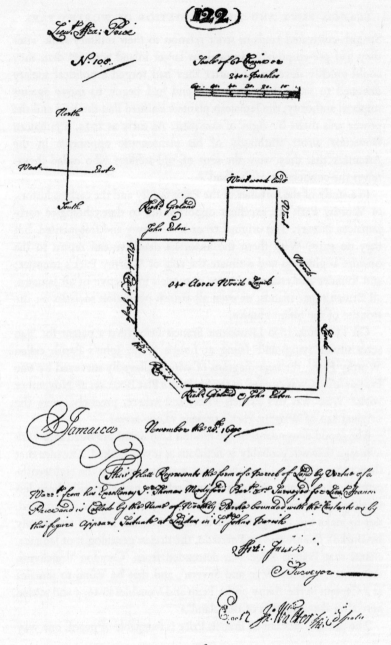

Lieut. ffra: Price

N° 108.

Scale of 60 Chains or 240 Perches
60. 50. 40. 30. 20. 10.

North

West — East

South

Richd Gyroland
John Eaton

Wast wood Land

West

West

240 Acres Wood Land

West Land Part

East

Richd Gyroland & John Eaton.

Jamaica November the 28.th 1690

This Platt Represents the form of a Parcel of Land by Vertue of a
Warr.t from his Excellency S.r Thomas Modiford Bart. &c.r Surveyed for Lieut. ffrancis
Price and is Called by the Name of Weekley Parke bounded with the Contents as by
this figure appears Situate at Guides in St Johns Parish

ffra: Price

Surveyor

Exd Jn Walter D.p Sr John

or the other. His military credentials, however, are more easily checked. Officer under General Venables Francis Price may have been, but Captain he was not. The most complete roll of the English forces of 1655 lists all officers of the rank of Captain and above by name, but Francis Price is not among them.[5] It is quite likely that Price was one of the 110 unnamed junior officers in the regiment of Colonel Anthony Buller which later became the Guanaboa Regiment. His name, however, does not appear on the first muster of that regiment, taken before leaving England in 1654.[6] This list, on the other hand, only contains the names of 26 officers and 92 men, those 'persons allready paid their first Moneths pay for theire Respect & qualityes under the Command of Generall Venables In the West Indies'—little more than a tenth of the regiment at its full strength of 1,046 on leaving Barbados to make its descent upon Hispaniola.

Clearly, Francis Price was a late recruit to the Cromwellian Army. Penn and Venables left England with 2,500 men, no more than 1,500 following later in two detachments under Robert Sedgwick and William Brayne.[7] Some 3–4,000–a majority of the original expedition —were recruited in Barbados, and a final 1,200 in the Leewards. Most of the officers came out from England, and Francis Price may have been one of these, whom Robert Venables called either 'godly men, eminent for their piety . . . though not able and fit for employment', or 'lazy dull officers that have a large portion of pride, but not of wit, valour or activity'. The reinforcements scraped up in the Antilles were predominantly indentured 'servants', though there were some freemen among them and a handful of officers.[8] It is quite feasible, therefore, that Francis Price—like many of the first British settlers in Jamaica— came from Barbados or the Leewards, where the surname Price was by no means uncommon.[9] It is even possible that the founder of Worthy Park was not originally an officer, but, having some pretensions towards gentility, was commissioned later to help fill the awful gaps torn in the ranks by disease.[10] The speed with which promotion came in the early days may be gauged by the fact that the Major and four of the seven Captains in Buller's regiment died in the first two years.[11] Besides this, neither Thomas Ayscough nor Whitgift Aylmer, who were both Francis Price's seniors when we first hear of them in the 1660s, appears on the list of officers in 1655.[12]

The first certain references to Francis Price are in the patents taken out for land in St. Catherine's and St. John's in 1665–7. On 15 October 1665 Francis Price, along with his 'mate' Nicholas Philpot, filed a patent for 150 acres at Flamingo Savanna, St. Catherine's, and on 20 December in the same year Francis Price alone—here styled Lieutenant—filed a patent for 175 acres at Guanaboa in St. John's.[13] The second patent stated that 'Francis Price hath transported himself together with his servants unto this Island of Jamaica in pursuance of our proclamation before made', and that 'for his better encouragement for being one of the planters there' he and his heirs were granted the land for ever, subject only to the usual provisos and the payment to the Crown of one penny per year at Michaelmas for each acre of land cultivated and manured. This would seem to indicate a recent arrival in 1665, but for the fact that the phraseology was a formula common to all patents—even those granted to favoured Spaniards who stayed on in Jamaica—down to 1672, when land grants were authorized by an Act of the Jamaican Assembly rather than by a Proclamation of the Crown.

Since Francis Price was one of the first Jamaican patentees it would be reasonable to suppose that he had held his lands at Flamingo Savanna and Guanaboa for some time before 1665. This supposition does not hold true, however, at least in the case of the holding at Guanaboa, for though Francis Price was the original patentee, he had only obtained the land in 1663. The first holder was a Captain William Clee, who bequeathed his 175 acres on his death in 1663 'to my Loveing Kinsman Mr ffrancis Price'.[14] The nature of the kinship between Prices and Clees and the details of the bequest of 1663 will probably remain forever obscure, but it is interesting to note that it was eight years after the English seizure of Jamaica that 'Mr' Francis Price first became a substantial landowner in the Vale of Guanaboa.

The land at Flamingo Savanna—to the west of Spanish Town in what became St. Dorothy's Parish—was obviously of limited value, but the 175 acres at Guanaboa Vale were fertile land which offered a modest basis for gradual expansion. This cradle of the Price fortune can be located quite easily from a comparison of the St. John's Parish land plats and from the Harper map of Jamaica of the 1670s, the first to identify plantations by the names of their owners. Price's plantation originally consisted of a rectangle of land about a mile long by a quarter-mile wide, extending from the Mountain River gully north of Guanaboa Church north-westwards as far as the escarpment of Cudjoe Hill. In this same loop of the occasional river lay the lands of Colonel John Cope and Major Thomas Ayscough, while those of Captain Whitgift Aylmer, John Laugher, William Thorpe, and Timothy Dodd—all later to be Price's neighbours at Lluidas—were adjacent or nearby.[15]

On Francis Price's plantation at Guanaboa there were cocoa walks and provision grounds,[16] and in this it appears to have been typical of the very earliest English Jamaican plantations. In the first flush of optimism the cacao tree was regarded as 'the most profitable tree in the world', needing little capital outlay for works and slaves, and thus ideal for planters beginning in modest circumstances.[17] In 1670, however, a disastrous blight fell upon Jamaica's cacao trees and the switch to sugar became inevitable.[18] Certainly, by 1673 Francis Price's plantation at Guanaboa was chiefly producing sugar. An inventory of that year lists the following items—almost the sum total of the Price estate: '4 coppers, 2 stills, 1 mill and millhouse, boiling house, dwelling house, 8 horses, 6 mules, 200 sugar potts, 8 hoggs'.[19]

This inventory indicates a striking resemblance between Price's Guanaboa plantation and the plantation at Sixteen Mile Walk set up by Carey Helyar between 1669 and 1672. This estate, called Bybrook from then until now, was fashioned 'Barbados style' on the advice of Helyar's associate Sir Thomas Modyford (owner of a model estate in Barbados), and is the earliest of which we have detailed knowledge in Jamaica. By comparison with Bybrook, it would seem likely that Price's Guanaboa plantation produced no more than 25 hogsheads of sugar a year from its mule-driven mill, and maybe 1,500 gallons of rum from its two stills. With sugar commanding perhaps £8 a hogshead and rum some 1/6 a gallon, this indicates an annual income of only some £310. None the less, even such an embryonic sugar operation represented a considerable investment of capital for that period. It could not have cost less than £1,200 to set up and would have taken at least three years to start bringing in a profit.[20]

It would be extremely interesting to know how the humble Lieutenant accrued the capital necessary to start up as a sugar planter. Governor Modyford in 1664 wrote that most of the old soldiers had become hunters of wild horses, cattle, and boar, which they sold in Spanish Town and Port Royal for a handsome profit, with which:

... some of them buy servants and slaves and begin to settle brave plantations; others like idle fellows, drink all out; but now the hunting begins to abate, more have settled land than ever, for there's scarce any place near the sea but is settled and many are gone into the mountains.[21]

The 'inferior officers' at Guanaboa were particularly noted as horse and cattle hunters, and special rules were passed by the Council of Jamaica in 1661 to regulate them.[22] It is a pleasant speculation to imagine the adventurous young Lieutenant roaming the forests and glades around Guanaboa with his dogs, in search of a four-footed fortune. Thus perhaps Francis Price first came upon the forested stretch of the Vale of Lluidas to which he was to lay claim in 1670, just as Carey Helyar penetrated the Rio Cobre Gorge with his dog in 1669 to discover the future route into St. Thomas-ye-Vale. Francis Price was evidently neither the type of witless officer described by General Venables, nor the drunken idler depicted by Governor Modyford; and having been ingenious, industrious, and fortunate enough to have survived and become a landed proprietor, he naturally joined in the speculative rush for land that characterized the second stage of Jamaica's development.

Since the original 840 acres of Worthy Park were surveyed in an extremely rudimentary fashion and the estate has changed its size and shape almost constantly since 1670, it has proved difficult to locate with absolute accuracy the area claimed by Francis Price three hundred years ago: difficult, but not impossible. After juggling with the capricious jigsaw of the St. John's plats, with their tantalizing scraps of information, a rough pattern of original holdings emerges. Study of the relevant deeds in the endless stream registered at Spanish Town by which lands were constantly chopped and changed, modifies the pattern and brings it closer to the earliest detailed maps, which date from 1715. Yet it is only Worthy Park's incredible constancy—with Bybrook and Sevens one of only three Jamaican sugar estates with a continuous history of three hundred years—as well as its unparalleled collection of estate maps running in a steady series from 1715 to the present, that enable us to proceed from likelihood to certainty, so that original grant and present patterns click into identity.

As late as 1667, conditions in Jamaica were sufficiently unsettled for it to be necessary to possess a pass to leave Guanaboa for places farther north,[23] and it is likely that the Vale of Lluidas was not thrown open to general development until after this. Francis Price in early 1670 was able to select the most desirable land in Lluidas because he was only the second patentee in the valley. He had been preceded by Richard Garland and John Eaton, partners who previously held little more than the bare minimum of the original grant of thirty acres each, with a hundred acres in lower St. John's.[24] The first Garland and Eaton patent in Lluidas had been filed as early as 1665, for a crudely delineated rectangle of 140 acres, situated astride the 'Rio Cobre' gully, from a point near the present Anglican church diagonally north-eastwards.[25] Bought by Francis Price and Peter Beckford in 1676, it passed later to Thetford Estate and can easily be traced on maps as late as 1879.[26] The second area patented by Garland and Eaton was a parcel of similar size just over a mile to the north, and on the western side of the great bend of the Rio Cobre gully.[27] Described, as was the first plot, 'waste woodland', this second area once cleared and developed, turned out to be excellent sugar land.

The land patented by Francis Price, and named Worthy Park by him from the beginning,[28] was situated in the area of rather more than a square mile between the two plots claimed by Richard Garland and John Eaton. Divided into two almost equal parts by the northwards-running Great Gully, it too consisted of 'woodland', though bounded on the western side by the two square miles of the Lluidas Savanna. Today no boundary markers define the limits of the original Worthy Park. The trees blazed by the first surveyor have all disappeared and fields and field roads all, of course, came later. The north-eastern bend of the Great Gully and the continued existence of the 'Old Road' as a modern cart-track in the south-west, however, enable us to super-impose the 1670 plat on the modern map. Immediately it can be seen how astutely Francis Price selected his land at Lluidas: of the 840 acres, no less than three-quarters are now in cane, producing each year some 3,500 tons of sugar. Over the long history of Worthy Park, they may have produced sugar totalling half a million tons.

With the benefit of hindsight it can be seen that besides the prime requirements of land, labour, and capital, there were at least three secondary prerequisites for the successful development of a sugar estate anywhere in the West Indies: conditions conducive to consolidation towards optimal size, good communications and a workable connection with the mercantile community. Worthy Park's was the largest and most suitable, as well as the most central, block of land in Lluidas Vale. If the dates of the original patents are an accurate indication, the development of Lluidas spread out from Worthy Park's fertile nucleus towards the less desirable fringes of the valley. The twenty or so patentees who followed Francis Price into Lluidas took out lands immediately adjacent to those already patented, and they were fortunate if their holding proved as fertile and well-watered as those selected by earlier patentees.[29]

Where land speculation was such a lottery, consolidation was inevitable, though the limitations of sugar technology restricted the optimal size of the area served by a single factory in the eighteenth century to a maximum of about 600 acres of canes. Worthy Park, as we shall see, became the only estate in Lluidas to survive in an unbroken line, and eventually dominated the valley, yet down to the middle of the nineteenth century it was no more than one of five or six estates within the circumference of the limestone walls of Lluidas Vale. All of these estates were themselves agglomerations of original holdings, consolidated in an attempt to reach the optimal size of a sugar factory-

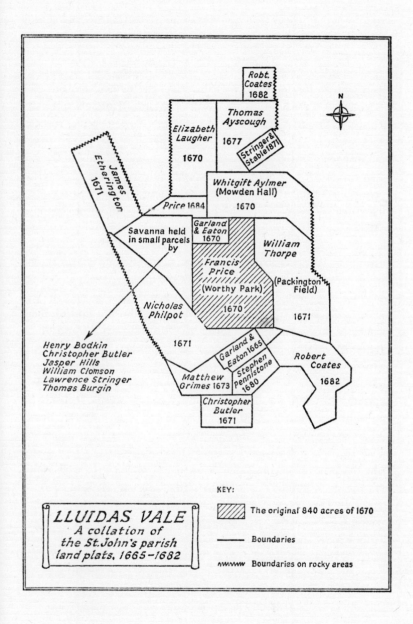

Robt.
Coates
1682

Thomas
Ayscough
1677

Elizabeth
Laugher
1670

Stringer &
Stable 1871

Whitgift Aylmer
(Mowden Hall)
1670

James
Etherington
1671

Price 1684

Savanna held
in small parcels
by

Garland
& Eaton
1670

Francis
Price

(Worthy Park)

1670

William
Thorpe

(Packington
Field)

1671

Nicholas
Philpot

1671

Henry Bodkin
Christopher Butler
Jasper Hills
William Clomson
Lawrence Stringer
Thomas Burgin

Garland &
Eaton 1665

Stephen
Pennistone
1680

Robert
Coates

1682

Matthew
Grimes 1673

Christopher
Butler
1671

N

KEY:

////// The original 840 acres of 1670

——— Boundaries

wwwww Boundaries on rocky areas

LLUIDAS VALE
A collation of
the St. John's parish
land plats, 1665–1682

35

estate. Four of them achieved some degree of success, and during sugar's heyday there was a certain uniformity in their character and operations.

Successful estates required good sugar land, grazing land for working steers, forests for fuel, and perhaps some surplus land for growing provisions. Of the lands to the north of Worthy Park, the 478 acres held by Whitgift Aylmer were the closest and most fertile, and this block—which Aylmer called Mowden Hall—was later joined to the rock-fringed and less plantable holdings of five adjacent patentees to form Swansea Estate. Third in importance in the course of development came Thetford, but this sprawling estate, based on the 600 acres first patented by William Thorpe in 1671, only achieved economic viability in the best years of the sugar industry, by the gradual consolidation of many small parcels of savanna and plantable land almost surrounding Worthy Park itself. To the south, the estate of Murmuring Brook grew up by the accumulation of the mixed grazing and plantable land watered by the only permanent stream in Lluidas Vale. But while fertile, Murmuring Brook was hilly and did not flourish independently, being swallowed up by Thetford towards the end of the eighteenth century, the two factories being worked for some years in harness. Tydixon, to the north-west of Worthy Park, with good grazing but only marginal sugar land, appears to have survived as a separate entity into the twentieth century chiefly because its lands did not sufficiently attract its more acquisitive neighbours. Finally, Shady Grove, to the south-west, though it grew a fair amount of sugar, was never large enough to develop as a factory-estate.

In the process of consolidation upon Darwinian principles which was already well under way by 1680, the followers of Juan de Bolas appear to have been early victims. There are only three Spanish-sounding names in the St. John's Parish list of patentees, two of whom, Bartholomew and Bastian Angolo, held land in the vicinity of Lluidas Vale; and the fact that Stephen Pennistone and Robert Coates (old Guanaboa hands) held hundreds of acres 'in Juan de Bolas pelincos' by 1682 seems to indicate that the followers of the great guerrilla leader had either died out already or, in the sad tradition of most 'natives' in

the face of white encroachment, been ousted from their lands. The
mention of 120 acres held in 1680 by 'Spanish Negroes' westward of
Lluidas Vale by the boundary of Clarendon may indicate that the survivors of Juan de Bolas's band may have begun a westward migration
that brought them towards gradual identification with the fugitive
Maroons of Trelawny.[30]

The future of Lluidas, as of Jamaica as a whole, belonged not to
casual smallholders growing provisions and raising hogs, nor to such
small cattle farmers as grazed Lluidas Savanna, but to sugar and its
planters. The transformation of Lluidas, however, did not occur
during the lifetime of the founder of Worthy Park. Indeed, Lluidas
remained joined to the rest of St. John's by the scantiest of tracks until
about 1715, and there is no certain evidence that sugar was grown for
export from Lluidas much before 1720. A great deal had to be
achieved, in road-building alone, before forest and savanna could
become canefields and pasture. The last two decades of the life of
Francis Price and much of the lives of his three sons was dedicated to
the accumulation of capital derived from the sugar plantation at
Guanaboa and speculations in land, so that the valuable holding at
Lluidas—which Francis Price more than doubled by judicious acquisitions—could in its turn be developed. Meanwhile, Worthy Park was
gradually cleared, and its broad acres were made to pay for themselves
by the production of beef and pork, and during the lifetime of Francis
Price the first 'Great House' was built and became the main residence
of the patriarch and his wife Elizabeth.[31]

Unfortunately, it is only the dry bones of the life of Francis Price
that can be reconstructed from his land patents, the deeds recording his
land transactions, and his will, written in 1688, the year before his
death. The fleshing out of his character must be left to inference and
the imagination. One thing is certain: that personal relationships played
an extremely important part in the life of Francis Price, as in that of all
such pioneers. The early histories of the successful founding families of
the Jamaican plantocracy were characterized by fruitful business connections and dynastic bonds, and the Prices were no exception. Francis
Price was sufficiently able and popular, or became of sufficient sub-

stance, to rise in rank from Lieutenant to Major in the militia and to be chosen twice as one of the Members of the Assembly for St. John's, and he always retained the friendliest relations with his neighbours at Lluidas and Guanaboa.[32] But more important than these were his amiable partnership with Peter Beckford and the friendship, cemented by marriage, between the Prices of St. John's and the Roses of St. Thomas-ye-Vale.

Peter Beckford, holder of 2,238 acres in Clarendon, was scion of a family already established in the City of London, and co-founder of the largest of all Jamaican fortunes. Successively, he was Assemblyman for several parishes, Councillor and Acting Governor of Jamaica.[33] For twenty-one years after 1667, Beckford and Price were partners, and their friendship survived Beckford's rise to eminence and even Price's death.[34] The link with the Government which Peter Beckford provided could have done his associates no harm, but Beckford was as much merchant as planter and legislator, and it was doubtless his familiarity with the channels of trade and his ability to raise capital that proved most useful to the Prices.

The first, and key, transaction in the partnership between Francis Price and Peter Beckford occurred in November 1667 when Price sold Beckford a half share in his Guanaboa sugar plantation for £300 cash.[35] With this capital (no inconsiderable sum in the money-starved Jamaica of the 1660s) as a basis, and in almost continuous association with Peter Beckford, Francis Price was able to develop and expand his holdings. Together, Price and Beckford added 274 acres to the plantation at Guanaboa, in five transactions between 1673 and 1677, and built a storehouse at Spanish Town for their produce. In 1675, when the parishes of St. Mary's and St. Ann's were opened to development at quit rents of only ½d. an acre, they speculated together in huge acreages. It was also with Peter Beckford that Francis Price in 1676 bought out the original 140 acres in Lluidas owned by Richard Garland and John Eaton, part of which is still called Beckford's.[36]

With the exception of the single parcel bought in 1676 from Richard Garland, the illiterate survivor of the partnership with John Eaton, Peter Beckford was not directly involved in the expansion of Worthy

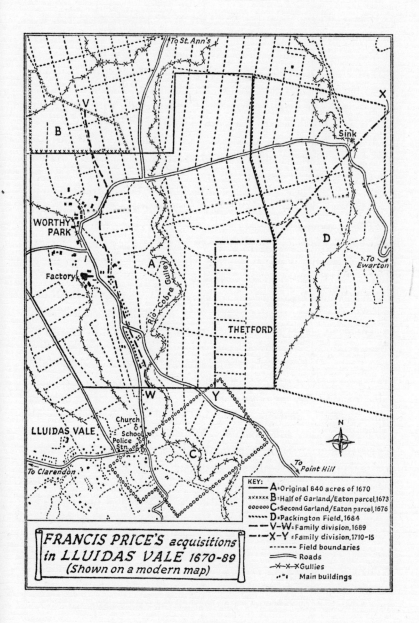

To St. Ann's

V

B

X

Sink

WORTHY
PARK

A

D

To
Ewarton

Factory

Rio Cobre Gulley

THETFORD

W

Y

Church

School

Police
Stn.

P.O.

LLUIDAS VALE

C

N

To Clarendon

To
Point Hill

KEY:

A = Original 840 acres of 1670
xxxxxx B = Half of Garland/Eaton parcel, 1673
ooooooo C = Second Garland/Eaton parcel, 1676
······ D = Packington Field, 1684
— — V–W = Family division, 1689
—·—·— X–Y = Family division, 1710-15
------- Field boundaries
——— Roads
–×–×–× Gullies
··°· Main buildings

FRANCIS PRICE'S acquisitions
in LLUIDAS VALE 1670-89
(Shown on a modern map)

Park. It may have been that Beckford, as an acute businessman, was only interested in active plantations, or in speculations in which partnership would obviate such inconveniences as the limitation of 2,000 acres on North Side patents imposed by the Government. Alternatively, it may have been that Francis Price, foreseeing the potential of Worthy Park, kept it, even while expanding, free from those partnerships that are always less welcome to heirs than to present incumbents. Whatever the reason, Francis Price alone added to Worthy Park's original 840 acres half of Garland and Eaton's northern parcel in 1673, a further 123 acres of unpossessed adjacent land in Lluidas Savanna in 1682 by patent, and, finally, the 600 acres of Packington Field in 1684, bought from William Thorpe for the princely sum of £100.[37] This spread of 1,774 acres, extending across Lluidas Vale at its centre from mountain to mountain, included approximately half the valley's present sugar land, but practically all those areas where sugar has been grown in Lluidas Vale for the past 250 years.[38]

While Francis Price was making his modest beginnings at Guanaboa and Worthy Park, similar estates were being developed at nearby St. Thomas-ye-Vale by two brothers called Fulke and Francis Rose. These gentlemen-adventurers enjoyed even better connections than Peter Beckford, being sons of a prominent London apothecary, John Rose, whose eldest son and namesake made a fortune as a merchant. Fulke, considerably the older of the two, was doubly unique in being both a doctor of medicine and already a landowner in England, with holdings at Oxney and Nonington in Kent. Both Fulke, who died in 1693, and Francis, who survived until 1720, were successively Assemblymen and prominent Members of the Council of Jamaica. Francis, as his memorial in the Cathedral at Spanish Town tells us, even rose to the height of President of the Council towards the end of his life.[39] The fortunes of Prices and Roses were destined to be intertwined by marriage, though not in the manner described by some genealogists, who state that Francis Price married Elizabeth, the widow of one Colonel William Rose.[40] In fact, Francis Price married Elizabeth Coxon,[41] who may have been a Bermudian related to the notorious buccaneer-turned-pirate of that surname. Besides their three sons, Francis, Thomas, and Charles, the Prices had a daughter, Elizabeth, and it was this young lady who married Francis Rose, the younger of the brothers, and owner of extensive lands in the vale of Linstead and elsewhere, which in 1724 were bequeathed by their son to the other grandsons of Francis Price on the extinction of the male line of the Roses in Jamaica.[42]

The sons of Francis Price had received far less when their father died in 1689. None of them had yet attained their majority and the Price patrimony was held in trust by their mother, Elizabeth, who survived her husband by only four years. The 'estate and plantation at Luidas' was intended for the eldest, also called Francis, who for the time being was bequeathed only 'six breeding Cowes and halfe of the Negroes, hoggs and fowles' that were to be found there. The remainder of the lands and possessions of Francis Price the elder, 'that is to say the moyety of half part of the plantation I have in company with Col. Peter Beckford at Guanaboa together with the negroes utensills cattle and Horses on the said Estate as alsoe my land at Mountain River likewise my land at the Northside and my land in St. Dorothy's parish . . . together with my part of the Store House in town', were destined for the other two sons, Thomas and Charles, on the death of their mother. Francis Price's daughter Elizabeth would receive all the property if the sons should die without 'heirs of their bodyes legally begotten', but for the present was bequeathed simply 'Twenty pounds Current money'. The only cash bequest was a similar one of twenty pounds to Elizabeth's first-born son, Francis Rose Price.[43]

Francis Price was still a poor man when he died, and whatever capital he possessed was largely invested in the unrealized potential of his lands at Lluidas. What was this 'estate and plantation' like in 1689? It was likely that much of the land was already cleared, but the planted parts probably grew little more than provision crops and pasture grass, for there is no mention of the 'utensills' necessary for the production of sugar which were to be found at Guanaboa. The mention of breeding cows, hogs, and fowls—which is echoed in the will of Elizabeth Price in 1692[44]—indicates an extremely modest pioneer farm, such as might have been found in the backwoods of Virginia or the Carolinas at much the same time.

Perhaps the best impression of Worthy Park and its neighbouring 'estates' in Lluidas Vale at the time of Francis Price's death can be gained from the pages of Sir Hans Sloane, who in 1702 described Jamaica as he had found it in 1688 (and who, incidentally, married the widow of Dr. Fulke Rose).[45] 'These sort of remote Plantations are very profitable to their Masters,' wrote Sloane, before going on to describe the rustic husbandry of the Jamaican backwoods. Swine, augmented by those caught wild in the mountains, were kept in 'crawles' until they were ready to be slaughtered and smoked into 'jerked pork'. Poultry, such as turkeys, were kept in 'palenques' and likewise carried down to market in Spanish Town. But Lluidas was notable during the early days of English settlement chiefly for cattle and their meat, particularly veal. Hans Sloane described graphically how the wild cattle had almost disappeared through indiscriminate slaughter, or by being penned by rural cattle farmers. Cattle had to be tended and kept at night inside palisado fences because they would disappear into the unexplored interior or be rustled by unscrupulous neighbours. Nor could they be allowed to graze freely even during the day, for their flesh would become tainted if they fed on the guinea hen weed and calabash grasses which they relished. Instead, they were best grazed upon good 'scotch grass', and this may have been what Francis Price planted as he gradually cleared his trees.

'Veal is very common,' wrote Hans Sloane, 'but none thought good but what comes from *Luidas*, where the Calves are very white flesh'd; whether this comes from the place being mountainous, or bleeding and giving them Chalk, as in Essex, I cannot tell, but the price of it was so extravagant, that in the Assembly they past an Act that it should not be sold dearer than twelve pence per Pound.'[46]

NOTES

[1] Compare, for example, A. P. Thornton, *West India Policy under the Restoration*, Oxford, 1950; H. Orlando Patterson, *Sociology of Slavery*, 15–51; Edward Long, *History of Jamaica*, 3 vols., London, 1774. The best account of the early development of Barbados is now Richard S. Dunn, 'The Barbados Census of

1680: Profile of the Richest Colony in English America', *William and Mary Quarterly*, January 1969, 3–30.

[2] Governor Hamilton to B.T., 30 August 1715, C.O. 137/11, 10.

[3] Land Patents, *Liber* IV, *Folio* 20; St. John's Plat Book, No. 105, p. 122. The patent was actually enrolled on 24 May 1671.

[4] W. A. Fuertado, *Official and Other Personages of Jamaica, 1655–1790*, Kingston, 1896, 78, 125, a mine of misinformation; *Burke's Peerage*, London, 1898, under 'Price of Trengwainton'.

[5] 'A Perfect list of all the Forces under the Command of his Excellency Generall Venables, taken at a Muster, March 21st., 1654/5', Portland MSS., Hist. MSS. Comm. Report, 7628, II, 90, given in C. H. Firth (ed.) *Venables*, op. cit., Appendix B, 116–22.

[6] C.O. 1/32, 56–7.

[7] S. A. G. Taylor, op. cit., 90–3, 123–8.

[8] C. H. Firth (ed.), op. cit., xvii–xxix.

[9] *Caribbeana*, III.

[10] The list of St. John's landowners as late as 1670 accords Francis Price no rank though there is at least one person given the title Lieutenant; *C.S.P. Col. A.W.I., 1669–74*, 102.

[11] Though Whitgift Aylmer's tombstone in Guanaboa Church makes great play of the fact that he arrived in Jamaica on the very day of the first soldiers' landing.

[12] C. H. Firth (ed.), op. cit., 119, 2–6.

[13] Land Patents II/92, 94, enrolled 1 and 20 January 1666–7; St. John's Plat Book, 95, p. 119, dated 7 May 1666.

[14] Jamaica, Island Record Office, Wills, *Liber* I, *Folio* 5. Clee's ownership is borne out by a study of the adjacent land patents of Thomas Ayscough and William Thorpe, which antedated that of Francis Price; St. John's Plat Book, I/240; 150/11. William Clee was listed as a Captain in the Guanaboa Regiment in December 1662; *C.S.P. Col. A.W.I., 1661–8*, 397.

[15] The Harper Map, Institute of Jamaica, 1727ED, is not dated, but was authorized by Thomas Lynch, Governor, 1671–5, 1682–4. The information contained in the map appears to be from the period of Lynch's earlier tenure rather than the later.

[16] Deed, Francis Price to Peter Beckford, 3 October 1673, I.R.O. Deeds, Grantors, *Liber* I, *Folio* 115: '. . . all edifices, houses, woods & underwoods, cocoa walks & canes, provisions, water, watercourses. . . .'

[17] J. Harry Bennett, 'Carey Helyar, Merchant and Planter of Seventeenth-century Jamaica', *William and Mary Quarterly*, June 8 1964, 53–76.

[18] Minutes of Jamaican Council, 31 August 1670; Lynch to Secretary of State, 2 July 1671; Lynch to Joseph Williamson, 7 July 1671; *C.S.P. Col. 1669–1674*, 84, 238–9, 241.

[19] Deed, Francis Price to Peter Beckford, 3 October 1673, I.R.O. Deeds 1/115.

[20] Lord Vaughan estimated the cost of setting up a 1,000-acre sugar estate in 1676 as being no less than £5,000; Vaughan to Secretary of State, C.O. 138/3; Patterson, op. cit., 20. Bybrook, with 60 acres of canes, was valued by Carey Helyar in 1672 at £1,858, though not less than £1,170 of this was the value of the 55 slaves and 14 indentured servants employed. The 'millwork' was valued at £199. Helyar, however, reckoned that the market value of the property was probably no more than £1,300, since the full value was beyond the means of

anyone 'that cums to settle in thes parts'; J. Harry Bennett, 'Cary Helyar', 74, fn. 47.

21 Modyford, 'A View of the Condition of Jamaica', op. cit., quoted in Patterson, op. cit., 19. Some of the profits of privateering may have been 'laid out in plantations', but there is no evidence that Francis Price was ever tempted to join the English freebooters.

22 The Guanaboa officers alone were allowed to pen and sell horses, for a maximum of £2 each. For the rest: 'All hunters called in within one month; no one to hunt or kill cattle or free gangs of dogs unless he have 10 acres planted and his licence', C.S.P. Col. A.W.I., 1661–8, 108; Minutes of Council of Jamaica, 18 June 1661.

23 The Council of Jamaica in November 1667 forbade the inhabitants of Guanaboa to 'pass to the north side without tickets', ibid., 1634, p. 519.

24 Indeed, the survey of 1670 listed them as holding only 60 acres, though the St. John's Plat Book shows a plat for 100 acres dated 26 December 1665; C.S.P. Col. A.W.I., 1669–74, 102; St. John's Plat Book, 66/72, Copy in Plat Book Two.

25 Ibid.

26 Jamaica S.S., St. Catherine's, Worthy Park Estate, Reference No. 11, at Worthy Park.

27 St. John's Plat Book, 71/47, dated 26 November 1670.

28 Why Worthy Park? The origin is as mysterious as that of the Welsh-sounding Lluidas, and made more so by the spelling 'Worthly Park' on the original patent (presumably a misspelling). There is a Worthy Park near Winchester in England, but as far as is known it has no connection with Jamaica. Lluidas may be a corruption of Lloyd's—there was at least one officer-landowner of that name among the Cromwellian settlers—though from early spellings the pronunciation would seem to have been originally 'Lewdas' rather than the present 'Loo-ai-duss'. The double 'L' also appears to be a later addition, first appearing on maps in the mid-eighteenth century. To confuse the issue further, one of the early plats is inscribed 'Luidas, alias Loonardia'; St. John's Plat Book, 47/216, dated 1682.

29 After Garland and Eaton, no one took out lands in Lluidas that did not have a patented holding on at least one boundary. The sequence, as far as can be judged, was as follows: St. John's Plat Book, Garland and Eaton I, 66/72; II, 71/147; Price I, 122/105; Aylmer, 7/144; Laugher, 105/128; Stringer and Stable, 140/151; Thorpe, 148/157; Philpot, 123/150; Etherington, 59/?; Butler, 26/168; Grimes, 72/170; Clomson and Stringer, 51/179; Ayscough, 2/200; Pennistone, 124/201; Burgin and Bodkin, 23/242; Coates I, 47/216; II, 48/206; Price II, Patents, 9/36.

30 St. John's Plat Book, 46/204; 102/228; 124/201; 109/223; 47/216; 23/242. It is worth noting that most of the trouble with Maroons between 1680 and 1720 appears to have occurred in the Clarendon hills. The great Maroon leader Cudjoe, for example, is thought to have been a runaway since the time of the slave outbreak at Sutton's near Chapelton, in 1690. Carey Robinson, The Fighting Maroons of Jamaica, London, Collins, 1969, 30–5.

31 'Great House' in the Jamaican context, implies simply the residence of the proprietor, often a very modest dwelling and even inferior in construction to the buildings of the nearby factory. For a description of the clearing of Jamaica's virgin timber (in St. Thomas-ye-Vale) see J. Harry Bennett, Carey Helyar, op. cit., 62–3.

32 References in deeds, wills, and the minutes of the Assembly indicate promotion to Captain around 1675 and to Major around 1685. Francis Price was Member during the brief session of 1675 and for the sessions of 1679–1684. Although his name does not figure prominently in the Journals, the Assembly deliberated many matters in which he had a direct interest, and passed Acts in that period relating, *inter alia*, to the preservation of savannas, the fixing of meat prices, the building and repairing of highways, the government of 'servants' and Negroes, the regulation of hunting, securing of land titles, quit rents and the militia; *Journals of the Assembly*, 26 April 1675 to 8 September 1684.

33 *Caribbeana*, V.

34 I.R.O. Deeds, Grantors, 1/115. Although signed on 28 November 1667 this deed was not enrolled until 3 October 1673. The list of chattels then appended is presumed to date from 1673 rather than 1667; above, n. 16.

35 'Collonel Peter Beckford' along with Francis Price and Robert Coates were designated her executors by Elizabeth Price in 1692, and styled 'my beloved friends'; I.R.O. Wills, 7/60, 1 August 1692.

36 I.R.O. Deeds, Grantors, 1/123; 6/63–4; 6/202–3; 6/206' 6/253; 7/49; 7/145; 8/95; 8/142; 8/152; 8/165; 8/124. Francis Price, however, did patent 49 acres of land at Mountain River in 1677 which he did not share with Peter Beckford; Land Patents, 7/6, dated 27 October 1677. See also Land Patents, 6/275, dated 24 November 1675.

37 I.R.O. Deeds, Grantors, Garland to Price, 5/94–5, 5 February 1673–4; Thorpe to Price, 15/121, 4 August 1684; Jamaica Archives, Land Patents, 9/36, 27 May 1682.

38 Jamaica S.S., St. Catherine's, Worthy Park Estate Map, 1879.

39 *Caribbeana*, V, 130–5.

40 W. A. Fuertado, op. cit.; Institute of Jamaica, Young Collection, 'Price', 45.

41 And perhaps daughter of the William Coxon, 'vintner' of Port Royal, who died 22 January 1684. I.R.O. Wills, III–V, 66.

42 See below, III,54.

43 I.R.O. Wills, 6/68, 8 May 1689.

44 *Ibid.*, 7/60, 1 August 1692.

45 Sloane, *A Voyage*, op. cit., I, vii–cliv.

46 *Ibid.*, I, xvi. Sloane was probably referring to either the 31st Act passed by the Assembly of 1675, or the 4th Act passed by the Assembly of 1679–84, both of which attempted to peg the prices of meat; *Journals of the Assembly*, I.

CHAPTER THREE

Consolidation and the Advent of Sugar, 1689-1730

Progress at Worthy Park was painfully slow at first. Situated in the very centre of Jamaica, it was as far inland as any British sugar estate developed in the eighteenth century. Hemmed in by forest, cockpits, and the looming mass of Mount Diablo, and twenty-five miles from Spanish Town, it must have seemed in the first decades of the eighteenth century very much a frontier settlement, extremely vulnerable to attacks from the defiant Maroons to the west. Yet so great was the energy and enterprise of 'Colonell' Charles Price, the last of the sons of Francis Price, that when he died in 1730 he was one of Jamaica's more substantial planters. The Price fortune was based as much upon the holdings in St. Thomas-ye-Vale as those in Lluidas Vale; but Worthy Park (where the first Charles Price lived all his life) had already attained the dimensions and shape it was to retain for a hundred years, was producing sugar, and only needed better communications and more water to take part fully in the fantastic prosperity of Jamaica's 'Golden Age of Sugar' in the third quarter of the eighteenth century.

That estates such as Worthy Park expanded rather than being subdivided like Irish land holdings was due both to the determined expansionism of the early settler families and to the awful mortality with which they were afflicted.[1] The Prices were prolific beyond the average, but their expectation of life in the first three generations seems to have been no more than 24 years.[2] With all the advantages, the white plantocracy was little more durable than the slaves, and the reservoir they had to draw upon was much less deep. Consequently, the compilation of wills was more than a melancholy responsibility: it was an important branch of the business of estate management.

When Francis Price died in 1689 his land was held in trust for his three sons by his wife Elizabeth. The central block of 500 acres 'good valley woodland'[3] was destined for the oldest son, Francis, while Thomas and Charles were to inherit equally the surrounding savannah and forest, as well as Francis Price's holdings in Guanaboa and elsewhere shared with Peter Beckford.[4]

Elizabeth Price died in 1692, but Francis Price the second enjoyed the proprietorship of Worthy Park for only five years, dying after a sudden illness in September 1697.[5] A short while before his death he had married Dorothy Pennistone, the daughter of a neighbour, but they had no children. Despite the provision in his mother's will that his land would revert to his brothers if he died without 'heirs of his body', Francis Price sold his patrimony on his deathbed. Having made over all his worldly goods to his wife in the shortest of the Price wills on 9 September 1697, he sold his 500 acres at Lluidas, along with thirty-three Negro slaves, to one John Goffe for £1,000 current money of Jamaica on 15 September, just before he died. Nine days after this, John Goffe re-sold the land and slaves to Dorothy Price.[6]

Obviously, the intention of Francis Price the younger was to provide for his widow against the provisions of his mother's will; yet had it not been for the prompt action of Charles Price, this irresponsible subterfuge might have alienated the heartland of Worthy Park from the Price family for ever. Shortly after the death of her first husband, Dorothy Price married another neighbour, Samuel Bromley, and for a while the couple owned the central 500 acres of Worthy Park, as well as the Bromley and Pennistone lands in the Murmuring Brook valley.

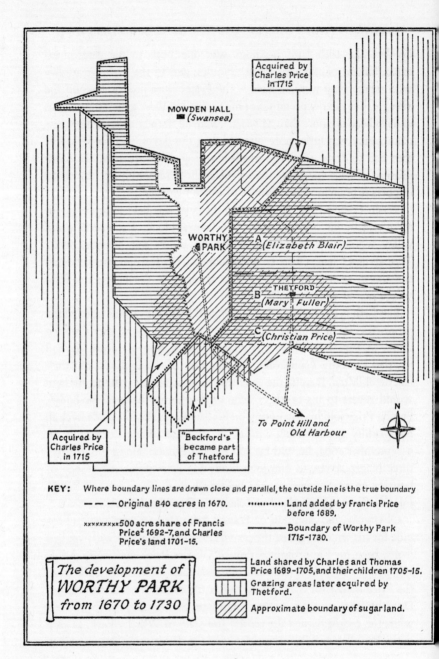

Acquired by
Charles Price
in 1715

MOWDEN HALL
▦ (Swansea)

WORTHY
▦ PARK

A
(Elizabeth Blair)

B
THETFORD
(Mary Fuller)

C
(Christian Price)

To Point Hill and
Old Harbour

N

Acquired by
Charles Price
in 1715

"Beckford's"
became part
of Thetford

KEY: Where boundary lines are drawn close and parallel, the outside line is the true boundary

— — —Original 840 acres in 1670.   ∙∙∙∙∙∙∙∙∙∙∙∙ Land added by Francis Price
                                                          before 1689.

xxxxxxxxx500 acre share of Francis   ———— Boundary of Worthy Park
Price² 1692-7, and Charles   1715-1730.
Price's land 1701-15.

The development of
WORTHY PARK
from 1670 to 1730

Land shared by Charles and Thomas
Price 1689-1705, and their children 1705-15.
Grazing areas later acquired by
Thetford.
Approximate boundary of sugar land.

48

On 10 November 1701, however, the 500 acres were re-purchased by Charles Price for £775 Jamaica currency, along with the surviving twenty-two Negroes and all buildings, cattle, hogs, and planted crops.[7]

Although moderate, the sum that Charles Price contrived to raise to pay for Worthy Park in 1701 still represented as much as an eightfold appreciation of land values in Lluidas Vale over the previous twenty years.[8] Had the estate already been producing sugar for export—with such a tiny work-force this was out of the question—the price would have been far higher. As it was, it was Charles Price who made Worthy Park into a sugar estate, so that whereas to find even £775 had been a financial strain in 1701, he was able when he died twenty-nine years later to bequeath ten times that amount in cash, as well as estates in Lluidas Vale and St. Thomas-ye-Vale alone worth more than £22,000.[9]

The second of the sons of Francis Price the elder, Thomas Price, died in 1705, and once his estate had been settled, Charles Price the survivor became the sole owner of Worthy Park in its entirety. Thomas Price bequeathed his share of the lands to his two sons, Francis and Thomas, but neither survived him long and the property devolved upon his three daughters, Mary, Elizabeth, and Christian.[10] All three married, and some time between 1710 and 1715 an arrangement was made between them and Charles Price by which each young lady and her husband were allotted one of three adjacent parcels of 100 acres 'good valley land', as their share of the divided inheritance. This prime acreage was later consolidated as the nucleus of Thetford Estate by the husband of Mary Price, Thomas Fuller, and their descendants.[11]

The two earliest extant maps of Worthy Park, found in the Institute of Jamaica and the Public Record Office in London, are both dated 1715, but the former is obviously earlier than the latter.[12] Since it does not show the division of land between Charles Price and the daughters of Thomas Price, the Institute of Jamaica map probably records details of boundaries for the period 1710-15. There is also a fragment in the Institute of Jamaica containing a collation of land plats and the details of the allocation of land to Elizabeth Blair, Mary Fuller and Christian Price that, from internal evidence, appears to date from the early 1720s. From these invaluable maps, which have few parallels in

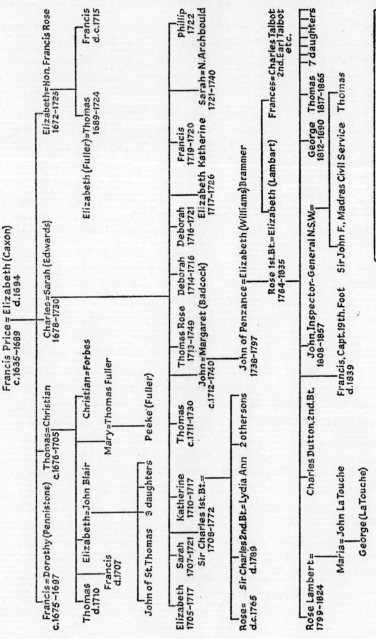

Francis Price = Elizabeth (Caxon)
c.1635-1689   d.1694

Francis=Dorothy (Penniston e)   Thomas=Christian   Charles=Sarah (Edwards)   Elizabeth=Hon. Francis Rose
c.1675-1697   c.1676-1705   1678-1730   1672-1725

Thomas   Elizabeth=John Blair   Christian=Forbes   Elizabeth (Fuller)=Thomas   Francis
d.1710   1689-1724   d.c.1715
    Francis   Mary=Thomas Fuller
    d.1707
                                        Peeke (Fuller)

John of St. Thomas   3 daughters

Elizabeth   Sarah   Katherine   Thomas   Thomas Rose   Deborah   Deborah   Francis   Phillip
1705-1717   1707-1721   1710-1717   c.1711-1730   1713-1749   1714-1716 1716-1721 1719-1720   1722
             Sir Charles 1st.Bt.=   John=Margaret (Badcock)   Elizabeth Katherine   Sarah=N.Archbould
             1708-1772   c.1712-1740   1717-1726   1721-1740

Rose= Sir Charles 2nd.Bt.=Lydia Ann   2 other sons   John of Penzance=Elizabeth (Williams) Brammer
d.c.1765   d.1789   1738-1797
                                                                    Rose 1st.Bt.=Elizabeth (Lambart)   Frances=Charles Talbot
                                                                    1764-1835   2nd.Earl Talbot
                                                                                                                 etc.

Rose Lambert=   Charles Dutton,2nd.Bt.   John,Inspector-General N.S.W=   George   Thomas   7 daughters
1799-1824   1808-1857   1812-1890 1817-1865

Maria=John La Touche   Francis,Capt.19th.Foot   Sir John F., Madras Civil Service   Thomas
                           d.1839
    George (LaTouche)

THE PRICES OF WORTHY PARK 1635-1890

Jamaica, we can identify the boundaries of Worthy Park, not only as they were established after the death of Francis Price the elder but also as they existed during the crucial last fifteen years of the life of Colonel Charles Price. Worthy Park consisted then of a spread of 1,314 acres with the Great Gully as its spine and with arms extending entirely across Lluidas Vale at its centre, approximately 40 per cent of which is now in cane, some 30 per cent grassland and 30 per cent mountainous or rocky.[13]

A half dozen ponds and 'springs' were scattered across Worthy Park in 1715, but the only running water was normally the last few yards of the Great Gully just before it plunged into the sink-hole at the north-east edge of the estate. The 'Old Road' still skirted the property to the south-west, but a 'Broad Road' now ran right through Charles Price's land from south to north, passing on its way the single building labelled Worthy Park. To the north lay the 700 acres belonging to Whitgift Aylmer[14] which, after his death in 1720, passed to John Halstead, on whose land in the map of the 1720s was depicted a simple dwelling called 'Mouden Hall'. This estate, the nucleus of the later Swansea, shared with Worthy Park the 'running rivulet' under the Blue Mountain, as well as enjoying adequate standing water, including the huge circular pond several acres in extent still found in the angle of the Great Gully surrounded by giant bamboo. In 1715 the area that became Thetford Estate was completely lacking in running water, and even many of the ponds later found on the property were artificial; yet the presence of the label 'Thetford Works' on the map of the 1720s seems to indicate that it was this estate rather than Worthy Park which was the first to produce sugar in Lluidas Vale in any quantity. To the north-west and south-east of Worthy Park were the lands of John Laugher, which developed, in time, into the estates of Tydixon and Murmuring Brook.

The period from 1715 to 1730 was one of crucial relative growth in the history of Jamaica and Jamaican sugar.[15] From the nadir of 1696 after the departure of the privateers and the depredations of the French on the eastern end of Jamaica, the white population slowly began to increase again, so that by 1730 it numbered about 8,000. This was the beginning of a rise that, accelerated by sugar prosperity, reached a peak of about 25,000 by 1787, though never fast enough to satisfy the provisions of the 'Deficiency Laws', which required a ratio of one white man to every thirty Negroes on each estate.[16] The impracticality of recruiting sufficient white 'servants' had been finally recognized, and African Negroes accepted as the only personnel suitable for working the sugar plantations upon which Jamaica's prosperity was obviously to be based. Between 1700 and 1730 the Negro population probably doubled to about 80,000, though there were not yet nearly enough to open up all the fertile lands.[17]

A constantly reiterated plea by the planters was for a large and constant supply of cheap slaves, and while this demand was never satisfied the supply increased considerably between 1715 and 1730. Slavers and provision ships alike stopped at Barbados and the Leewards before Jamaica, and it was only with the increase of shipping and the 'saturation' of the sugar economies in those windward British colonies that Jamaican planters had a chance to expand rapidly. In 1700, Jamaica, though thirty times the size, produced only half as much sugar as Barbados and the Leewards; yet by 1730 it had equalled the production of Barbados and by 1740 exceeded the production of Barbados and the Leewards combined. By 1763 Jamaica produced four times as much sugar as Barbados, and more than half the combined total for all British colonies.[18]

Situated to leeward of the Lesser Antilles, Jamaica was not only at the farthest point of the orbit of British Caribbean trade, but was also highly vulnerable in wartime. The ending of the Spanish Succession War in 1713 removed the preoccupation with coastal defence and freed the seas for British commerce. All was not gain, however. The Treaty of Utrecht, in granting the *Asiento* and the right to send an annual ship to Spanish Porto Bello, opened up a floodgate of speculative British trade that diverted capital, ships, and slaves from the British colonies to the Spanish Main.

Over the slightly longer period, however, the British West Indian colonies benefited from the expanded trade in the Caribbean region. Shipping, capital, and capitalistic expertise built up as a result of the trade with the Spanish colonies, and with the bursting of the 'South Sea' boom in 1720 and the growing activity of the Spanish *guarda costas*, much of these were redirected to the British colonies, particularly to Jamaica.

The sugar and slave trades grew immensely in extent and sophistication during this formative period, and with the invention of new systems of credit, commission, and factorage, the first West Indian fortunes were established in London, Bristol, and Liverpool, if not yet in the island of Jamaica itself. Reinvestment of sugar profits, as Eric Williams has shown,[19] produced a 'snow-ball' effect. Besides this, the British American colonies began to play an invaluable part in the quadrilateral of British West Indian trade, providing provisions and lumber in return for sugar, for consumption, processing or re-export.[20]

As a result, or an index, of these changes, Jamaican sugar production increased rapidly. As we have seen, sugar only became the major product just before 1700. Then, from a level around 4,500 tons a year, it had only risen by about a third before 1715; but in the subsequent 15 years it more than doubled to an annual level of about 13,000 tons.[21]

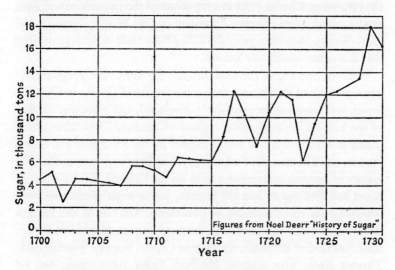

JAMAICAN SUGAR PRODUCTION, 1700-1730

It was during this period that Worthy Park began to contribute its share, and Charles Price, the struggling planter, emerged from his chrysalis a man of considerable substance, owner of a coach-and-four, and able to send his children to England for their education.

Charles Price, like most of the Jamaican planters, was already rich in land but poor in capital and poorer in slaves. The deeds in the Island Record Office bearing his name include many transactions augmenting his work-force of slaves in parcels as small as a single Negro.[22] And with the demand, the price of Negroes rose from an average of about £25 in 1700 to £50 or more in 1730. At least one of the skilled slaves whom Charles Price bequeathed at his death was valued at £70, and since even the most elderly Negroes were worth as much as many acres of land, the acquisition of estates may often have been as much for the slaves as for the land itself.[23]

In 1719, Charles Price purchased 1,000 acres in Old Woman's Savanna from John Laugher his neighbour, for the paltry sum of £150;[24] but the key event in the development of the Price fortune did not occur in Lluidas Vale and westwards, but in St. Thomas-ye-Vale to the east, when Charles Price in 1725 acquired the valuable trio of Rose family estates called Savanna Plantation or Old Works, Burton's, and New Works, thereafter generally called Rose Hall, an acreage so large that it was not specifically known.

With the opening of the road through the Rio Cobre gorge around 1700, the Vale of St. Thomas, four times the size of Lluidas and 600 feet lower, was bound to be extensively developed, and it became the first of the interior sugar-growing regions of Jamaica. Large areas of the parish of St. Thomas had been patented by the Rose brothers, Fulke, Francis, and Thomas, all of whom played an important part in the early history of Jamaica and served a term on the Council. Yet by 1725, all Roses had died out or had left Jamaica, just as sugar plantations were becoming the most desirable of possessions. The last of the Jamaica Roses was the Hon. Thomas Rose, the surviving son of the Hon. Francis Rose, husband of Elizabeth, the sister of Charles Price of Worthy Park. Thomas Rose, who married Elizabeth Fuller (1699–1722), had no children, and in his will, signed on 7 November 1724, he nominated

Guanaboa Church, founded before 1670.
The site of the St. John's Parish Vestry, this was the
nearest church to Worthy Park until the nineteenth
century.

Rio Cobre Gorge at Bog Walk, with Sugar Wain (Hakewill Print). (*See Chapter Three*)

his nephews Charles and Thomas Price the heirs of his holdings in St. Thomas-ye-Vale.[25] These estates, however, were not entirely his to bequeath. When his mother made her will in the following year, she pointed out that her husband had bequeathed Rose Hall to his son Thomas only for his life, and had stipulated that in default of 'heirs of his body' the property should go first to Elizabeth, his mother, for her lifetime, and then to John Rose, merchant of London, the nephew of Francis Rose and son of another John Rose, also a London merchant.

Once more, as in 1701, Charles Price moved quickly to avoid the loss by a testamentary accident of valuable land intended for the Prices. Even before his sister Elizabeth died, he bought out John Rose of London's interests in Jamaica for the remarkable sum of £10,000 sterling, equivalent to £14,000 Jamaican currency.[26] Included in the transaction were not only the three contiguous estates in the Vale of St. Thomas and large undeveloped areas in 'Bagnall's Thicket', St. Mary's, where later was built the famous Decoy, but also a large parcel of 'pen land' at Halfway Tree (now an important crossroads in Kingston itself) and two dwelling houses in Spanish Town formerly belonging to Francis and Thomas Rose respectively.

Charles Price continued to live at Worthy Park in the modest 'Great House', though at the time of his death he was in the process of building a far more elaborate establishment in Spanish Town, the capital.[27] He continued to build up Worthy Park until he died, to the detriment of Guanaboa, with its inferior and exhausted soils. He also seems to have used the assets of Rose Hall, which was managed by an overseer, to the benefit of Worthy Park. Only five years after the transaction with John Rose of London, Worthy Park was more than the equal of Rose Hall, producing almost as much sugar, and with 257 slaves compared to 244. In contrast to the animals flourishing at Lluidas Vale, the 32 steers and 16 mules remaining at Rose Hall were listed as 'very poor and low' or 'past labour', and the assessed value of Rose Hall had fallen to £6,878, though the value of Worthy Park—admittedly including the Great House—was assessed at £15,395.[28]

From the Inventory of Charles Price's effects drawn up in 1731 it is possible to ink with considerable detail the nature of the Great House at Worthy Park first built by his father, and to gain some notion of the estate in its early sugar years.[29] Probably constructed of wood with a stone base, Worthy Park House consisted merely of three main rooms on the ground floor with a hall and a closet, and three rooms on a second storey. Out back were a kitchen, wash house, buttery, and modest coach-house, and in the stone basement was a 'Hurrycane House' which was normally used for the storage of linen.

The furniture of Worthy Park House in 1730 was walnut or mahogany, the curtains of blue and white dimitty or speckled linen. For ordinary use there was pewter, but for more formal occasions there were '2 Tankards, 12 Chocolate Cups, 2 Water Cups, 3 pairs of Candlesticks, 1 pair Snuffers and Dish, 6 good Salts and 4 old ones, 6 Rose Waiters, 2 Soop Ladles, a sett of Castors, 2 large Sauce Pans, a Bason, 2 Hand Salvers, 12 Knives and 12 Forks and 26 Spoons, all silver' and valued at £350. Other vestiges of elegance were many 'looking glasses', a clock, ten 'family pictures', and a 'spinet'. Charles and Sarah Price had thirteen children in all, and such a moderate-sized house must often have been overcrowded. There were beds listed in every room, including the 'Great Rooms' above and below, and two 'cotts' in the closet. Also hidden away in the closet were the reminders of the pleasures of the hunt or the dangers of Negro insurrection or Maroon raids: a case of silver-mounted pistols, nine guns, two silver-hilted swords, a cane, and two bags of powder.

Worthy Park in 1730 was at least as much a stock farm as it had been in the latter days of Charles Price's father. Grazing on the savanna land on the west of the estate were 106 steers and 64 cows and calves. In addition to 90 mules, there were 17 horses and innumerable hogs, sheep, and 'small stock'. The great difference from the time of Francis Price was the production of sugar. With a field-force of at least 200,[30] there were probably as many as 200 acres already in cane, as well as 75 acres in provision crops such as plaintains, eddoes, yams, cassava, and corn. The presence in the Inventory of 1731 of 2,000 'sugar potts' (ten times the number found on the Price-Beckford estate at Guanaboa in 1673) indicates a production of at least 250 hogsheads of sugar a year. It may have been more, for Rose Price in 1795 said that Worthy Park land, properly tended, would produce two hogsheads of sugar per acre.[31]

Already, by 1730, Worthy Park was so close to the optimal size for sugar estates described by later eighteenth-century experts that we can estimate from their writings the profits which boosted the fortune of Colonel Charles Price. Writing in 1793, when there were more than 700 such sugar estates in Jamaica, Bryan Edwards calculated that an 'average' spread of 900 acres (with 300 in sugar-canes, 200 in guinea grass, 100 in provisions, and the rest waste woodland, requiring 250 slaves and 80 steers to work it) represented a capital outlay of £30,000 and would make returns of £1,500, or 5 per cent per year.[32] The chief obvious difference between the 1793 figures and those for Worthy Park sixty years earlier was that Bryan Edwards estimated the capital cost of land at £10 an acre,[33] which meant that the cost of slaves represented approximately 42 per cent of the total capital outlay. The fact that planters such as the Prices obtained their lands far more cheaply than this, and had held them long before 1730, probably meant that the proportional cost of the slaves was higher than 42 per cent, but that the total capital outlay was far lower. Taking into account the much lower costs of provisions, supplies, carriage, and credit, it is likely that the annual return on capital in the earlier period was not much less than 15 per cent.[34] This handsome return was doubtless the chief explanation for the tremendous expansion of Jamaican sugar planting and production in the early eighteenth century, an expansion that was accelerated by the high prices maintained by imperial protection.[35]

The transition to sugar suggests one reason why Charles Price was so eager to build a house for himself in Spanish Town towards the end of his life. From the maps of 1715 it seems that the first Worthy Park House was close to the site of the present factory, and the habitation built by Francis Price to be open to the fresh breezes of Lluidas Vale—the stock pens were probably some way to the north—was now beset in season by the sickly stink of the boiling sugar.[36] Another reason for Charles Price's decision to shift from the house where he was born, was that Spanish Town was the seat not only of what passed for island fashion, but also—more potent indeed—of power. Charles Price the elder was chiefly notable as an estate builder, but like his father and brothers he too served dutifully in the St. John's militia, on the parish bench as J.P. and in the Jamaican Assembly. As Colonel of the St. John's Regiment at the end of his life, he could even have aspired to be Custos and Member of the Council, like his brothers-in-law Rose. But this was not to be. Indeed, in 1725 Charles Price was expelled from the Assembly for persistent non-attendance.[37]

Backsliders, even if detained on their estates by important business, were not tolerated by the self-important Jamaican Assembly, especially if they were likely to side with the Governor in his almost occupational conflict with the elected house. For this was the last stage of the great constitutional struggle between Assembly and Governors which lasted intermittently from 1672 to 1728 over the questions of whether the Assembly could pass its own laws and whether the Governor had the right to a permanent revenue, or was forced to come cap-in-hand to the Assembly at the start of each session.[38] The first dispute was resolved in 1680 with an unequivocal victory for the Assembly, and though the revenue question was settled in 1728 by a compromise, the temporary era of better feelings between the Governor, with his nominated Council, and the elected landowners which followed, added to the immense power exercised by the plantocracy through the legislature. Though Governors were now rarely planters, they normally preferred, or were forced, to identify with the planter class, and to back up legislation which was almost exclusively designed to promote their interests.

One of the most obvious ways in which the revenue of Jamaica was voted to aid directly the interests of the planters was in the provision for roads, and tracing the spread of the Jamaican network through the records of the Assembly is one of the most vivid ways of illustrating the way in which the island was opened up. On the English pattern, public works were originally the responsibility of the parishes, which, in effect, meant the local planters gathered together in the vestries. But from the beginning of the eighteenth century the Jamaican House of Assembly took upon itself the duty of passing bills to 'empower and oblige' the parishes to build and mend particular roads and bridges.

Ruins of Thetford Factory, out of operation since 1820. From foreground (*right to left*): windmill, mule-mill, trash-house, boiling-house, distillery. (*See Chapter Five*)

Eighteenth-century windmill and boiling house, from contemporary prints.

Somewhat later, from the 1740s, the Assembly started voting money from the Public Treasury under the supervision of commissioners to pay for the development of roads, particularly in the undeveloped inland areas, or even to reimburse planters for expenditures already made on roads. Finally, from 1797, large blocks of money were voted by the Assembly nearly every year to each of the three counties of Jamaica, to be distributed as directed by a Committee of Public Works upon petition. From the beginning there was an incentive for a planter who was also a Member of the Assembly to promote a bill to oblige his fellow parishioners to build or keep up a road that served the Member's plantation. Later on, a position in the House of Assembly helped to ensure that the money issuing out of the Treasury was channelled in the right direction. In the final stage, monies were issued to groups of three trustees; but almost invariably the trustees were the planters through whose lands the roads passed, and often one of them was planter, petitioner, Assemblyman, and roadbuilder all at once.

One development that was absolutely essential for the success of Worthy Park was the construction of an adequate road over Point Hill to Guanaboa and Old Harbour, and it was not until December 1740, when Charles Price the younger was a Member of the Assembly, that a bill was brought in 'for enlarging, widening and repairing the road from Spring Garden, in the parish of St. Dorothy, to Captain Thomas Fuller's plantation in Lluidas, in the parish of St. John'.[39]

As we have seen, a road of some sort entering Lluidas Vale from the south had existed when the very first English settlers arrived there, but this bridle path required much improvement before it was suitable for sugar wains carrying four hogsheads or puncheons weighing up to 1,500 pounds apiece. Before 1740 the road had apparently been made passable—presumably by the parish and the planters themselves—for in 1731 there were two wains listed at Worthy Park, and Charles Price even had an old coach and a chariot in his coach-house. But even after 1740 improvement was not rapid, for in May 1744 the Assembly was forced to pass a Motion, 'that a committee be appointed to inspect the act . . . concerning the road from Spring Garden to Lluidas to enquire what the commissioners have done pursuant thereto, and what is become of the money raised by the said law, with the reasons why the same hath not been executed'. Even in 1774, Edward Long reported that the Point Hill road was not yet worthy of Worthy Park.[40]

A journey on wheels to the Assembly in Spanish Town, or even to church and vestry in Guanaboa, must have been a boneshaking and deterring experience. The account given by 'Monk' Lewis of his passage by Mandeville and Porus on his journey from Westmoreland to Portland in 1817, must have been more than applicable to travel in the parish of St. John almost a century earlier.[41] The road was fringed by wooded chasms and often blocked by fallen rocks or trees. A gentleman in a coach or chariot had to send an outrider up ahead to clear the way of sugar wains, though on the many steep inclines there was no way of stopping the wagons, with their four, eight or even sixteen oxen, hitched for and aft. Coming down the steepest gradients, the drivers would blow on their conch shells to warn all comers, and at certain times of year the valleys would echo and re-echo with the urgent hollow hoots of many drivers.

The route taken by the Worthy Park sugar wains, and the pannier mules that carried down smaller quantities of sugar and rum and brought back provisions and lumber, can still be followed, and some of the road is in much the same condition as—or even worse than—it was in the eighteenth-century heyday of the sugar industry. Until the very end of the eighteenth century when Port Henderson came into operation, Old Harbour was both the nearest and most convenient port for Worthy Park. The distance is 27¾ miles, and though the road rises to 2,000 feet, nowhere is the gradient greater than one-in-twelve, the steepest regarded as practical for ox-drawn wains.

Leaving Worthy Park by a ford over the Great Gully, the road passed through Thetford property before snaking steeply out of the valley to Point Hill. In 3½ miles, the road rose 800 feet, levelling out for more than a mile to give the exhausted animals a rest, before a plunge every bit as steep the eight miles down to Guanaboa Vale. Midway on the descent, at Watermount, the gradient eased as the road splashed through the ford of the Mountain River, where the oxen could drink;

and at the bend of Cudjoe Hill the welcome sight of the sea appeared for the first time. Four hundred feet below was the curving basin of Guanaboa Vale, its church and vestry-house hidden by tropical greenery; beyond it the uncultivable cockpits of the Spanish Town Red Hills and, on the distant skyline, the silvery sea, with the hump-backed whale of Great Goat Island and its attendant dolphins guarding the approaches to Galleon Harbour, Jamaica's 'old harbour', which the Spaniards had once called Puerto Esquivel.[42]

For the patient oxen, the fourteen-mile slog from Lluidas Vale to Guanaboa was a good day's journey, and as the years went on the

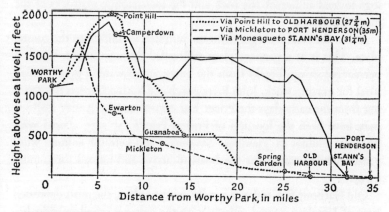

WORTHY PARK TO THE COAST: Comparative Gradients

Guanaboa holdings became less important as plantations and were turned into 'pens' or 'gardens' to rest and refresh the Lluidas Vale animals and to 'season' the Negroes off the boat from Africa and on their way into servitude on the interior estates. Even in the 1952 revision of Harrison's Jamaica map of 1883, these functions are still remembered, for around Guanaboa are listed 'Price's Pen', 'Fuller's Rest'—once owned by Thetford—and a piece of land labelled 'Swansea'.[43]

From Guanaboa to the coast was a comparatively easy journey, whether it were the 13½ miles to Old Harbour or the nine to Spanish Town and sixteen to Passage Fort. Today it is a venturesome driver who takes the road from Guanaboa where it forks off towards Old Harbour at Bamboo Junction, for since the decay of the port more than 150 years ago the roadway has scarcely been improved. On the few level stretches, the red laterite has been pressed flat into a reasonable roadbed, but where the road thrusts through the many steep ridges of the limestone foothills, the surface is naked, rain-loosened rock. Nonetheless, enough remains of the road to remind one of its former importance and the painstaking skill of the early roadbuilders, particularly the many cuttings hacked through the solid rock. These were not cut out with high explosives, but with 'Jamaican dynamite'—a fire of logs to heat and crack the rock and the metronomic mattocks of the inevitable slaves.

At last the road emerges from the jumbled foothills into the coastal plain. This is at a pleasant place still called Spring Garden, where a permanent stream breaks from the limestone to water a grassy valley ideal for grazing stock. John Price purchased Spring Garden in 1776,[44] but from the early days the Prices had owned nearby Amity Hall—it may have been the location of Francis Price's 150 acres shared with Nicholas Philpot in 'Flamingo Savanna'—and here the animals were grazed while waiting for the boats to arrive and unload three miles away.

Old Harbour Bay today is a sadly decayed place, the most depressed type of Jamaican coastal village, with the cottages raised on stilts because of the frequent floods; but in the eighteenth century it must have been a bustling place of wharves and warehouses, a vendue house for the slaves and amusement places for the seamen. Here during the shipping season might have mingled the very different dialects of Cockney, Bristolian, Liverpudlian, as sailors, often straight from the horrors of the Guinea Coast or the Middle Passage, waited to take on muscovado or molasses; or the harsh accents of Newfoundland and Acadia, the Yankee twang and southern drawl of the North Americans who had come to the tropics with saltfish, corn, shingles, or lumber for making casks. Old Harbour was always shallow, and most ocean-going vessels stood some way out, while barges shuttled their cargoes to and fro. Doubtless there was also a thriving coastal traffic between Old

Harbour and the burgeoning port of Kingston, thirty good sea miles to windward.[45]

Although Worthy Park and Rose Hall were little more than eight miles apart as the john crow flew, the only way to travel by coach or cart between the two chief Price holdings before Rose Price built the

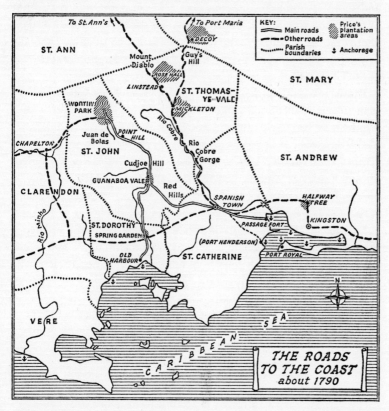

road to Ewarton in 1793 was by way of Guanaboa, a journey of twenty-five miles. From the eighteenth century maps we can see that until well after the death of Charles Price the elder, the Point Hill road was the only route better than a bridle path into Lluidas Vale. As the valley became more fully developed and its planters more vocal in the Jamaican Assembly, however, the paths to west and north were improved to the status of roads: that out of Dodd's Valley to Old Woman's Savanna in the 1760s, and the route by Camperdown to the Moneague and thereby to St. Ann's Bay in the early 1790s.[46] Neither of these was shorter or easier than the Point Hill road, however—though St. Ann's Bay had the advantage of being on the North Coast and more accessible to shipping than Old Harbour—and it was not until the construction of the Ewarton road that Worthy Park had an alternative route with reasonable grades, a lower ridge and the additional benefit of travelling by way of the Price holdings in the Vale of St. Thomas.[47]

By the standards of his day, Colonel Charles Price was an elderly man when he died at the age of 52 on 23 May 1730, but by any standards he had lived a fruitful life. Worthy Park developed more in his lifetime than at any period in its history, save perhaps in the half century after 1918. Charles Price made no great impact on the public life and history of Jamaica, but he died full of the golden opinions of his neighbours and the gratitude of his surviving children. In many ways he was the archetypal Jamaican planter of the better sort. Some years after his death his more illustrious son and namesake ordered a memorial carved that, although as much a memento to filial piety and the benefits of an English education, tells us much of his character:

> Near to this Mournfull Marble lies Interr'd
> the Body of the Hon. Coll: CHARLES PRICE
> who was divested of the Robe of Mortality
> on the 23ᵈ day of May 1730 Aged 52 Years
> Who was a Loving Husband, an Indulgent Parent,
> peaceable Neighbour, & a faithfull Friend:
> Just, Charitable, Courteous, Affable to his
> Inferiors, patient of Injuries & Slow to wrath
> A Man of Integrity, & so firm to his word, that he
> inviolably preserv'd the same even to the
> strictest Nicety of Honour, meek he was but
> truly Brave, & every way fitted for his Hon.
> station, & for a Loyalist was second to none.
> He was possessed of such a singular ingaging
> temper & sincerity of mind which rendered him
> a very desirable Companion to all, but more

especialy to those who had the happyness of
being intimately acquainted with him for he
knew no guile neither was deceit found in
his heart if he had any Enemies they must have
been the Sons of Envy, & became such not
thro any real cause by him given, but from
some invidious & Malignant seeds planted and
foster'd in their own turbulent & uneasie Breast
To say more of him would be but still to say
too little, only that he is now gone to that place
which alone knows how to reward those vertues
of which he was here the happy possessor.
O may we then like him resign our breath
In life his vertues share, be like him in Death
Pallidae mors aequo pulsat Pede pauperum
Tabernas Regumq Turres.

This 'Mournfull Marble', surmounted by a crest that may be as
fictitious as the princely descent of Francis Price, was found 'in a wood
near Aylmer's' in the middle of the nineteenth century and translated
to the parish church at Guanaboa, where it now rests. Fittingly
adjacent is the most pathetic of all the Price relics, the marble slab that
covers the last resting place of eight of the thirteen children of Charles
and Sarah Price. It speaks for itself:

Under this Tomb are deposited the Bodys
of 2 Sons and 6 Daughters the Children
of Coll: CHARLES PRICE
and SARAH his Lady

DEBORAH	13 June 1716		2 Years
KATHERINE	23 Nov: 1717		7 Years
ELIZABETH	25 Nov: 1717		12 Years
FRANCIS	died 10 July 1720	Aged	9 Months
SARAH	30 July 1721		14 Years
DEBORAH	17 Nov: 1721		5 Years
PHILLIP	4 Jan: 1722		3 Weeks
ELIZ. KATHERINE	9		9 Years

The houseful of chattering children at Lluidas Vale had become this
quiet monument; yet four sons and a daughter still remained in 1731,

as well as Sarah, the Colonel's 'lady'. There was enough in Charles Price's estate to leave all six survivors in comfortable circumstances, but the good Colonel, businessman to the last, made sure that the lands were not split into more than two almost equal portions.[48]

To Sarah Price his wife, Charles Price left the house then under construction in Spanish Town, with orders that it should be completed at the expense of his estate at Lluidas Vale, and nine house slaves. For the education and dowry of his daughter, also Sarah, he left £5,000; £3,000 to be taken from the profits of Rose Hall and the remainder from Worthy Park. His daughter was also to inherit the land at Old Woman's Savanna and eight house slaves, and in the event of the death of her mother before she reached the age of 21 or was married, she was entrusted to the guardianship of Charity Edmunds, her maiden aunt, who was bequeathed an annuity of £60.

Rose Hall, Halfway Tree, the Rose houses and storehouses in Spanish Town and the other Rose holdings in St. Ann's parish were bequeathed to Charles Price's oldest sons, Charles and Thomas, 'share and share alike'. Worthy Park and its Great House, and the reversion of the new house in Spanish Town—later called Lluidas House—were bequeathed to the youngest sons, John and Thomas Rose, then still minors, along with 'all other my lands in the parishes of St. John's St. Mary's, St. Ann's, and St. Dorothy's and elsewhere within this Island', to be shared equally. Charles Price's wife and his eldest son were nominated executors of his estate, but three trustees or guardians were also chosen from among the planter's many friends, to serve while the heirs were under age; Dr. John Charnock and Thomas Corker of St. John's,[49] and George Thorpe of Spanish Town, son of the William Thorpe who had sold Packington Field for £100 to Francis Price in order to enter the more reliable business of merchant in 1684, and had apparently become the local commission agent for the Price estates. Charnock, Corker, and Thorpe were fully empowered to manage the Price holdings, to buy and sell produce, stock and slaves, to invest money and even sell off land if necessary.

The most notable features of the will of this Jamaican patriarch, however, were the provisions for the education abroad of his surviving children, or even the buying of land in England 'in fee simple' if any of them chose to desert Jamaica and become an absentee. Colonel Charles Price had never seen the land of his ancestors, nor even left Jamaica, but in the tradition of his class he never quite came to regard Jamaica as his motherland. Hurricane, earthquake, disease, the constant threat of the revolt of the African blacks, and the fear that even the land might revert to bush and the Crown if economic and political conditions changed, made it natural that Jamaican whites should look with nostalgic longing to the comparative security of Britain's milder climate and more polished society.

Colonel Charles Price was merely among the first of a long line of those who saw sugar wealth not as a solace for residence in Jamaica but as a means of escape; if not for them, for their sons and daughters. All of Charles Price's surviving children went to England—where Charles' sister Elizabeth Rose had gone to die in 1725—though all returned to their lands in Jamaica for most of their lives. The eldest son, Charles, aged 22, had already come back to Jamaica when his father died, with the memories of his classical education 'at some of the best schools in England', Trinity College, Oxford, and that summit of an eighteenth century grandee's upbringing, the Grand Tour, fresh in his mind.[50]

NOTES

[1] The Price example illustrates the fact that primogeniture was not an inflexible rule in the British plantations, let alone a law.

[2] Francis Price had at least eighteen grandchildren, 15 of whom died at an average age of 23·9 years. Not one of the Jamaican Prices of the first five generations appears to have lived out his 'allotted' three-score years and ten.

[3] The phrase is used on one of the early collations of land plats, dating from about 1720.

[4] Wills of Francis Price and Elizabeth Price, 8 May 1689, August 1692, I.R.O. Wills, 6/68, 7/60. The oldest child, Elizabeth, wife of Francis Rose, was merely bequeathed £20 by her father and £10 by her mother, though she was to receive all the land if her brothers all predeceased her without issue.

[5] The brevity of his will and the hasty settlement of his affairs testify to this; I.R.O. Wills, 8/331; Deeds, Samuel Bromley to Charles Price, 33/89–90.

[6] *Ibid.*; 27/38–9, Francis Price to John Goffe.

7 I.R.O. Deeds, 33/89–90, Samuel Bromley to Charles Price. Of the 11 men, 9 women and 13 boys and girls—all named—7 men, 7 women and 8 boys and girls remained.

8 Compare, for example, the £100 paid by Francis Price for the 600 acres of Packington Field in 1684; above, II, 40. There is, of course, the chance that Samuel and Dorothy Bromely settled for a practicable sum to avoid the danger that Charles Price would go to Chancery to uphold the provisions of his mother's will.

9 I.R.O. Wills, 18/76, 14 January 1730.

10 Francis was to obtain the land shared with Charles Price at Lluidas and Thomas the land at Guanaboa and elsewhere—as well as £700 apiece—but on the death of Francis around 1707, Thomas Price the younger was briefly the sole heir of his father's lands. On his death in 1710, his sisters—hitherto bequeathed only £500 apiece—became, jointly, their father's heiresses.

11 Even by 1715, Christian Price was a widow and her sister Elizabeth had died and left her husband, the Hon. John Blair, a widower. P.R.O., MPGG 56 (C.O. 441/4/4 (3)).

12 I.J. St. Catherine's Maps, surveyed 1 September 1715 by Henry Nelson; P.R.O. MPGG 56, a copy with changes by Stephen Latin.

13 See Diagram of Development of Worthy Park, 1670–1730, 48. The boundaries of the 500 acres inherited by Francis Price the younger and bought by Charles Price in 1701 are easily detected on the Nelson–Latin map of 1715. These boundaries are almost impossible to trace on the present topography, though they are easy enough to place in general.

14 The son of Whitgift Aylmer the elder, who had died on Sunday, 20 July 1701, after having lived—according to his tombstone in Guanaboa Church—'46 years, 2 months, and 10 days in this Island'.

15 Contrary to most accounts, which see the period, especially 1720–30, as one of serious decline in the sugar trade.

16 Governor Hunter to B.T., C.O. 137/19, 124 (1730); Long Papers, B.M. Add. MSS. 1827, f. 93 (1786). Although an Act to maintain a ratio of one white man to every twenty Negroes was passed as early as 1703, this was chiefly to encourage white immigration, and its penalties were, apparently, never invoked. The first effective Deficiency Act was passed in 1720 and thereafter annually. By 1750, the penalties levied through the Deficiency Laws had become an invaluable source of revenue. Pitman, 35–6; 50–4.

17 See above, I, 24, n. 28; Pitman, 373.

18 L. J. Ragatz, Statistics, VII, xv; Noel Deerr, History of Sugar, 2 vols., London, 1949—50. As early as 1729 it was reported that Barbados 'has many Yeares been all clear'd and the necessary Works fix't; Francis Freelove to William Wood, July 1729, C.O. 28/21.

19 Eric Williams, Capitalism and Slavery, University of North Carolina Press, 1944.

20 Richard Pares, Yankees and Creoles, London, 1956.

21 See accompanying graph of sugar production, 53.

22 I.R.O. Deeds, 1717, 54/246 (5); 1719, 59/160 (16); 59/57 (8); 60/20 (4); 60/30 (1); 1722, 67/19 (1); 1723, 69/148 (1); 70/1 (1); 1724, 70/243 (1).

23 As late as 1717, slaves could be had in Jamaica for from £25 to £40; Sir Nicholas Lawes to B.T., C.O. 137/11, 178. For eight slaves bought of John Garland in August 1719, Charles Price paid £320; for 1,000 acres of Old Woman's

Savanna bought of John Laugher in April of the same year, he paid £150; I.R.O. Deeds, 59/57; 58/108. In the Inventory of Charles Price's possessions at Worthy Park in 1731, able-bodied male slaves were assessed at £50, females, £45, Indian men and women, £30, boys and girls, £25, old men and women, £20, and an Indian child, £10. Archives, *Inventories*, 15/147.

24 I.R.O., Deeds, 58/108.

25 I.R.O., Wills, 16/152.

26 20 July 1725, I.R.O. Deeds, 73/45.

27 I.R.O. Wills, Charles Price, 14 January 1730, 18/76.

28 Archives, Inventories, 15/147–51, dated 21 June 1731.

29 *Ibid.* This original Great House appears to have been built near the site of the present factory at Worthy Park, on the mound to the north-east on the other side of the main estate road, near the present house of Mr. Owen Clarke. Rose Price considerably extended the Great House in the 1790s. The foundations may still be seen.

30 Of the 257 slaves at Worthy Park in 1731, 92 were abled-bodied men, 56 able-bodied women, 57 boys and girls, and 52 old men and women. It is worth noting that there were 145 males to 112 females. At the same time, of the 244 slaves at Rose Hall, 50 were able-bodied men, 63 able-bodied women, 26 'old men', 15 'old women', 17 'superannuated' men and women, 23 boys and girls, 36 'children' and 14 'house negroes'. Six of the slaves were 'Indians' and the two Indian men may have been among those Amerindians imported into Jamaica about that time to track down Maroons. Archives, *Inventories*, 15/147.

31 *Worthy Plantation Book, 1791–1811;* Library of Congress. The average was closer to a ton of sugar, or 1·54 hogsheads, in 1787. In some fortunate areas, such as the French islands, two acres were cultivated per slave. This would have given Worthy Park a potential of four hogsheads per slave, or a total of 800 in 1730. Pitman, 62 n. 6.

32 Bryan Edwards, *History of the West Indies,* 1798, II, 87, quoted in Deerr, II, 333.

33 William Beckford (1790) placed the average cost of land as high as £12 an acre (cane-land £22, provision land £14, grazing £8, woodland £4); *A Descriptive Account of the Island of Jamaica,* London, 1790, II, 15.

34 A modern writer has estimated that the annual profit *to the Empire* of the British West Indies during the eighteenth century averaged 8·4 per cent on invested capital; R. B. Sheridan, 'The Wealth of Jamaica in the Eighteenth Century: a Rejoinder', *Economic History Review,* 2nd series, XXI, April 1968, 46–61.

35 See below, IV, 71. Governor Hamilton in 1715 mentioned that most of the valuable sugar land was already patented, though the enemies of the established plantocrats long maintained that the land was under-employed. Hamilton to B.T., C.O. 137/11, 10; Pitman, 124–6.

36 Having to live right on top of the factory, especially during the season, was regarded as one of the sorest trials of being a factory manager; Beckford, 11.

37 He was Member for St. John's, 1711 and 1725, Fuertado, W. A., *Official and Other Personages of Jamaica, 1655–1790,* 78.

38 A. M. Whitson, *The Constitutional History of Jamaica, 1660–1729,* Manchester U.P., 1929.

39 *Journals of the Assembly of Jamaica,* III, 16 December 1740.

40 *Ibid.,* 9 May 1744; Long, II, 51.

41 Matthew Gregory Lewis, M.P., *A Journal of a West Indian Proprietor*, London, Murray, 1834, 359–66.

42 See accompanying map of eighteenth-century roads, derived from that published by Edward Long in 1774 and copied by Bryan Edwards (1794) 63. Long, whose chief estate, Sevens (Longville), was in the neighbouring Minho Valley, described the ascent of the Lluidas Vale road from the other direction, including the magnificent view from 'Cudjue Hill', though he does not seem to have gone far beyond the newly built barracks at Point Hill, except to look on Lluidas from afar. *History of Jamaica*, II, 51–2.

43 Institute of Jamaica.

44 Originally belonging to Sir John and Hender Molesworth, Spring Garden's 2,001 acres were sold to John Burke in March 1759, by Burke to Robert Mason in 1764, by Mason's executors to Malcolm Laing 'for the use of John Price' on 19 July 1776, and by Robert Laing outright to John Price on 5 September 1786. I.R.O. Deeds, 277/159; 350/77; 'An Account of all the Lands Belonging to or in the Possession of John Price Esq. of Penzance in Great Britain, Situated in the Island of Jamaica', Worthy Park.

45 Though the shipping rate, which in 1790 was 7s. 6d. per hogshead, puncheon or 1,000 shingles, was doubtless a deterrent. For a description of Old Harbour Bay as a port, see Cynric R. Williams, *A Journey through Jamaica . . . 1823*, London, 1827, 199–200.

46 *Journals of Assembly*, VI, 15 December 1768, X, 448, etc., 1797.

47 *Journals of Assembly*, IX, 10 December 1794; and below, VII.

48 I.R.O. Wills, 18/76.

49 The tombs of John Charnock, M.D. (died 1730) and of Deborah, the wife of Thomas Corker (died 1727, age 19) are also in Guanaboa Church. Charnock was married to Frances, the daughter of 'Captain' John Rose of London.

50 *D.N.B.*, under Charles Price.

CHAPTER FOUR

Sir Charles Price: Apogée of the Price Fortune, 1730-1775

During the period from 1730 to 1793, and particularly between the end of the Seven Years' War in 1763 and the outbreak of the American War of Independence in 1775, the word 'Jamaica' became synonymous with a certain style of ostentatious luxury based upon absentee fortunes made in sugar. From this period dates the famous anecdote concerning George III out riding on horseback near Lyme Regis with William Pitt the Elder. Spying a magnificent coach with postillions and retinue crossing the heath, the King, in amazement, asked who it might be.

'That is Mr. —— the West Indian sugar planter, Your Majesty,' replied the Great Commoner.

'Sugar, sugar, eh, all that sugar?' muttered the King. 'How are the duties, Mr. Pitt? How are the duties?'[1]

The sugar duties remained moderate, for the West India Committee of absentee planters, merchants, and Agents of the islands represented a lobby in London that convinced the Government that what was good for the West Indies was good for the Empire. When Caribbean matters came up in Parliament, the 'West Indians' had ample influence to see that their interest was made into law. The North Americans, for example, had no comparable lobby.[2]

The planters who resided in Jamaica also tended to dabble in politics as a function of their 'interest', like their landed counterparts and cousins in England. Indeed, although the parallels between English and Jamaican politics have often been noted, the direct connections may have been even closer than has hitherto been realized. The evidence is patchy, but suggests that the factional skirmishing between 'planter' and 'merchant' classes in Jamaica may have been closely related to the factional manoeuvrings at Westminster, such as that between the 'Tory' adherents of the Crown and the 'patriotic' opposition which formed around the charismatic personality of the elder William Pitt.

In all British West Indian legislatures, the interest of the planters became gradually more dominant, submerging any imperial doubts and overcoming, for a time, the not entirely concurrent interests of the merchant class. In Jamaica this was largely the achievement of the eldest son of Colonel Charles Price, Sir Charles Price, grandee, faction politician and perennial Speaker of the Assembly; just as the favourable position enjoyed by Jamaica in Whitehall was largely the work of his cousins Rose Fuller, M.P., and Stephen Fuller, for thirty years the Agent of the island.[3] At the family level, the Jamaican Prices also enjoyed a useful connection, through their absentee relatives in borough-rich Cornwall, with the tangled web of English politics.

The golden evening of Sir Charles Price's career coincided with the Golden Age of Sugar, but in the formative and factious forties and fifties he epitomized the planter or 'Spanish Town' interest in the conflict with the 'Kingston' or merchant interest, with which several of the Governors sided. In building up his estates, Sir Charles Price's legislative position was of inestimable use and, paradoxically, he combined territorial megalomania with an exaggerated sense of duty. It was typical of that expansive and uncritical age that while becoming one of the five greatest Jamaican magnates he could be accorded by his peers the grandiose title, 'The Patriot'.[4]

In one respect, Sir Charles Price was almost unique. Unlike the majority of his fellow planters, including his own nephew John, he chose not to become an absentee when fortune offered the chance. In the short term his presence in Jamaica was a positive asset in building up his holdings; but in the long run even this greatest of the 'native' Jamaican plantocrats overreached himself. In contrast to such splendid absentees as Alderman William Beckford—great-grandson of Peter Beckford the first—who died in 1775 worth over a million sterling and £100,000 a year (and was consequently able to dabble in the luxury of radical politics on the side of John Wilkes),[5] Sir Charles Price died on the eve of the American War with his real estate empire staggering under the weight of mortgages. The collapse was delayed, and when it came, Worthy Park was carefully shielded from the worst of the damage. For even when the Price fortune was at its optimistic apogée, this model estate in the heart of Jamaica, though less than a tenth of the total holdings of the Prices, was regarded as the most valuable jewel in the whole necklace of estates.

The graph of Jamaican sugar production between 1730 and 1775 presents a pattern remarkably similar to that for the years between 1700 and 1730 on a rather larger scale.[6] The trend was ever upwards, but a long period of steady increase was followed by a shorter period of soaring production after 1759. In the twenty-nine years following 1730, the increase was merely by two-thirds, from 13,000 to 21,000 tons a year; yet in the sixteen years immediately after 1759, sugar production rose in zigzags to a peak of over 50,000 tons in 1773, with an average of 36,000 tons a year between 1760 and 1775.[7]

During the period from the death of Colonel Charles Price until the outbreak of the Seven Years' War, Jamaican plantations continued steadily to increase in numbers and production. That the progress was not more spectacular was attributable to several factors. Jamaica, unlike Barbados and the Leewards, had much undeveloped land; but capital and credit were still in short supply, and the large patentees were unable to obtain sufficient slaves and machinery to develop rapidly. During the frequent wars, the carriage of produce and supplies was hampered, and in peacetime slaves and supplies were diverted to the foreign West Indies and Spanish Main. The white population in the interior increased less rapidly than the number of slaves, and in the weakness of the militia and the absence of regular troops, Maroons and runaway slaves harassed the back-country regions. In the late 1730s friction with the Maroons amounted to an actual war, though by Cudjoe's Treaty in 1739 the Maroons, in return for concessions. promised to hunt down runaways and return them to their owners.[8]

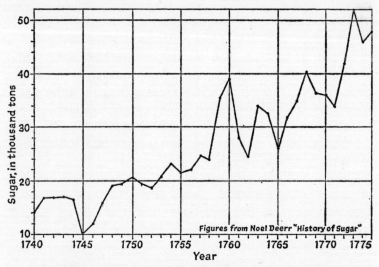

JAMAICAN SUGAR PRODUCTION, 1740–1775

Distrust, however, remained on both sides, and progress in the interior did not immediately accelerate. The enemies of the planters maintained that it was the selfish jealousy of the original patentees which limited production,[9] but the planters and their representatives claimed in reply that the lack of protection—in the double sense—meant that sugar prices were not high or stable enough to guarantee a safe return or to extend plantations. Perhaps the real reason was that the West Indian plantocracy had not yet quite gained the ascendancy in local government, nor become the most powerful single lobby at Westminster.

By the 1733 Molasses Act, some effort was made to deter the North Americans from trading with the foreign West Indies for cheaper sugar, and in 1739 the direct exportation of British West Indian sugar to southern Europe was permitted by the Act of 12 Geo. II, c. 30. Largely as a result of these enactments, the price of West Indian muscovado in England rose from a nadir of under 17s. a hundredweight in 1733, to 32s. in 1740, from which point it maintained an average of some 36s. (exclusive of duty) right down to the time of the American War.[10]

The most important event in the development of Jamaican sugar prosperity, and that which confirmed the notion that the British Empire was dominated by its sugar plantations, was the Seven Years' War (1756-63). With the establishment of British naval hegemony in the Caribbean and the extinction of rival colonies, Jamaican sugar production soared while the war was still in progress, and continued to increase thereafter. By the Treaty of Paris, the captured enemy

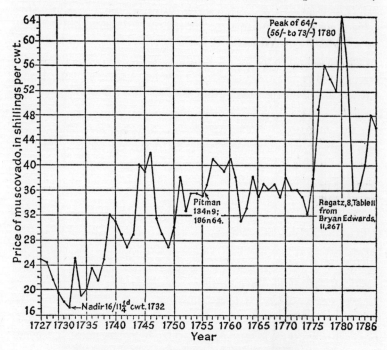

AVERAGE PRICE (EXCLUSIVE OF DUTY) OF
MUSCOVADO IN ENGLAND, 1727-1786

sugar islands of Martinique, Guadeloupe, Cuba, and Puerto Rico were all returned, so that Jamaica was not damaged by further competition within the protective system; and by the Sugar Act of 1764, the North Americans were more effectively penalized for the benefit of the British West Indies than they had been in 1733.[11]

Between 1763 and 1775, the British West Indian planters luxuriated in optimal conditions. They enjoyed steady high prices that resulted from protection and a strong demand. Peacetime freight and insurance rates were the lowest ever, and provisions and slaves were relatively plentiful and cheap. Because of the increased trade with the Spanish colonies now encouraged by the Free Port Act of 1766, even gold and silver coin were in better supply. Success bred success, and success, concord. Capital and credit became more readily available than ever before, and with the almost complete dedication of metropolitan capital to the West Indian system, an unrivalled political nexus grew up at Westminster that was not to be severely challenged until after the American War. On the local Jamaican scene, faction evaporated in an era of good feelings, characterized by votes of loyalty to the British Crown and of conspicuous gratitude to the likes of Sir Charles Price. Sugar, it seemed, had become the philosophers' stone of economics: but two human flaws remained, too soon to become apparent; the propensity of Jamaican planters to desert their island and dissipate their fortunes in vulgar expenditure, and the tendency of those who remained to expand their holdings far beyond their power adequately to finance them.

The second Charles Price returned to Jamaica early in 1730, leaving behind in England his younger brothers Thomas Rose and John. The latter, who was consumptive, settled in Cornwall for the sake of his health and founded an absentee branch of the family active in English politics,[12] though all three brothers actually died in Jamaica. In 1732 Charles Price was elected to the Jamaican Assembly, and by 1739 he was one of its most prominent Members. Over the following six years he effectively gained control of the legislature by means of an alliance with Governor Edward Trelawny (1738–52), a Cornish protegé of Walpole's who appears to have infected Jamaica with the kind of petty faction politics with which he had been familiar as M.P. for West Looe.[13] As a reward for his efforts, Charles Price was elected and confirmed as Speaker in 1745, a position he retained almost continuously for eighteen years. In 1749, Trelawny, who was a frequent visitor to Price's estates, even pressed for the appointment of his friend as Lieutenant-Governor, despite the typical eighteenth-century calumnies of Price's enemies that he was a chronic debtor 'of no abilities or Experience' who 'frequently Lyes with Black women'.[14]

In the event, Trelawny did not leave the West Indies until after the arrival of his successor, Admiral Charles Knowles, in 1752, and by that time the worst of the factional rifts had been patched over. This was partly due to Trelawny himself, who, like most West Indian Governors who served long terms, came to identify with local interests so completely that factions could no longer form for and against the Governor as a function of the rift between imperial and colonial interests. In his last Assembly Trelawny signed many controversial Acts without a murmur, though seven—including one appointing Judges on good behaviour rather than at the Royal Pleasure—were immediately overturned in London, and at his departure he received a vote of thanks of almost unprecedented fulsomeness.

The chief aim of the Assembly was now to consolidate its ascendancy over the Governor. In October 1751, twelve of the leading Jamaican politicians met at Charles Price's house in Spanish Town to form a coalition, called the Jamaica Association, that would present Trelawny's successor with a united front. Among the signatories were three merchants, of whom Henry Archbould was the husband of Charles Price's sister Sarah.[15] But nine of the members of the Jamaica Association were planters of the Spanish Town clique, of whom three were so dominant as almost to comprise a triumvirate: Charles Price, his cousin Rose Fuller—who had been one of the bitterest opponents of Trelawny and Price in previous years—and Richard Beckford, the brother of Alderman William Beckford. Since William Beckford was one of the closest confidants of William Pitt, and Rose Fuller and his four brothers in London were close to the ear of the Duke of Newcastle, the Jamaica Association wielded unprecedented power.[16]

77

With inferior connections with the Ministry in London, the unfortunate Governor Knowles had little chance of reasserting the power of the Executive in the affairs of Jamaica, and after provoking one of the most severe crises in the political history of Jamaica, he was recalled in 1756. So virulent was the opposition of the planters to Governor Knowles that he shifted his seat 'for safety' from Spanish Town to Kingston. Once there, he drummed up the support of those merchants who felt that the capital should be moved from plantocratic Spanish Town to the island's chief commercial centre. By adroit political manoeuvring, Knowles obtained a temporary majority in the Assembly that elected a merchant to the Speaker's chair and voted the transfer to Kingston early in 1755. The subsequent session was characterized by scandalous conflict between merchants and planters which led to the arrest and imprisonment of Charles Price and fifteen of his supporters and, when the planters' complaints reached London, to the summary recall of Governor Knowles.[17]

The planters now counterattacked. With a majority reinstated in the new Assembly—and Charles Price once more in the Speaker's chair—they passed a vote of thanks for the removal of Knowles and loyally petitioned for the return of the capital to Spanish Town. Assent reached Lieutenant-Governor Moore in September 1758, and amid scenes of jubilation that included the burning in effigy of Charles Knowles and certain prominent merchants, Charles Price and his supporters returned in triumph to their home town.[18]

For five years after the return of the Assembly to Spanish Town, Jamaica was preoccupied with the events of the Seven Years' War. As usual in wartime, the disputes between merchants and planters, and even between the islanders and the Royal Navy, were submerged by the common exigencies of defence and the need for convoys for 'the Trade'. In October 1763, Charles Price—now 55—retired from the Assembly on the grounds of ill-health, to be voted a present of plate worth £500 by a grateful House.[19] He left the Assembly in friendly hands, for the Members voted unanimously to elect his son and namesake to the vacant Speaker's chair. Charles Price Junior, who held the Speakership for most of the time until he returned to England in 1775, carried on the 'patriotic' fight for the powers of the Legislature over the Executive, and won a notable victory for the privileges of the Assembly over Governor Lyttleton in 1765.[20]

Charles Price Senior did not retire for long. After a brief return to the Assembly in 1765 he was nominated to the Council in 1768 by Governor Sir William Trelawny, Edward Trelawny's naval cousin, and in the same year was made a baronet by George III. He died, full of honours, in June 1772, having for the last period of his life also been Custos of St. Catherine's, Judge of the Supreme Court, and Major-General in the militia. Charles Price's praises were sung eloquently by Edward Long in 1774, and extravagantly by the marble memorial raised to his memory at the Decoy and now in the Cathedral at Spanish Town.[21] But perhaps his chief monument was the unprecedented power of the Jamaican Assembly and its position in relation to the Crown and its colonial Governors, which was expressed in its most extreme form by the 'Loyal Address' to the King on behalf of the grievances of the North Americans in December 1774.[22]

The objective historian who examines the basis of Sir Charles Price's fortune, however, is not likely to be impressed by his altruism. Sir Charles Price was probably the most flagrant beneficiary of the system whereby the control of the Jamaican Government enabled the planters to obtain cheap land. Despite the Order-in-Council of 1735 limiting grants to 1,000 acres,[23] Price patented between 1738 and 1769 no less than 8,707 acres. He also bought up adjacent land whenever it became available cheaply, and at his death possessed 26,000 acres—perhaps the largest portion of Jamaica ever owned by a single individual.[24] Had it been possible for all these holdings to have been planted, Price might have become the richest planter in the world; but it is obvious from the transactions recorded in the Island Record Office and Archives of Jamaica that many of his land dealings were speculative investments.[25]

The most damaging fact that emerges from a study of the 164 deeds and 11 patents bearing the signature of Charles Price the second is that he obtained, during periods of good relations with the Governors, large tracts of Crown Lands which he later, where possible and convenient, sold in smaller parcels. Two periods when Charles Price notably failed to obtain Crown Lands were the years of party faction early in the tenure of Edward Trelawny, and during the period of conflict with Governor Knowles. Before he became Speaker in 1746, Charles Price patented 1,500 acres of Crown Lands in four separate parishes, and after 1769 a final 1,307 acres in three parcels of 1,000, 227, and 80 acres. But his largest acquisitions were during the brief heyday of the Jamaica Association coalition, when he patented first 600 valuable acres in St. Mary's and then, having convinced his friend Edward Trelawny that Britain's dependence on the troublesome Honduras Shore would thereby be obviated, was granted the patent for about 5,000 acres at Lacovia and Black River in St. Elizabeth 'for growing logwood'.[26]

Between 1738 and 1771, Sir Charles Price acquired 21,641 acres in eleven of Jamaica's nineteen parishes, of which 8,707 acres were patented, 2,590 acres leased, and the remainder bought outright. The cost of the 10,984 acres purchased was approximately £30,400, or an average of £2. 15s. 6d. an acre. In all, Sir Charles Price disposed of 6,072 acres, as well as house lots in Kingston, Spanish Town, Port Royal, Bath, and St. Ann's Bay, which appear to have realized some

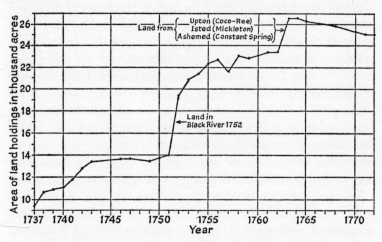

SIR CHARLES PRICE I'S TOTAL LAND HOLDINGS
1737–1772 (INCLUDING LEASEHOLDS)

£30,600, an average of £5. 8s. 6d. per acre. One of his most notable transactions was to sell to the Government itself, in 1760, 240 acres at Salt Pond, St. Catherine's, for £3,880, which had been sold to Thomas Rose Price in 1748 for £498.[27]

Thus, Sir Charles Price the 'Patriot' managed, overall, to recover almost his total investment in land of £30,400 in selling off only 58 per cent of the area acquired. When his land dealings are broken down by parishes, however, he appears in an even less scrupulous—or more businesslike—light. Sir Charles Price speculated chiefly in the highly developed areas of St. Catherine's or St. Andrew's, and in the rapidly-developing back-country areas of St. Mary's and St. Ann's. When these parishes are considered separately, it can be seen that 57 per cent of the land acquired was sold off for 131 per cent of the total purchase price. Of the 'heartlands' of St. John and St. Thomas-ye-Vale, where Sir Charles Price had spent £12,325 in acquiring 4,170 acres—including the Cocoree in Lluidas from Samuel Upton in 1753 and Mickleton, the last of the Rose holdings from Thomas Isted in 1766[28]—hardly any were disposed of out of the Price family at all.

	Total Acres acquired	Acres patented	Acres leased	Acres bought	Price £	Acres sold	Price £
St. Elizabeth	5,300	5,300					
St. Mary	3,970	600	250	3,120	5,659	1,217	1,487
St. Ann	3,656	1,300	820	1,546	250	1,980	1,063
St. Catherine	3,379		700	3,309	11,523	1,367	17,863
St. Thomas-ye-Vale	2,141	80	820	1,241	9,802	1,308	4,911
St. John	2,029	300		1,729	1,000	50	100
St. David	600	600					
St. Andrew	300	300			100		2,676
St. Dorothy	227	227				150	94
St. Thomas in the East	23			23			200
Port Royal	16			16	2,025		2,025
TOTALS	21,641	8,707	2,590	10,984	£30,359	6,072	£30,419

Although a land speculator on a grand scale, Sir Charles Price did develop a considerable proportion of his lands. Indeed, had he not cleared and planted at least some of his patented acres even he would not have been able to have prevented their reversion to the Crown. Some indication of his stature as a true planter can be gauged from the huge number of slaves he possessed. As early as 1744 he owned 1,353 slaves on Burton's (543), Shenton (43), Rose Hall (321), Wallins (199), Decoy (112), Amity Hall (12), and Cutthroat Gully (21), and altogether probably owned 1,800 by the time of his death in 1772.[29] This swarm of Negroes almost certainly made him the largest Jamaican slaveholder during the eighteenth century, as well as the most substantial land-owner.[30] To replenish the supply was a constant concern, and although normal sales at the vendue houses were not recorded in the Island Record Office, there are twenty-four transactions recorded involving Negroes bought by Sir Charles Price between 1741 and 1771. In December 1755, for example, Charles Price was one of three partners who purchased a whole cargo of slaves—perhaps 500 souls—for £16,000, payable in sugar and bills of exchange.[31]

Sir Charles Price was also a great roadbuilder, though in under-taking the construction of the roads without which his new estates would have been worthless, he was not slow to ask reimbursement from the House of Assembly, or even to levy tolls where public roads passed over his lands. As we have already seen, an Act was passed in 1740 to improve the road from Old Harbour into Lluidas Vale, and within the following thirty years, similar Acts were passed to build or improve the roads from Lluidas to Croft's Hill, and from Guanaboa to St. Thomas-ye-Vale.[32] Charles Price was more directly involved in constructing the two roads connecting the Vale of St. Thomas with the north coast of Jamaica for the first time, innovations that were ex-tremely important after the development of the northern parishes and the creation of ports of entry at Port Antonio and Montego Bay in 1758.[33] Charles Price was particularly interested in connecting his estate at the Decoy in St. Mary's with Spanish Town and with the north shore. As Member of the Assembly for St. Thomas, he managed to persuade the freeholders of his constituency to form a unique parochial road committee, and between 1764 and 1772 the House of Assembly almost annually voted money to construct and complete a carriage road over Guy's Hill to the newly established harbour of Port

Maria, by way of the Decoy and Bagnall's Thicket, in sums that escalated gradually to £1,000, for a total of £2,265.[34] More important for the general economy of Jamaica—it is now the island's A1 Highway—was the spectacular carriage road over Mount Diablo to St. Ann's Bay, which would have the additional benefit of connecting more of the Price estates. Charles Price was closely involved with this road from its beginning in 1769, though it was not completed until several years after his death.[35]

Following the English pattern, there was considerable pressure in Jamaica from the middle of the eighteenth century to finance road-building by turnpike trusts.[36] Indeed, from their promotion of turn-pikes and tollgates it seems that Jamaican landowners were less concerned with opening up commerce than with turning the roads over their lands into another form of income. At different times tolls were suggested for the roads through the Rio Cobre gorge and over Mount Diablo,[37] but potentially the biggest revenue-maker was the road between Kingston and Spanish Town where it was made impassable by the mouth of the Rio Cobre. Here a toll-ferry had existed since 1749, but some time before 1762 Charles Price built a road between Passage Fort and the Ferry upon which, by an Act of 16 February 1762, he was empowered to levy a toll of 5s. for each coach or wagon and 3s. 6d. for every sugar wain, the income being intended for the cost of building and upkeep of the road. The inhabitants of Spanish Town and the parish of St. Catherine petitioned the Assembly in November 1763 that the tolls were 'an insupportable burden' and brought 'excessive gain' to the tollkeeper. Charles Price agreed to surrender his 'contract' in return for £700, which, he computed, was his expenditure on the road.[38] Attempts were made in November 1764 and September 1766 to pass bills to reimburse Charles Price, but they were unsuccessful, perhaps because since he continued to enjoy the tolls, it was not to Price's interest to force them through. It was not until the end of 1767 that Charles Price was voted the £700 by the Assembly and the Act was passed that taxed the parish of St. Catherine for the money in return for the abolition of the tollgate.[39] The present road was con-structed as the result of an Act passed in December 1774 to raise £6,000 for a causeway and bridge by means of subscriptions and a public lottery.[40]

Sir Charles Price owned one of the largest houses in Spanish Town, the location of which, on a whole-block lot on Red Church Street, can be traced from old maps, though the building has since disappeared.[41] This was his home during the sessions of the Assembly and the Supreme Court, nearly always held in November and December, which was also the Season in the Jamaican capital. 'They live after a gay Manner', wrote Leslie of the Spanish Town planters in 1740,

'tis surprising to see the Number of Coaches and Chariots which are perpetually plying, besides those which belong to private Persons; they have frequent Balls, and lately have got a Playhouse, where they retain a Set of extraordinary good Actors. In short, they live as happily as if they were within the Verge of the *British Court*: and to do them Justice, they seem perfectly polite, and have a Delicacy of Behaviour which is exceedingly taking.[42]

In this society, Sir Charles Price was outstanding. 'In private life,' wrote his admirer Edward Long,

his complacency of manners, accomplished knowledge of books and men, and delicacy of humour, rendered him the polite, instructive, and entertaining companion: here he shone the inflexible lover of truth, the firm friend, and the generous patron. His mind was amply stored with the treasures of a liberal erudition. But theology seemed his favourite science; and the Great Author of nature, the chief object of his study.[43]

For a man of such sensibility as Sir Charles Price, Spanish Town could not have been permanently congenial; for most of the clergy of the established church had strayed far from the designs of the Great Author, and the members of the Jamaican plantocracy who had not the 'Advantage of a polite generous Education' in Great Britain despised any learning beyond an ability to 'read, write and cast up Accounts'. They were also addicted to gambling, and to such heavy drinking that the creation of the Jamaican Bath in St. Thomas in the East in 1731—Sir Charles Price was later a Director—was more a medical necessity than the result of an attempt to reproduce in Jamaica the society of Bath or Tunbridge Wells in England.[44]

Spanish Town, moreover, was fatally unhealthy, and Sir Charles Price preferred to spend most of the year on his country estates, particularly at the magnificent mansion he built at the Decoy some time around 1765. This house was described by Edward Long in 1774 as being constructed:

... of wood, but well finished, and has in front a very fine piece of water, which is commonly stocked with wild-duck and teal. Behind it is a very elegant garden disposed in walks, which are shaded with the cocoanut, cabbage and sand-box trees. The flower and kitchen-garden are filled with the most beautiful and useful variety which Europe or this climate produces. It is decorated, besides, with some pretty buildings; of which the principal is an octagonal saloon, richly ornamented on the inside with lustres, and mirrors empanneled. At the termination of another walk is a grand triumphal arch, from which the prospect extends over the fine cultivated vale of Bagnals quite to the Northside Sea. Clumps of graceful cabbage-trees are dispersed in different parts, to enliven the scene; and thousands of plantane and other fruit-trees occupy a vast tract, that environs this agreeable retreat, not many years ago a gloomy wilderness.[45]

Sir Charles Price, who was so attached to the Decoy that he left instructions that he should be buried there, was famous for his hospitality. The Decoy 'was constantly open to the reception of worthy men, whether of the island or strangers: and few gentlemen of rank, whether of the Army or Navy, on service here, quitted the island without having passed some of their time at the Decoy'.[46] Although sold by the Prices in the 1790s, the Decoy remained a favourite retreat of Governors, Admirals, Judges, and important visitors to Jamaica until well into the nineteenth century, and Lady Nugent provides memorable descriptions of two visits in 1802 and 1803.[47] Since that time, however, every trace of the Decoy has disappeared.[48]

Closer than the Decoy to Spanish Town, and in a situation just as impressive, Worthy Park might well have been chosen by Sir Charles Price as his country seat had he ever owned it completely. He lived there for some time after his return to Jamaica in 1730 and appears to have been attorney or manager of the estate for most of the next two decades; but by his father's will the estate had been bequeathed to John Price and Thomas Rose Price, and only on the death of the latter in 1750 did Charles Price inherit a share of Worthy Park. John Price had died on a last visit to Jamaica in 1740, but his share of the estate fell to his infant son, also John, who spent all but a few months of his life in Cornwall, on the lands purchased by the terms of his grandfather's will.[49] Thomas Rose Price appears to have spent most of his short adult life in London, but on setting out on the risky voyage to Jamaica in September 1747 he made his brother Charles his sole heir. He survived the journey but died little more than two years later, making his brother half-owner of Worthy Park.[50] The management of Worthy Park and its related holdings was now entirely in the hands of Charles Price, the last survivor of the thirteen children of Colonel Charles Price, and the direct management was carried on by his son and namesake after his death. On the death of the second Sir Charles Price without issue in 1789, however, it was only through the tenuous Cornish link—provided by the first of the true Price absentees—that the Price inheritance was carried on at all.[51]

Despite his non-residence, Sir Charles Price after 1750 was instrumental in supplying Worthy Park, and two neighbouring estates, with the commodity in which they were chiefly deficient: running water. Once more, his powerful position in the Legislature was doubtless invaluable. Between 29 September and 13 October 1752 a bill was introduced and passed through three readings in the Assembly, the preamble to which read:

WHEREAS the Conveying the Water by a Trench Gutter or Aquaduct from one of the Heads of the Rio Cobre known by the name of Murmuring Brook in the Parish of St John through the lands of Thomas Fuller Esquire William Halsted Esquire George Maddix Carpenter Whitegift Samuel Aylmer Gentleman Elizabeth Bonny a Minor and Susannah Elletson Laugher a Minor, to a Plantation called Worthy Park situate lying and being in a certain Vale in the said Parish called Luidas will be a great Benefit and advantage to Charles

Price Esquire Speaker of the present Assembly Proprietor of the said Plantation by enabling him to make water Mills for grinding of Sugar Canes and will also be a means of settling and improving the uncultivated land of the said Charles Price and will also be a further Benefit and Advantage to Sundry Proprietors of other Plantation Lands and Settlements adjoining to and near the said Planation called Worthy Park which are now destitute of running Water. . . .[52]

The bill was passed by the Assembly after the Members had satisfied themselves that the adjacent owners and the guardians of the two minors approved of the aqueduct. The Council was rather less tractable, pointing out that one of the guardians of Elizabeth Bonny and Susannah Laugher was also a mortgage-holder of their estate of Murmuring Brook, and that notice of the intended bill should properly have been posted in the parish church of St. John's for three weeks; but the bill passed the Council with one amendment on 17 October and was signed by Governor Charles Knowles on 21 October 1752. The Act was not confirmed by the King until August 1760, but by that time the aqueduct had probably already been some years in existence.[53]

The Worthy Park 'gutter wall' still exists in working order, with much of the eighteenth-century brick and stone work still intact, providing the chief water supply for Lluidas Vale village as well as the Worthy Park factory. It was an impressive engineering feat for the Jamaica of its day, and to follow its curving $2\frac{1}{4}$-mile course is to become convinced of the importance of Worthy Park during the Golden Age of Sugar. The Murmuring Brook stream was tapped at the top of the Laugher lands, just before it petered out in the tumbled porous rocks of the Great Gully. The aqueduct followed the sinuous walls of the Gully, easing the gradient, so that it is often near the top of precipitous slopes 50 or 60 feet high. Three-quarters of a mile from the source, it was first harnessed by the Murmuring Brook factory, the huge housing of the water-wheel and the ruined buildings of which can still be seen.[54] A mile farther on the aqueduct passed briefly through the Thetford lands of Thomas Fuller, perhaps to be drawn off for irrigation, but not, it seems, for driving cane mill wheels.[55] The water may also have been utilized by Shady Grove, the small estate built up around the present site of Lluidas Vale village by Dr. John Quier between 1767 and 1822.[56] Finally, the aqueduct reached Worthy Park sugar mill, where a huge dormant water-wheel may still be seen, though it dates from 1866. From the Act of 1752, it appears possible that the 'Trench Gutter or Aquaduct' was intended to pass through Worthy Park a further mile to the Mowden Hall factory of the Halsted–Aylmer lands, but this was never accomplished, and Swansea, like Thetford, was faced by the growing technical predominance of Worthy Park.

For doubtless waterpower revolutionized the operation of Worthy Park and, once the huge expense of the building of the aqueduct had been overcome, her profitability was enhanced as well as her productivity. Unfortunately, few figures remain for this crucial period of development. The only official accounts of production were those handed in by managers for absentee owners or minors and recorded in the Island Record Office. We therefore only have figures for Worthy Park in 1741, 1743, and 1744 on behalf of the infant John Price, and for the years after 1775 when Sir Charles Price the younger left for England. These alone, however, are significant. In 1741, the 'produce of the late Charles Price on Worthy Park' amounted to 8,201 potts of sugar and 3,000 gallons of rum, or approximately 265 hogsheads of sugar and 27 puncheons of rum. In 1743, the estate produced 8,578 potts of sugar and 5,000 gallons of rum, amounting to perhaps 276 hogsheads and 45 puncheons,[57] and in the following year, 288 hogsheads of sugar (of which 140 were shipped and 148 sold locally) and 3,712½ gallons, or about 33¾ puncheons, of rum.[58] In 1776, Worthy Park, the 'Estate of John Price', produced no less than 354 hogsheads of sugar and 130 puncheons of rum, which indicates an increased productivity of approximately 46 per cent over the period between 1744 and 1775.[59] In gross income, the gain was even more impressive. In 1776, the 354 hogsheads of sugar produced at Worthy Park were sold in Jamaica for £8,731, an average of approximately 38s. per hundredweight in a year when the average London pre-duty price was 47s. 6d. per hundredweight.[60] If the relative Worthy Park production figures and London prices are taken into account, the value of sugar produced in the earlier period can be calculated at £3,997 for

1741, £4,521 for 1743, and £7,862 for 1744, an average of £5,460 a year, at 27s. 9d. for each of the 3,926 hundredweight produced in an average year.[61] The 130 puncheons of rum produced in 1776 were sold for £1,823, making a total for sugar and rum of £10,554. Taking into account the average of 35¼ puncheons of rum produced in 1741-4, it is likely that the gross income from Worthy Park's sugar and rum in the earlier period averaged about £5,848 a year.[62] This would indicate an increased gross income of £4,685, or almost exactly 80 per cent. It should be remembered, however, that the sugar prices for 1776 were particularly good.[63]

One thing is certain: that after the construction of adequate roads into Lluidas Vale and the building of the Murmuring Brook aqueduct, no Price would be able to persuade his neighbours at Lluidas Vale to give up his sugar land as long as the sugar boom lasted. Even that tireless and ingenious empire-builder, Sir Charles Price, was not able to add to Worthy Park's sugar acreage. The only additions made to Worthy Park between 1730 and 1772 were the 584½ almost inaccessible acres of Cocoree grazing land bought from Samuel Upton for £300 in 1753, and 600 acres of mountainous land at Riverhead purchased from John Lunan in 1766 for £200, though from 1776 onwards, the Prices had the use of the invaluable estate of Spring Garden on the road to Old Harbour.[64]

The most important contribution to the development of Worthy Park made by Sir Charles Price, however, was not in the acquisition of fresh land but in assuring that whatever happened to all his other holdings, Worthy Park, and its related lands, would not be further subdivided, and would suffer the depredations of Price creditors last of all. By the terms of Sir Charles Price's will,[65] enrolled on 20 August 1772, the lands at Cocoree and Riverhead acquired by Sir Charles were declared indissolubly part of Worthy Park; yet at the same time, Sir Charles renounced any interest he or his direct heirs might have in the half share of the estate held by John Price of Penzance. Moreover, the will declared that on the death of the second Sir Charles Price without issue, his half share of Worthy Park would revert to John Price. This was to be of immense importance later, for when Sir Charles Price the second died without children in 1789, the whole of Worthy Park passed to his cousin John Price of Penzance and was spared the ignominious fate of the rest of the old Price holdings.

NOTES

1 Quoted by Richard Pares, *Merchants and Planters*, 38.

2 'For Interest with you we have but little. The West Indians vastly outweigh us of the Northern Colonies'; Franklin to Collinson, 30 April 1764, *Franklin Writings* (ed. Smythe), IV, 243, cited by Pitman, 334 n. Namier, *Structure of Politics at the Accession of George III*, London, Macmillan, 1957.

3 1764–94. Stephen Fuller was the grandson of Fulke Rose, brother-in-law of Colonel Charles Price.

4 The epithet—redolent throughout eighteenth-century British politics of opposition to the Crown—was recorded by Edward Long, the most fervent of Price's admirers; Long, II, 76–7 n.

5 D.N.B., under William Beckford.

6 Above, III, 53.

7 See accompanying graph of sugar production, using figures from Noel Deerr, II.

8 Carey Robinson, *Fighting Maroons of Jamaica*, 36–52.

9 '... I have daily Application for further Grants, which upon Surveys taken thereof not Exceeding Five hundred Acres in One Grant is by Custom Esteemed as of right. Tho' indeed often there is little Intention of Settling the Same; but rather to form themselves a Sort of Barrier against an approaching Neighbour ... the greatest part of the Valuable Lands Unsettled has been long since patented and now in hands who neither Cultivate nor care to dispose of it, I shall endeavour all I can procure proper remedys which I'm afraid will meet the greatest opposition'; Governor Hamilton to B.T., 30 August 1715; C.O. 137/11, 10, quoted in Pitman, 110.

10 See accompanying graph of sugar prices, 1727–86, from Pitman and Ragatz.

11 The fact that the returns from the sugar duties of 1733 were pitiful has often been pointed out. Their deterrent effect is less easily gauged. The 1764 Act halved the duties on foreign sugar, but was more effectively collected.

12 For the Cornish activities of the Prices, see VII and VIII, below.

13 George Metcalf, *Royal Government and Political Conflict in Jamaica, 1729–1783*, London, Longmans for the R.C.S., 58–9; L. B. Namier, *Structure of Politics*.

14 Trelawny's agent Francis Gashry faintly defended Price by pointing out that these defects might be said to apply to any West Indian planter; Gashry to Trelawny, 25 July 1749, B.M. Add. MSS. 19038, f. 48, quoted by Metcalf, 100.

15 From whom Charles Price was to buy the magnificent property of Constant Spring (2,011 acres) in 1766, for £13,565. I.R.O. Deeds 213/180.

16 *The Jamaican Association Develop'd*, London, 1757. Rose Fuller left Jamaica in 1756 on the death of his brother John, and thereafter sat as M.P. for Sussex; Metcalf, 109–38.

[17] *An Historical Account of the Sessions of the Assembly . . . Containing a Vindication of . . . Charles Knowles*, London, 1757. During this session, Charles Price and his supporters attempted to overthrow the Governor's suspending power and to assert the right of the Assembly to appoint commissioners to receive revenue. Both of these pretensions were severely censured by the House of Commons in 1757; *House of Commons Journals*, xxvii, Metcalf, 136.

[18] Metcalf, 141. Henry Moore was Jamaican-born, a schoolfriend of William Beckford and the brother-in-law of Edward Long. He had acted as intermediary between Edward Trelawny and his opponents in 1751. It is worth noting that the shift back to Spanish Town was accompanied by important administrative decentralization. By the same Order-in-Council, Jamaica was divided into three counties and three additional ports of entry created: Middlesex (Kingston), Surrey (Port Antonio), and Cornwall (Montego Bay and Savanna-la-Mar).

[19] *Journals of the Assembly*, V, 385, 11 October 1763. Charles Price had already been voted testimonials of plate worth 200 *pistoles* in 1748 and £200 in 1760, *ibid.*, III, V, 248.

[20] Metcalf, 160–9.

[21] '. . . with an honest loyalty to his sovereign, which none could surpass, he possessed a truly patriotic attachment for his country; and though ever ready to assist and facilitate administration, while conducted on the great principle of public good, he was always the steady, persevering, and intrepid opponent to illegal and pernicious measures of governors. If it were at all necessary to produce testimonials in justification of his character, I might refer to the very honourable marks of approbation which were so deservedly conferred upon him, both by the crown, and the different assemblies in which he presided, for so many years, as speaker, with an integrity, candor and dignity, that were almost unexampled', Long, II, vii, 76 n. The Decoy monument was transferred to the church at Port Maria in September 1932, the tombstone to Spanish Town; *Daily Gleaner*, 9 April 1963. The inscription on the tombstone reads: *CAROLUS PRICE, Baronettus, multis vir ornatus virtutibus; in omnibus enim vitae officiis ita se probavit ut et civibus et sociis gratissima esset ejus integritas et fides. Memoriae tanti viri Carolus Price, filius natu maximus et quattuor solus superstes, fortunae et honoris, utinam ac virtutem haeres, hoc monumentus posuit.*

[22] *Journals of the Assembly*, VI, 569–70; C.O. 137/70; Metcalf 187–90.

[23] Order-in-Council of 30 July 1735 approving the instruction to Governor Cunningham, C.O. 137/22, 1; Pitman, 119–20.

[24] The oft-quoted statement that Sir Charles Price was the fifth of sixty Jamaican planters owning more than 5,000 acres, with 13,651 acres, behind William Beckford, James Dawkins, Henry Gale, and Francis Sadler Hals (*Caribbeana*, IV, 95, quoting B.M. Add. MSS. 12436) dates from 1750. Charles Price acquired at least 18,564 acres after 1750, disposing of 6,227, leaving 25,998; I.R.O. Deeds and Archives, Patents.

[25] In 1754, Governor Knowles estimated that there were no less than 1·6 million acres of uncultivated plantable land in Jamaica. The Crown still held about 0·6 million acres of plantable ground, but of the 1,671,569 acres patented, only about 0·5 million were in cultivation; Knowles to B.T., 31 December 1754, C.O. 137/28, 43, quoted in Pitman, 124–5. The total area of Jamaica was estimated at 3·84 million acres, of which 1·71 million acres were held to be 'mountainous, inexcessible, rocky or barren land'.

[26] Archives, Patents 21/29; 21/170; 22/11; 23/139; 25/140; 25/150; 26/29;

26/30; 28/159; 30/133; 32/34. Although granted thirty years' grace, neither Sir Charles Price nor his son appear to have done much actual logwood planting in St. Elizabeth; Metcalf, 77.

27 I.R.O. Deeds 134/152; 184/150.

28 *Ibid.*, 142/176–8; 199/159; 216/181. Mickleton consisted of 1,050 acres with 125 slaves, for which Price paid £9,800.

29 *Ibid.*, 120/114. Sir Charles Price's major sugar estate acquisitions after 1744 included Plum Grove (1754), Magotty Savanna (1756), Bagnall's Thicket (1761), Mickleton + 125 slaves (1766), Riverhead (1766), Constant Spring (1766).

30 R. B. Sheridan, 'The Wealth of Jamaica in the Eighteenth Century', *Economic History Review*, 2nd series, XVIII, 2, 1965, 292–311, does not mention anyone with more slaves than Henry Dawkins, who died owning 1,062 in 1743, nor anyone holding more than the 22,021 acres of William Beckford in 1754.

31 *Ibid.*, 162/27. Price's partners were Peter Furnell and Edward Manning, fellow member of the Jamaica Association. The vessel was the *Lime* of Liverpool, owned by John Knight and Company.

32 Above, III, 59, n. 39. *Journal of the Assembly*, IV, 10 October 1750; VI, 15 December 1768.

33 Order-in-Council 29 June 1758; C.O. 137/31, 27; Pitman, 21, 306–7. Previously, the easiest route from Linstead to the North Coast was by way of Kingston and a boat—a mode that was dangerous during wartime and tedious and expensive at all times.

34 £300 in November 1764, £120 in November 1766, £140 in December 1767 and December 1768, £565 in December 1769, and £1,000 in December 1772; *Journals of the Assembly*, V, VI. A further £500 had to be voted in 1783 because the road had been washed out by floods; *ibid.*, VII, 6 December 1783. In 1774, Edward Long described the Guy's Hill road as 'inferior to none in Great Britain, if we consider the difficulty of the ascent which was to be gained, a great part being cut through perpendicular rock; the judgement with which it is traversed, and the safety and ease with which so high a mountain is rendered passable to wheeled carriages', Long, I, 468. Unusually, Sir Charles Price used dynamite in constructing this road, some of the £565 voted in 1769 being for this.

35 *Ibid.*, VI, 16 December 1769 ('... towards finishing and completing a carriage road from the plantain-walk of Sir Charles Price in St. Thomas in the Vale to the Gate of Joseph Price in St. Ann ... £300'). Further sums, either of £300 or £600 were levied in 1770, 1772, 1775, 1776, 1777, 1780, 1784. In November 1787 an Act was passed to create a toll-road over Mount Diablo; *ibid.*, VI–VIII.

36 Though Edward Long came out strongly against them in 1774; Long, I, 468. The first toll-gate was established at the Ferry in 1749; *Journals of the Assembly*, IV, 30 November 1749; the first true turnpike road appears to have been erected from the Pindar's River in Clarendon to Old Harbour, by way of Bodle's Pen, in 1760; *ibid.*, V, 10 November 1760.

37 In April 1741 and November 1787 respectively, *ibid.*, III, VIII. The first was rejected, the second passed.

38 'Petition of the Justices and Vestrymen of the Parish of St. Catherine, in behalf of themselves, and the other parishioners ...', 12 November 1763; *ibid.*, V.

39 *Ibid.*, 23 November 1764; 29 August, 5 September 1766; 4 November, 17 December 1767.

[40] *Ibid.*, VI, 24 December 1774.

[41] Sir Charles Price's house was on the block he owned formed by Red Church, Jew, and Monk Streets, and the meadows bordering the Rio Cobre—only a short walk from the House of Assembly and the King's House where the Governor resided. Map of St. Jago de la Vega, by John Pitcairn, London, 1786, Institute of Jamaica, 727.35EDE.1786.

[42] Charles Leslie, *History of Jamaica*, London, 1740, 28-39, quoted by Pitman, 26 n. 42.

[43] Long, II, vii, 77 n.

[44] Leslie, 28-39, quoted in Pitman, 24-5. The Act creating the Bath at St. Thomas in the East is in C.O. 137/12, 36.

[45] Long, II, vii, 76-8. Sir Charles Price's son wrote the following doggerel in praise of the Decoy:

> To dust and suffocating heats,
> Well pleased, we bade adue;
> To taste your gardens roll sweets,
> And pay respects to you. . . .
>   Wright, *Nugent*, 109, nl.

Sir Charles Price also almost certainly imported deer for the park at the Decoy, the wild descendants of which were still roaming the more remote parts of Jamaica in 1850. They were either Mexican *guazuti* or European fallow deer; Philip Henry Gosse, *A Naturalist's Sojourn in Jamaica*, London, Longmans, 1851, 433-40. The legend that Price also imported a large species of rat to eradicate the native species is of less credence, though Gosse identified a Cane Piece Rat *Mus Saccharivorus*, 18 inches long, which may have been eradicated by the mongeese introduced in the nineteenth century. A large rat is still popularly called a Charles Price rat in Jamaica.

[46] Long II, vii, 76-8.

[47] *Lady Nugent's Journal* (ed. P. Wright), July 1802, 109-10; March 1803, 151-2. The ten-hour journey from Spanish Town to the Decoy was a particular ordeal for such a tremulous lady. On one occasion, the Nugent's coach was swept off a bridge by a flood of the Rio Magno and on another, a 'kitareen', or small coach, was lost over a precipice on Guy's Hill during a violent thunderstorm.

[48] In 1965 the National Trust of Jamaica attempted to find the site of the Decoy, but without success.

[49] I.R.O. Wills, 27/143, written in London, 2 September 1747 and 'entered' in Jamaica on 4 May 1750. One of the witnesses was John Serocold, London merchant, whose father had been a friend of Colonel Charles Price, and who was to become a major Price mortgage-holder. In February 1753, during one of Charles Price's periods of land expansion, for example, Price mortgaged Burton's New Works with its 242 slaves to John Serocold for a debt of £14,000; I.R.O. Deeds 170/7.

[50] Above, III, 66. Thomas Price, the second son of Colonel Charles Price, seems to have died shortly after his father in 1731.

[51] Genealogy, above, III, 50.

[52] Motion to bring in the bill and committee appointed, 29 September; presentation of bill and first reading, 6 October; read for second time and sent to committee (committee having power to send for persons, papers, and records), 11 October; report, amendments, third reading, and emgrossment, 12 October; passed, 13 October; *Journals of the Assembly*, IV.

53 *Worthy Park: Extracts from Slave Journal, 1670–1787*, 23–6.

54 *Ibid.*, 23.

55 Murmuring Brook factory, scarcely smaller than Thetford, was in a closed valley and there is no trace of the route used to carry out the processed sugar to the Point Hill Road.

56 The Thetford works—with their two mule-mills and windmill—are a mile to the north-east and at a higher elevation.

57 Archives, Crop Accounts 1/168; 2/95, both sworn to by John Forsyth, overseer. A 'pott' was 56 pounds gross, which would have indicated production of 300 and 320 hogsheads respectively. But the wastage apparent in the figures for 1744, when 501,000 pounds was said only to have produced 288 hogsheads, reduces the net product.

58 *Ibid.* 2/95. Sworn to by Charles Price 'as received by John Jump in Spanish Town'.

59 *Ibid.* 8/92; figures for 31 December 1775 to 31 December 1776, sworn to by Malcolm Laing, 'Attorney of John Price'. A puncheon of rum is calculated at 60 per cent of a hogshead. The average production of Worthy Park 1741–4 was 302 hogsheads of sugar and 34¼ puncheons of rum.

60 Ragatz, 8 (part 4, table II) from Bryan Edwards, II, 267, above, 4. 38s. is 80 per cent of 47s. 6d., the difference being accounted for by freight, insurance, and commission.

61 The London average prices for muscovado were 29s. per cwt in 1741, 31s. 6d. in 1743, and 40s. in 1744, giving approximate Jamaica prices of 23s. 3d., 25s. 3d., and 32s. respectively.

62 Calculating the price per puncheon between 1741–4 at £11, against £14 in 1776.

63 From a London pre-duty price of 32s. 6d. in 1774, it rose to 38s. in 1775 and was to go to 57s. 6d. in 1777 and a peak of 64s. in 1781. The average between 1745 and 1775 would seem to have been about 36s. No figures are available for the income for cattle farming, if indeed this was still carried on.

64 I.R.O. Deeds 153/2; 227/170; 277/159. The 600 acres at Riverhead were later reduced to 297 in a dispute with Thetford. Later still they were grazed by John Quier.

65 I.R.O. Wills 40/152. In what, ironically, is one of the shortest Price wills, Sir Charles bequeathed all his lands to his only surviving son. Among minor bequests were £200 to Lydia Ann, the wife successively of Sir Charles Price's two sons Rose and Charles, a marrying ring to every freeholder of St. Thomas-ye-Vale 'as a grateful acknowledgement of the many favours I had at their hands', and an annuity of £10 to 'a Mulatto woman named Margaret residing at Rose Hall and to her two Elder children'.

CHAPTER FIVE

The Sugar Economy of
An Eighteenth-Century Estate

After 1750, sugar dominated the existence of Worthy Park at the same time as sugar monoculture began to characterize—if not blight—the economic life of Jamaica. With the completion of the aqueduct and watermill and the inability of the estate to expand into the neighbouring arable lands of Thetford, Murmuring Brook, and Mowden Hall, cattle rearing for beef dropped into insignificance and even provision raising on the estate was virtually ignored. The production of sugar, and its by-product rum, offered prospects of splendid wealth, and the late eighteenth century was a period of tremendous optimism in the sugar colonies; yet at the best of times sugar was a fickle enterprise. As in all industries, technical expertise, good management, and an adequate labour force were mandatory; but sugar was additionally susceptible to the influence of variables beyond the control of planters; beyond the control even of their more strategically placed partners, the merchants. The only certainties were the uncertainty of London sugar prices, the caprices of the West Indian climate, the apparent inevitability of war, and the ever-rising cost of credit. As time went on, the system of absentee proprietorship and indirect management, which applied to Worthy Park as to the vast majority of West Indian estates, appeared more and more a luxury which the estates could ill afford.

Growing sugar-cane, and extracting and processing its juice, 'the most uncertain production upon the face of the earth',[1] was a sophisticated operation, complicated by the fact that the sugar-cane took rather more than a year to come to maturity. The Jamaican climate was sufficiently equable to allow for continuous growth and to permit planting at almost any season, but the optimization of climatic, market, and mechanical conditions determined a traditional pattern of operations, with its associated changing tempo of employment. The harvest, or 'crop', period was that which demanded the most sustained burst of manual activity from the slave work-force; but a well-managed estate was one in which the inter-crop period was most practically utilized, in factory as well as field. In this way, not only was productivity maintained or expanded, but slaves were kept from dangerous, if only comparative, idleness.

In Jamaica, the cane-tops were sometimes planted between Christmas and June, but it was the cane planted from August to October which gave 'with tolerable seasons, the most certain returns'.[2] All plantations in Jamaica, however, allowed the roots of the cane recently harvested, the ratoons, to grow out again, rather than to replant every cane-piece each year, because it was thought that ratoon cane—especially of the variety first imported from Tahiti by Captain Bligh, the Otaheite[3]—would 'upon all properties and in all seasons, generally make the best produce'.[4] Further ratooning was commonly employed in the most fertile or freshly worked soils, and in most areas of Jamaica, the practice was to divide cane land, one part 'in plants, one in first ratoons, one in second ratoons and sometimes a fourth division in fallow'.[5] Excessive ratooning, however, progressively exhausted the soil, and unless an estate was able to rotate its fallow land and assiduously manure its heavily worked soils before replanting, its productivity would decline. Worthy Park was fortunately much more fertile than average, never quite grew sugar on all its plantable lands, and always had a sizeable population of animals to manure its young planted cane.[6] Yet here as elsewhere there was a temptation to expand cultivation unwisely when sugar prices were high or debts pressing, and to flog the most productive lands repeatedly with third, fourth, or even further ratoons. In the later 1780s, Worthy Park's sugar production slumped, though study of the field records which fortunately still exist for 1786–8 shows that it may have been mismanagement (or lack of management) and external conditions as much as soil exhaustion which accounted for the indifferent results.[7]

None the less, Worthy Park's cane husbandry between 1786 and 1788 cannot have been much different from the majority of Jamaican estates owned by absentees, and even in the poorest years its average yields were well up on the averages calculated by the contemporary writers Long, Beckford, and Edwards.[8] The cane land totalled 456 acres, divided into 21 cane-pieces, averaging 21·7 acres apiece. In each year, only 12 cane-pieces were harvested, for an average total of 263 acres, between five and seven cane-pieces being in plant canes and the remainder in ratoons. In 1786 and 1787, all but two of the latter were in first ratoons, and 1788 apparently there were no cane pieces in second ratoons. The reasons for this may have been the disclosures concerning production found in these very records. The contention that ratoons could produce more than plant cane appears to have been a myth, at least as far as Worthy Park in the 1780s was concerned. In 1786, the five cane-pieces in plant canes, totalling 100 acres, produced an average of 2,210 pounds of sugar an acre, whereas the 131 acres of the five cane-pieces in first ratoons averaged only 463 pounds per acre, and the two cane-pieces of 46 acres in second ratoons, a paltry 305 pounds per acre. In 1787 the differential was considerably less; but whereas the seven cane-pieces, totalling 151 acres, in plant canes produced an average of 1,270 pounds of sugar to the acre, the three cane-pieces of 79 acres in first ratoons averaged 1,140 pounds per acre, and the two cane-pieces of 40 acres in second ratoons only 860 pounds to the acre. 1786 and 1787 were notoriously bad years, but the figures available for 1791, when the overall production was almost doubled, corroborate the general pattern. In 1791 the six cane-pieces totalling 122 acres in plant canes produced an average of 2,910 pounds

97

to the acre, but the six cane-pieces of 109 acres in ratoons averaged only 1,450 pounds to the acre. For the three years studied, the average production for plant canes was 2,060 pounds to the acre, for first ratoons 970 pounds to the acre, and for second ratoons 561 pounds to the acre. At Worthy Park in the late 1780s, first ratoons seem to have been about 51 per cent as productive as plant canes, and second ratoons only about 26 per cent as effective, though this was before the introduction of Bourbon canes, from which great improvements were expected.[9]

	Cane-pieces in plant canes	Acres	1,000 lbs sugar	Average	Cane-pieces in 1st rattons	Acres	1,000 lbs sugar	Average	Cane-pieces in 2nd ratoons	Acres	1,000 lbs sugar	Average
1786	5	100	220·6	2·21	5	131	60·6	0·463	2	46	14·1	0·305
1787	7	151	191·7	1·27	3	79	90·7	1·14	2	40	34·2	0·860
1791	6	122	354·4	2·91	6	109	157·8	1·45	–	–	–	–
TOTALS	18	373	767·2	2·06	14	319	309·1	0·970	4	86	48·3	0·561

It is worth noting that at Worthy Park in the 1780s cane was only planted in land that had lain fallow for at least one season. In 1788 there were even three pieces planted which had not grown cane for the previous two seasons. Worthy Park's soils were mainly 'stiff yellow clays' or 'brick mould' with very little sand, which were not only difficult to work and drain but also needed much fertilization for the best results. The fallow cane-pieces were grazed by the stock animals, the dung of which was invaluable for the replenishment of the soil. The area for grazing was systematically rotated by moveable fences, though animals were even penned on fallow land after they had eaten away the pasture, being fed on guinea grass cut in neighbouring savannas by gangs of the younger slaves.

When land was being prepared for planting it was first 'hoe ploughed' three or four times before the 'holes' or trenches for the cane were dug, in rows some 6 feet apart.[10] At the same time, drainage trenches were carefully cut to carry off excess rainwater. The whole field was manured as heavily as possible, always during the planting and sometimes also during the initial 'ploughing' as well, the slaves

Worthy Park: Sugar Production by Cane-Pieces, 1786–1791

	Acreage	1786	Cop-pers	Potts	1787	Cop-pers	Potts	1788	1791	Cop-pers	Potts	Hogs-heads	Acreage (where different)
Sorrel Hill	13	P	155	647	2R	48	206						
Pond Piece	31	P	211	788	R	74	346						
Harry Hill	27	P	276	1131	R	98	405		R	139	7	22	(25 acres)
Craddock's Piece	6	P	35	174	R	358	881*		R	24	3	4	(5 acres)
Fuller's Side Piece	27	P	281	1198	R	116	392		R	142	24	22	(25 acres)
Dry Gully	40	R	80	396	P	137	422		R	67	7	10	(13 acres)
Fig Tree	26	R	14	79				F	P	213	23	29	
Pasture Piece	29	R	67	282									
Overgully Piece	26	2R	34	103				P	P	376	394	22	(25 acres)
Limekiln Piece	21	R	58	228				P	P	298	68	41	
Little Middle Piece	20	2R	36	148				P	P	255	7	39	
Crawfish Gully	15	R	19	97									
Two Bullet Tree	22				P	201	772	R	R	92	5	12	
Little Pasture	14				P	111	430	R					
Bristow Hole	23				P	82	260	R	R	129	7	16	(19 acres)
Cabbage Tree and Flower Piece	25				P	101	372	R					
Fuller's Garden Side Piece	22				P	124	415	R	P	174	14	21	(12 acres)
Unclassified	20				P	117	453						
Will's Pen	10							P					
One Bullet Tree	19							P	P	213	12	29	
Middle Piece	30							P					

P = Plant Cane; R = First Ratoons; 2R = Second Ratoons; * Includes 15 acres in second ratoons in Dry Gully.

carrying the noisome dung mixed with rotted trash, ashes and 'dunder' from the factory generally in baskets on their heads.

Once the 'holes' were prepared, 'perfectly sound succulent healthy canes' were selected, either from the cane nursery or from the old cane tops, and planted 'not less than six nor more in general than eight inches below the surface', sufficiently far apart 'as to allow the air a free passage between them and admit of hoeing around the roots'.[11] The planting method which had been found best at Worthy Park was one called 'four canes lapped', which proved more fruitful than 'two canes lapped' or a third method tried in the 1790s called 'double cane lapped close and the canes . . . spread in the hole'.[12]

After planting was done, the field gangs were kept busy in 'banking' the holes as the green shoots emerged and then, as the shoots burgeoned into swaying verdure taller than a man, in 'cleaning' the lines of weeds, though this task became progressively easier as the voracious cane monopolized the shade and the substance of the soil. Workers were also employed in additional drainage and in cutting trash, or super-fluous leaves, from the growing cane.[13] There was also guinea grass to be planted, compost to be mulched, and some plantains and other pro-visions to be grown for the white workers on the estate.

At Worthy Park, fresh planted cane was fourteen to eighteen months old when harvested. Ratoons would be ready for cutting after a twelve-month, but were usually fourteen months in the growing. Canes cut at the beginning of one crop and left to ratoon would be ready for the middle or end of the subsequent crop, but cane freshly planted after the middle of one year when crop was finished would not be ready until the beginning of the next year but one.

The period of the cane harvest was kept as short as possible, begin-ning soon after the New Year and extending preferably no later than May or the beginning of June. This was the driest period of the year when rain would least interrupt the cutting or cut down the sugar content of the cane by excessive moisture. It was also the period easiest for carting the sugar over roads that could well become boggy during heavy rains, and for shipping produce to England, before the onset of the hurricane season. After July, vessels could not be expected to risk being caught off the coasts of Jamaica, being forced to scurry northwards to avoid both the dangers of tropical storms and the imposition of the prohibitive seasonal insurance rates.

Once the factory was started up it was important to keep it at capacity until the crop was finished. It was extremely uneconomic to prolong operations unduly or to operate the factory intermittently. Besides this, cane deteriorated rapidly after cutting, just as cane juice spoiled if not processed almost immediately after crushing. A well-managed estate was therefore one in which the rate of cutting was geared to the capacity of the mills, and the production of the mills to the capacity of the rest of the factory. A good year at Worthy Park was one in which the entire crop was cut and processed between January and June: a bad year was one in which inclement weather, a delayed crop or trouble with the machinery might prolong operations past midsummer and into the autumn. In 1789, for example, the field gangs were cutting until October, and the factory, though it actually worked only 118 days, was in operation from February until December. In 1787, in contrast, the factory had worked not many fewer days but only between February and June, and in 1791, when 60 per cent more sugar was produced than in 1787, an almost identical period. All in all the sugar harvesting and processing between 1783 and 1791 averaged 179 days from beginning to end, beginning in an average year on 31 January and ending on 28 July, during which period the factory appears to have worked an average of approximately 120 actual days, to produce an average of roughly $2\frac{1}{2}$ hogsheads a day, with a maximum of $5\frac{1}{2}$.[14] Even with consistent methods, sugar production varied quite widely from year to year. Production in 1786 and 1787, for example, when Worthy Park like the rest of Jamaica suffered from a succession of hurricanes, only reached 181 and 176 hogsheads; but in 1788 it rose to 294 hogsheads from even fewer acres in cultivation, and this appears to have been about the average annual production between 1776 and 1796.

For the backbreaking and oppressive tasks of field and factory were reserved the healthiest slaves. Of the 338 slaves at Worthy Park in 1789, 56 were children below the age of six and therefore not capable

Worthy Park: Factory Operations and Output 1789–91

1789				1790 (figs. deficient)				1791			
	Days	Hh	Av.		Days	Hh	Av.		Days	Hh	Av.
Feb 4– 7	4	12⅔	3·16	Feb 7–13	7	19	2·71	Jan 31–			
8–14	7	17	2·42	14–20	7	25	3·57	Feb 4	4	–	–
15–21	7	26	3·71	21–27	7	19	2·71	8–12	4	9	2·25
22–24	3	7	2·33	28– 6	7	14	2·00	14–18	5	18	3·60
Mar 1– 6	6	21	3·50	Mar 7–13	7	25	3·57	21–25	5	20	4·00
12–14	3	7	2·33	14–20	7	28	4·00	28– 1	1½	4	2·70
15–21	7	22	3·14	21–24	4	1	0·25	Mar 7–12	6	22	3·66
22–28	7	23	3·28	28– 3	7	–	–	14–19	6	21	3·50
29– 4	7	18	2·57	Apr 6–10	5	–	–	21–26	6	23	3·83
Apr 5–12	8	26	3·25	11–17	7	17	2·42	28– 2	6	16	2·75
14–18	5	16	3·20	18–23	6	14	2·33	Apr 7– 9	3	7	2·33
19–20	2	7	3·50	May 2– 8	7	23	3·28	11–16	5	14	2·80
29– 2	4	7	1·75	9–14	6	16	2·66	18–23	6	13	2·16
May 3– 9	7	14	2·00	17–22	6	–	–	26–30	5	10	2·00
10–16	7	11	1·57	July 18–21	4	5	1·25	May 2–27	6	17	2·83
17–21	5	11	2·20	25–29	5	5	1·00	9–14	6	21	3·50
28–30	3	11	3·66	Sep 9–11	3	–	–	25–28	4	17	4·25
July 29–31	3	11	3·66	Oct 1– 2	2	–	–	31– 3	4	7	1·75
Aug 12–15	4	11	2·75	12–13	2	–	–	Jun 7–11	4	12	3·00
16–20	5	11	2·20	29–30	2	–	–	13–18	6	15	2·50
Sep 1– 5	5	11	2·20					20	1	1	1·00
29– 2	4	11	2·75								
Oct 23– 4	2	11	5·50								
Dec 1– 3	3	11	3·66								
TOTALS	118	333⅔	2·83		31	211	2·61		93½	267	2·85

Crop Accounts for 1790 give 248 hogsheads, which at 108 days operation averages 2·29 hogsheads per day.

of useful work, 29 were elderly or sick men used as watchmen, and 25 were listed as 'old and infirm' or 'good for nothing'. Only 133, with five 'drivers', were in the permanent field force, but these included 102, or 70 per cent of the 146 Negroes on the estate officially listed as 'able'. The factory employed 38 men, of whom exactly half were skilled and half unskilled labourers. One remarkable fact was that of the field force in 1789, no less than 89 were women, quite capable of weeding and carrying, and perhaps of hoeing and holing, but surely not of the strenuous monotony of cutting the cane. Accordingly, 24 able-bodied Negro men were hired in 1789 to assist in the crop, augmenting the work-force to something like 60 cutters.[15]

As soon as the overseer decided that the first cane was ready, the

Cane-holing and Cane-cutting. Two contemporary prints.

Eighteenth-century building in Overseer's Yard, Worthy Park, believed to have been the slave hospital.

factory workers began to prepare the machinery while the cutting gangs were turned out each day like machete-wielding shocktroops to reduce the tall acres of rippling greenery to the piles of yellow-brown stalks ready for the cane mill. Called from their cabins at dawn by the weird alarm of a blown conch shell or by the crack of the driver's whip the cutting gangs were led to the canefields by their drivers while the invariable mist still hovered in Lluidas Vale. Although it was the overseer—usually the first man out in the fields—who decided which area should be cut each day, it was the driver 'with his knotted stick and his whip slung carelessly across his shoulder'[16] who was chiefly responsible for the adequate fulfilment of the cutting tasks. William Beckford, the most candid of the writers on the Jamaican sugar industry in this period, found something 'particularly picturesque and striking in a gang of Negroes when employed in cutting canes', but a modern reader is chilled by his description of the whip-cracking slave-driver who 'takes care to chequer the able with the weak ... intimidates some, and encourages others; and too often, perhaps, a tyrant in authority, he imposes upon the timid, and suffers the sturdy to escape'.[17]

As the cutters advanced, severing the cane near the ground and clearing the stalk of its leaves in almost one rhythmic movement, they were followed by a gang of 'tyers' who bundled the fallen cane into manageable loads for mules or other slaves to move to the mule wains waiting on the nearest roadway to carry them to the factory yard. By modern standards it was not an efficient operation. Although the vast majority of Jamaican cane is still cut by hand, each modern worker may be as much as five times as productive as his ancestor in the days of slavery, just as the land of Worthy Park is probably at least five times as productive in tons of sugar per acre as it was in 1790. The huge differences may be accounted for by greatly improved varieties of cane, better factory methods, mechanical loading and carrying, and by much more closely-spaced 'intervals' for sugar wains; but they are also an indictment of the economic inefficiency of a system based on slave labour.

At Worthy Park between 1776 and 1796, approximately 250 tons of sugar were produced in a good year from 260 acres of canes, in a crop that averaged 120 cutting days. On an average, some two tons of sugar were produced from 2·2 acres of cane per day, at an average of just under a ton of sugar per acre. Going on the assumption that the cutting gangs totalled 60 men and that 20 tons of cane were needed to produce a ton of sugar,[18] this indicates an average of 40 tons of cane cut per day, or about two-thirds of a ton of cane per cutter. In the 1968 crop, an average of 410 tons of cane were cut daily from Worthy Park's cane-pieces by 120 cutters, an average of 3·42 tons per man, producing one ton of sugar for every 7·3 tons of cane, at a rate of five tons of sugar to the acre. 1968 was an exceptionally good year, but eighteenth-century planters would have been incredulous of Worthy Park's production of five tons, or roughly six hogsheads, per acre. In 1790, William Beckford estimated that an estate giving two hogsheads an acre was 'uncommonly great yielding', and even 1½ hogsheads an acre was 'more than one estate in ten will give'.[19] In the 1790s, Rose Price claimed that Worthy Park would 'always' produce two hogsheads per acre 'if well put in and dunged',[20] but this may well have been an exaggeration to encourage an overseer. The available figures do not bear out Rose Price's assessment. In 1788 and 1791, production was as high as 1·13 hogsheads per acre, but in 1786 and 1787 it had been as low as 0·72 and 0·62 hogsheads. Even in 1795, the last year of Rose Price's personal management of Worthy Park, the assessed production was no higher than 0·64 hogsheads per acre, though by the last year of his life it had reached 1·11 once more.[21]

Despite the comparative inefficiency of the system in the eighteenth century, cane cutting—along with hole-digging—was regarded as the most onerous of the tasks required of the slave, and impossible for Europeans. 'The white man cannot labour under a burning sun, without certain death,' wrote Rose Price in 1832; 'though the negro can in all climates with impunity.'[22] William Beckford, somewhat earlier, had asserted that 'the climate is congenial to their natural feelings', since 'the careful benevolence of Providence has thickened their skins'.[23] And so the cutters and carriers toiled, without choice, all the hours of daylight as the cane progressively ripened; out of the comparative coolness of January towards the broiling heat of midsummer, and sometimes beyond. Then, as the last cane was cut, they turned, with little respite, towards the innumerable chores in the fields which a 'benevolent Providence', through the agency of their overseer, had designed for them. Nothing, however, could be as arduous as crop time, when practically every waking hour was spent in the fields. Some index of the drudgery then can be gauged from William Beckford's smug comment that the Negroes' 'exertions out of crop are seldom required for more than thirteen hours a day'.[24]

At Worthy Park, as on most Jamaican plantations, the time of the slaves was almost as valuable to the proprietors as the land of the estate. During crop time, for example, the factory worked continuously whenever possible, and the field slaves were kept working seven days a week in order to keep the mills and boilers supplied.[25] Even out of crop time, when Sundays were normally free, few were the hours and less the energy that the slaves had to cultivate the tiny vegetable plots that surrounded their huts, let alone those distant pockets of marginal land which they cultivated when they could, with the primitive methods of slash-and-burn and hoeing which they remembered from their African past. Only after 1787, when the Assembly decreed that masters should allot provision grounds for their slaves, were the owners constrained to employ any of their invaluable acres and slaves in the production of provision crops. When sugar and rum had become the sole source of income for the estate, all resources were single-mindedly dedicated to their greater production. In Worthy Park's case, the 1787 enactment meant the estate's formal adoption as Negro provision grounds of the 580 remote acres of the Cocoree purchased by John Price in 1753 and probably worked informally since that time.[26]

During crop time the lot of the factory worker was scarcely preferable to that of the field slave, for the hours were as long and the heat and stench were nearly intolerable. Out of season, there was a more noticeable lull in activity, and the indispensable craftsmen in the factory were often rewarded when the sugar produced was of exceptional quality. Of the nineteen skilled men working in the Worthy Park factory in 1789, ten were boilers, five distillers, three 'potters', and one a cooper, and the senior in each of these crafts was a member of the estate's highest Negro élite. Indeed, the head boilerman, presiding over the supreme mysteries of the craft of sugar production, was probably as important to the estate as anyone save the overseer and attorney.

Just as the owner's and overseer's houses at Worthy Park were situated on adjacent knolls with an excellent oversight of factory and fields, so the Worthy Park factory was an integrated knot of buildings strategically placed at the centre, though to one side, of the cane land. Worthy Park did not suffer from the need to grind cane or even boil cane juice in different parts of the estate as was common in more mountainous areas and other islands, the longest journey for cane-carts being little more than a mile. The fact that fertile Lluidas Vale was neatly subdivided in the eighteenth century into four or five estates each with its own factory, was not entirely fortuitous. Each factory worked almost to capacity, and amalgamation of estates would not necessarily have led to the consolidation of factories, since the technology of those days was not sufficiently advanced to take off the produce of more than about 600 fertile acres, or to produce more than about 600 hogsheads of sugar in a four-month crop. It was only with the introduction of more sophisticated crushing rollers in the late 1790s, of steam engines after 1810 and of sundry other technical advances later in the nineteenth century that further consolidation was feasible. It was during this latter period that Worthy Park gradually expanded to swallow up the whole of Lluidas Vale, though this was less because of technical innovation than the decay of the adjacent estates.

Within the present compass of Worthy Park can be examined the substantial remains of two eighteenth-century factories, which were abandoned before mechanical improvements could save or even change them. Worthy Park factory—a product of twentieth-century technology which has multiplied eighteenth-century capabilities forty-fold—has changed out of all recognition, save for some ancient foundations, the brickwork of the disused distillery, and the 30-foot water wheel brought from Constant Spring in the 1860s. Mowden Hall and Swansea factories have disappeared without trace, but the ruins of

Murmuring Brook and Thetford enable us to imagine what Worthy Park factory must have been like in the later eighteenth century. At Murmuring Brook still stands the massive masonry that housed the wheel of the water mill, above the swift-running conduit that two miles farther on turned a similar wheel at Worthy Park; but the most evocative ruins are at Thetford, where walls still stand as high as roof level and rusted coppers and cogwheels can still be discovered in the tangled undergrowth.

Thetford did not share the Lluidas Vale mill-race, but relied chiefly on a windmill, the masonry of which is still intact, though the wood has decayed and the machinery has long since been removed. This mill stood proudly at the prow of an elongated hillock, where its sails could turn and catch all available breezes. Adjacent to the windmill was an octagonal mule or cattle mill 40 feet in diameter, such as was found on almost all Jamaican plantations, to augment the wind and running water or to use when these elements failed.[27] Originally, the animal mill, consisting of a circular walk and a central well containing the crushing rollers, was covered by a conical roof, to keep the rain and the rays of the sun from machinery, animals, and workers. At one time there were two such mills at Thetford, the octagonal foundations of the second standing close to the first; but from the absence of an animal walkway and a central machinery well it seems that this was converted into a covered store for the chopped firewood and squeezed cane-stalk 'trash' used as fuel in the boiling house and distillery.[28]

Close to the octagonal animal mill and fuel store at Thetford, and at a slightly lower level, was the huge T-shaped building that was both boiling and curing house, and below that the smaller distillery, the brick-lined chamber which once housed the condenser coils being still in excellent preservation. Behind boiling house and distillery was the artificial pond, now dry, which once contained the water for cooling; and below the distillery the sump into which were discharged the malodorous factory wastes. The survival of so much of the Thetford factory while all traces of Great House and other buildings have passed away is visible proof of the assertion made by many contemporary writers that the factory buildings were far and away the most substantial and imposing constructions to be found on most West Indian estates.

The ancient Great House at Worthy Park has also disappeared, but from an estate plan surveyed in 1794 it is possible to reconstruct all the plantation's buildings as they were during the later eighteenth century.[30] The Great House was within 200 yards of the factory and no more than a quarter mile from cattle pens and slave quarters, but separated from them by the main road and surrounded by a large garden, or small park, of about 35 acres. The estate offices were among the out-buildings in the Great House yard. The overseer's house, in parts of which doubtless lived the book-keepers and other white workers, was a slightly greater distance to the north, backed by the canefield called Hot House Piece—named for the nearby 'hot-house' or hospital—which was apparently the cane-plant nursery. The hospital for the sick slaves was also placed on the overseer's hillock, for this was regarded as the healthiest spot on the estate. Normally, the slaves lived in the semi-circle of forty to fifty huts just to the west of the factory.

The heart of the plantation was the factory compound, dominated by the mill with its huge wheel, and the boiling house—larger than the Great House itself—with its tall chimney belching smoke during crop-time. Adjacent to the boiling house was a separate curing house, and next to that the distillery. On the other side of the boiling house were no less than three 'thrash' houses, as well as the mule mill used to supplement the watermill.[29]

Once the cane arrived from the fields it was not chopped as in modern processing, but fed entire through the vertical rollers of one of the mills, unskilled slaves being employed in a continuous chain carrying in the succulent fresh stalks and clearing the mills of the desiccated trash. From the mills, the spurting cane-juice coursed through lead-lined wooden gutters straight into the boiling house. In this steaming and smoking inferno it was crystallized by evaporation. After being held in one of several large reservoirs or 'receivers', the juice was first heated in shallow round pans called 'clarifiers', during which it was 'tempered' with lime. The calcium carbonate acted as a catalyst, causing the sediment to sink and other impurities to rise to the top of

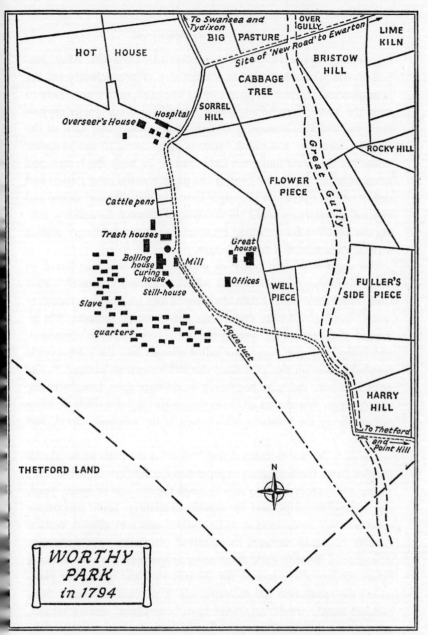

From 'Worthy Park Estate, in the Parish of St. John, Jamaica, the
property of John Price Esq., of the County of Cornwall in the Kingdom of Great Britain. Surveyed in 1794. Kirkwood & Sons Surveyors'
P.R.O. C.O. 441/4/4, No. 3.

the seething liquid. This 'crust' was constantly skimmed. After tempering, the juice was boiled in a succession of progressively smaller hemispherical cast-iron 'coppers', up to five in all, until it was ready to enter the 'tache' ('tayche' or 'teache'), in which it was finally crystallized, or 'struck'. Constant fires were maintained under each of the coppers, from the 300-gallon 'great copper' down to the 75-gallon tache, but the flame under the tache had to be both the hottest and steadiest of all, for the striking of the sugar was the most critical and delicate of the operations in a sugar factory. Only the most skilled and vigilant of boilermen could tell the optimal moment for striking, testing the bubbling brown liquid between thumb and forefinger until it formed a filament of a certain length.

The sugar was now ready to granulate, and was transferred to 'coolers', further coppers around which water was constantly circulated. From these it was originally scooped into 56-pound earthenware 'potts', from which were drained the residue liquid molasses. But by the end of the eighteenth century the use of potts had been outmoded, and instead the raw sugar was ladled straight into the 1,800-pound hogsheads, though this operation was still known as 'potting'.[30] The potts, and later the huge hogsheads, stood over stone troughs in the curing house, where after 48 hours they were tapped and left draining and maturing for several weeks before being weighed, carted, and shipped.

The dark brown molasses drained off from the potts or hogsheads gurgled down further gutters or pipes into the distillery or 'still-house', where it was processed into rum through the addition of water, yeast, and sugar-skimmings, and by double distillation. Some plantations exported their molasses raw, to be distilled into rum abroad, but the carriage of liquid molasses from inland plantations was extremely difficult, and Worthy Park seems never to have exported her molasses before modern times. Indeed, for Worthy Park and most other plantations the production and successful sale of the rum they made from molasses which would otherwise have been almost always wasted, provided the difference between a handsome and a bare profit on their operations, or between a bare profit and none at all.[31]

The sugar produced at Worthy Park, as on most Jamaican plantations, was the coarse brown muscovado, much of which was further refined once it reached Great Britain. Muscovado travelled better and was regarded as more economic than the semi-refined or 'clayed' sugar produced in a few Jamaican factories; but the fact that their sugars usually had to go through the hands of refiners as well as shippers and factors before they reached the consumer was an enduring grievance to West Indian planters, particularly when the sugar refiners began to form a parliamentary lobby implacably opposed to the West India Interest. Moreover, even the production of adequate muscovado required endless pains at every stage, an expertise from the skilled and a dedication from the unskilled that was not expected from the average slave.[32] Out of crop there was much for the factory workers to accomplish; cutting and fetching wood, lime-burning, cleaning and mending machinery. The cooper, for one, was employed continuously throughout the year making up and repairing his casks. Fortunately for the planters, most of their factory slaves remained remarkably cheerful, particularly near the beginning of crop, often singing away the oppressive monotony of their work,[33] and many of their craftsmen slaves demonstrated a degree of enterprise and industry that belied the sneering stereotype of the Negro usual in plantocratic writings.

Yet, despite the invaluable exertions and skills of the slaves, much still devolved on every estate on the overseer and his 'legal guardian', the attorney. During crop-time the factory worked 24 hours a day, and such unremitting vigilance was demanded of the overseer that not only did he take up a station in the factory from which he could survey all operations, but he also often slept in the factory for the duration of the crop. At Worthy Park the overseer was particularly overworked for there was not a separate overseer for factory and field as on some of the larger estates; and it is small wonder that there was an almost annual turnover in the overseers between 1785 and 1791, despite the considerable salary of £200 (currency) a year.[34]

At Worthy Park there was normally a three-week gap between the initial cane-cutting and the dispatch of the first batch of muscovado to market. To hold 16 or 17 hundredweight of sugar in a hogshead 'forty-two inches in height and thirty-six across the head' on the jolting 4,000-mile journey to Britain required well-seasoned wood and stout hoops. But the worst section of the entire journey was the first, from Worthy Park south to Guanaboa, and until 1789 the estate did not risk the collapse of its casks on the boneshaking passage over Point Hill, but rather packed its muscovado into hessian bags weighing either one or two hundredweight. At the height of the crop, batches of thirty to thirty-eight bags, totalling 5,000 to 6,000 pounds of sugar, arrived each day at Price's Pen, Guanaboa, where the sugar was repacked into the traditional hogsheads. In 1784, for example, Worthy Park's crop commenced on 12 January and the first sugar left the factory on 9 February. The same day, thirty bags of muscovado, weighing 5,400 pounds, were

Worthy Park: Crop and Shipment Periods, 1781–1791

Crop and Processing	Dispatch to Guanaboa, Spring Garden, and Old Harbour
1781 —	'Sugar Received from Worthy Park', March 1–16
1782 —	'Sugar Received from Worthy Park', February 7 1782–February 27 1783
1783 January 27–June 1	'Sugar Sent to Market', March 4–April 31 (incomplete) 'Received from Worthy Park', March 5–October 29
1784 January 12–June 27	'Sugar Sent to Market', February 9–October 10 'Hogsheads filled up', February 10–October 20 'Sugar Received from Guanaboa', February 12–October 21
1785 January 20–June 16	'Sugar Sent to Market', February 21–August 1
1786 January 31–June 26	'Sugar Sent to Market', February 9–July 15
1787 February 9–June 2	'Sugar Sent to Market', March 23–July 30
1788 February 13–September 16	'Sugar Sent to Guanaboa and Spring Garden', March 12–December 16
1789 February 4–December 3	'Sugar Sent to Guanaboa and Spring Garden', February 26–January 4 1790
1790 February 7–October 30	'Sugar Sent to Guanaboa and Spring Garden', March 1–November 16
1791 January 31–June 20	'Sugar Sent to Guanaboa and Spring Garden', February 22–July 20

Taken from: Worthy Park Books, 1783–7, 1787–91; (1) 'Sugar Produced at Worthy Park', 1783–8, 1790–1, (2) 'Sugar Sent to Market from Worthy Park', 1783–91, (3) 'Account of Sugar Received from Worthy Park', 1781–2, (4) 'Account of Sugar Received at Spring Garden from Guanaboa', 1782–4, (5) 'Account of Hogsheads filled up', 1784.

hauled south to Guanaboa, being repacked there on 10 February into three hogsheads before dispatch along the relatively gentle road to the estate's provisioning ground at Spring Garden, where it arrived on 12 February. After 1789, however, either because the road or the quality of the Worthy Park casks had improved, or as a result of the switchover from potts to hogsheads at the curing stage, all sugar was sent out of Lluidas Vale in hogsheads, reaching Spring Garden easily in two days, with only a pause for refreshment at Guanaboa Vale. Rum, it must be presumed, was always carried all the way from Worthy Park in puncheons, this size of cask being handier, though scarcely less heavy, than the sugar hogshead. Before 1794, however, nearly all of Worthy Park's rum was sold in Jamaica and not exported.

Until 1794, when the transfer was made to the new port of Port Henderson in Kingston Harbour, Worthy Park's sugar was all exported through Old Harbour, being stockpiled at Spring Garden, three miles from the coast. As soon as he had accumulated enough produce and had negotiated, where necessary, with the master of a visiting vessel or the local agents, the Spring Garden overseer dispatched his cargo to the quayside, where it was commonly exchanged for provisions brought to Jamaica in the same vessel. These arrangements had their drawbacks; the difficulties of the journey to the coast being compounded by the somewhat haphazard facilities at Old Harbour. Often, Worthy Park's produce had to wait weeks until transport was found to take it to Britain, and sometimes the shipping season ended with produce unshipped. In 1783, for example, the sugar which first left Worthy Park on 4 March did not find a berth until 12 May, when 80 hogsheads were put aboard the *Lord Rodney* for London. In the two months after 12 May a total of 231 hogsheads from Worthy Park were shipped aboard no less than eight vessels, but after the last one sailed on 10 July, Worthy Park sugar continued to arrive at Spring Garden as late as October. Finally, 38 hogsheads remained, and, had they not found a purchaser in Jamaica, they might have proved unsaleable in the spring of 1784.

As time went on, vessels stopped less regularly at Old Harbour, preferring the safer shelter, deeper water, and better facilities of

Kingston Harbour. Competition for the available vessels increased, and the three miles journey from Spring Garden to Old Harbour became a positive disadvantage. Sometimes whole consignments were transported to the waterside only to fail to find a berth, and since warehouse facilities at Old Harbour were inadequate, this meant either returning laboriously to Spring Garden or leaving the produce to deteriorate on the quayside.

In the days before the American colonies were sundered from the British Empire, masters or supercargoes of vessels in the West India trade were commonly authorized to sell provisions and buy sugars where they could obtain the most favourable prices, and Worthy Park, like most West Indian plantations, negotiated many of its purchases and sales on the very dockside, dealing in direct commodity exchange, or in bills of exchange drawn on London, Bristol, Boston, or Baltimore. Consequently, before 1775 Worthy Park's produce left Jamaica for North America or Europe in a bewildering diversity of ships, and much depended on the business acumen of the manager on the spot, even if—as was generally the case—the actual transactions went through the hands of local commission agents. Even after 1783, Worthy Park's provisions came and her produce departed in a variety of vessels; but the sudden stoppage of the chief source of cheap provisions and the closure of one of the most certain markets for sugar by the achievement of American independence greatly reduced the flexibility of the West India trade. Partly for simplicity and efficiency, but mostly because each plantation's trade, along with its credit, was being concentrated in the hands of fewer factors, and further in advance of production, larger consignments were made in fewer vessels and all arrangements came to be made by agents in the metropolitan ports. At the same time, plantations were compelled by the forces that drove them into sugar monoculture and debt to sell all their produce abroad, though a planter able to sell locally was said to be able to 'make 100 hogsheads of sugar produce more than he can when he is obliged to consign 150 to Europe'.[35] Even more damaging was the tendency of conditions to enforce that provisions and supplies were purchased in the same market as that in which the sugar was sold. The one advantage of the growing concentration on the metropolis was that the proprietors—the vast majority of whom were now absentees—had the chance, or at least the illusion, of personally managing their sales and purchases in the home market, to offset the disadvantages of having to rely so heavily upon attorneys and overseers for the direct management of their estates.

These general processes were well illustrated by the example of Worthy Park, the business operations of which were finally rationalized about the time the switch was made from Old Harbour to Port Henderson in 1794, during the resident managership of young Rose Price. At one time, most of Worthy Park's rum and some of her sugar had been sold in Jamaica, but from the middle of the 1790s almost all produce was consigned to Great Britain. London was always the principal destination, though before 1791 some produce was from time to time shipped to other British ports. In 1783, for example, a single hogshead was sent to Bristol, and in 1788 and 1791 large consignments of eighty and forty hogsheads went to Liverpool.[36] Thereafter, all of Worthy Park's exports for more than a hundred years were sent to market in London, where their handling was managed entirely by a single agent. Towards the end of the eighteenth century this agent was one Thomas Smith, merchant, of whom it was said in 1794 that he had been receiving 'all the Sugars and produce of the said plantation [Worthy Park] . . . for many years'.[37]

The concentration of business in the hands of a single factor was indicated by the repeated use of a single ship for the carriage not only of the estate's sugar and rum but the bulk of her provisions also. One such vessel was the *Betsey*, captained by George Laurie, which arrived regularly between April and May every year between 1783 and 1791 with provisions for Worthy Park, carrying away a week or so later between fifty and a hundred hogsheads of the estate's first sugar. The remainder of the produce was carried away in from five to ten other vessels, in consignments averaging about thirty hogsheads. Few of these vessels were used more than once and none regularly, the space in their holds being negotiated for as occasion demanded, mainly in June and July.[38]

The trade of English plantations was governed by the mercantilist 'compact'—intended to be reciprocal but so often to the disproportionate benefit of the mother country. Jamaica's muscovado and rum went to satisfy the growing demand from Britain's soaring population; and Jamaica in return took the products of embryonic British industries, which flourished from the demand and from the infusion of capital generated by the slave and plantation trades. Colonies like Jamaica were always economically dependent on the mother country, but became increasingly so as time went on. Hardwares and yard goods had always to be imported, for manufacture was denied to mere plantations. Lumber and foodstuffs also had always been obtained mostly from abroad, for the plantations were never self-sufficient in these commodities; and after 1783 these too were largely obtained from across the Atlantic.

Thus, in return for Worthy Park's muscovado and rum, the delivery ships—notably the *Betsey*—annually discharged tons of supplies at Old Harbour or, later, Port Henderson: hardware vital to the factory operations such as coppers, boilers, condenser coils, anvils, paints and oil; the axes, cutlasses, bills and hoes essential to operations in the fields; the linen oznaburghs and checks, the coarse woollens, baizes, blanketing and hats to clothe both slave and free. Food too was imported in huge annual purchases, mainly from Cork in Ireland; the bulk of it salt-fish for the slaves, but also relative delicacies, beef, biscuit, butter, pork and tongue, destined for the plantation's whites. The English sugar ships, however, did not entirely satisfy Worthy Park's enormous appetite for provisions and supplies. Each year the management had to buy in Kingston more food for slaves and whites, cooperage lumber, coal and tallow for heat and light. Most of these items were also imported into Jamaica, though acquired by the estate by way of an agent in Kingston rather than directly from the sugar factor in England.[39]

The growing extent of the dependence of West Indian estates upon the metropolis was, of course, a crucial financial weakness in the long run. It was brought about originally, however, by the huge profits that could be made from sugar and rum—and from few other West Indian products—by planters, merchants, and investors alike, and the basic flaws were only shown up when these profits declined. From the data available at Worthy Park we should be able to estimate just how profitable Jamaican estates could be before their inexorable decline set in, and to decide whether the bondage to sugar monoculture was the result of selfish mismanagement or an unavoidable tragic dilemma.

By 1775, almost the sole income for Worthy Park was from sugar and rum. In the years from 1776 to 1796 for which figures are, for the first time, fully available, the estate produced an annual average of 296·9 hogsheads of sugar, averaging 16·88 hundredweight apiece, and 102·8 puncheons of rum. Since the average price received for each hundredweight of sugar once all transport and factorage charges had been deducted appears to have been about £1. 11s. per hundredweight, and for rum approximately £15. 11s. per puncheon, this indicates an average annual income of about £7,300 for sugar and £1,160 for rum, or a total of some £8,960 per year; possibly double the income of the estate before 1750, but very little if any more than during the period immediately before the American war.[40]

The key to the profitability of any estate was the control of its out-goings: the cost of supplies and slaves, local expenditure, and other contingent charges. Around 1800, Sir William Young calculated that for a plantation with 200 slaves producing 200 hogsheads of sugar a year, the imported supplies would cost £1,000 a year. To eliminate this debt, the supplying merchant, if he were the purchaser of the sugars, would deduct £5 from the net proceeds of each hogshead con-signed.[41] Young's estimate dated from years when two wars and the loss of the American trade had greatly increased prices, yet Worthy Park's slave population was, on the average, twice that of Young's model, and over the period of the last quarter of the eighteenth century it is unlikely that Worthy Park's annual bill for supplies was less than £1,500 on the average. As to other charges, Worthy Park was certainly not crushed, at least before the 1790s. From the apparent weakness of the slave work force and the need to import labourers during crop-time it seems that purchases of slaves were not heavy, and the bill for the salaries of white supervisors was probably smaller than on most estates. In an average year, the cost of new and hired slaves and white workers was probably no more than £1,000, though to this should be added the £150 paid to the doctor and the 5 per cent commission on sales, or approximately £450, paid to the estate's attorney.

The total of running expenses at Worthy Park during the 1780s was probably some £3,100 a year, or 36 per cent of income. The profit margin of nearly all estates, however, was greatly burdened by accumulated amortised debts, consisting of the payment of interest and the repayment of principal on sundry advances, loans, and mortgages. Worthy Park was no exception, though the estate before the 1790s was fortunate in that it had been largely shielded from the crushing load of mortgages carried by the rest of the Price estates. The estimate made by Edward Long in 1774 that an estate making £6,000 a year would be burdened with contingent expenses totalling £2,000, or 33⅓ per cent of income,[42] while it was made before the general weight of plantation debts had become insupportable, was almost certainly an exaggeration in the case of Worthy Park in the 1780s. Even if Worthy Park's debt charges had amounted to 20 per cent of income, the average profit for the estate was some £4,000 a year, and all in all it is likely that it was expected to make at least £5,000 a year for its proprietors between 1775 and 1800, representing as much as 15 per cent or even 20 per cent of the assessed value of the estate.

In the case of the Prices, as with most West Indian planters, this figure was, as time went on, more of an optimistic expectation than an actual reality. While costs remained constant or gradually increased, income fluctuated, failed to keep pace or actually declined. For example, although the slave population remained static for many years, representing a steady demand for imported provisions, the production of sugar and rum could vary by as much as 50 per cent from year to year, and the prices received by very much more.[43] In some years the income from produce barely covered expenses, and in the 1780s there seemed to be evidence that productivity was in an irreversible decline.

The system by which factors were paid on commission provided planters with some guarantee that their interests were safeguarded; but nearly all the myriad risks which threatened sugar profits were borne by planters, not by merchants. Prices on the London exchange fluctuated widely, but, because of distance, individual estates were never able to play the market in the manner possible—and indeed indispensable—150 years later. Worthy Park was not even able to enter the race to get the year's sugar first to market, both because of her distance from the coast and the fact that her sugar generally matured a week or two later than that in the hotter southern lowlands of Jamaica. Although London prices between 1775 and 1800 varied by some 100 per cent, the prices received by Worthy Park remained constant within 5–10 per cent, being determined by the lowest average prices rather than the highest.[44]

Even at the best of times, planters were forced to borrow money on the security of their estates and crops, and this practice invariably worked to the benefit of the lender rather than the borrower.[45] The valuation of estates for mortgages and of crops—so commonly committed far in advance—for loans was determined on the figures for the previous five years. While this stood the West Indian planters in relatively good stead during boom periods such as the 'Golden Age' between 1763 and 1775, it was mainly after a run of bad years that the planters were most in need of credit. In periods of slump, such as that which accompanied and followed the American War of Independence, credit proved particularly expensive for the planter. Associated as it was with steeply rising import costs, the period was one in which the average planter was unable to take advantage of improved production and produce prices by selling when and where he liked.

For a factor, debts owed by a planter represented a doubly secured investment: not only had he a guaranteed income as high as 5 per cent from the interest on mortgages advanced, but he also enjoyed a guaranteed supply of sugar out of which a 2½ per cent commission was regularly levied.[46] The position of the factor was additionally secured because the British Parliament had passed laws which ordained that factors could pay themselves first out of the proceeds of sugar committed to them, without special court orders.[47] For the planter, the very availability of credit encouraged extravagant habits that he was generally unwilling or unable to forsake when profits declined and capital migrated to areas other than the West Indies. The only solution which most planters faced with crippling charges and declining income were prepared to adopt was an assiduous increase in the production of sugar and rum, even at the cost of monoculture, over-production, and the grossest exploitation of resources, especially slaves. Increased efficiency, further investment, and, particularly, resident owner-management, few were prepared to consider.

The absenteeism of the owners was the most notorious of all the burdens laid upon West Indian estates. Not only were the expenses of an absentee geared irremediably to a style of living based on the years of greatest profit, but the absentee generally had no direct control over, or even direct commitment to, an estate which often he had never seen and had come to regard as nothing but the foundation of his wealth. He was forced to rely upon the financial management of an attorney who through his payment on commission might have an interest in productivity but seldom had any concern for the long-term well-being of the estate, and on the farm and factory management of an overseer with neither the commission incentive nor the competence to make expensive, though necessary, capital improvements. Predictably, the interests of owners and the operations of attorneys and overseers were rigidly protected and controlled by Jamaican law, and faithful servants could provide an owner with a better return than he deserved; yet attorneys and overseers had no more control than proprietors themselves over the effects of war, the vagaries of prices and costs and the inexorably increasing burden of plantation debt. Bad attorneys and overseers—and the general level of honesty and managerial ability was not high—might visibly accelerate a plantation's decline.

In 1791, Worthy Park had been an absentee's estate for most of the previous fifty years. Soundly established as a sugar plantation by Colonel Charles Price, and provided with the means to more efficient production through the supervision of his son, Sir Charles, the estate had enabled Sir Charles Price's brother John to migrate to Cornwall for the benefit of his health, and his nephew John to live the life of a Cornish squire throughout the years of sugar's affluence. Yet all was not so well as it seemed. The years after the American War, which saw the collapse of Sir Charles Price's empire and the defection and death of Sir Charles Price's only son, also showed the cumulative effect on

Worthy Park of the system of indirect management and absentee plunder. The only possible cure for the problems of the estate—and this is a theme which runs consistently through the history of Worthy Park—was dynamic resident owner–management, coupled, if possible, with a fresh infusion of capital. These were provided between 1791 and 1795 by young Rose Price, the son of the second John Price, and we shall consider the value and limitations of this brief episode after looking in some detail at Worthy Park's slaves.

NOTES

[1] Beckford, II, 11.

[2] *Ibid.*

[3] In 1789. See Clement Caines, *Letters on the Cultivation of the Otaheite Cane,* St. Kitt's, 1792, quoted in Pares, *West India Fortune,* 109–11. What West Indian planters learned by bitter experience was that new varieties of cane, after promising magical returns, often declined rapidly. 'Bourbon' cane from Mauritius succeeded Otaheite cane in popularity in the 1790s.

[4] Beckford, II, 86.

[5] Long, *Jamaica,* I, 442.

[6] The exact number of cattle at Worthy Park during the eighteenth century is not known, but in 1814, when the sugar production had risen by 70 per cent, there were 162 'road cattle', 147 'cane cattle', 54 mules, and 2 horses; *Worthy Park Plantation Book, 1811–17,* 117–19. Most of Worthy Park's cattle were bred at Spring Garden until 1793 and from then at Spring Garden and Mickleton.

[7] See below, VII, 169.

[8] *Worthy Park Sugar Production, 1786–1791*

	Acreage	Sugar pro- duced, Hh	Hogsheads per acre	Pounds per acre
1786	257	181	0·72	1,296
1787	270	172	0·63	1,134
1788	258	294	1·14	2,052
1791	236	267	1·13	2,034

These figures compare with those of 1,600 pounds/acre given by Long (1774), 1,333 by Beckford (1777), and 1,066 by Edwards (1791). Ward Barrett, 'Caribbean Sugar Production Standards in the Seventeenth and Eighteenth Centuries', in J. Parker (ed.), *Merchants and Scholars,* Minnesota, 1966, 147–70. Barrett actually gives figures for Worthy Park, derived from U. B. Phillips, 'A Jamaican Slave Plantation', *American Historical Review,* 1914, 543–47; but these, only 888 pounds/acre, were derived from an exceptional year, 1792. See below, VII.

[9] In calculating this data, the pott has been assumed to contain 59 pounds of

sugar, the hogshead 1,800 pounds. Detailed production figures for 1788 are missing.

[10] Ploughs and animal-drawn harrows were not commonly used in Jamaica before the days of labour shortage following Emancipation. This was almost certainly because it would keep slaves under-employed out of crop-time, though some writers strenuously maintained that ploughing and harrowing required skills beyond the aptitude of praedial slaves, and that hoeing was much more effective for sugar land, especially in upland regions. See Pares, *West India Fortune*, 111.

[11] Long, I, 442–5.

[12] (a) Four canes lapped   (b) Two canes lapped   (c) Double cane lapped close

```
— — —            — —              — — —

  — — —          — —                — —

  — — —          — —                — —

— — —            — —              — — —
```

from *Plantation Book*, 1791–1811 (1795).

[13] One of the best summaries of cane cultivation, drawn largely from Roughley, Whitehouse, Henry, and Wentworth, is in W. L. Burn, *Emancipation and Apprenticeship in the British West Indies*, London, Cape, 1937, I, 40–2. Ward Barrett, op. cit., also gives an excellent brief account of many aspects of sugar husbandry, factory as well as field, though his chief concern is to compare standards throughout the foreign as well as British West Indies. Moreover, his Worthy Park figures, taken from U. B. Phillips, are clearly misleading.

[14] See accompanying Table for 1786–91.

[15] Analysis of bound 'Slave Book' figures for 1789.

[16] Beckford, II, 47. 'The driver's whip, (which is generally slung round his shoulders, which he cracks as a signal to call the negroes in the morning to work, to breakfast at ten, to dinner at twelve, to turn out again at two, to go home at six o'clock, *and with which* they are punished with thirty-nine lashes for felony or any *great crime*, by the manager. . . .') Rose Price, *Pledges on Colonial Slavery* . . . Penzance, T. Vigurs, 1832, 1. It should be noted that the hours and standard of punishment indicated here date from the Amelioration period, and follow the Jamaican Slave Codes of 1815 and 1831.

[17] *Ibid.*, 48.

[18] It may have been more. Beckford reckoned that twenty cartloads were needed to produce each hogshead. If each cart carried rather more than a ton of cane, this would indicate a ratio of closer to 30:1, with the average cutter producing a ton of cane a day. Beckford, II, 85.

[19] Beckford, II, 87.

[20] *Worthy Park Plantation Book*, 1791–1811 (1795).

[21] That is, 359 hogsheads from 564 acres. It should be noted, however, that Rose Price always calculated yield from the total acreage planted. *Ibid.*, and below, [22–4]. The figures for 1795 may be somewhat low since Rose Price divided production by the total potential cane acreage. The production for 1834 was 490 hogsheads from 441 acres actually reaped. See below, VII.

[22] Rose Price, *Pledges*, 30.

[23] Beckford, II, 65.

[24] *Ibid.*, 67. See also the evidence of Messrs. Fuller, Long, and Chisholm to the House of Commons Inquiry of 1789, P.P., H.C., A. & P., XXVI, 646A, iii

[25] In 1790, for example, the factory worked non-stop forty-five days from the

beginning of crop on 7 February, during which 131 hogsheads were produced at an average of about three hogsheads a day. This average would have greatly pleased John Pinney on Nevis, who considered that ten hogsheads a week (for a cattle mill) was quite satisfactory. Pares, *West India Fortune*, 115.

[26] Laws for the Government of Negro Slaves, 1787, II, cited in F. R. Augier and S. C. Gordon, *Sources of West Indian History*, London, Longmans, 1962, 169, For the use of the Cocoree as provision grounds see VII below.

[27] According to the Musgrave Papers, BM Add. MSS. 8, 133, ff. 95–6, of the 648 sugar plantations in Jamaica in 1768, 369 were equipped only with cattle mills, 235 with water-mills, and 44 with windmills; Ragatz, *Statistics*, I, V. The average production of each estate in 1768 was 105·2 hogsheads, with an average work-force of 153 persons. Although water-wheels could grind at least twice as much cane as cattle-mills, the latter were most efficient of all in extracting juice, being slow but sure. Mule mills normally extracted 65 per cent juice by weight with double-crushing, whereas the intermittent windmills could rarely manage 50 per cent, water-mills coming somewhere in between. Even steam-mills in the early nineteenth century could only expect to extract about 62 per cent with double-crushing, or 47 per cent with single-crushing. Ward Barrett, op. cit., 154–5.

[28] The trash, from which probably no more than two-thirds of the juice had been extracted by the rather inefficient crushing rollers, had to be kept dry and even then could not be used for fuel for about six weeks. In the early weeks of the crop therefore a considerable quantity of cut firewood was normally consumed; Burn, 47.

[29] See accompanying map, derived from P.R.O. C.O. 441/4/4/3. The mule-mill is not shown on most maps, but is mentioned as a fixture of long standing in the *Worthy Park Plantation Book, 1811–17*, 66 (1813).

[30] The change from potts to hogsheads seems to have been made at Worthy Park around 1791, for in that year sugar production figures hitherto calculated in potts was now calculated in hogsheads as well as potts. By 1800, calculation in potts had disappeared altogether.

[31] Again, the most lucid account of sugar production is in Burn, 43–5, which is derived from Roughley, Whitehouse, Wray, Martin, Belgrove, and several other contemporary writers. See also Pares, *West India Fortune*, 103–40.

[32] Beckford, II, 32.

[33] See below, IV.

[34] Beckford, II, 89.

[35] Appendix, I, 320.

[36] I.R.O. Deeds 423/68.

[37] The *William Beckford*, Cundall, was used in four years; the *Clarendon*, Barnes, in three; the *Lord Rodney*, Stimpson, *Phoenix*, same master, *Nancy*, Treluda, *Lord Hood*, Whedon, and *Queen*, Goodwin, twice each; and twenty-four other vessels once apiece.

[38] A vessel brought food supplies for Worthy Park from Cork each year between 1785 and 1791, and in addition to the *Betsey* smaller consignments of hardware and yard goods were made in two other vessels from London and two from Bristol in the course of these seven years. For a full list of the goods supplied to Worthy Park from London, Bristol, Cork, and elsewhere in Jamaica in the year 1789, see Appendix I below, 320.

[39] For a discussion of the fragmentary figures available for the earlier period,

see above, IV, 88; and for a discussion of profitability in the early sugar years, III, 57.

⁴⁰ Young, *West India Commonplace Book*, 46.

⁴¹ Long, *Jamaica*, I, 462.

⁴² The highest production between 1776 and 1796 was 371 hogsheads in 1778; the lowest, 172 in 1787. The peak of production before the twentieth century was 1812, when 702 hogsheads were produced.

⁴³ Even the bottom prices for sugar in London varied between £1. 9s. and £2. 11s. a hundredweight between 1776 and 1781 alone; but during the same period, the prices received by Worthy Park merely fluctuated between a low of £1. 9s. 11d. and a high of £1. 12s. 5d.

⁴⁴ As early as 1756, Patrick Browne wrote that Jamaican planters, 'though rich and in easy circumstances, are seldom out of debt; for the charges attending a sugar settlement are very considerable and constant; the interest of money very high and their natural propensity to increase their possessions constantly engaging them in new disbursements and contracts. . . .' These remarks might almost be a commentary on the activities of the two Sir Charles Prices. Browne, *The Civil and Natural History of Jamaica*, London, 1756, I, 23, quoted by Burn, *Emancipation*, 23.

⁴⁵ *P.P.*, *H.C.*, XXVI, 646a, v (1789).

⁴⁶ Pares, *Merchants and Planters*, 48. William Beckford maintained that a planter was better off to borrow money at 6 per cent from any other person than to accept a loan at 5 per cent from his factor if thereby he tied up all his produce. Planters in this case were dependents for life. Beckford, II, 357, quoted by Pares, *Merchants and Planters*, 47, n. 69, the fourth chapter of which is invaluable for an understanding of credit arrangements.

CHAPTER SIX

Slave Society on an Eighteenth-Century Estate

The magnitude of the Price estate by the last quarter of the eighteenth century was largely the result of the economic aggressiveness and political eminence of Sir Charles Price. Yet to attribute the rapid growth of the Price empire solely to the dynamic energy of its most illustrious owner is to ignore the contribution of its humble co-progenitors, the myriad Negro slaves. Sir Charles Price planned and schemed, but the pyramid of his family's fortune was based firmly on the backs of African blacks. It was the slaves who axed the matted virgin timber, tilled the land with hoes, swathed the standing cane with cutlasses, sweated in the odorous hell of the boiling-houses, cutting, digging, and carrying under the ever-present reality or threat of the gangman's lash. To proprietors and outside observers alike, the fact was axiomatic: the enslaved majority formed the very 'sinews of West Indian property'.[1]

To develop his properties Sir Charles Price was bound to invest in slaves. The young, the aged and the diseased were harnessed to the innumerable exhausting tasks necessary to make the empire pay. Slaves were allowed, or expected, to breed without the apparatus of marriage or formal family life: families were split by economic dictate alone. Like the land, the factory plant and the cattle, the slaves were regarded simply as units of economic value. In law (so often the reflection of, or mandate for, economic fact), they were simply property, chattels with few or no legal rights as humans.[2] Collectively the slaves formed an ever-expanding, shifting, and volatile labour force that was vital to the economy. Yet it must be remembered that the bare statistics relating to the slaves conceal the lives of thousands of forgotten people.

When he took over the estate at the time of his father's death, Sir Charles Price (then simply Charles) owned hundreds of slaves scattered throughout Jamaica, and in the course of the next forty years he was to add considerably to this labour force. Fortunately for the development of Jamaican plantations during the Golden Age of Sugar, the average price of slaves remained fairly stable. The spiralling inflation in prices occurred later, under the influence of war and the abolition of the trade, just as earlier the foreign demand for slaves had inflated prices. But prices of healthy slaves were always high, and varied widely, depending on age, sex, and technical skills as well as the degree or expectation of health. For example, in three groups of slaves purchased by Sir Charles Price between 1741 and 1742, the first coffle of 55 cost £1,365, an average of only £25; in the second, the prices varied from £48 to £101 per slave; the third, a group of seven, cost £364, an average of £52. Upon analysis the reasons for the price variation become obvious: the first purchase was a heterogeneous parcel, the second consisted of skilled males, the third of six women and a single male.[3]

In their purchases of slaves the plantocracy showed a marked preference for men, who were therefore more expensive than women. In 1744, six females could be bought for a mere £125, an average of less than £21 apiece. Even at their most desirable women slaves never cost as much as comparable able-bodied men.[4] The potential economic value of male children did not substantially raise the market value of a woman and her offspring. Boys, and even girls, might mature into useful adults, but this, to say the least, was uncertain, and slave children were valued in terms of immediate economic returns.[5] Still more distressing than this crude evaluation of offspring was its corollary, the breakup of slave families to satisfy the needs of their owners' estates. The frequency with which female slaves, with or without their children, were bought as a job lot is an indication of the inevitable dependence of such women on more than one mate.[6] Cohabitation approximating marriage was frequently impractical, and children were often sundered from their mothers as soon as they were useful in the fields, normally at the age of six. In 1744, for example, one of the Price properties employed children who had already lived on two other Price estates.[7]

In addition to the traumatic severance from the African homeland, the tribal, kin, and family disintegration occasioned by the Negro trade, plantation slaves even when 'Creole', or island-born—almost invariably suffered dislocation and instability in personal, sexual, and familial relations. The resulting alienation from plantation life must have been particularly severe on estates such as those of the Prices, controlled as a unit but scattered widely over Jamaica. Plantocratic commentators often remarked on the natural 'promiscuity' of Negroes: in fact it was the slaveowners themselves who provided the conditions which made 'promiscuity' inevitable.[8]

What the plantations needed above all were healthy male slaves, and the resulting sexual imbalance exacerbated the social malaise. In the mid-eighteenth century the Price estates were no exception to the general rule that men outnumbered women, though the sexual imbalance evened out naturally in time as the proportion of creole, or Jamaican-born, slaves increased. On four of the Price properties, Burton's, Rose Hall, Wallins, and the Decoy, the numerical superiority of men was particularly striking; out of a total of 1,141 slaves only 356, or 30·4 per cent, were women.[9] On Worthy Park itself, it seems that the percentage of men was never higher than 60 per cent, for even as early as 1730 there were 112 females out of 257 slaves, amounting to 44 per cent of the total. By the 1780s this had risen to 47·5 per cent, and the numbers of males and females was almost certainly equalized by the time the slave trade was abolished in 1808. Thereafter, the ratio was gradually reversed.[10] From being in a minority of 9:11, the female slaves moved inexorably towards a ratio of 9:7, and from a situation in which one in three male slaves could not expect a stable monogamous relationship, conditions changed so that one female slave in three had a similar lack of expectation. These fluctuations obviously had a deleterious social effect, and if extended to the whole of Jamaica may help to explain much of the instability of sexual relationships that characterized island society after Emancipation as well as during slavery days.

The fluctuating ratio between the sexes also, of course, had a potent effect upon the trend towards the natural increase of the Negro population. Clearly, as the proportion of females rises so does the chance that the society will reproduce itself and increase naturally. At Worthy Park over the period of slavery the proportion of females rose from about 40 per cent of the total to approximately 60 per cent, implying a potential fertility increase from this factor alone of at least 20 per cent.[11] Taken in conjunction with the decreased demand for the importation of fresh slaves from Africa because of the failure of some estates, this is obviously worth considering when estimating the motives for the abolition of the slave trade and the improvement in the conditions of the creole slaves.

On the whole the more arduous tasks on sugar plantations fell to the male slaves, though at Worthy Park at least, women also worked hard in the fields. It was the men, however, who bore the brunt of the heavy work of cane cutting and holing, and men alone tended the blistering operations in the factories. Women, children and the aged normally undertook the less demanding, though no less essential, tasks.[12]

Besides the most gruelling manual tasks, men also monopolized the plantation crafts. Skilled craftsmen were no more essential to the functioning of a sugar estate than were the hordes of enslaved labourers; but their particular skills commanded a higher market value.[13] In 1761 Sir Charles Price purchased ten slaves for the staggering figure of £912, a sum accounted for by the fact that six of the slaves were skilled men; two were bricklayers and four carpenters.[14] A similar number of unskilled slaves acquired five years earlier had cost only £500.[15] Whatever the sex, skill, or strength of slaves, their rôle in plantation society was conditioned by their economic usefulness.

To complement the development of his territorial empire, Sir Charles Price the elder embarked on a massive investment in slaves. Between 1741 and 1772 he sunk, at the very least £13,730 into the purchase of 742 slaves.[16] In addition slaves passed into the Price empire when they were resident on property purchased by Sir Charles. Thus in 1766 when Mickleton in St. Thomas in the Vale was bought, 1,050 acres and 124 slaves were added to the family assets.[17] The end result of these two forms of investment, one in slaves alone, the other in properties containing slaves, was the emergence of a formidable slave population owned by the Price family. The pattern of slave ownership on the Price lands in the lifetime of Sir Charles the elder reflects the island-wide correlation between rising sugar prosperity and the expansion of the slave labour force.[18] At the time of his death in 1772 Sir Charles the elder, as we have already seen, owned eleven properties consisting of some 26,000 acres, surpassing even the Beckfords as the largest of Jamaican landowners.[19] These vast tracts of Jamaica were worked by no fewer than 1,800 slaves.[20] The largest single group of these slaves toiled away their lives on Worthy Park. From 1783, when Sir Charles the younger was supervising the liquidation of his father's over-extended empire, to Emancipation we are fortunately able to examine Worthy Park's slave community in great detail.

The factors which affected the lives of the slaves in the forty years culminating in Emancipation were international and parochial. While the West Indies as a whole became increasingly sensitive to the repercussions of British humanitarian politics and the changes in the British economy, the slaves lived out their lives beset by more local pressures. It was the social structure of each particular estate which conditioned the daily existence, the fears, aspirations, and customs of the captive labour force.

In 1783 Worthy Park was run by the labour of 318 slaves, a workforce that was expanded laboriously in the absentee years of the 1780s until it reached a figure of 357 in 1791. In these years the natural decrease in population was only 0·8 per cent, although in only two years, 1785 and 1787, did the number of births on the estate outstrip the number of deaths.[21] In the five years after 1791, the years of Rose

Price's resident ownership, the demographic pattern of Worthy Park's slave society changed dramatically. A natural decrease of 3·4 per cent in population made a striking contrast to the much more stable pattern under absentee ownership. The birth-rate of 2·3 per cent for 1792–6 compared favourably with that of 2 per cent for the period 1783 to 1791 but the death-rate, which had averaged 3 per cent in the earlier

Worthy Park slave population, 1783–96

	Total population	Births	Deaths
1783	318	2	11
1784	316	10	18
1785	313	5	4
1786	307	–	–
1787	339	10	7
1788	338	9	12
1789	339	7	16
1790	345	–	6
1791	357	8	18
1792	359	13	14
1793	450	6	26
1794	528	8	56
1795	483	13	19
1796	470	8	22

From *Worthy Park Plantation Books*, 1783–87; 1787–91; 1791–1811.

period, jumped to 5·7 per cent. The reason for this lay in the massive purchase of new slaves after 1792.

New slaves were needed throughout the eighteenth century both to keep up with the expansion of the sugar industry and to make good the overall decrease in the slave population. In the last two decades of the century Worthy Park's slaves failed to keep up their numbers, and their rate of natural decline makes a sharp contrast to the healthy surplus of local births in the period following abolition.[22] Although the total number of slaves gradually climbed to 357 in 1791, the figures available for the years preceding the arrival of Rose Price, show that 43 children were born into slavery on Worthy Park but 74 slaves died. Only the purchase of new slaves enabled the labour force to expand. Under Rose Price's energetic control the slave population soared from 357, to 528 in 1794, a total increase which came at a time of rising mortality rates. Between 1792 and 1796, 48 slaves were born but 137 died. In brief, the mortality under the resident master became noticeably worse. The reasons for this are to be found not in the harshness of the owner's personal rule, but in his determination to expand his labour force by the wholesale purchase of new slaves.

The eighteenth-century plantocracy faced apparently insuperable problems with their labour force. Only by adding to it could they hope to expand their sugar lands and yet they were aware that freshly imported slaves were notoriously prone to fatal illnesses. Edward Long noted that it was a fact of life that up to a third of the Africans would die within three years of arrival in Jamaica and that a majority of all slave deaths could be accounted for among new slaves.[23] Worthy Park's doctor pointed out that this phenomenon resulted from '. . . the bad habit of body these people have contracted from long confinement, bad food and improper treatment on the voyage'.[24] Dr. Quier also suggested that '. . . the treatment of new negroes in this island has been greatly altered for the better. . . .'[25] The evidence of the 1790s on Worthy Park suggest that, on the contrary, the plantocracy were helpless in the face of widespread illness and death among new slaves.

In 1792 and 1793 Rose Price invested £13,472 in 225 slaves.[26] Almost immediately the death-rate rose dramatically, and although slaves succumbed to a variety of illnesses it was the 'bloody flux' which exacted the most serious toll.[27] By the end of 1794, 40 men and 16 women had died over the course of the year, a death-rate of 10 per cent of the total population. The majority of these deaths took place among the new Congolese. In a desperate attempt to save lives, many of the Africans were sent to Worthy Park's provisioning ground at Spring Garden '. . . for a change of air . . .'[28] and by 1795 the death-rate had fallen to a more 'normal' proportion of 3.9 per cent. At the end of the three years' seasoning of the new slaves almost a quarter of them had perished. In the period of Rose Price's residence no fewer than 115 slaves had died on his estate. Such horrifying figures raise, in a dramatic fashion, the more general problem of the health of Worthy Park's slaves. The years preceding the enforced immigration of new slaves with their attendant epidemics, illustrate a remarkably different pattern of health. From a population of 339, of whom 177 were men and 162 women, in 1789, 36 men and 16 women suffered a wide variety of complaints; sores, bone-ache, distemper, or they were simply infirm. That there were twice as many sick men as women suggests that the more onerous tasks performed by male slaves were more detrimental to their health. Similarly, 33 women were classified as old compared to 29 men, a reversal of the actual proportion between the sexes on the estate.[29] There were in fact more old slaves than sick slaves, itself an indication that treatment of the slaves was not so bad that longevity was only a remote possibility. Old age did not however bring the rewards of rest. In 1787 in a field gang of 70 slaves, 10 were elderly. Likewise illness offered no escape from toil. In another work gang of 45 slaves in that same year, 12 suffered from various complaints.[30]

Far from having an exceptionally severe ratio of sick to healthy slaves, there is good reason to believe that Worthy Park had a better record than other estates. In the context of Jamaican slavery, Worthy Park's medical care of its slaves was impressive. From 1767 the estate had in attendance a doctor who was both a general practitioner and a researcher into tropical slave diseases. After studying in London and Leyden, Dr. John Quier made his home in Lluidas where, in a career that spanned fifty-six years, he treated thousands of slaves.[31] His experiences with them formed the basis for an important publication in 1789 in which Quier analysed slave conditions and complaints. Quier's findings corroborate the statistical evidence for Worthy Park in the 1780s.[32] Among new-born slaves he failed to find any evidence of excessive mortality.[33] Worthy Park's records reflect the same pattern, showing that only two of the estate's new-born slaves in the 1780s died immediately, both in 1783.[34] At the same time, the low natural increase of slaves in Lluidas was as striking to a contemporary doctor as it is to latter-day historians. Such low birth-rates were partially explained by '. . . the promiscuous intercourse which the greater number of negro women indulge themselves in with the other sex'. Quier wrote of the '. . . frequent shifting connection between the sexes' which resulted in the death of children '. . . through neglect and the want of maternal affection which mothers seldom retain for their offspring by a former husband'.[35] Once again Quier's comments bring us face to face with the harsh human facts of the Price empire. Slaves were transferred from one property to another, inevitably sundering any stable sexual unions they had developed in one place and ensuring that new relations would emerge wherever the slave was finally deposited. The initial disintegration of sexual relations between slaves was hence frequently brought about by the plantocracy. Coupled to the over-abundance of men, the transfer of slaves provided an ideal climate for the 'promiscuous' life of slaves. Sexual freedom was moreover the only area of individual freedom left to the slave; the social and economic atmosphere in which slaves lived guaranteed that they would enjoy it to the full. But the cost of this freedom was to be found in the incidence of venereal disease and its accompanying abortion[36] and miscarriage rates.[37]

It was, however, in the field of practical medicine that Quier made perhaps his greatest contribution to the slaves at Worthy Park. Measles, an epidemic '. . . almost equally dreaded with the smallpox',[38] had blighted Jamaica's slaves in the 1770s. During that time Quier perfected a diagnosis of measles that was not adopted in Europe for another century.[39] Smallpox, the most horrific of slave diseases, also attracted Quier's research energies. Using his slave patients as guinea-pigs he was able to perfect inoculation against the disease.[40] By 1774 Edward Long felt confident that the '. . . late method of inoculation, happily practised in this island promised fair to put an end to such dreadful examples of mortality'.[41] Never in the 1780s and 1790s did Worthy Park suffer a renewed attack from either of these two scourges. Quier had evidently insulated the estate against them, but he was powerless to cope with the appalling death-rate among the new slaves in the 1790s. The physical trauma of the Middle Passage and the related problem of acclimatization was so severe that it could not be eradicated or solved simply by improving the material conditions of the slaves on the estate. Despite the attention of the best slave doctor in the island, Worthy Park's African slaves died wholesale on arrival.

The conditions in which the Africans found themselves were no different from those of the resident slaves. Contrary to the findings of Worthy Park's earlier historian no evidence exists to show amelioration under Rose Price.[42] The new Negro housing was simply to cater for the 25 per cent increase in the working force. The houses were, moreover, '. . . sometimes suffocating with heat and smoke; at others, when the fires subsides, especially at night, admitting the cold damp air through innumerable crevices and holes of the walls . . .'.[43] Provision of a nurse for the Africans was not an improvement but rather an essential element in the battle against epidemic.

At the height of the dysentery epidemic the startled Rose Price took the opportunity to inquire into the fertility of his slaves. In 1794 and 1795 he noted the numbers of miscarriages suffered by his female slaves; the fact that he should undertake such a survey indicates a degree of concern about the reproductive patterns of his work-force. His findings must have puzzled and alarmed him. The figures for 1793 showed that only four miscarriages had taken place at Worthy Park,[44] but looking into the past history of all the women more thoroughly revealed a picture of entirely different dimensions. Of the 240 resident female slaves 89 had given birth, but of these, 35 had suffered miscarriages. More appalling still was the fact that only 19 of the 89 women had managed to keep alive all the children born to them. 70 women had lost various numbers of children. Of the exceptional 19 women whose children had all survived, 15 had in fact been delivered of only a single child. Two women had each given birth to, and managed to keep alive, two children and one lucky woman still cared for all three children born to her. At the time the ownership made these investigations there had been, in all, 345 babies born to slaves at Worthy Park. But only 159 children were still alive.[45] More than one half of the babies had died. Quier, as we have already seen, noted that new-born mortality was rare. This being so, it is evident that the majority of fatalities among slave children born at Worthy Park occurred not at birth, but in the children's early years. A female slave was thus beset by hazardous emotional and physical problems during and after pregnancy. While pregnant she stood a good chance of aborting. After delivery, her child's grip on life was precarious in the extreme. A pregnant slave must have been acutely aware that her child would probably never join its parents in a life of unremitting toil.

Many of the physical complaints suffered by the slaves, and handed down by sick mothers to their young children, derived from a combination of excessive work and deficiencies in diet. The food given to the slaves '. . . was generally the roots and other vegetable substances which at all times make up the greatest part of their nourishment such as yams, cocos or eddas, potatoes, plaintain, bananas etc. Their drink was water or beverage (so they call here a drink made up with water and sugar or with the addition of some lime or lemon juice)'[46] Yet, at least until the time of Rose Price, little of the staple diet of Worthy Park's slaves was grown on the fertile lands of the estate itself because the slaves were too fully occupied working the sugar lands to be diverted to food cultivation and most of the Jamaican food was bought not grown. Yams, plaintain, and cocos were not produced at Worthy Park in sufficient bulk to feed the slaves, but had to be transported via the provisioning ground at Spring Garden.[47]

In addition large quantities of food were bought from England and Ireland. Both whites and slaves relied on imported foods for their basic diet; the better, more expensive food passing inevitably into the Great House and the Overseer's House.[48] While the whites enjoyed their beef, cheese and porter, the slaves had to depend for their protein upon a monotonous supply of herrings.[49] Throughout Jamaica, wrote Long, the slaves not only relied on salt fish, but actually enjoyed it, '. . . and the more it stinks the more dainty'.[50] At Worthy Park the slaves had no choice about their diet or the degree of its putrescence. Frequently herrings were given out to the slaves long after the barrel had been opened. Herrings exposed to the Jamaican climate for as long as two weeks would indeed have provided a stinking if none-too-dainty morsel. At other times, the slaves' fish had turned bad on the long voyage from England. Herrings which were found to be '. . . quite rotten and mashed . . .' were none the less passed on to the slaves.[51] Christmas for the slaves, at least before the arrival of Rose Price in 1791, far from being celebrated with a seasonal change of diet, simply brought a massive and seemingly indigestible increase in herrings.[52]

Only at times of emergency, as in 1791 when an epidemic threatened the community, could a slave hope for a slight improvement in diet. Unlucky enough to fall seriously ill, a slave was nursed back to a working health on a diet supplemented by tongue and flour.[53] When newly arrived slaves received slightly better food than resident slaves it was not a gesture of improvement by the ownership so much as an essential measure. The new slaves harboured the most serious illnesses and without special care were more than likely to enter the mortality figures.

To supplement the fish, roots and vegetables, the slaves were provided with guinea corn and rice, items which were also transported through Spring Garden.[54] Two further commodities given to the slaves could however be produced in abundance on Worthy Park itself. Provision was always made for the allocation of sugar and rum to slaves and whites alike.[55] Annually some seven to eight puncheons of rum were drunk on the estate, the bulk of it by the slaves.[56] Similarly some 48 hundredweights of sugar were consumed by Worthy Park's population in the course of a year.[57] Rum may have given a pleasant stimulus to work while involving the estate in no great expense but it in no way compensated for the deficiencies in the slaves' diet, deficiencies which, when allied to the work load, reduced the slaves' resistance to disease.

Worthy Park, like any other eighteenth-century estate, relied to a large extent on cattle for the heavy work of cartage and ploughing, in addition to using the manure as fertilizer for the cane,[58] but no attempt was made to provide the estate with home-grown beef. None of the hundreds of heads of cattle were beefstock and the estate had to rely on local butchers for fresh meat. Rose Price gave instructions that each white man on the estate should receive 2 pounds of fresh beef each day[59] and since, in the last three months of 1793, meat for the tiny band of white men alone cost over £55[60] it was economically unthinkable that Price should order similar allowances for the hundreds of slaves. Only on one occasion, at Christmas, did the slaves ever savour the nourishment of fresh meat, when 357 slaves shared a cow and a steer.[61]

The years of resident ownership made little difference to the diet of

Worthy Park's slaves, and they continued to suffer from those diet deficiencies which made West Indian slaves so prone to illness. Since 1753, the estate had owned the fertile enclave in the hills to the west of Lluidas Vale called Cocoree, and this was probably worked for 'ground provisions' by the slaves whenever they had the spare time and energy—providing a continuous training in 'African' methods of cultivation that was to prove invaluable when emancipation came. Until the arrival of Rose Price, however, there were too few slaves adequately to work even the sugar lands, and such a labour shortage made it highly unlikely that the management would divert vital labour to the task of growing food. Rose Price, with an augmented labour force, under pressure from the Assembly and bearing the interests of economy in mind, began to turn more attention to the formal production of ground provisions on the estate itself.[62] And yet Worthy Park was as dependent in the 1790s as it had been in the previous decade on the importation of saltfish to feed the slaves. Such a reliance on foreign food placed a continuing strain on the estate's finances; increasing indebtedness to British merchants and bankers. Although the normal years of the 1780s suggest that illness was common though not widespread, it was in the years of epidemic in the 1790s that the slaves' inability to resist a tidal wave of disease stood revealed. At the time of the severe death-rate in the 1790s Worthy Park made greater efforts to grow its own food, following the attempt of the Assembly to promote self-sufficiency by passing a law requiring the estates '. . . to put in every year so many acres of provisions for the negroes . . .'.[63] In August 1792, 1,674 pounds of 'coco heads for planting' were brought by the estate.[64] Similar strides towards self-sufficiency in guinea corn were also taken under Rose Price. Working on the assumption that three pints of corn for each Negro was the ideal, it was found that 2,053 bushels '. . . will feed more than one hundred and twenty negroes for one whole year—as many of them cannot consume three pints per day'.[65]

Compounding the deficiences in slave diet were the related problems of work and punishment. The work, carried out seven days a week in crop and six in the out of crop period, was compelled by the constant threat of physical punishment. According to Beckford the 'instrument of correction' was '...heard...to resound among the hills and upon the plain'.[66] In the 1790s Rose Price refined the punishment of recalcitrant slaves by introducing the 'Vagabond Gang' designed to accommodate persistent offenders against the system. Slaves were condemned to the gang as they would be to prison, even to the extent of serving life sentences.[67] In May 1795 thirteen slaves were serving various terms in this gang. Whatever the task of the slave in the fields, the rawhide, used as much as an inducement to work as an instrument of punishment, could literally be heard across Lluidas valley.[68]

The marshalling of slaves into groups suitable for work on a plantation was to a large degree dictated by the nature of the work itself. In the 1790s, at the suggestion of Rose Price, Worthy Park's slaves were divided into seventeen categories; the Great House people, the Overseer's House people, cooks, watchmen, carpenters, coopers, sawyers, masons, blacksmiths, ratcatchers, cattlemen, weed gang, pen workers, the field workers (in three gangs), invalids, young children, and lastly the idle.[69] Although these groupings were a rationalization for book-keeping purposes, it merely confirmed the pattern of work groups in existence in the 1780s. As the new Africans arrived they were slotted into these divisions but, lacking the essential skills for the artisan trades, they found their way almost inevitably into the field gangs.

Proportionally more women worked in the fields than men. In 1789, 70 women out of 162 worked in the fields compared to 29 men out of a total of 177.[70] Similarly in 1793, although the total slave population had increased, this pattern remained; 107 women out of 244, worked in the field compared to 92 of a possible 284 men.[71] Fewer than one half of the estate's labour force toiled in the fields. In 1795 when the estate owned 483 slaves only 219 were employed in the fields.[72] While the work of the female slaves was concentrated in the fields the energy and skills of the men had to be channelled into the great variety of functions vital to sugar production. No single occupational group could claim greater importance in the functioning of the estate. Although artisan slaves were more costly, because of their much-sought-after skills, the contribution of the human beasts of burden in the fields was equally vital to the unending work of sugar cultivation.

If any group of slaves could be said to be expendable it was the domestic workers, a group which became substantially inflated under the residence of Rose Price. Before his arrival in 1791 the Great House, with its seventeen rooms easily the largest habited building, had been run by only two slaves.[73] Between 1791 and 1793 this figure increased each successive year, from eleven to twelve and then to seventeen slaves. On Rose Price's departure this work-force fell back to the original two slaves.[74] Even more notable was the increase in domestic slaves working in the Overseer's house. In 1789 a single slave worked there.[75] In 1791 ten slaves worked there; two years later this had risen to twenty-seven and in 1795 no fewer than thirty-six were employed in the Overseer's house, some drafted perhaps from the now unoccupied Great House.[76] Such an excessively large number of domestics catered for the needs of a mere six whites in 1795.[77] The habitual extravagance of the eighteenth-century Jamaican whites in surrounding themselves with domestics was wasteful but explicable. At the social level it was compensation for the barrenness of their leisure hours and an aping of the grand manner and the bloated retinues of the English class to which white Jamaicans aspired.

Although there were few persons of mixed blood on the plantation—no more than 5 per cent were so listed before about 1800[78]—these almost invariably filled domestic positions, and none worked in the fields or factory as labourers. The reasons for this were partly because the coloureds were the offspring of domestic liaisons, and partly because manual labour was regarded as fitted only for the darkest Negroes. Consequently, the notion that social mobility was related to fairness of skin was perpetuated.

Within the slave community there was, however, a degree of occupational mobility that was not necessarily related to colour. Most notably, this came from the enforced movement of slaves according to the exigencies of the seasons.[79] But such movement was strictly limited. Recently seasoned Africans could clearly not be drafted into skilled occupations. Making puncheons, repairing equipment, or maintaining buildings—tasks for the carpenters, blacksmiths, and masons—required skills which precluded the field slaves. It was, moreover, unlikely that skilled men would be put to work at menial tasks because of the shortage of skilled labour on the estate. In 1792 and 1793, for instance, a carpenter, stonemasons, and sawyers had to be hired from outside Worthy Park.[80]

Where opportunities for mobility existed, they were open to only a handful of slaves. Clearly some slaves would always be called on for training in the various skills needed on the estate. Since the number of artisans was small, the prospects of a young slave being apprenticed to such a career were very restricted indeed. Men could be moved from field work to the job of watchman but such a transition was normally a function of advancing age. Ratcatchers could also be recruited from the field workers but since, in 1795, the estate employed only two men in that capacity,[81] once again little or no possibility of transfer existed. Wherever prospects of changing jobs existed, they simply involved a transfer from one form of unpleasant manual labour to another; it was generally a lateral rather than an upwards movement. With the right kind of disposition, however, a slave could at least avoid the heat of the midday sun by winning the confidence of the whites and gaining entry to the domestic staff. The qualities needed in a servant would not be found in every slave, thus restricting yet again the chances of movement between jobs. On Worthy Park occupational mobility was a very restricted feature of slave society.

Women, perhaps more than men, suffered the fate of almost inevitable restriction to an original job. Technically a female slave could gain release from work by producing a large brood of children. Unfortunately she gained no credit for miscarriages or children who died in early life, the fate of half the children born at Worthy Park. Slave motherhood was a painful experience and one that was rarely rewarded. The eight slaves who gave birth in the course of 1794 each received a dollar.[82] Coming at the time of serious slave mortality, this exceptional gesture was more a sign of thankfulness than of munificence on the part of the owners. So high was the miscarriage rate, however, that had the gift of a dollar to new mothers been a regular practice many pregnant slaves would none the less never benefit from it. Nor were they likely to be released from work to care for their children, since too few of their young survived. Like their male counterparts, female slaves had little hope of changing their jobs, their style of life or their economic prospects. Occupational and social mobility were ideals which few slaves understood and to which even fewer aspired.

Set above the mass of the slaves was a small group of privileged slaves who held the key to the effective control and the efficient management of the working body of slaves. This élite of 'Head People' consisted in 1795 of twenty-five slaves, including the headmen of each artisan trade and the drivers of the field gangs.[83] To this élite was given the incentive of preferential treatment and the lion's share of material goods set aside for the slaves. In 1795, for instance, 932 gallons of rum were set aside for the slaves but since the 'Head People' were, on Rose Price's instructions to receive two quarts a day, a total of 274 gallons were consumed by only twenty-five slaves.[84] Thus from a total slave population of 480, a mere twenty-five absorbed a quarter of the rum allocation.

Similar privileged treatment for the 'Head People' had long been a feature of the management of the estate. Slaves were regularly issued with various lengths of oznaburghs, baize, check, and blanketing from which they made their own clothes, as well as hats, caps, coats, and knives. When these distributions took place, normally on an annual basis, the 'Head People' received more than the ordinary slave. Quashie, the head carpenter, though old and infirm, received a notably bigger clothing allowance than the field slaves.[85] Conversely the withholding of an allocation could be used as punishment for wayward slaves. Arthol and Betty, both 'good for nothing', were rewarded for their laziness when they received no clothing allowance in 1789, though technically it was not illegal for masters to withold essential clothing from their slaves.[86]

Under Rose Price the distribution of the slaves' basic protein dish, saltfish, was divided into two groups. Some received their food by the day, others by the week.[87] Evidence here is tantalizingly fragmentary but it is reasonable to assume that the 'Head People' were fed more regularly and more substantially than the majority of slaves. Distribution of food, drink, and clothing was more than a means of keeping the slaves alive. It was both a reward and a punishment. Those slaves in positions of special responsibility were rewarded for their contribution to the well-being of the estate. Preferential treatment was the means by which the management set the 'Head People' apart from the mass of slaves. The slave élite supervised, cajoled, and marshalled the black labour force and received in return a little more of life's essentials.

Unless forcibly moved around between estates by the ownership, the slaves were predominantly static; they had little hope or prospect of improving their lot. Life was apparently unchangeable. Bought, transported, and listed like animals, their family structure destroyed, slaves were dragooned to work at unfamiliar tasks for long periods on inadequate diet and with no material or spiritual reward in sight. They were, in brief, dehumanized and reduced to a common level of passivity. It is remarkable that, given this syndrome of dehumanization, any spark of resistance should remain in the slave community. In fact many refused to be bowed by the system and made determined efforts to escape, legally or illegally, from slavery.

Means of escape for slaves were few. The most obvious yet most infrequently used was the legal freedom bestowed by manumission. Between 1784 and 1797, only twenty-two of Worthy Park's slaves were freed, and of these, four bought their own freedom.[88] That slaves were able to raise sums of £150 and £65[89] is perhaps explicable by reference to the liaisons which inevitably developed between white men and female slaves and the affection which sometimes grew for a domestic servant. When children were born from the illicit affairs of white men and slave women, financial provision was very often made for their future in deeds or wills.[90] Such arrangements were the slaves' only chance of acquiring large sums of money. Only one white woman lived at Worthy Park in the 1790s,[91] making it inevitable that local white men would turn to their slaves for pleasure and companionship. It was the bastard offspring of such liaisons which provided the mothers, and the children themselves, with the best chance of escape from slavery. But whenever freedom was offered to the white man's children, to his black mistress, or simply to his most faithful servants, it was an expensive gesture. Manumission drained labour from the estate and was, furthermore, a continuing expense to the man who released the slave; for the upkeep of a freed slave a substantial sum had to be lodged with the wardens of the local vestry.[92]

More frequent than manumission was the escape of slaves from captivity, but such escapes were dangerous and mostly unsuccessful. Escaping from Lluidas Vale was in itself a feat of desperation and endurance that must have sapped the resistance and determination of many 'runaways'. Furthermore, since Jamaica's legal code demanded that Negroes be able to prove their freedom,[93] and because they could no longer rely upon sanctuary among the Maroons, escapees were forced to avoid all contact with civilization. Runaway slaves were hence obliged to head for the safety of the almost impenetrable and inhospitable forests and mountains. The Robinson Crusoe qualities of ingenuity, determination, and technical knowledge must have been rare among slaves whose physical power and spirit had often been corroded by illness, poor diet, and hard work. Recapture was almost inevitable and the annual quota of escapees represented a regular turnover in slaves; those recaptured simply filled the gaps left by new runaways. Some slaves were habitual offenders in which case they were simply 'worthless'; regular runaways were in the same economic category as the weak and the aged.[94]

The numbers of runaways would naturally depend on prevailing conditions. It is significant that the largest number fled in 1794, the year of the terrible mortality figures. An uncertain and lonely fate in the hills was better than an apparently inevitable death on the estate from the 'bloody flux'. But most of the runaways soon returned, either forcibly or voluntarily. One slave, Ann, made two escapes in 1794. Longer spells of freedom may have lulled slaves into a false sense of security. Cesar who escaped early in 1794 was not brought back for more than a year.[95] The hills rarely offered a permanent escape from slavery.

Suicide offered the last escape for the desperate or the disturbed who lacked the energy or the will to flee. For at least one Worthy Park slave, self-inflicted death was preferable to servitude; in 1791, an unfortunate man 'hanged himself in the woods'.[96] It may be that the occasional deaths recorded as being due to 'dirt-eating' should also be classified as suicide.[97] Cynical commentators might suggest that slave revolts, not known at Worthy Park, were tantamount to mass suicide, of a particularly painful kind.

It is, however, the runaways and disaffected who offer the best guide to the incidence of slave unrest at Worthy Park. In 1795 the Vagabond Gang contained thirteen offenders, nine men and four women, at a time when nine other slaves were still at large as runaways.[98] Twenty-two slaves from a community of 480 (a proportion of 4½ per cent) may not indicate a significant degree of unrest unless the rapid turnover in runaways is borne in mind. The group of runaways changed quarterly. Thus in the period 1785 to 1790 no more than seven slaves were fugitives from Worthy Park at any one time but over that same period twenty-nine slaves tried the lonely freedom of the hills. The quarterly returns of runaways is only the visible tip of a deep-rooted slave malaise that was more widespread than it appears on first examination. Considering the harshness of the slaves' daily experiences it is perhaps to be wondered why unrest was never on a wider and more violent scale. What militated against widespread violence was not the mildness of conditions, but effective forces of control which stemmed from the social structure of the estate. The power of the controlling whites was evidenced in the regular pathetic sight of returning runaways, but this power was both more complex and more subtle than numerical or military superiority.

Unlike the slave community, the white personnel on Worthy Park changed with bewildering speed. Most whites stayed in their jobs only for a matter of months. There was never more than a very small group of whites on the estate at any one time, a fact of central importance when attempting to understand the control they exercised over the slaves. Throughout the last two decades of the eighteenth century a group of slaves, never smaller than 300 and at times more than 500 strong, was kept at work and in check by a rapidly changing handful of whites in times of great internal and external stress. Between 1783 and 1796 no fewer than 85 white men lived and worked on Worthy Park. But, until the arrival of Rose Price, there was only one instance where the white community went into double figures. For the rest of the time the slaves were controlled by a white group that fluctuated between five and nine members. At the worst point, there was one white to 63 slaves; at the best, one to 34.[99] After 1791 Rose Price never allowed the white community of which he was master to fall to the dangerous levels of the late 1780s, but even he managed to keep within the deficiency laws on only two occasions.[100] To maintain the already inadequate ratio, Price had to employ more whites after 1791 to keep up with the influx of new slaves and to look for white tenants not actually employed on the estate, who could be used to 'save the deficiency.' With his departure in 1795, the proportion once again slumped. From being within striking distance of a legal balance between blacks and whites, Worthy Park dropped to a ratio of 68 slaves to each white man.

The fundamental cause of this situation lay beyond the control of the estate. Worthy Park was beset by the problem, common to the whole of the island, of the mobility of white labour. Overseers, book-keepers, and white artisans were transitory to the point of being nomadic. Jamaica was apparently full of peripatetic whites who failed to develop occupational roots. This problem was not simply a question of inadequate salaries. Central to the running of an estate was the Overseer to whom Worthy Park paid the handsome salary of £200 a year. Despite this high pay, no fewer than five overseers managed Worthy Park between 1783 and 1791. Later, under Rose Price, this salary was increased to £300, more than twice that given to the estate's medical practitioner, Dr. Quier.[101] Wages for the other whites were low. Book-keepers, distillers, carpenters, millwrights, smiths, and ploughmen, some of whom worked cheek by jowl with equally skilled slaves, could expect no more than £50 a year and very often would draw only £30. While they may have felt underpaid, they would have found wages little better elsewhere in the island.

There were obviously factors other than the purely economic which had an unsettling effect on the whites. Geographical isolation and lack of a social life must have weighed heavily on them. In 1795 all the whites, with the exception of Rose Price and the Reverend Vinicombe, were accommodated in the Overseer's House where their lives were materially barren; their rooms contained nothing but the basic essentials.[102] Austere simplicity compounded the loneliness and the poor pay. Moreover, no one could oblige a white man, unlike a slave, to stay on a plantation. In comparison to the master in his spacious house,[103] with his books sent to Jamaica from Oxford[104] and with his vested interest in the estate, the white workers spent an apparently depressing, impecunious and austere life on the estate. No man could survive solely on the natural splendours of the setting, and slave women must inevitably have become one of the few tolerable recreations. Men resolved the problem of isolation and alienation by quitting their jobs.

In economic terms it is mistaken to group together all white men on the estate simply because of their colour and their freedom. Whites had group coherence and solidarity only in relation to the slaves; the whites were the obvious instruments of control over the slaves. But in terms of vested interest, the majority of white men had little more commitment to Worthy Park than the slaves themselves. The life of most white men at Worthy Park was purely functional; the estate offered a job, and not a very rewarding one in the main, to which they pledged little or no commitment. Where the white workers shared a community of interest with the ownership was in the preservation of the clearly defined social and racial barriers erected in the course of Jamaican history between black and white. What separated the two communities was the freedom of one versus the slavery of the other. Jamaican slavery existed because of its crude economic value. Yet by the late eighteenth century, when the plantocracy was increasingly absentee, the plantation system needed not simply an enslaved labour force but a relatively small, literate white élite to control and manage the estates. This élite on Worthy Park, despite its racial and social affinities with the ownership was quite clearly alienated from its work. In its turn this alienation produced an instability which a plantation could ill afford.

The rôle of the whites on Worthy Park raises a paradox: a transitory and alienated nucleus of workers, sharing no common economic ground with the ownership, was able to hold in subjection a massive body of restless slaves. Such a dominance cannot be explained purely by the firearms owned by the whites.[105] Although tools were controlled as carefully as possible, slaves often had access to these potentially fearful weapons; hoes, bills, axes, knives and cutlasses.[106] Yet, although slave revolts in Jamaica as a whole were frequent, bloody, and always latent,[107] Worthy Park never suffered an open upheaval, despite the number of factors the estate held in common with more rebellious areas. Slaves were undernourished and frequently sick; they were hit by periodic waves of fatal epidemic and they constantly harboured a groundswell of unrest. Set against the unstable collection of drifting whites, the slaves thus posed a continual danger to the *status quo*.

The whites on such estates as Worthy Park must have been acutely sensitive to the tenuousness of the control they exercised over the slaves. The Jamaican Government and the forces at its disposal were too distant to make an impression on slaves in remote rural areas, and there must have been more immediate sanctions against revolt which impressed themselves on the slaves. The return of runaways offered tangible proof of the hopelessness of individual revolt. More difficult to assess, but no less important, was the rôle played by the slave élite in controlling the slave community. The immediate sanctions against failure to work or a desire to escape were implemented by the small group of artisans and slave drivers.[108] It was to the élite's benefit not only to produce the finished goods, but, following from this essential point, also to mould the slaves beneath them and to keep them as pliable and reliant a group as possible. In return for better facilities, the slave élite was the agent which impressed a work discipline on to the slave community.

To distil the social attitudes and identity of the slaves from the statistics available is a difficult task. Among dehumanized people it is difficult to find traces of human and social sentiment. That there was still a proportion of slaves who rejected their social situation by escaping from it, speaks for the power of their feelings. Their alienation from plantation society stemmed from the friction between memories of an African past, whether experienced personally or relived by Creole slaves through the folklore of the slave community, and the harsh reality of Jamaican experience. As long as the slave trade existed, Africa and African memories would perhaps remain the most powerful element in the make-up of the slave mentality, if only because the constant infusions of new African blood brought fresh reminders of that lost, distant continent. It must be remembered that even ten years after emancipation, a third of all the slaves on Worthy Park had been born in Africa.[109]

Naturally, in the records drawn up by the masters, evidence of the African-ness of the slaves is sadly lacking. Little evidence remains of the tribal origins of Worthy Park's Africans, and next to no evidence of the persistence of African customs. In walking miles to the Cocoree and in clearing and cultivating the provision grounds there beyond the oversight of the plantation whites, the slaves doubtless continued West African methods such as described by the literate ex-slave Equiano. But how much more we would like to know from Worthy Park of those lingering remnants of African cooking, religion, language, and folklore described, for example, by M. J. Herskovits in Trinidad and Haiti. Traces of *obeah* and African folklore remain even today, though Jamaican cooking and the 'Creole' language, while distinctive, are hardly African at all.

One tenuous strand of evidence relating to the acculturation of Worthy Park Negroes, however, does remain in the records: the evidence of names. When they first came to the plantations, slaves retained their African names and were generally known by them by their masters as well as their fellows. In the earliest Jamaican lists of named slaves, found for the most part in inventories, African names predominate. At Worthy Park in 1730, for example, no less than 62 per cent of the listed slaves were given recognizably African names. The remainder, either to avoid duplication or because the African names were difficult for the whites to remember, were given common Christian names, or nicknames derived from qualities apparent in the Negroes, towns, or (with a contemptuous sense of irony) from classical mythology.[110] Some of these nicknames may have been English approximations of African originals, and it is highly likely that all African-born slaves retained their native names among their fellows.

Fifty years after the death of Colonel Charles Price in 1730, the proportion of creole-born slaves at Worthy Park had probably risen from about 25 per cent to 65 per cent, and the proportion of non-African names in the records increased accordingly. Between 1783 and 1792 (after which fresh influxes of new Africans occurred) the proportion of African names, at least as listed in the records by the masters, had fallen below 20 per cent. Nicknames also had become less frequent, the greater majority of the slaves (regrettably like the working steers recorded on adjacent pages) being known by common Christian names, though doubtless few of them were ever baptized.[111]

The third stage in the naming of West Indian Negroes, extremely significant in the process of acculturation, occurred during the period of Amelioration. Gradually after about 1810, with an acceleration after 1830, the Worthy Park Negroes assumed surnames as well as Christian names. In the last records before 'full freedom' in 1838, practically all of Worthy Park's blacks are accorded surnames, taken from nearly every white man who had ever served in the estate's peripatetic white managerial class. In many cases this process may have been the delayed result of miscegenation; but in the majority it was probably fortuitous; the Negroes assuming the surname of a white to whom they were not related and may not have admired, but some of the status of whom they wished, by association, to acquire.

From the example of Worthy Park, it is evident that the sociology of an eighteenth-century plantation was much more complex than a simple economic *apartheid*. The whites formed a house that was continually divided against itself. On the other hand, the slaves were never able fully to exploit their numerical and physical strength because of a complexity of social and psychological controls that were placed over them. Their immediate enmity was no doubt evenly divided between their black drivers in particular and the whites in general. Most whites, however, did not stay long enough at Worthy Park in the late eighteenth century to incur a lasting wrath from the slaves. With more permanence among the whites, slave frustrations and complaints would have been given a sharper and more personal focus. As it was, their antagonisms remained inchoate and were dissipated in acts of individual desperation. Their feeling of general malaise could be directed at few specific targets.

It was, in brief, virtually impossible for the slaves—themselves depersonalized—to personalize hatreds, which thus remained hopelessly diffuse. This, in turn, highlights the major problem facing slaves and slave owners alike. At Worthy Park, both consciously and unconsciously, individual white men changed the lives of the slaves only by a matter of degree and not in any qualitative way. Even in a period of rigorous resident ownership between 1791 and 1795, deep-rooted problems could not be solved. The social system was sick and out of kilter. The white managerial and administrative workers remained alienated from their work at the same time as the slave community suffered an irradicable *anomie*. Tinkering with the mechanisms of slavery—improving the diet, living conditions, lightening the work load—was not only expensive at a time when frugality was called for, but it could in no way cure basic ills. No amount of rationalization by Rose Price in the 1790s could eradicate the imperfections that had been evident in the absentee years of the 1780s. Nowhere was this more apparent than in the life of the slave community. Life was much the same for the slave at the end of the century as it had been at the end of the American War.

The plantocracy were shackled to a system which required constant investment in labour at a time of marked decline in income. The planters still felt that they could not survive without slavery but they appeared incapable of solving its obvious economic and social imperfections; they saw slavery as their sole remaining hope of salvation but at the same time they were damned for its continuing existence. Now that slavery had become an issue, it was increasingly obvious that it had corruped—even enslaved—the owners as much as it had debased the Negro.

NOTES

[1] Long, II, 502.
[2] For a discussion of the legal basis of slavery; Patterson 72–3.,
[3] I.R.O. Deeds 109/190; 115/99; 114/1.
[4] *Ibid.*, 217/20.
[5] *Ibid.*, 124/85.
[6] *Ibid.*, 122/60; 124/85; 131/353; 136/149.
[7] *Ibid.*, 120/124.
[8] *Ibid.*, 122/60; 124/85; 131/353; 136/149.
[9] *Ibid.*, 120/114. The male–female ratio on these properties was: Burtons 440:127, Rose Hall 137:120, Wallins 102:59, Decoy 112:50.
[10] Percentage of Males at Worthy Park 1730–1836:

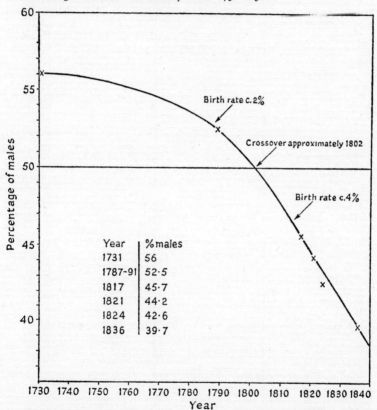

Year	% males
1731	56
1787-91	52·5
1817	45·7
1821	44·2
1824	42·6
1836	39·7

[11] Since men cannot bear children, it should probably be higher. Taking monogamous pairs as the norm, the potential increase at Worthy Park was more

like 40 per cent. To be more precise, demographers prefer to take the total number of females of child-bearing age as the annual fertility potential of a society. With pains this could be assessed at Worthy Park, though only for the period 1783–1838.

[12] Patterson, 61.

[13] I.R.O. Deeds, 120/103.

[14] Ibid., 185/103.

[15] Ibid., 162/234.

[16] Ibid., 109/190; 115/99; 114/1; 122/60; 122/108; 124/85; 136/149; 162/27; 164/139; 162/234; 185/103; 185/110; 230/195; 232/91; 230/95.

[17] Ibid., 216/181.

[18] R. B. Sheridan, 'The Wealth of Jamaica', op. cit., 301–2.

[19] Ibid., 308; also see above, IV.

[20] At about the same time the total slave population of Jamaica was approximately 180,000; Patterson, 95. Thus the Price family controlled a one-hundredth part of the total population.

[21] This rate of decline was less than that described by Edward Long on one of his own properties where it ran at 1·75 per cent. 7 March 1788. Chatham Papers, P.R.O. 30/8/153, p. 40.

[22] See below, VIII.

[23] Long, II, 432–4.

[24] Quoted in Goerke, 'The Life and Scientific Works of John Quier', op. cit., 25–6.

[25] Ibid., 26.

[26] I.R.O. Deeds 402/92; 408/172; 406/102; 407/198; 416/14; 422/120; 426/172; 437/128.

[27] 'Increase and Decrease in Negroes, 1793–5', Plantation Book, 1791–1811.

[28] Ibid., 1794.

[29] List of Negroes on Worthy Park, 1 January 1789, Plantation Book, 1787–91.

[30] Ibid., 1 January 1787.

[31] Goerke, 'The Life and Scientific Works of John Quier', op. cit., For evidence of Quier's residence on Worthy Park see Vestry Returns, 1783–95, Plantation Books, 1783–7; 1787–91; 1791–1811.

[32] The Code of Laws for the Government of the Negro Slaves in the Island of Jamaica, London, 1789. Quoted in Goerke, 24–6.

[33] Goerke, 24.

[34] Increase and Decrease in Negroes, 1783. Plantation Book, 1773–87.

[35] Quoted in Goerke, 25.

[36] Patterson, 108–10.

[37] Ibid., Goerke, 25.

[38] J. Quier, Letters and Essays . . . on the West Indies, London, 1778, 113.

[39] Goerke, 23–4.

[40] J. Quier, Letters and Essays, 63–4.

[41] Long, II, 436.

[42] U. B. Phillips exaggerated the element of conscious improvement imposed by the management. While conceding the fact of general amelioration, the present authors see Rose Price's measures—increased provision for housing, increased medical services, even the extension of provision growing—simply as essential attempts to cope with an expanded population.

[43] Quoted in Goerke, 25.

44 Increase and Decrease in Negroes, 1793, *Plantation Book*, 1791–1811.
45 List of slaves on Worthy Park, 1794, *ibid.*,
46 J. Quier, op. cit., 20–1.
47 'Supplies received from Spring Garden', *Plantation Books*, 1783–7; 1787–91.
48 *Ibid.*
49 See, for example, 'Account of the disposal of 100 barrels of Herrings', 1787, *Ibid.*
50 Long, II, 413.
51 'Accounting of Herrings Opened', 5–6 June 1791, *Plantation Book*, 1791–1811. Paradoxically, as with American Negroes, the enforced diet of slavery days has been transmuted into modern ethnic delicacies: saltfish—preferably cooked with ackee—is 'soul food' in Jamaica today, as are chitlings, ham hocks, and collard greens in the U.S.A.!
52 *Ibid.*, 25 December 1787.
53 'Distribution of food', 1791, *ibid.*
54 'Account of Guinea Corn and Rice', 1791, *ibid.*
55 'Rum Account', 1791, *ibid.*
56 Puncheons of rum consumed by slaves 1787–91, 8; 7; 7; 8; 9, *ibid.*
57 Sugar account, 1791, *ibid.*
58 Long, I, 155–6.
59 'Contents of the Plantation Book', 1795, *ibid.*
60 Provisions Account, 29 December 1792, *ibid.*
61 Cattle Account, 1792, *ibid.*
62 Forty acres of land turned over to guinea corn, 1795, *ibid.*
63 Long, I, 164.
64 Provisions Account, 6 August 1792, *Plantation Book, 1791–1811.*
65 'Calculations of the provisions for the negroes', 1795, *ibid.*
66 Beckford, II, 51.
67 'Contents of the Plantation Book', 1795, *ibid.*
68 B. M'Mahon, *Jamaica Plantership*, London, 1839, 61.
69 'Contents of the Plantation Book', 1795, *Plantation Book*, 1791–1811.
70 List of Negroes, 1 January 1789, *Plantation Book*, 1787–91.
71 List of Negroes, 1793, *Plantation Book*, 1791–1811.
72 List of Negroes, 25 October 1795, *ibid.*
73 List of Negroes, 1 January 1789, *Plantation Book*, 1787–91.
74 Annual lists of Negroes, 1791–5, *Plantation Book*, 1791–1811.
75 List of Negroes, 1 January 1789, *Plantation Book*, 1787–91.
76 Annual lists of Negroes, 1791–5, *Plantation Book*, 1791–1811.
77 List of whites, 1795, *ibid.*
78 Listings of 'mulattoes', 'quadroons', 'sambos', 'mestizos' in annual 'Lists of Negroes', *Plantation Books*, 1787–91, 1791–1811.
79 Patterson, 61.
80 Accounts, 20 December 1792; 9, 10 January 1793, *Plantation Book*, 1791–1811.
81 List of Negroes, 25 October 1795, *ibid.*
82 Accounts, 1794, *ibid.*
83 'Contents of the Plantation Book', 1795, *ibid.*
84 *Ibid.*
85 Distribution of Provisions, 26 April 1789, *Plantation Book*, 1787–91. P.P. (*1789*) op. cit., Evidence of Fuller, Young and Chisholm.
86 *Plantation Book*, 1787–91, 1 January 1789.

[87] Distribution of Provisions, 8 March, 29, 20 June 1792, *Plantation Book*, 1791–1811.

[88] Jamaica Archives, Manumission Records, 15/138; 16/9/11/183; 17/15/23; 18/25/185; 19/215/153; 20/99/00; 22/20; 23/193/152.

[89] *Ibid.*, 16/11/183.

[90] I.R.O. Deeds, 312/230.

[91] Vestry Returns, 1791–99, *Plantation Book*, 1791–1811.

[92] I.R.O. Deeds, 417/112; these provisions were laid down in an Act of 1774, Patterson, 90.

[93] Patterson, 90.

[94] Decrease of Negroes, 1785; List of Negroes, 1 January 1789, *Plantation Books*, 1783–7; 1787–91. Two regular female runaways in the 1780s were called Whore and Strumpet, pejorative nicknames that were almost unique at Worthy Park. It would be extremely interesting to know why, precisely, they were accorded these brutish labels, and whether their names had any connection with their running away. Vestry Returns, *Plantation Book*, 1787–91.

[95] Vestry Returns give the following runaway quarterly figures: 1783 (5), 1785 (3), 1786 (10), 1787 (2/6/6/1), 1788 (2/1/3/2), 1789 (1/1/1/2), 1790 (2/2/1/1), 1791 (2/7/2), 1792 (2), 1793 (3), 1794 (9/9/9), 1795 (9/7/9/7), 1796 (8/7/5/5), 1797 (6). *Plantation Books*, 1783–7; 1787–91; 1791–1811.

[96] Decrease in Negroes, 1791, *Plantation Book*, 1787–91. There is no evidence on Worthy Park to show that slaves of a particular tribe were more prone to escape than others. The '... fugitives were utterly miscellaneous...' (Phillips, 555). Worthy Park's Africans had completely conflicting characteristics. The Congolese were famous for being mild and light-hearted (Phillips, 556) but the Coromantees were known and feared for the '... martial ferocity of their disposition' (Long, V, 446). See also Patterson, 226; 269; 271; 272.

[97] Increase and Decrease of Negroes, *Plantation Books*, 1783–7, 1787–91.

[98] Vestry Returns, 1795, *Plantation Book*, 1791–1811.

[99] Vestry Returns, 1783–96, *Plantation Books*, 1783–7; 1787–91; 1791–1811.

[100] Vestry Returns, 1792; 1793, *Plantation Book*, 1791–1811.

[101] Wages of Whites, *ibid.*

[102] Worthy Park Inventory, 1795, *ibid.*

[103] *Ibid.*

[104] Invoice of goods, 13 July 1793, *ibid.*

[105] Accounts, 1795, *ibid.*

[106] Delivery of hoes, bills, knives, 1785, *Plantation Book*, 1783–7.

[107] Patterson, 266–83.

[108] *Ibid.*, 62–3.

[109] See below, VIII, 196.

[110] Inventory tacked to Will of Colonel Charles Price, I.R.O. Wills.

[111] There is no reference to slave baptisms before 1811, in which year nine baptisms were recorded. *Plantation Book*, 1791–1811. See below VIII, 201.

CHAPTER SEVEN

Worthy Park Narrowly Preserved, 1775-1815

Between 1775 and 1815, the British Empire in the West Indies was beset by an almost Egyptian sequence of afflictions. Three great wars, the threat of revolution, competition, rising costs, and an unprecedented succession of natural disasters were serious enough; but these might have been overcome by the resilient plantocracy. The insuperable bane was a subtle and inexorable mutation in metropolitan attitudes and imperial policy which changed the planters' optimism into pessimism and, finally, despair.

American independence increased rather than decreased imperial resolve. The influence of the West India lobby was devalued, largely because it was a purely colonial interest group now that the interests of the metropolitan merchants had diverged from those of the planters, who were so often their debtors. While merchants were looking eastwards rather than to the west and refiners were eager for cheap sugar from whatever source, American trade was now legally foreign, and the special protectionist privileges enjoyed by the West Indies were progressively whittled away. Provision costs soared and sugar prices decreased, while West Indian technology was hamstrung for want of capital. Investment increasingly migrated to new industries and new colonies, and credit consequently grew tighter year by year. To add to the burden of the West Indian planter, the anti-slavery lobby achieved its first great success, the abolition of the slave trade in 1807, itself a symptom of West Indian sugar's declining power and prestige. The West Indian honeymoon was over, but all was by no means lost. Over-extended estates had their superfluous fat drastically trimmed, marginal estates began to close and weaklings to consolidate. The sturdiest, however, survived by increasing production and efficiency, being able to command whatever capital was still available for West Indian investment. These developments can be clearly traced in the contrasted story of the two branches of the Price domains in Jamaica between 1775 and 1815. The pretentious fabric of Sir Charles Price's empire collapsed into rubble by 1790, while Worthy Park survived and even, relatively, prospered as the result of the retrenchment and re-organization undertaken by young Rose Price between 1791 and 1795, achieving peaks of production in 1805 and 1812.

Since the creation and expansion of West Indian estates was only possible through the infusion of British capital, it is not surprising that the two Sir Charles Prices, for a few years the greatest of Jamaican

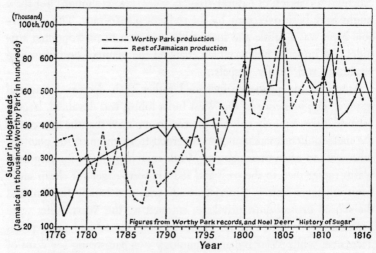

SUGAR PRODUCTION OF WORTHY PARK
AND JAMAICA, 1776–1816

landowners, should also be among the most extensive and frenzied borrowers. Long before he reached the zenith of plantocratic power, Sir Charles the elder was inextricably in debt, though it was his son who was to be faced by the inevitable nemesis. As early as 1753, Charles Price's dealings with John Serocold, a London merchant and sugar factor, had resulted in a debt of £14,000 sterling, which after John Serocold's death survived in the form of three bonds to Serocold's widow and son. Far from repaying the principal, it was said that owing to the exigencies of the Seven Years' War, Charles Price was unable even to find the interest payable at the modest legal limit, then fixed at 5 per cent. As a result, when the bonds matured in 1758, Price was forced to pledge the 658 acres and 242 slaves of Burton's New Works as security, thus setting a dismal pattern for the future.[1] Each new borrowing for purchases of slaves and supplies, new building or yet more land was henceforth backed by the security of the estates themselves. Repayment was pledged in produce, but where and when this became insufficient and defaulting occurred, mortgaging and re-mortgaging inevitably followed, until the entire estate was committed beyond the limit of the most patient creditor, and ownership was finally lost.

When Sir Charles Price the elder died in 1772, his huge estate was already disastrously compromised, but it was the onset of the American War which brought about the final collapse. Despite the hopelessness of the general position, Sir Charles Price the younger was able to continue borrowing, almost on the security of his debts, for at least eight more years, though under progressively more rigorous conditions. By the time conditions in the sugar industry eased after the American War in the later 1780s it was too late to rescue all but the rump of the Price estates. Long before his death in 1788, the second Sir Charles was to see most of the family estates not simply mortgaged, but leased, sold, or seized to satisfy impatient creditors.

Within three years of his inheritance, Sir Charles Price the younger was hopelessly grappling with his father's debts. In 1775 he made a desperate journey to England to untangle the affairs of the estate; yet in that year alone, nine different Price properties, including Rose Hall,

Halfway Tree, and Worthy Park itself, were conveyed to Serocold and Jackson, the successors of John Serocold.[2] Formal ownership and a semblance of control remained in the hands of the Prices, but a depressing pattern emerged: initial agreements conveying property on trust to a creditor until such time as outstanding debts could be met were invariably revised within a few years to incorporate unpaid interest. Although this secondary agreement was strictly a new and separate document, it was quite clearly a form of illegal compound interest against which the planters had no defence.[3] When, in its turn, this second arrangement failed to bring any diminution of the debt, either land was offered, and accepted, in lieu, or else another creditor would absorb the debt, coming to new—and yet harsher—terms with the unfortunate debtor.

For no less than four years Sir Charles Price was forced to remain in England juggling with the Price finances, yet he returned to Jamaica in 1779 with the situation worse than ever.[4] For example, in 1776 Sir Charles Price borrowed £8,000 from three London merchants, transferring his 528-acre Gayle plantation to them as collateral. Within eight years he owed £13,655 to the same merchants, who by then had 'become very pressing in their demands to the said Sir Charles to pay off and satisfy the same'. Accordingly, the hard-pressed baronet fully conveyed Gayle plantation to another London merchant, Davidson, to whom he already owed £8,273 for sundry supplies, on the understanding that Davidson would assume as his own the larger debt. This particular transaction was further complicated by the fact that Price's original debt to Davidson was not erased, but merely transferred to yet another group of creditors; an excellent instance of the interlocking complexity of West Indian investment.[5]

Over-extended planters like the Prices in the 1770s and 1780s were, simply, sellers in a buyers' market. Once their produce was committed, they had nothing but their real estate to offer their creditors, and as their debts accumulated they were eventually forced to sell for crippling losses. Besides this, estates starved of money and threatened with foreclosure inevitably deteriorated, losing even more value.

The syndrome of frenetic ingenuity, tortuous complexity, and inevitable disaster was repeated in one after another of the Price holdings, until almost all were gone. Serocold and Jackson, the major creditors, not only squeezed exacting property guarantees from the Price family, but also levied extra annual contributions on certain holdings. In 1777 they agreed to advance Charles Price two modest annuities of £100 from the proceeds of Mickleton estate; but within eleven years the money was 'considerably in arrears', and Price was forced to sell a portion of that invaluable estate.[6] Again, in 1779 when Price borrowed only £1,500 from two Liverpool merchants, he was not only obliged to guarantee the debt with the 1,181 acres and 218 slaves of Burton's plantation, but he also had to consign 300 hogsheads of sugar annually to pay off the debt. Were he to fall below this target, Price was committed to pay an indemnity of £1 for each hogshead below 300 a year. By 1782, his debts to the same Liverpool merchants had soared to £10,821 and he had to hand over Burton's to them, lock, stock, and barrel.[7]

Another sugar house to which Sir Charles Price became heavily indebted was the London firm of Hankey, which, with its successors Thompson, Hankey Limited, has retained financial links with Worthy Park down to the present. In 1779, Wallins estate, of 1,038 acres and 171 slaves, was offered to Hankey's as collateral for a debt of £8,078. The slaves alone were valued at £11,335; but when after eight years the debt had not been reduced at all, the entire estate was forced out of the Price family's hands for the cash payment of a mere £1,400.[8] Amity Hall, consisting of 700 acres in St. Dorothy, went much the same way. Initially handed over to one William Bleamire 'as a Collateral Security for the payment' of £3,477 in 1776, its control was to remain in Price's hands, but if no attempt was made to pay off at least the interest owing on the debt within a year, Bleamire was given the right of auctioning the property on his own behalf. Some time later the debt was taken over by Serocold and Jackson, who in 1786 forced the sale of Amity Hall for £8,589. None of this money, needless to say, could by then be credited to the Prices themselves.[9] The valuable estate of Plantain Walk at Magotty in St. Thomas-ye-Vale was likewise sold in 1786 as the result of non-payment on a loan of £2,196 made in 1779.[10]

Debts bombarded Sir Charles Price from all directions during the American and Maritime War, threatening his most valuable properties with the fate already suffered by the lesser. By 1778 he was forced to put up Rose Hall, the slaves alone on which were valued at £16,850, as security for a debt of £18,000 owed to certain London merchants, to pay off which he committed the entire produce of the estate for the subsequent five years. This produce, thanks to good sugar prices, was enough to eradicate the debt, but Rose Hall was merely released from the clutches of one set of merchants to be available to act as collateral for yet another debt in 1782.[11] In 1779 the 1,047 acres of Shenton's was used to cover a promissory note for £10,000, and New Works another for £7,000.[12] With the pledging of the family's domestic property in Spanish Town about the same time, the fund of Price credit was practically exhausted.[13] Even the most famous of all Price properties, the Decoy in St. Mary's, was mortgaged to the hilt. In 1777 Sir Charles Price the younger was able to raise a loan of £5,000 using as collateral the 3,025 acres and 105 slaves of his favourite retreat, the slaves by themselves being valued at £6,390. Yet twelve years later, his widow, Lydia Ann Price, was forced to sell the Decoy for exactly half the money originally borrowed.[14]

Ostensibly, Sir Charles Price the second had inherited a territorial empire from his father in 1772, but its disorganized resources proved indefensible, and his entire life as a planter was spent in constant retreat before the irresistible advance of an army of creditors. The deeds made between Sir Charles Price the younger and his various creditors from 1777 to 1786 reveal debts amounting to £118,283,[15] but even this huge sum did not represent the total Price indebtedness. Although most expenditure, like income, was in the hands of creditors, the accumulated bill for normal plantation expenses not so included must have been considerable and, moreover, all paper debts were, to say the least, dynamic, constantly being added to by unpaid interest at 5 and 6 per cent. By 1786 these additional debts amounted to no less than £89,000, including current account debts of £12,455 run up with

Serocold and Jackson since 1780 and a long-standing debt still owing to the correspondents of Sir Charles Price the elder in London, amounting to £76,485, which had not been reduced at all since 1777.[16]

The mark of the grandee, it is often jokingly said, is the grandness of his debts. Certainly, the extent of his great-grandson's indebtedness would have hugely impressed Francis Price, the founder of Worthy Park. To Sir Charles Price the younger, however, it must have seemed an insupportable burden which he had done little to bring upon himself. By 1786 he was at the end of his tether, faced by only two desperate alternatives: to make an appeal to the sympathy and generosity of the Jamaican Assembly, or to take refuge from his responsibilities in flight to England.

On 2 December 1786 Sir Charles Price made an impassioned plea before that tribunal which had been the seat of his father's authority and of which he too in turn had once been Speaker. He threw himself, he said, 'on the munificense of the house, hoping they will, on consideration of the premises, assist him with the loan of a small sum of money or grant him such relief as to their wisdom shall seem meet, that a remnant may be saved'.[17] His supporting book-keeping, however, showed that nothing short of a considerable fortune could now save the majority of the Price lands. By 1786 Price had already been 'dispossessed of property to the value of many thousands of pounds', and in addition his six remaining properties were loaded with brutal mortgages. Price's chief argument was that having had to raise money in a depressed market he had been forced to sell property far below its true value and to accept mortgages based on savage undervaluation, so that he was faced with the prospect of disposing of a splendid inheritance for a pittance. By his own calculations, Sir Charles Price's remaining six properties were worth more than a quarter million pounds. Their mortgages, however, totalled only £90,404, leaving Price with potential assets, or losses, of £134,743.[18]

Sir Charles Price's creditors, however, told an entirely different story. Serocold and Jackson, in a counter-petition to the Jamaican Assembly, averred that not only had Sir Charles grossly exaggerated the value of his property, but he had also greatly understated the sum of the advances made by his sundry creditors. In the case of 'The Farm', for instance, the merchants showed that 'Sir Charles Price hath actually received value of £7,971 for the mortgage, more than the estimate of the mortgaged premises, tho' he states an overplus in his favour of £22,674'.[19] Similarly, Price's account of the Rose Hall mortgage had suggested that he was still owed £19,484, whereas in fact he had received within £363 of the actual valuation.[20] In the case of Burton's, Sir Charles had even included the valuation of goods and slaves which had already been deducted to pay for other debts, thus boosting the true value of the estate by £16,000; and in assessing the value of Goshen he had also neglected to deduct the procceds from a portion already sold.[21] According to Serocold and Jackson, far from being owed £134,743 in devalued mortgages, Sir Charles Price, 'deducting for the number of negroes and stock which had been taken off the properties and sold to pay prior judgement creditors', had received an actual excess of £12,403.[22]

In laying his ravelled affairs before the Jamaican Assembly, Sir Charles Price had dropped a heavy stone into an already troubled pool. The plantocracy which the Assembly represented was already deeply unsettled by the economic effects of American independence,[23] but these new revelations made them fear for the very foundation of the socio-economic system. Price's debts were referred to a Committee of the Whole House, which was ordered 'to inquire into and take further into consideration the state of the island'.[24] The assembled planters were sympathetic to Price's plight, but the underwriting of such manifold debts was not only a dangerous precedent but financially impossible. After a heated debate lasting three days, Sir Charles Price's petition was turned down, though the Assembly voted a loan of £5,000, to be administered by trustees, in order to save the Decoy, in recognition of the gratitude felt by the Assembly for the services rendered by the Prices, father and son.[25]

Yet even this act of sentimental generosity was later revoked. In October 1787 the House was called upon to 'observe the strictest frugality in the disposal' of public funds, and it was resolved that the vesting of public money in loans to individual Members was 'unconstitutional and of dangerous example'. The original motion was even more strongly worded, declaring that such loans were 'destructive of public confidence and a breach of trust towards our constituents, the good people of this island'; yet, despite the modification of the motion, the £5,000 already voted in 1786 was withdrawn and the Decoy doomed to extinction.[26]

Unable now to offer his creditors even the crumbs of official support from the Jamaican legislature, Sir Charles Price was finally besieged by a humiliating series of cases in the Court of Chancery that extended almost continuously from 1787 to 1789. One after another, most of the remaining properties were ordered to be sold, including Rose Hall, which was auctioned for £18,000 in 1788; and the Decoy, sold by Lady Price in 1789 for a paltry £2,500.[27] Yet so heavy was the weight of debt and consequent decay that even properties bought at auction after orders of the court were found to be incapable of profit and still encumbered with the dead hand of ancient mortgages. For example, even after Sir Charles Price had died, the new owners of the Decoy were pursued by Serocold and Jackson for debts owing on the estate since 1776. In a mournful plea, the defendants told the Court of Chancery that far from extracting a profit on what had so recently been a splendid estate, they were now pouring in new capital into a drain, since the Decoy had been 'in a great measure suffered to remain uncultivated and the buildings to go to decay owing . . . to the Distressful state of the said Sir Charles Price's circumstances and affairs'.[28]

The Jamaican Assembly's change of heart in October 1787 was almost certainly related to Sir Charles Price's decision earlier in that year to forsake the island of his tribulation. What had doubtless impressed his fellow Assemblymen and the other 'good people' of Jamaica hitherto was the tireless manner in which Sir Charles had sought remedies for the distemper of his father's affairs. Unlike the majority of Jamaican proprietors he had resolutely returned to the source of his troubles, though the case was hopeless, even attending the interminable sessions of innumerable cases in the Jamaican Court of Chancery, that saddest of courts. Now, however, the last straw of litigation had been laid on his aching back. Henceforward, Sir Charles

Price followed the cases, if at all, from the elegant refuge of Grosvenor Place in London.[29]

Yet Sir Charles Price the younger was no ordinary absentee, fleeing Jamaica as soon as he had garnered sufficient wealth to live in ostentatious luxury abroad. Instead, he was a battered victim of an implacable system, seeking relief from the daily mounting weight and tension of plantation debt, in abdication. Relief, if he found it, was not long lived: within two years of leaving Jamaica, Sir Charles Price the younger was dead.

His parting shot was a shrewd one: the confirmation in detail of the arrangements initiated by his father sixteen years before, by which Worthy Park was to be preserved. Sir Charles and Lady Price had had no children to whom to pass on their dubious heritage, and Lydia Ann, even when all of the remaining holdings in Jamaica owned entirely by Sir Charles had been sold, had no more than a competence. Yet Sir Charles Price's share of Worthy Park, with its associated 'penns' at Guanaboa and Spring Garden, was bequeathed to his cousin, John Price of Penzance, almost free of all 'encumbrances', and this solvent fraction of the Price domains was even able in 1793 to purchase Mickleton, which, by judicious management, had been merely leased not sold after Sir Charles Price died.[30]

John Price of Penzance was a more conventional type of absentee than Sir Charles Price the younger, having, in a life that extended from 1738 to 1797, made but one brief visit to Jamaica, the fount of his wealth. He was the only child of that John Price who, sent to England by Colonel Charles for his education, was advised by his doctor to stay on in Cornwall for the sake of his health, being perhaps 'the first invalid ever sent from a distance to breathe the soft air of this all but island of the Atlantic'.[31] Modestly lodged in Penzance town with Mr. Henry Badcock the Customs Collector, John Price married Margery, one of the daughters of the house, in 1736, leaving her with an infant son when he went off to Jamaica in 1739 to die.[32]

Educated locally and at Trinity College, Oxford, the second John Price visited Jamaica just after the end of the Seven Years' War, staying only long enough to reassure himself that Worthy Park was in the capable hands of his uncle Charles, and to marry Elizabeth Williams Brammer, the daughter of an island physician. A son, christened Charles Godolphin, was born at Worthy Park in 1765, but he died young, and John Price's heir, Rose, was born in 1768 back in Cornwall, where John Price was destined to spend the rest of his life. For a dozen years, without any notable effort on his own part, he saw his income from a half share of Worthy Park grow steadily as a by-product of the Golden Age of sugar, and with its increase his importance in the county of his residence magnified accordingly. An associate of the Cornish Godolphins and Trelawnys who provided innumerable M.P.s, as well as the two Governors of Jamaica friendly to his uncle Sir Charles the Patriot, John Price was doubtless a minor minion of the intricate Pitt–Newcastle 'connexion'. In 1774, at the age of 35, he was made High Sheriff of Cornwall, reaching the plateau of his modest career.[33]

Virtually assured of an income that may have been as high as £2,500 in a good year, John Price was thereafter able to spend the life of a gentleman of leisure, busying himself only in those affairs which interested him. Living in a town house in Chapel Street, Penzance which has since disappeared, he built a 'pretty retreat' called Chi-owne in the parish of Paul, near which can still be seen the monument in the shape of a sugar loaf which he erected to commemorate the discovery of an antique Cornish gold ring.[34] The author of a painstaking Cornish genealogy and a MS. history of St. Michael's Mount, John Price patronized such local celebrities as 'Peter Pindar' and John Opie, and even corresponded with that distant luminary Horace Walpole.[35] Rose Price, who was to become a far more dynamic—and probably unpleasant—person, gained his first rudiments at Penzance Grammar School before being sent first to Harrow and then to Magdalen College, Oxford, as a 'gentleman commoner'. In both latter places, by the curious custom of the day, he was allowed as private tutor and companion a protégé of his father, the Rev. John Vinicombe who, like John Opie, was a brilliant natural product of the Cornish proletariat. Successively Scholar and Fellow of Pembroke College, Vinicombe accompanied young Price first on the Grand Tour and then to Jamaica, after which he was permitted to resume his career at Oxford.[36]

Rose Price's elaborate education spanned the tumultuous period of the American and Maritime War and its troubled aftermath, and was not completed until 1790. Ever since the death of the first Sir Charles Price in 1772, the news from Jamaica and Worthy Park had been progressively more disquieting, and with the reappearance in England of the defeated Sir Charles the younger in 1787 came a sense of immediate foreboding. Before leaving Jamaica, Sir Charles had ordered the overseer at Worthy Park to keep more systematic accounts, but these, arriving at Penzance each year after 1787, did little to dispel the feeling that West Indian planting—and with it the income of John and Rose Price—was gravely threatened.

During the years of war, conditions for West Indian sugar had been precarious, especially in the period between 1778 and 1782 when Britain's command of the seas had been extremely tenuous. The cost of provisions soared by as much as 400 per cent and the freight and insurance charges on the sugars which penetrated the blockade by almost as much. With the coming of peace these costs decreased, but not to pre-war levels. The decision of the British Government in 1783 not to allow free trade with the Americans compelled the West Indians to obtain their provisions from across the Atlantic, and from a source—Ireland for the most part—with which there was little reciprocal trade. As the Governor of Jamaica reported to the Colonial Office in 1785, flour which before the war had cost 15s. to 20s. per hundredweight and had risen to 50s. at the worst time of shortage, had only fallen to about 30s. by 1785. The price of the lowest quality of imported beef and pork in 1785 was approximately the price that the best had been in 1775. Likewise, white oak staves, as low as £10 per thousand before the war and as high as £40 during it, could not be obtained for less than £12 in 1785 and generally cost closer to £20.[37] Moreover, land, now that the most fertile parts of Jamaica were intensively cultivated and some areas were already worked out, had risen insensibly in price over the previous decades, as had the cost of imported slaves now that the practical monopoly of the Liverpool traders was having its effects.[38]

To add to the burden of the increased costs of provisions, land, and

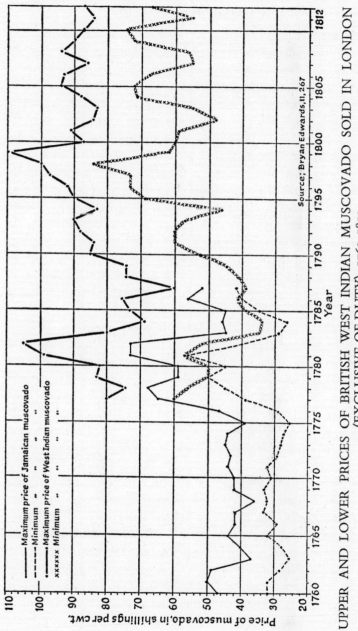

UPPER AND LOWER PRICES OF BRITISH WEST INDIAN MUSCOVADO SOLD IN LONDON (EXCLUSIVE OF DUTY), 1760–1812

slaves, the high prices obtained for West Indian produce during war-time shortages did not continue after the signing of peace. In 1782, the price charged for muscovado by the London sugar wholesalers rose to 106s. per hundredweight, and the gross price received by the planters to between 40s. and 73s. In 1783 these prices, respectively, fell to 80s., 29s. and 45s., and this trend was maintained until 1787, when the median price charged by London wholesalers reached 50s. The prices received by the West Indian planters in the 1780s were not substantially lower than those obtained in the early 1770s, but when coupled with the general 25 per cent increase in the costs of operation, they made disastrous inroads upon plantation profits, and many planters faced imminent bankruptcy. A general inquiry conducted by the Jamaican House of Assembly in October 1792 discovered that although the number of sugar estates in operation in 1791 had only fallen by eight from the peak of 775 in 1772, only 451 remained in the hands of their original proprietors, 177 had been sold for debt since 1772 and 92 were in the often reluctant hands of their mortgagors.[39]

Worthy Park, though more firmly than ever under the control of its absentee owners, was in at least as perilous a plight as the majority of Jamaican estates. The war years had been bad enough, when sugar exports had been difficult and costly, but in 1786 and 1787 Worthy Park's sugar production fell to 181 and 172 hogsheads at a time when the London prices were no more than two-thirds those obtained at the height of the war. With a gross income of less than £4,000 for those two years, it is unlikely that there was any profit at all for the Prices to draw upon.

With Sir Charles Price as well as John Price absent from Jamaica, or otherwise distracted, Worthy Park had obviously been allowed to deteriorate sadly. The plea of an unprecedented series of hurricanes, earthquakes, and fires which severely affected southern and eastern coastal parishes, did not apply equally to inland regions. A scrutiny of the Worthy Park records discloses to us—as it did to John and Rose Price—many basic faults in the plantation's husbandry as well: haphazard planting, reaping, processing and shipment patterns, and an unhealthy weakness in the slave labour force, as well as a disappointing return of sugar and rum produced. Worst of all was the evidence that gradually came to light that the estate was probably being milked, as well as mismanaged, by its attorney, Malcolm Laing.

When leaving Jamaica, Sir Charles Price had given his attorney £17,000, 'with a view to indemnify the said Malcolm Laing against any expences or advances which he might sustain or incur in the conduct or management' of Worthy Park and the other Price lands. After Laing's death four years later it was revealed by his will that the £17,000, far from being used to cover Price's expenses and debts, had been transferred to Laing's own personal estate. Despite this malversation, Laing's executors had the temerity to maintain that Price actually owed his attorney money, and one of them, John Jacques, used this spurious debt to enforce the sale of Goshen plantation 'at a price far short of the real value'.[40] Malcolm Laing had acted as attorney for the affairs of John as well as Sir Charles Price. Under his dubious supervision and the management of five different overseers in the six years after 1785, it is not surprising that Worthy Park was badly in need of reform. Accordingly, Rose Price, at the age of 23, set sail for Jamaica in 1791, accompanied by the Rev. John Vinicombe, for more than three years of dynamic residence at Worthy Park, during which he was said to have 'nearly doubled the value of the estate'.[41]

Rose Price and his clerical companion, doubtless armed with the latest treatises on sugar estate management, established themselves in Worthy Park Great House, one of the rooms of which was converted into a chapel for the benefit of Mr. Vinicombe. Since Rose intended to manage Worthy Park entirely on his own, both attorney and overseer were dispensed with, at an immediate saving to the estate of some £650 a year.

Rose Price's overriding purpose was the increase of the profits from Worthy Park by improved efficiency, but his first concern was to increase production. Consequently, the acreage under cultivation was rapidly extended, while that in fallow was drastically reduced. Within three years, nine new cane-pieces were created, totalling 161 acres, raising the number to twenty-nine and effectively increasing the arable acreage by at least 25 per cent. Three new areas were opened to sugar cultivation; the reddish clays 'full of springs' north of the Overseer's house, some 30 acres close under Lluidas Blue Mountain south of the sinkhole, and 30 acres more surrounding the unpromising promontory of Rocky Point. These were all marginal areas, greatly in need of fertilization, and Price consequently established four 'manuring pens', located close to each of the three new areas.[42]

The increase in sugar land utilization was largely achieved by much greater use of ratooning. As the result of the introduction of Bourbon canes and more intensive fertilization of the soil, it was hoped to obtain much better yields from first and second ratoons, and to extend viable ratooning almost indefinitely. From an average of 259 acres in canes between 1786 and 1791, of which 124 were in plant canes and 135 in first and second ratoons, Rose Price raised the acreage in canes almost to 500 acres in some years, while actually decreasing the acreage re-planted each year. In December 1814, for example, only 53 of the 433 acres then in canes were in plant cane and no less than 380 in ratoons. Of these, there were similar acreages in first, second, third, and fourth ratoons, but considerable acreages also in fifth, sixth, eighth, and ninth ratoons, and even 40 acres in fifteenth ratoons.[43]

The hopes for the productivity of ratoons were not entirely fulfilled, and by the 1820s it seems to have been the practice to re-plant up to a third of the cane-pieces each year and not to ratoon often beyond the sixth year; but a Worthy Park crop map dating from the very last days of slavery—and of Rose Price's life—shows that of the 488 acres then in cane, still only 134 were in plant canes and 353 in ratoons. Of these, 78 acres were in first ratoons, 61 in seconds, and 71 in thirds. No less than 140 acres were in fourth, fifth, and sixth ratoons, and one small piece of three acres, Craddock's, had been ratooned for fourteen successive crops, though with a meagre yield.[44] At the time of this map, at least twenty-five of Worthy Park's thirty-one cane-pieces were in cultivation, with only four acres of Crawfish Gully marked 'fallow', and it is obvious that it was Rose Price's ideal to eliminate fallow cane land altogether. Certainly he measured the production of sugar by the total acreage of the cane-pieces, which in the last year of his residence he calculated as 564, out of the total of Worthy Park's 1,145 central acres of 'canepieces, common pasture, copperwood land and buildings',[45] though it is unlikely that even with the drastic cropping he introduced after his arrival in 1791 he was ever able to crop much more than 500 acres.

Worthy Park: Plant Canes and Ratoons, 1786–1834

	Plant canes	1st ratoons	2nd	3rd	4th	5th	6th	7th	8th	9th	10th	11th	12th	13th	14th	15th	Total canes	Sugar produced (Hogsheads)
1786	104	104	46														254	181
1814	53	56	61	61	42	8		20	8							40	433	
1822	128	61	62	62	62	36	22										434	533
1834	134	78	61	71	140											3	488	

In fact, the total area of Worthy Park land when Rose Price arrived in Jamaica was no less than 2,922 acres. Of the 1,777 acres not contiguous with the central block of land in Lluidas Vale, much was uncultivable mountain; but Rose Price had it carefully surveyed by Messrs. Kirkwood and Low in 1792 and systematically assessed its economic potential. At Riverhead and on the Point Hill road there was useful grazing land to add to the 429 acres of planted guinea grass in the central block, and on one side of the Ewarton road were 90 acres possessed by one Philips and his wife 'who save deficiency at Worthy Park'. But the most interesting of the marginal lands of Worthy Park were those 577 acres 'laying to the westward of Tydixton Park or at Coco Ree', which Rose Price hoped would help to make Worthy Park more self-sufficient. This land, which even today can only be reached on foot or horseback, was, according to the surveyors' report, 'very Rocky & inaccessible unless in Glades, great part of which is now in Negro grounds & plantain walks—Beyond the Plantain walk there is plenty of Broad leafed Trees, Sta. Marias & timber for Shingles, Staves, Board & heading and a few Cedars but distant. The part called Sarah's Bottom is good provision land abounding with hard Timber difficult of access.'[46] It was the almost inaccessible parts of Cocoree which Rose Price utilized to fulfil the requirements of the Jamaican Assembly that each plantation do its best to produce its own provisions. Hitherto, what provisions had been grown at Worthy Park probably came from the hilly acreage of Plantain Walk which Rose Price had converted into sugar land, and Rose Price was doubtless prouder of this conversion, and of the 33 fresh acres of sugar land which he squeezed out of the even less promising 689 tumbled acres of Dry Gully, than of all the provisions grown in Cocoree. For, as one of the earliest Jamaican planters discovered, one acre of sugar could grow enough to pay for five acres in ground provisions.

If all sugar land was to be utilized, excessive ratooning was a necessary recourse, for no estate could maintain sufficient field slaves to re-plant all its sugar acreage every year. In fact, the rapid expansion undertaken by Rose Price at Worthy Park, even with its heavy reliance on ratooning, could only have been possible with a great expansion and reorganization of the existing field labour force. Two years before Rose Price went to Worthy Park, the slave population was 338, of whom only 133, including 89 women, were field labourers. In each year of his residence, Price purchased large numbers of new slaves, including 144 in 1792 and 81 in 1793.[47] By 1794, the slave population of Worthy Park was 528, a level that was approximately maintained until Emancipation. Of these, 219 were field labourers, divided into three gangs, over 190 being healthy adults, mainly men.

By almost doubling his praedial labour force, Rose Price was not only able to accomplish his plans for greatly expanded cultivation, but also, apparently, to dispense with the gangs of expensively hired labourers hitherto necessary during crop. To carry out many construction tasks on the estate, however, Rose Price was occasionally constrained to hire carpenters, masons, and bricklayers, at least until the skill of Worthy Park's craftsman slaves had risen sufficiently, as a result of Price's new régime.[48]

Besides expanding his labour force, Rose Price was extremely concerned to ensure that his slaves became much more productive. In a manner far in advance of his times he gathered vital statistics concerning the slaves he owned at Worthy Park and, with the aim of improving

Jeffreys' Map of Jamaica, 1794, showing roads as developed before the time of Rose Price. Notice that Port Henderson was not yet constructed.

Eighteenth-century watercolour of Worthy Park, believed to have been by Hakewill. The Great House is located to the left of the tree, the Overseer's Yard to the right. The buildings of Thetford Works are hidden behind the trees to the left.

their health and morale and reducing their awful mortality, he made considerable improvements in their diet, built numerous new hutments and a barrack-like new slave hospital close to the overseer's house. These improvements placed Worthy Park in the forefront of 'enlightened' Jamaican estates, but it is unlikely that Rose Price's motives were more than nominally humanitarian. Healthier and humanely treated slaves were invariably more efficient and cheerful at work, and the closer to the ideal of natural increase achieved by the slave population of an estate, the lower would be the annual bill for new slaves to the wise proprietor.

Certainly, Rose Price's slaves were made to work even harder in the fields and factory and, besides, were kept incessantly active in building projects. As well as the new slave living quarters and hospital, new cattle pens, including a mule pen at Rocky Point for 100 animals, three new trash houses and sundry other buildings were erected. But the most notable innovations at Worthy Park between 1791 and 1795 were in road building. Many miles of new 'intervals' were laid to facilitate the collection of cut cane, until nearly every cane-piece was not only surrounded but also divided by all-weather cart tracks, and very little cane was more than 100 yards from a road. Yet these important improvements were overshadowed by the ambitious construction of the New Road, running from the central buildings eastwards across the width of the estate and over Lluidas Blue Mountain to Ewarton.

As soon as he arrived in Jamaica it was apparent to Rose Price that the old system by which sugar was hauled laboriously over Point Hill to Old Harbour was extremely uneconomical, and that the easier gradient towards Jamaica's main inland road in St. Thomas-ye-Vale, and thence to Kingston Harbour, would be greatly preferable. A bridle path already existed, running by way of Thetford Works,[49] but this took a route up the mountainside with a gradient of about one-in-five: difficult enough for horses, and impossible for sugar wains. Starting in 1792, Rose Price set his slaves building a carriage road diagonally bisecting Worthy Park's canefields to the foot of the hill by the Rio Cobre sinkhole. This section alone greatly improved the links between the factory and the most distant fields, though the bridge over the Great Gully at the factory end was not constructed until 1815, and the ford must have been impassable in times of flood. From the sinkhole, the New Road ingeniously serpentined its way, with a maximum gradient of one-in-twelve, up and over the ridge to Riverhead, and thence to Ewarton, seven miles distant from Worthy Park. For its first four miles, the road ran entirely through land belonging either to Worthy Park or Thetford, but once it had been gouged and graded as far as Riverhead, where some sort of road already existed, in 1794, Rose Price and Peek Fuller (the owner of Thetford) were able to prevail upon the Jamaican Assembly to take on the responsibility for its completion and upkeep.[50]

Two miles south of Linstead Tavern, and thirteen miles from Worthy Park by the new road, lay the 600 acres of Mickleton, the holding purchased by Sir Charles Price the elder in 1766 and by John Price from the estate of his cousin in 1793. This was to serve a very similar purpose on the 34-mile journey to and from Port Henderson as had Guanaboa and Spring Garden on the route to Old Harbour. By 1793, Mickleton grew very little or no sugar and was no more than a 'penn'; but it proved an invaluable stopping place for the Worthy Park wains, and a seasoning ground for newly-imported Negroes. It also grew some of its mother-estate's ground provisions, which were sent over the mountain in the returning sugar wains, and shared with Spring Garden the duty of breeding replacement cattle.[51]

An essential feature of the new route to and from the coast was the existence of a port that was a great improvement on Old Harbour. Port Henderson, directly opposite Port Royal at the mouth of Kingston Harbour, had only been developed in the late 1780s, when silting from the Rio Cobre made Passage Fort, the traditional barcadier for Spanish Town, impractical. Efficiently run by a company, Port Henderson offered excellent wharfage and warehousing. For Worthy Park this meant much more reliable import and export arrangements, though at the cost of greatly increased annual charges for port handling and storage. Almost immediately, Worthy Park became one of Port Henderson's most important customers, paying no less than £222 out of the £1,708 total income for the new port in 1796, and £292 out of £1,801 in the following year.[52]

By that time Rose Price was no longer in Jamaica, having returned to England in 1795, certain that he had placed Worthy Park on a footing more than sound enough to withstand the buffets of the war with revolutionary France. In his thorough manner, Price had left behind exacting instructions, including orders to record and forward every detail of the estate's transactions. This meticulous supervision would have been intolerable to the type of overseer from which Worthy Park had suffered before 1791, but by raising the salary from £200 to £300, Rose Price assured himself of a much more reliable class of manager in his absence.[53]

The results, at first, must have been distinctly disappointing. Newly worked marginal lands and poorly fertilized acreage could not produce sugar purely by an effort of will, nor could the factory suddenly process beyond its capabilities. During Rose Price's residence, Worthy Park's production rose steadily from 248 hogsheads of sugar and 85 puncheons of rum in 1790 to 371¼ hogsheads and 162 puncheons in 1794, but even these figures, being derived from 564 acres of cane represented a very poor acreage yield. Moreover, Price's departure was followed by a two-year recession that saw sugar production fall to 306 hogsheads in 1795 and 269 in 1796. After this, however, the improvements in husbandry set afoot by Rose Price began to fructify. In 1797, production soared to 468 hogsheads of sugar, easily a record for the estate, and this was surpassed by 498½ hogsheads in 1799, 590½ in 1800, 624 in 1804, 673 in 1805 and a wonderful peak of 705 in 1812. From an average annual production of 296·9 hogsheads between 1776 and 1796, Worthy Park, thanks almost entirely to Rose Price's reforms, averaged 508·2 hogsheads between 1796 and 1815. To produce more than this would have required a complete reformation in the factory, which was not actually achieved before the decline of planting made the necessary capital almost impossible to come by.[54] Even the improvements in ratooning, while not dramatic, bore witness to the effectiveness of Rose Price's husbandry. The results delineated in the crop map of 1834 show that while plant canes were at last able to produce two

Worthy Park: Cane-pieces and Productivity, 1786-1834 (in hogsheads)

A. 1791	Acres	1786	1787	1791	1834
1 Sorrel Hill	13	P 20	2R 6½		XR 15
2 Pond Piece	31	P 24½	R 10¾		3R+XR 14+6
3 Harry Hill	27	P 35	R 12¾	R 22¼	XR 6
4 Craddock's	6	P 5⅓	R 6	R 4	14R 1
5 Fuller's Side	27	P 37	R 30¼	R 22⅔	3R 23
6 Dry Gully	40 (13)	R 12⅓	P 13	R 10¼	P 56 (33 acres)
7 Fig Tree (Halsted)	26	R 2½		P 29⅔	R 47
8 Pasture Piece	29	R 9			R 33
9 Overgully	26	2R 3¼		P 34	P 74
10 Limekiln	21	R 7		P 43	P ?
11 Little Middle	20	2R 4½		P 39¼	P ?
12 Crawfish Gully	15	R 3			part fallow
13 Big Bullet Tree	22		P 24	R 12¼	P ?
14 Little Pasture	14		P 13⅓		3R 10
15 Bristow Hill	23		P 8	R 16¼	2R 23
16 Cabbage Tree	20		P 11½		2R 24
17 Flower Piece	5				XR 5
18 Fullers Garden Side	22		P 13	P 21½	XR 5
19 Well Piece	10				R 19
20 Little Bullet Tree	19			P 29⅓	R 32
21 Big Middle	30				2R+XR 16+8
22 Unclassified	20		P 14		
B.1794					
23 Plantain Walk	8				} P 45
24 Big Plantain Walk	23				
25 Sawpit Piece	7				
26 Rocky Hill Side	6				} XR 18
27 Rocky Hill Bottom	22				
28 Pope's Pasture	20				
29 Little Pope's Pasture	8				Nursery
30 Old Hot House	14				
31 New Hot House	21				3R 10
C. 1834					
32 Bamboo Canes	30				

hogsheads to the acre, first ratoons produced an average of 1·38, second ratoons just about a hogshead, third ratoons 0·61, and even the further ratoons an average of 0·54 hogsheads to the acre.[55]

To add to Rose Price's complacency, the comparative slump in sugar prices during the middle 1780s came to an end in 1788 and, as the effects of the devastating revolution in St. Domingue began to be felt in a reduction of competition after 1790, prices moved steadily upwards to a new peak in 1799, almost unaffected by the outbreak of war with France in 1793. With an annual production of rum that averaged

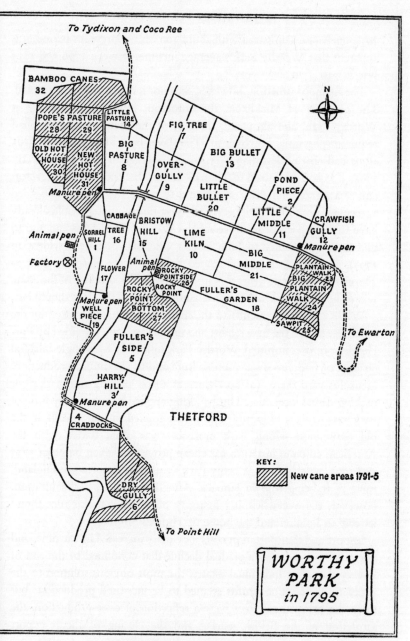

To Tydixon and Coco Ree

N

BAMBOO CANES 32

POPE'S PASTURE 28 / 29

LITTLE PASTURE 14

FIG TREE 7

OLD HOT HOUSE 30 / NEW HOT HOUSE 31

BIG PASTURE 8

OVER-GULLY 9

BIG BULLET 13

Manure pen

POND PIECE 2

LITTLE BULLET 20

LITTLE MIDDLE 11

CABBAGE TREE 16

BRISTOW HILL 15

Animal pen

SORREL HILL 1

LIME KILN 10

CRAWFISH GULLY 12

Manure pen

Factory

FLOWER 17

Animal pen

ROCKY POINT SIDE 26

BIG MIDDLE 21

PLANTAIN WALK 23

ROCKY POINT

ROCKY POINT

FULLER'S GARDEN 18

BIG PLANTAIN WALK 24

Manure pen

WELL PIECE 19

ROCKY POINT BOTTOM 27

To Ewarton

SAWPIT 25

FULLER'S SIDE 5

HARRY HILL 3'

Manure pen

4 CRADDOCKS

THETFORD

KEY:
New cane areas 1791-5

DRY GULLY 6

To Point Hill

WORTHY PARK in 1795

FROM C.O. 441/4/4, 5, 12

203 puncheons, compared with about 100 for the previous period, it is apparent that Worthy Park's average income between 1796 and 1815 was at least £20,000 a year.[56]

The financial situation, however, was not quite so rosy as it seemed. The purchase of Mickleton, the numerous improvements made at Worthy Park, and above all, the cost of the many new slaves, had required substantial borrowing. The slaves bought in 1792 and 1793 alone had cost no less than £13,472, an average of £60 a head.[57] By 1794, £18,000 was owed to Thomas Smith, the Price's London factor, and as a result John Price was forced to make the type of one-sided agreement without which nearly all West Indian estates would already have folded up. In order to cover the Worthy Park debts and also to guarantee an annuity to John Price's wife (she became a widow in 1797), Worthy Park and its related holdings were placed in trust to Thomas Smith for 99 years.[58] Naturally, the entire produce of the estate was to be consigned into Smith's hands as long as the debt should last.

While this arrangement had the merit of simplicity, backed by the reliability which the new export and import facilities provided by Port Henderson, it committed Worthy Park inflexibly to a single bilateral channel of trade, to sugar monoculture and to maximum production. Henceforward there was no chance at all of 'playing the market' or making casual local sales. This had long applied to sugar, very little of which was ever sold locally; but now it applied to rum as well. In the old days, rum—along with molasses—was often traded with the American colonies in return for cheap provisions. Even between 1775 and 1791, very little of Worthy Park's rum was exported to England, most of it being sold in Jamaica. After Rose Price's reorganization, however, the overwhelming majority of Worthy Park's rum found its way to London and the house of Thomas Smith.

Import and transportation costs inevitably increased in wartime, and after 1800 prices began a gradual decline that continued to the end of slavery days. For individual estates, the most obvious solution to the problem of declining profits seemed to be increased production; but since the prices themselves were a reflection of over-production, the saturation of the British market and the closing of the re-export markets by the extension of the war, this was not a permanent cure. In 1805, for example, Worthy Park produced far more sugar than ever before, but since this was also Jamaica's year of greatest production before 1937, the returns were disappointing. In the final decade of the Napoleonic War, Worthy Park's proprietor enjoyed only two periods of moderate solace. In 1807, when Parliament abolished the British trade in slaves, Rose Price could reflect that, thanks to his foresight, Worthy Park's labour force was more than adequate and her slave population was at last approaching stability through natural increase; and in 1812 the estate produced her record crop in a year when the general Jamaican production was decidedly meagre, and prices were relatively high.

By 1815, Rose Price, now middle-aged, must have looked back with nostalgia to 1795 when, as an optimistic youth of 27, he had returned in triumph from Jamaica. Then, as the sole heir of an ailing father, he must have seemed a very eligible bachelor indeed, and within three years of his return he had married in typically West Indian style. His bride was Elizabeth Lambart, a genteel though impoverished young lady of County Meath, whose chief asset—a kind of delayed dowry— consisted of the fact that, through her sister Frances, she became sister- in-law of Charles, the second Earl of Talbot.[59] This family connection was to prove invaluable to Rose Price and Worthy Park in the stormy years ahead.

NOTES

[1] I.R.O. Deeds, 170/7, 281/86.
[2] Ibid., 268/200, 271/187, 273/64; and D.N.B. under Sir Charles Price.
[3] Pares, Merchants and Planters, 44.
[4] D.N.B.
[5] I.R.O. Deeds, 320/152, 320/209.
[6] Ibid., 286/70, 361/105.
[7] Ibid., 299/25, 314/3.
[8] Ibid., 294/215, 380/176.
[9] Ibid., 297/1, 272/178.
[10] Ibid., 343/212.
[11] Ibid., 286/64, 307/207.

[12] *Ibid.*, 292/40, 294/164.

[13] *Ibid.*, 299/45, 343/24.

[14] *Ibid.*, 285/1, 364/206.

[15] These deeds involved the following properties: Gayle (1777, 1784), Decoy (1777, 1789), Rose Hall (1778, 1781), Mickleton (1778, 1788), Shenton's (1779), Amity Hall (1779, 1789), New Works (1779), Wallins (1779, 1787), Burton's (1779, 1782, 1787), Spanish Town (1779, 1786), Plantain Walk (1779, 1784), Goshen (1781, 1782), and three unnamed properties (1778, 1779).

[16] *Journal of the Assembly*, VIII, 2 December 1786.

[17] *Ibid.*

[18] *Ibid.*

[19] *Ibid.*, Petition of John Jackson.

[20] *Ibid.*, 'Rose Hall Mortgage'.

[21] *Ibid.*, 'Burton's Mortgage', 'Goshen Mortgage'.

[22] *Ibid.*, 'Wallins Mortgage'.

[23] A telling example of this concern was the investigation of a Committee of the Jamaican Assembly into the activity of the Vice Admiralty Court, held early in 1789 under the chairmanship of Mr. Redmond. See C.O. 137/88.

[24] *Journal of the Assembly*, VIII, 2 December 1786.

[25] *Ibid.*, 20–21 December 1786.

[26] *Ibid.*, October 1787.

[27] I.R.O. Deeds, 285/1, 364/206.

[28] Chancery Records, Lib. 130, No. 120, pp. 328–32.

[29] I.R.O. Deeds, 340/81.

[30] Crop Accounts, 8/92, 162; 9/60, 114; 10/10, 59. The first new borrowing on the security of Worthy Park appears to have occurred on 13 June 1789 from Thomas Smith and William Cardale, in order to finance the improvements carried out by Rose Price after 1791; I.R.O. Deeds, 822/1.

[31] Davies Gilbert, *Parochial History of Cornwall*, London, Nichols, 1838, III, 85. Educated at Winchester, John Price apparently contracted tuberculosis there, being advised to settle in Cornwall by Dr. Nicholls, the physician of George II, who came from Trereiffe, just outside Penzance. John Price died at Worthy Park on 4 February 1740 but his body was carried back to Penzance and buried in St. Mary's Church; G. C. Boase, *Collecteana Cornubiensis*, Truro, Netherton and Worth, 1890. Davies Gilbert, alias Giddy, had a close connection with the Prices, since he had been one of the trustees of Rose Price's marriage settlement in 1798 and then one of Worthy Park's numerous creditors.

[32] *Ibid.*, and above, IV, 86.

[33] Gilbert, III, 86–7.

[34] Edgar A. Rees, *Old Penzance*, Penzance, privately printed, 1956, 26–7. The Chi-owne monument is locally called the Ring and Thimble. The ring itself, found in 1781 and inscribed *in hac spe vivo*, is now in the British Museum.

[35] Peter Pindar was the pseudonym of John Wolcot (1738–1819), Devon-born quack doctor, promoter, and satirist, who spent the years 1769–73 in Jamaica as a client of Edward Trelawny's. By coincidence, it was his doggerel elegy on young Lt. William G. Boscawen, drowned at the Decoy in April 1769 (Forlorn from shade to shade I rove / By friendship's sacred spirit led / Where horror wraps the twilight grove / That glooming seems to mourn the dead . . .), published in the *Annual Register* for 1779, that led to Wolcot's patronage by Admiral Boscawen's widow, the young man's mother.

The natural genius of the artist John Opie (1760–1825) came to public notice through the patronage successively of John Wolcot and Mrs. Boscawen. At different times he painted two portraits of Rose Price (1780, 1795), one of Lady Price (1795), and another of John Vinicombe (1800). They have not been traced.

John Price wrote to Horace Walpole from Penzance on 28 July 1776 concerning an impression of the Seal of Richard III as Lord High Admiral which he had acquired from the effects of an indigent tavern-keeper for 6d., and which he forwarded by way of 'Mr. Serocold of Hampton'; B.M. Add. MSS. 21553, f. 119.

John Price's writings are mentioned in C. S. Gilbert, *An Historical Survey of the County of Cornwall*, Plymouth, Congden, 1820, I, 159, 579–80, II, 733–4, and G. C. Boase, *Biblotheca Cornubiensis*, 526, 1318.

[36] Rapidly appointed College Tutor and Public Examiner, Vinicombe was on the threshold of great things when he was killed by a fall from a horse. His portrait by John Opie was presented to Pembroke College, Oxford by Rose Price; Gilbert, 88.

[37] C.O. 137/85.

[38] Goveia, *Slave Society*, 1–50.

[39] Ragatz, *Statistics*, I, x.

[40] Crop Accounts, 8/92, 162; 9/60, 114; 10/10, 59; Chancery Records, Jacques *vs.* Murphy, 19 February 1805, 194/78.

[41] Gilbert, III, 88.

[42] Maps No. 3 and 9 (1794 and 1834), C.O. 441/4/4, 5, 12.

[43] The actual acreages of ratoons were 56 in first ratoons, 61 in seconds, 61 in thirds, 42 in fourths, 8 in fifths, 19 in sixths, 20 in eighths, 8 in ninths and, 40 in fifteenths; Worthy Park *Plantation Book*, 1811–17, 31 December 1814, p. 141.

[44] See accompanying map and productivity table, 176–7.

[45] Map of 1792, C.O. 441/4/4 (7).

[46] *Ibid.* As late as 1814–15, the 40 acres of Plantain Ground were used for 'provisions for whites', though by 1834 they were at least partly growing sugar. In 1814 it was calculated that of the 433 acres in canes, 372 were due to be cut for the 1815 crop and 61 for the crop of 1816. At that time, Worthy Park had 452 acres of guinea grass (22 of which had been planted that year), 677 acres of common grass, 40 acres of provision grounds for whites, and 1,647 acres of woodland and 'Negro grounds'; a total of 3,250 acres. Worthy Park *Plantation Book*, 1811–17, p. 141.

[47] See above, VI, 131.

[48] Worthy Park *Plantation Book*, 1791–1811; Accounts, 20 December 1792, 9–10 January 1793.

[49] Institute of Jamaica Map.

[50] *A Plan of the road leading through Worthy Park Estate* . . ., by P. Keefe, 1814, C.O. 441/4/4, 8.

[51] Of Mickleton Pen's 600 acres, 548 were in common pasture in 1813, with 40 acres of 'Negro Land' and 12 acres of 'Corn Land and Provisions'; Worthy Park *Plantation Book*, 1811–17, 83. In 1811 Mickleton carried 96 breeding stock, compared with 303 at Spring Garden, a spread of 2,000 acres. Of the 399 total breeding stock, 8 were bulls, 124 cows, 39 heifers, 75 steers, 44 bull calves and 109 cow calves. In the same year there were 33 Negroes at Mickleton, compared with 74 at Spring Garden and 516 at Worthy Park; *ibid.*, 2, 7–8, 11–14.

[52] The charges rose to the formidable totals of £578 in 1799 and £645 in 1801.

Archives of Jamaica, *Port Henderson Account Book*, Vol. I, 1795–1804, 57, 71, 98, 166, 237.

53 The overseer also enjoyed a considerable number of perquisites, including special provision allowances, a large number of domestic slaves, and even several acres of grassland allocated to him to provide fodder for his horses. See above, VI, and C.O. 441/4/4, 12. Almost certainly, Rose Price left behind him at least one illegitimate coloured child. In his will in 1831 he bequeathed £50 Jamaica currency a year during her lifetime to a quadroon called Lizette Naish, 'formerly a slave at Worthy Park', and £25 sterling a year to her daughter Eliza Naish, 'otherwise Price', the wife of the Rev. Lockhart of Dumbarton. There was also a John Price Naish to whom in 1822 Rose Price gave three slaves and who in 1837 was one of the signatories of the agreed schedule of work tasks for apprentices in St. John's Parish. I.R.O. Wills, 116/11; Deeds, 713/66; *Jamaica Almanack* for 1838. In March 1794 Rose Price manumitted a female slave called Lisette, lodging security of £100 with John Quier and Samuel Queneborough the Church-wardens of St. John's to provide £5 a year, by the Act of 1774; I.R.O. Deeds, 417/112. In the Worthy Park records there is mention of a quadroon or mestizo domestic slave called Eliza working in the Great House in 1813, aged 15, who would have been born in 1795 or 1796, and she was probably the Eliza Naish who was allocated ten gallons of rum in 1821; *Worthy Park Plantation Books*, 1811–17; 1821–4. Eliza and John (Price) Naish, however, might have been the 'quadroon female slave named Biddy, and a mulatto slave named Jack of the value of £280' manumitted by Rose Price in May 1811; I.R.O. Deeds, 604/83. Samuel Queneborough was involved in this transaction, as in the manumission of the slave Lisette in 1794.

54 The only improvement at the factory during the lifetime of Rose Price of which we have record was the introduction of a cane-cutting mill near the Rocky Point mule pen in 1825; C.O. 441/4/4, 5. Steam engines, introduced into the West Indies as early as 1808, were not brought to Worthy Park before the 1840s.

55 Figures from the crop map of 1834, C.O. 441/4/4, 12, which indicate, respectively, 130 hogsheads from 66 acres, 176 from 127, 63 from 64, 51 from 83, and 64 from 118. The three acres of Craddock's in fourteen ratoons produced a single hogshead.

56 The production of rum between 1776 and 1815 was 3,449 puncheons in the seventeen years for which we have records, and for the period 1775–95, 1,601 in sixteen years. £20,000 is arrived at by multiplying 508·2 (hogsheads) by 16·9 (cwts) by £2, and adding 203 (puncheons) by £15. In 1796, Worthy Park was expected easily to bring in £6,000 clear profit a year; see below, VIII.

57 Above, VI, 131, n. 126.

58 I.R.O. Deeds, 423/68.

59 *Burke's Peerage*. The marriage settlement (4 August 1798) is referred to in I.R.O. Deeds, 665/31.

CHAPTER EIGHT

The Coming of Emancipation, 1815-1834

Trengwainton House shelters among trees at the head of a combe two miles out of Penzance, on the short road to England's rocky south-western extremity. Preserved, in contrast to the thousand lost Great Houses of Jamaica, by the National Trust (to whom it was deeded in 1961), it is the last remaining English evidence of the fortune made by the Prices from Worthy Park. Once owned by the ancient Cornish family of Arundell, it was bought in 1798 by Rose Price, who spent much of the remaining 37 years of his life extending the building and developing its grounds.[1] The house itself is undistinguished, its solid grey frontage more reminiscent of the stolid Bettiscombe of the Pinneys than the gothic extravagance of William Beckford's Fonthill Abbey.[2] Only the magnificent gardens, crammed with every sub-tropical tree, shrub, and flower it is possible to grow in England, are a reminder that it was once the home of a West Indian absentee; as if Rose Price had striven in the cooler humidity of Madron parish to reproduce at least a reminder of Lluidas in St. John, Jamaica.

Yet in the gardens at Trengwainton there is a sense of order that would be out of place amid the promiscuous luxuriance of Jamaican vegetation. If we came upon a scarlet parakeet or flickering vivid lizard at Trengwainton we would expect to find them caged. For this was

the home of Rose Price the indefatigable manager, to whom dis-
organization and disorder, like disobedience, were a personal affront,
and whose politics, philosophy, and very religion were a reflection of
his economic needs. Over Trengwainton House there also hangs an
aura of failure and frustration. For, despite Rose Price's abilities,
energy, and sense of order, Worthy Park could not continue to prosper, and his over-large family was, at his death, neither wealthy nor
harmonious. Significantly, Trengwainton, with its reminders of an
evaporated fortune based upon a slavery now abolished, was not
maintained after Rose Price's death in 1834 by any members of a
family that had split to the four corners of the earth and into many
different pursuits.[3]

In many ways Rose Price duplicated the life of his father on a
grander scale. For the first two decades of his married life he enjoyed
an income at least twice that of John Price,[4] and the comparatively
modest establishment in Penzance was inadequate for his rising aspirations. At first Rose Price intended to build his own house close to
John Price's cottage retreat Chi-owne, and went so far as to erect a
windbreak on such a grandiose scale that the locals christened it 'The
Chinese Wall'.[5] But shortly after the death of his father and his own
marriage he moved into Trengwainton, already one of the finest
properties in South Cornwall, and it was there that his six sons and
eight daughters were born and strictly raised. Besides rebuilding the
mansion, Rose Price lived as lord of the manor, keeping a private pack
of foxhounds and travelling in a splendid coach with no less than four
liveried and bewigged postillions. A special driveway led from Trengwainton across the fields to the parish church, where the Price
escutcheon and the monstrous Price mausoleum may still be seen.
'When Sir Rose and his fourteen beautiful children attended Madron
church it was a sight to see and remember,' wrote one local historian,
'the children walking down the aisle two and two, followed by the
portly squire and his very charming wife, to their special pews, the
girls plainly dressed, their straw bonnets having a single piece of ribbon
across. Folk said at that time that a finer family did not exist in the
county.'[6]

Following in his father's footsteps by becoming Sheriff of Cornwall in 1814, Rose Price was even more active than John Price in local affairs. First President of the Penzance Public Library, the West Penwith Savings Bank, and the local branch of the S.P.C.K., he busied himself with such parliamentary matters as the abolition of the salt duties, as well as those which more directly concerned his holdings in the West Indies.[7] Yet Rose Price was probably most remarkable not as a man of affairs but as a dynast in the classic West Indian mould. Despite the imposing coat of arms inherited from Sir Charles Price and the legend of a descent from Welsh princelings which began to gain currency about this time, Rose Price had little to offer save his £6,000 a year in lieu of noble lineage. Yet on the strength of his Jamaican fortune, this great-great-grandson of the obscure Lieutenant Price married a lady whose uncle was the second Lord Sherborne and whose great-uncle was the first Earl of Belvedere, while two of his sons and one of his daughters were to marry into the families of the Earls of Desart and Ducie and Lord Dunsany, the premier Baron of Ireland. Another dutiful daughter married John Basset of Tehidy, a member of a family that, though without titles, had made millions through the ownership of tin and copper mines and the harbour of Portreath.[8] These connections, however, were outshone by Rose Price's own fortune in becoming, two years after his own marriage, the brother-in-law of Charles, the second Earl of Talbot, whose son was to become in 1844, as Lord Shrewsbury, the premier Earl of the peerages of England and Ireland. It was almost certainly through this relationship, which ripened into a close personal friendship as well as business association, that Rose Price was made a Baronet in 1815, taking Trengwainton (rather than Worthy Park) into his title, as his descendants have done to the present day.[9]

Keeping up with his illustrious relatives and with the expenses of his huge family was increasingly difficult for Sir Rose Price in the face of declining profits from sugar. Worthy Park became progressively loaded with debt in the pattern already established by the estate of the two Sir Charles Prices, a process accelerated rather than retarded by the costs of sundry improvements undertaken on the estate and several speculations in land and slaves made by its proprietor in his declining years. As we have seen, advances were made in 1789 by Thomas Smith and William Cardale on the produce of the estate, but by 1794 this debt had escalated to almost £18,000 and by 1796 to over £30,000. Yet by his will in August 1796, John Price was able to bequeath £6,000 a year to Rose Price and his heirs, as well as £30,000 for the benefit of Rose's daughters and younger sons from the proceeds of Worthy Park, as well as £200 a year for the Rev. John Vinicombe from Spring Garden and Guanaboa. The cost of these bequests were mortgages of 1,000 years on Worthy Park to Cardale, Sir Christopher Hawkins, and James Perkins—all merchants of London—including an annual payment of 4 per cent on the £30,000 already owed, and of 99 years on Spring Garden to Sir William Lemon and Thomas Smith.[10]

In 1798, as the price of his advantageous marriage, Rose Price made a generous settlement that guaranteed £1,000 a year to his wife if she became his widow (in fact, she died before him, in 1826), as well as £20,000 for those children over five in number who might be born of the marriage, with provision for their education at 4 per cent of that sum invested. About the same time, Rose Price borrowed a further £15,000 on the security of the estate from Cardale and Francis Gregor, by increasing the terms of the main mortgage to 2,500 years and the rate on the money owed to 5 per cent.[11]

Between 1798 and 1834 the debts of Worthy Park grew ever more complicated as the original creditors died or transferred their interests. In 1811, however, the affairs of the Spring Garden segment of Rose Price's lands were somewhat streamlined when the Earl of Talbot took over the debt and mortgage from the heirs of Smith and Lemon, John Vinicombe having died, and with him the annuity of £200. Talbot became increasingly involved in all aspects of his brother-in-law's finances, but in the case of the much more heavily entailed debts of Worthy Park proper his intervention could not simplify matters. Over the estate loomed the guaranteed commitment of £6,000 a year to Rose Price and the approaching settlements to be made to his twelve surviving children. By 1812 the original debt of £30,000 left by John Price had almost been expunged, but this was merely an accountancy trick, and it was soon replaced by others of a harsher kind. In 1816, for example, when Ralph Dutton and Davies Gilbert, two of the original trustees of the marriage settlement of 1798, were persuaded to advance £10,000, they did so only on a second mortgage, raising the interest on the loan to 6 per cent.[12]

Yet, thanks to his superlative connections with the English and Irish landed interest, Rose Price was able to march resolutely across the quaking mire of West Indian finances, and his credit remained excellent almost to the end of his life. On the plausible evidence of the meticulous records kept of his absentee management of Worthy Park he was able to make further improvements while estates all around were collapsing, and even to speculate in the 'bullish' market for land and slaves. In contrast to Thetford and Swansea (which had not received improvements comparable to those undertaken at Worthy Park between 1791 and 1795), or even his own Mickleton Pen, Worthy Park was kept in excellent repair, and new building continued throughout the 1820s.[13] In 1822, Rose Price installed the most modern type of copper rum still capable of producing 680 gallons at a time, and three years later a mule cane-cutting mill that must have greatly increased the efficiency of the crushing of cane.[14] In 1815 he purchased Russell and Derry Pens, each with their complements of slaves and, as late as 1830, Arthur's Seat with its 127 Negroes. Besides this, he greatly increased the acreage of Coco-ree by four purchases of 300 acres each, raising the total of Worthy Park land to more than 4,000 acres.[15] These investments were almost certainly made with the help of the Talbots, whom Rose Price convinced that conditions were due for an upward turn and that land and slaves should be bought while prices were at their lowest point. The Talbot investment in slaves was particularly heavy, and when claims for compensation were entered after 1834, it was found that all the slaves at Worthy Park and Mickleton were owned by the Talbots, and only those at Spring Garden by the Prices.

Sir Rose Price, like his cousin Sir Charles, gravely underestimated the power of the market to decline below a level imagined possible and, like his forerunner, also greatly overestimated the value of his land and slaves. When he came to make his will in April 1831 his bequests, while not as splendid as they might have been 25 years earlier, were still beyond his means. Among the most favoured of his legatees were his brother-in-law the Earl of Talbot, Talbot's sons the Viscount Ingestre and the Hon. John Talbot, and Price's wife's uncle Lord Sherborne. But Rose Price's favours were double-edged, since his noble relatives were also appointed trustees. Conveniently provided with instructions to sell whatever was necessary to fulfill the financial bequests, they found themselves responsible for an estate that proved unsaleable, whose creditors now numbered over twenty and whose encumbering debts, constantly increasing, would take a further thirty years to determine.

The fortune of Worthy Park between 1815 and 1834 was that of a piece of flotsam rather more buoyant than average on a wave of general depression. With the coming of peace in 1815, Jamaica continued to over-produce, but the prices of sugar tumbled as sugar poured into England from the newly opened colonies of Trinidad, the Guianas, and Mauritius, and into the European market from Cuba and Brazil.

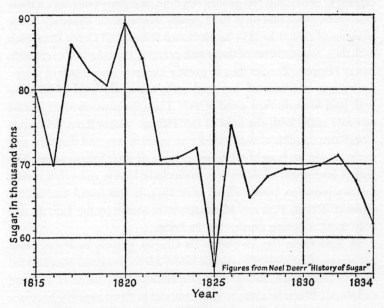

Figures from Noel Deerr "History of Sugar"

JAMAICAN SUGAR PRODUCTION, 1815–1834

Jamaica produced almost 90,000 tons of sugar as late as 1820, though the average price received had plunged from 61s. per hundredweight in 1815 to 36s. 6d. After 1821, the average annual production for Jamaica stabilized at around 70,000 for almost a decade, but the prices received fell yet further, averaging little over 30s. per hundredweight. Between 1829 and 1831, planters often received less than the 24s. 2d. which a Select Committee of the British Parliament in 1831 determined was the average cost of production.[16]

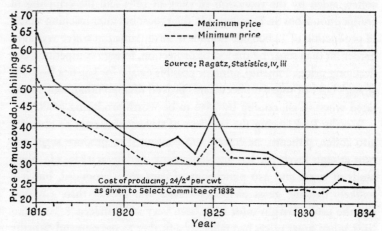

AVERAGE HIGHEST AND LOWEST PRICES OF MUSCOVADO SOLD IN LONDON (EXCLUSIVE OF DUTY), 1815-1833. (FIGURES FOR 1817-1819 AND 1827 ARE MISSING)

Despite the disastrous fall in sugar prices, the cost of provisions remained high, and the British Government displayed an increasing reluctance to pass protective legislation for the benefit of West Indian sugar producers. The rate of duty on British West Indian muscovado had risen steadily from 15s. per hundredweight in 1791 to 30s. in 1815, and declined thereafter far too slowly and only to 24s. in 1830. Likewise, the excise on rum, 5s. 7d. a gallon in 1792 and 13s. 7d. at the height of the war, actually rose to 13s. 11d. between 1819 and 1824, and was still 9s. in 1830. Although the preferential rate for British West Indian over foreign sugars rose to a peak of 39s. in 1830, the absolute duty of 63s. charged on foreign sugar was no greater than it had been in the last years of the war. Much more serious for the Jamaican planters were the removal of the drawback of 27s. 6d. on re-exports of their sugars from Great Britain in 1819 and the gradual whittling down of the preference they enjoyed over sugars produced in the British East Indies. This preference had been as high as 13s. per hundredweight in 1816, but was reduced to 10s. in 1818 and removed altogether in 1825. Many Jamaican estates had turned from sugar to coffee, aided by the reduction of duty in 1783 and the crippling of competition from St. Domingue in the 1790s; but after reaching a peak of production of 34,000,000 pounds in 1814, Jamaican coffee was even harder hit than sugar by the loss of protection, foreign competition and declining prices. Pimento, another possible escape for Jamaica from the stranglehold of sugar monoculture, proved disappointing, and cotton fared worst of all, ceasing by 1830 to be worth producing at all.[17]

Worthy Park during the last days of slavery chose not to diversify into coffee, pimento, or cotton and continued to produce sugar and rum at high levels for less and less return. As late as 1822, 533 hogsheads of sugar and 250 puncheons of rum were produced, but it is unlikely that the gross income received was greater than £16,000, and the profit margin must have been very small indeed.[18] Ten years later, when sugar prices had fallen by a further 25 per cent and Worthy Park was producing perhaps 10 per cent less sugar, normal profits were out of the question.[19]

The one advantage remaining to the West Indian planters was the cheapest possible labour force, and it is small wonder that with the sugar industry facing disaster the planters—including Rose Price— became almost paranoid in their defence of Negro slavery. In 1807 it had seemed that the deprivation of a never-ending supply of fresh African slaves was a serious blow to the plantations, and the successive campaigns for the registration of slaves and the amelioration of conditions appeared part of a steadily developing plot on the part of parliamentary liberals and sectarian missionaries to reduce the profitability of plantations and upset the delicate social stability of the British islands. By the 1830s, however, the situation had subtly changed. The established colonies, having over the registration question won the principle that slave legislation was a colonial rather than imperial affair, had all by 1831 passed acceptable new Slave Codes. Even had capital been available—and money was so short that in 1832 the Jamaican Government could only raise £5,430 of a loan of £100,000 at 6 per cent[20]—the purchase of new slaves was in most cases no longer strictly necessary. An increasing number of transactions in slaves were speculative in nature. Amelioration had actually begun to work in reducing Negro mortality and, in the face of a naturally increasing slave population and declining sugar production, planters were beginning to bemoan the large number of unproductive slaves they were forced by law to feed and clothe, and even to subscribe, at last, to the argument that slavery was an uneconomic system. The startling rise in the number of manumissions after 1825 was evidence not only of the liberalization of the manumission and property laws—so that slaves now owned money and could buy their freedom more easily—but also of the declining need for slaves in many areas and the eagerness of slave-owners to capitalize upon unwanted Negroes while yet they could.

What was, however, intolerable to virtually all slave-owners were the notions that the British Government might not only free the slaves and force the planters to pay wages for their labour, but also fail to compensate the owners adequately or even to coerce the free Negroes to continue to work on the sugar plantations. As the superb bibliography of the emancipist controversy by L. J. Ragatz[21] demonstrates, the 1820s and 1830s saw an almost inexhaustible efflorescence of polemical literature; yet there is no clearer exposé of the plantocratic point of view than the obscure broadside fired off by Sir Rose Price in 1832, published—at his own expense—in Penzance and entitled *Pledges on Colonial Slavery, to Candidates for Seats in Parliament, Rightly Considered.*[22] Ludicrous if it were not faintly horrific, Rose Price's pamphlet set itself the conflicting tasks of proving that while slavery was odious, it was preferable to the life of a free labourer in England, and that English slavery was infinitely superior to 'the dreadful slavery of foreigners'.[23] Negroes, moreover, while they alone were naturally suited to toils in the tropics were, paradoxically, of such a base indolent nature that it was necessary and right to force them to work. Members in the recently reformed House of Commons were therefore urged to continue slavery if they could, but if they could not, to coerce the emancipated Negro to continue in his labours, while at the same time to compensate the slave-owners handsomely.

It is some indication of the reforming temper of that era that Rose Price claimed, disingenuously, to be a radical reformer himself ('to the utmost extent that I trust *a man of integrity can be*') and a regular reader of Cobbett's *Political Register*, though he quoted Cobbett solely for the purpose of contrasting the miserable lot of the English labourer with that of the Jamaican slave. In a masterpiece of special pleading, Price asserted that for the ten 'necessities' which, in 1805, took up all but 2s. 1½d. of the English labourer's weekly wage of 26s.,

. . . the black man has ten articles which he prefers, as equivalents to them, *in any abundance he chooses to have them; his food depends not on the wages he obtains, or on the depreciation of a currency;* animal food is not his general diet, either in Africa or the West India islands. . . . *Providence has ordered it otherwise*—inflammation and putrid complaints would speedily attack the black labourer, in the tropics, if he made free use of animal food, in a climate where the meat turns putrid in twelve hours; though they have fowls and pigs in abundance, with which the markets are supplied *by them, for the whites, at high prices,* such as a dollar for a fine fowl, and £4, or £5, for a pig; these they kill, and use themselves, at their dances and festivals, but not as a general food.

In the room of Meat;—The negro has salt herrings, with which he seasons his mess of pottage, of vegetables; and substantial farinaceous roots, far superior to any produced in Europe.

For Bread;—He has yams.

For Butter;—He has honey and treacle.

For Potatoes;—The plantain *and substantial cocoa-root*, which, for its invigorating qualities, and delicious flavour, he prefers to all others; besides which he has the large sweet potatoe of the West Indies.

For a *little Sugar*;—He has ten times more than the European labourer.

For Tea;—He has abundance of coffee.

For Beer;—He has grog, or punch, made with limes or lemons,

which grow on the hedges in abundance, and he sweetens it with
sugar, or preserved tamarinds, at his pleasure.

For Coals;—He has as much wood as he pleases.

For Candles;—He has the castor oil in abundance, which we purchase *at a half guinea a pint, as medicine, of the druggist.*

For Rent;—He has his own house, which is as much his own, as any
building erected on a leasehold estate in England, *which goes to whom he
pleases at his death, with his other property,* which I firmly believe, was
never deviated from, *when no law existed to secure it to him.*[24]

Rose Price went on to elaborate the idyllic life of the slave on the
Jamaican plantation of 'a gentleman with whom I am acquainted'
which bore a remarkable superficial similarity to Worthy Park. Of the
4,450 acres of land on the estate,

... 400 of which are canes, and 600 are in grass, *all the rest,* wood-
lands, &c., amounting to 3,450 acres of land *are dedicated to the population of the estate* (500 in number) to cultivate in provisions, *of which
they take to themselves as much as they please;* and a negro and his family
generally cultivate annually a new piece of ground in provisions, of
about 40 laces or poles, besides having about three times that quantity
of ruinate provision ground, which require no further care, (the cultivation of former years) to produce him food, in all about an acre to a
family, *which is as much his own property as a freehold estate can be,* and
his return for seed is one hundred-fold ... more I need not say to
prove that the negro wants not to toil *for his victuals,* the greatest
object of a poor white man, many of whom both in England and
Ireland, have been starved to death.[25]

The only problem in this apparent earthly paradise was to discover
the way in which the black man was, '*to be made (advantageously to himself and his white brethren) a free labourer.* . . . It is a fact, *which cannot be
contradicted,*' wrote Price with his unquenchable optimism, '*that one
month's easy labour in the year, will provide a negro and his family, in the
island of Jamaica, all . . . necessaries of life in abundance. The important
question, therefore, is, how is he to occupy his time the remaining eleven
months of the year, when he is no longer compelled to labour? and what
inducement has he to labour as a free-man?*'[26]

As was the wont of the slave-owning negrophobe, Rose Price pointed to the examples of the 'free' colony of Sierra Leone and the republic of Haiti to illustrate the fate of the Negro freed from coercion. In Haiti, he pointed out, even Christophe (the darling of the emancipists) had been forced to introduce the savage strictures of the *Code Rural* in an attempt to rescue the languishing economy. Rose Price's idea of 'coercion' was clearly slavery in all but name, and would have included the generous application of the driver's whip. In the most distasteful—and salacious—section of his pamphlet, Price praised the mildness of the driver's whip when compared with the cat o' nine tails so frequently employed on 'free English soldiers and sailors'. The driver's whip was,

> . . . *made of the lightest substance of bark hemp*, which is taken from the pingwin or plantain tree, *and is not half as thick or heavy as the cart whip*, and the negroes are never flogged *above* the waistband of their trowsers, but like boys at Westminster and Eton schools, except when they are condemned to be flogged, *by a bench of magistrates, at the workhouse, and then it is with a cat o' four tails* (and not nine). . . . With respect to the severity of the driver's whip, and the boatswain's or drummer's cat, all men, and naval officers who have been in the West Indies, can testify that the cat o' nine tails *inflicts a punishment considerably more severe than the driver's whip*, and as a proof of it, at the late rebellion in Jamaica, the negroes who were, by the laws of the country, condemned to be flogged, *were punished a la militaire, with a cat o' nine tails;* and there is not a negro of credit in Jamaica, that will not testify to the severer punishment of the cat o' nine tails.[27]

Despite his nominal concessions to egalitarian sentiment, Rose Price clearly believed in the natural inferiority of the Negro, who was designed by a convenient Providence to be a hewer of wood and a drawer of water, while 'many an opulent English family' lorded it in their distant mansions. Price's *Pledges* ended with an intemperate attack upon the motion for immediate and unconditional emancipation recently passed by 'a meeting of the Wesleyan, Independents, and Baptist ministers of Truro', the spiritual brethren of those nonconformist missionaries commonly held to have stirred up the Negroes

of Trelawny to the rebellion of Christmas 1831. Unconditional freedom, thundered the lord of Trengwainton, was, 'utterly impossible,
unless it is intended to abandon the West Indian Islands to the negroes, to
live in idleness and vice!' The Negro should be 'coerced to labour, by
direct means, otherwise he will cultivate no land, except for the purpose
of procuring such necessaries and comforts for himself and family *as
he may desire*.

'. . . And as coercive labour *is not a state of freedom*', concluded Rose
Price with the most banal of his *non sequiturs*,

it would appear he is destined by Providence to labour in a state of
slavery, *of some sort or other*, till the curse of Adam is removed from the
face of the earth, and from the brow of man in God's appointed time.
The freedom of black men is attended with difficulties (by the laws of
nature and of God himself) *which never impeded the freedom of white men*.
Nature presents every reason for the white man's freedom as a *fellow
labourer on earth;* and every reason for the black man's bondage, *as
such, to cause the earth to produce its abundance. . . .*'[28]

The facts and figures available from Worthy Park in the period immediately before Emancipation do provide evidence that the lives of
the slaves on the estate were not quite so nasty, brutish, and short as
the emancipists maintained; but it should be borne in mind that this
was twenty-five years after the abolition of the slave trade and following at least a dozen years of legislated amelioration, points which were
carefully ignored in Rose Price's pamphlet. Moreover, the hypocrisy
of many of Rose Price's arguments is patent when we know of his
speculation in slaves in anticipation of compensation, and realize how
much worse the fate of Worthy Park might have been had the estate
suddenly been deprived of its labour supply in 1834.

In the years after 1807, and probably also in the period rather before
that during which Worthy Park did not rely heavily on fresh African
slaves, the ratio between the sexes achieved a healthier balance and the
birth-rate rose considerably. Besides this, the general health of the
slaves seems to have improved with the gradual improvement in their
diet and working conditions, and mortality declined, despite occasional

epidemics, such as the siege of measles in 1821. Consequently, the Negro population of the estate rose steadily, even without purchases, to a peak in 1817, maintaining itself roughly at this level until the increasing number of manumissions in the 1820s and 1830s brought about a steady decline. In 1811, the slave population of Worthy Park was 505, and this rose steadily to 527 in 1817. In 1821 it fell again to 505, in a year when at one time nearly 100 slaves were sick with measles, and thereafter, by steady stages, to 448 in 1827, as up to a dozen slaves were manumitted in each year.[29] In 1830, the population soared once more to 522 with the purchase of more than 100 Negroes from Arthur's Seat estate, declining gradually again to 467 in the year of Emancipation.[30]

By 1817, no less than 66 per cent of the slaves at Worthy Park were creoles, or island-born, and by 1831 this proportion had risen to 88 per cent.[31] As the flow of African Negroes—the majority of them males over 18 years of age—dried up, the ratio of women in the population naturally rose, a tendency that was accelerated by the greater number of manumissions and sales of males in the last days of slavery, and the perceptibly greater life-expectancy of the females.[32] By 1817 there were 286 females to 241 males at Worthy Park, and in 1824, 278 to 206, bidding fair to reverse the ratio between the sexes of the mid-eighteenth century altogether.

At the same time, the birth-rate rose to much more tolerable levels and the death-rate declined. In 1813, no less than 88 out of the 511 slaves, or 17·2 per cent, were under the age of six, having been born on the estate since the abolition of the trade in slaves. With an average of at least 18 successful births a year, this indicates a birth-rate of almost 4 per cent. Between 1811 and 1817, only 90 slaves died at Worthy Park, a death-rate of 12·86 slaves or 2·5 per cent a year, which predicates an annual net increase of practically 1·5 per cent. It should be pointed out, however, that 1811–17 was a period free from epidemics and that in bad periods, such as 1821–2 and 1830–3, the death-rate was almost double the earlier average. Nonetheless, for the years for which we have data over the whole period 1811–37, 250 slaves or apprentices died in 19 years, an average of 13·2 per year and a death-rate of 2·6 per

Worthy Park: Numbers of Slaves, 1810–35

	Worthy Park records Total	Males	Females	'Givings in' (Almanacks)	'Vestry returns'
1810				491	
1811	505	225	280		
1812	503	229	274		
1813	511	235	276		
1814	514	235	279		
1815	514	237	277	518	
1816	527	240	287	511	
1817	527	241	286	526	
1818					
1819					
1820				514	
1821	505	223	282	514	
1822	494	213	281	499	
1823	496	215	281	494	
1824	484	206	278	487	
1825					
1826				469	
1827				448	
1830	461			397 ('Labourers')	522 (503 taxable)
1831	334 ('Labourers')				517 (501)
1832	309 ('Labourers')				494 (478)
1833	296 ('Labourers')				483 (469)
1834	266 ('Labourers')				467 (454)
1835	260 ('Apprentices')				417

From *Worthy Park Plantation Books*, 1811–17; 1821–4; 1830–6; *Jamaica Alma-nacks*, 1811, 1816–18, 1821–5, 1827–31.

cent. Infancy and youth were the most vulnerable ages. Of the 88 slaves born between 1808 and 1812, apparently only 58 survived until 1821, and 39 to 1831, when they would have been between 19 and 23 years of age.[33] Yet even these rather depressing mortality figures only indicate an annual death-rate of 3·1 per cent, a mere fraction of the death-rate of unseasoned Africans in the days of the transatlantic slave trade.[34]

From the somewhat primitive diagnoses entered in the records, it seems that slaves died of a wide range of afflictions. Of 222 causes of death given between 1811 and 1834, 53 were from old age, 'infirmity', or 'debility' and 9 slaves were killed or died after accidents. Of the remainder, 23 died of 'fever' or dysentery, 22 of dropsy, 21 of yaws or 'ulceration', 15 of consumption, and 11 of various other pulmonary complaints, Worms and 'worm fever' accounted for 11 deaths, 10 died from 'convulsions' or 'palsy', seven from 'dirt-eating', and 4 each from measles, whooping cough, and smallpox. Six women died in childbirth and six infants were listed as having died shortly after birth for no specific reason. Among other causes of death given were lockjaw, scrofula, water on the brain, catarrh, a menstrual stoppage, and even 'a sudden Act of God'. Except for a single case of a 'lung abscess', nothing akin to cancer was diagnosed. But the most remarkable conclusions than can be derived from Worthy Park during this period are the high proportion of slaves who apparently died from natural causes, and the small numbers of those actually carried off by epidemics which in an earlier age would have proved widely fatal.

The expectation of life of Negroes at Worthy Park increased steadily during the early nineteenth century, though the average age, after rising considerably between 1813 and 1821, declined somewhat by 1831. The initial increase indicates a higher survival rate for the middle aged as conditions improved and the young were not yet numerous, and the subsequent decline the cumulative result of an improving birthrate after 1808. In 1831, the average age of the 40 African-born was 60·7 years, and of the 29 'superannuated', 67·0; and yet the average age of all slaves at Worthy Park was 29·3, and of the 227 listed workers, 28·3.

Combining the vital statistics, totalling 1,266 entries, available for Worthy Park in 1813, 1821, and 1831, provides a broad analysis of the slaves on at least one estate during the period of Amelioration. The average age of all slaves was 30·1 years, and of the workers—those between 6 and 65—32·7 years. Those under 6 years of age represented 15·5 per cent of the total, and those over 65, 5·1 per cent (with 1·6 per cent over 75 years of age). Those aged 6 to 15 comprised 22 per cent of the total, and the subsequent decades descending proportions of 15·9 per cent, 15·3 per cent, 13·8 per cent, 11·1 per cent, and 7·6 per cent. The oldest recorded slave was a 'nurse' called Dorothy, 92 in 1821, who had been born during the lifetime of Colonel Charles Price.[35]

The Worthy Park statistics bear favourable comparison with those

Worthy Park: Slaves in Each Year-Group

	1813	1821	1831		1813	1821	1831
1	21	19	5	47	1	12	7
2	18	5	4	48	2	6	2
3	6	16	3	49	10	9	2
4	15	14	7	50	2	4	4
5	28	14	7	51	4	1	6
6	14	14	4	52		8	4
7	8	10	3	53	1	10	3
8	17	13	8	54	9	3	1
9	5	8	3	55	6	1	2
10	7	14	12	56		3	3
11	9	4	6	57	1	11	7
12	5	13	8	58	1	4	1
13	9	19	8	59	11	1	5
14	3	13	11	60	2		
15	5	3	11	61		1	4
16	5	5	10	62		8	3
17	2		6	64	7		1
18	12	7	7	65			
19	5	2	10	66		1	2
20	11		8	67	1	8	4
21	3	4	7	68	1		1
22	4	2	5	69	6		1
23	8	2	9	70			
24	21	4	7	71		3	
25	12	2	6	72		4	5
26	13	3	3	73	1		2
27	11	3	10	74			
28	4	5	6	75		1	
29	10	2	4	76			1
30	4	2	5	77		4	1
31	11	5	6	78	2		
32	13	4	3	79	4		
33	8	12	5	80			
34	4	8	2	81		1	1
35	6	5	3	82			
36	3	5	2	83	2		
37	3	5	3	84	1		
38	8	3	3	85			1
39	17	8		86			
40	8	12	7	87			
41	13	9	4	88			
42	5	3	6	89			
43	1	3	4	90			
44	11	1		91			
45	8	5		92		1	
46	3	7					

produced for the first census of 'free' Jamaica in 1844, or even with the figures for modern Jamaica. They were almost certainly more healthy than those for the industrial cities of England during the same period.

	Worthy Park 1813–31	St. John's parish 1844	St. John's, St. Thomas, St. Dorothy, and St. Catherine, 1844	Modern Jamaica (1943)
Aged under 5	10·5	9·2	12·6	11·9
5–10	12·4	11·7	12·6	11·9
10–20	19·1	17·5	16·0	19·5
20–40	28·0	31·5	32·1	30·3
40–60	21·8	27·5	20·7	16·1
Over 60	7·8	9·8	5·0	6·2

Remarkable differences lie in the higher percentage of infants and lower percentage of aged in the four parishes when compared with Worthy Park; but this is almost certainly because of the urbanization around Spanish Town in St. Catherine's, Old Harbour in St. Dorothy, and Linstead in St. Thomas-ye-Vale, for the 1844 figures show even fewer young and more old in rural St. John's parish as a whole than at Worthy Park in the earlier period.[36] The most startling fact of all is the difference between the percentages of those aged 40 and over at Worthy Park in the last days of slavery and in Jamaica in 1943: 29·6 per cent to 22·3 per cent!

Although Rose Price was guilty of exaggeration in this respect, there is no doubt that the great improvement in the health of the Negroes even before Emancipation was due largely to the increase in the consumption of fresh 'ground provisions'. It is also likely that the work load expected of each slave was imperceptibly eased during the last three decades of slavery, so that the daily tasks expected of the ex-slaves during Apprenticeship were greatly less than those enforced during the eighteenth century.[37] At Worthy Park, for example, the traditional system of three field work gangs had changed to one of four by 1821. In that year, the Great Gang alone totalled 167 slaves, all over 17 years of age, with a Second Gang of 55 aged 10–17, a Third Gang of 52 of those between 8 and 13, and a Fourth Gang of 27 children aged 6–7, under the direction of a 'Driveress'. The total of 301 field

Loading sugar into ships. Old print showing coasting vessels.

'The New Road' over Lluidas Blue Mountain to Ewarton, built by Rose Price in 1794. An eighteenth-century watercolour, probably by Hakewill. (*See Chapter Seven*)

labourers represented an increase of about 37 per cent over those employed in 1795, without any noticeable increase in the amount of work required.[38]

The brutalizing aspects of the system, however, remained, particularly since after 1795 Rose Price obdurately continued an absentee. The violent disaffection that ran through western Jamaica at Christmas 1831, to be countered by a repression ten times bloodier, did not reach into Lluidas Vale; but this was more likely due to the backward remoteness of the region than to the benign nature of the plantocratic régime. Worthy Park was apparently spared the unwelcome attentions of sectarian missionaries, but even during the Amelioration period we hear practically nothing of religion, and no inkling at all of education, or the institution of marriage for the slaves. If pressed, Rose Price's fellow planters tended to claim that their rule of the slaves was justifiably paternalistic, pointing out that a smattering of education in Trelawny had merely led to dissatisfaction through a misreading of the newspapers by the few literate slaves. The Church of England, out of which sprang the disgracefully militant Colonial Church Union disbanded by Governor Lord Mulgrave in 1833, was so inextricably connected with the Establishment that its extension to the slaves was almost unthinkable, and formal marriage was a custom claimed to be distasteful to the slaves because it was inconvenient to the estates.[39]

Whipping and its threat remained an essential component of the slaves' existence. As Rose Price pointed out in his *Pledges*, the punishment of thirty-nine lashes by the whip 'for felony or any great crime' could, by 1832, only be legally administered by the manager of an estate 'and by no underling whatever';[40] but even the most indulgent of absentee proprietors could not ensure that the law was carried out properly, nor restrain a sadistic manager. Unfortunately, Worthy Park in the later 1820s seems to have suffered from such a creature in John Blair, who was attorney for four nearby estates as well as attorney and resident manager of Worthy Park.[41] An itinerant plantation bookkeeper called Benjamin M'Mahon, albeit scurrilous, wrote in 1839 that if John Blair 'had not the satisfaction of mangling the flesh of ten or a dozen negroes before breakfast every morning his countenance would be black and threatening; but on the contrary, after indulging in his morning's amusement, he would be cheerful and pleasant'. The manager himself told M'Mahon that if the Negroes were not seen to be wearing bloody breech cloths during crop time, the word would get around that the estate was 'going to hell'.[42]

Sir Rose Price's Cornish campaign for the West India interest was, initially, a signal failure. After the General Election of December 1832, the reformed House of Commons, already shorn of thirteen rotten boroughs in Cornwall alone, contained only sixteen Members with West Indian interests, compared with as many as seventy-five in 1780.[43] Emancipation was inevitable, but the right of property and landownership were still too strong for the demands of the emancipist extremists to be fully satisfied. The statesmanlike, if imperious, Lord Stanley, coming to the Colonial Office only in March 1833, steered through an Emancipation Act that included both substantial compensation for the slave-owners and coercion for the ex-slaves in the form of temporary 'Apprenticeship' for the Negroes of working age.[44]

The political astuteness of Stanley's Act of 1 August 1833 can be seen in the ease with which it passed its divisions at Westminster and the speed with which the colonial legislatures competed to comply with its requirements, and also in the virulence with which it was attacked from either wing. To the emancipists, Apprenticeship was but slavery cloaked: to the 'West Indians', the compensation, though much greater than the £15,000,000 loan originally proposed, was still inadequate. Twenty million pounds in direct compensation was the largest similar sum raised by the British Parliament before the twentieth century; but to such proprietors as Sir Rose Price and the Earl of Talbot a little arithmetic disclosed that however divided among the 675,000 slaves in the British Empire, this sum would amount to little more than a third of their market value, and only a fraction of the combined debts owed by the planters to their English creditors. To those who had speculated in Negroes in expectation of continued slavery or more generous compensation, the Emancipation Act was yet another disappointment.

To Rose Price, who still held his land and the command of the labourers to work it,[45] the Act was less disastrous than to the Earl of

Talbot and his associates, whose equities in Worthy Park were unredeemable mortgages and most of the slaves themselves. Yet Rose Price did not live to see the effects of the freeing of the slaves, since he died on 29 September 1834, just eight weeks after the Emancipation Act came into force.

In the inventory tacked to his will, Sir Rose Price was credited with 274 slaves, valued at £11,265, an average of £43 per head.[46] When the compensation claims were settled, however, his estate received only £1,662 for 79 slaves, or about £21 per head. The vast majority of the slaves were shown to belong to the Earl of Talbot, along with the Hon. J. C. Talbot and Lord Sherborne, who, proportionately, fared even worse, being awarded only £4,661 for 543 slaves, an average of less than £9 per slave.[47] All in all, Sir Rose Price's Jamaican estate was valued at no less than £133,823; but the general overvaluation was found to be as great as in the case of the slaves, with Worthy Park hopelessly committed to its many creditors.

For Rose Price's numerous surviving children, most of whom had already received their settlement from the estate during the lifetime of their father, the proving of the will must have been a bitter disappointment. The baronet's eldest son, Rose Lambart Price, had already died (in 1824), and the successor to the title, Charles Dutton Price, had long been alienated from the family. In a classic nineteenth-century manner, Sir Rose Price cut off his eldest surviving son, literally, with a shilling, 'which is more than his base and unnatural conduct towards me and my family deserves but I will and I hope that though he may for a time persist in the career of vice and infamy which now mark his conduct he may die a penitent sinner in the strict sense of our Blessed Saviour'.[48] The other sons, though rather more fortunate in their father's approbation, were also scattered. Francis, namesake of the founder of the family and great-grandfather of the present baronet, was a Captain in the 19th Regiment of Foot and 78th Highlanders, living only until 1839. John (1808–57) was a lawyer in the colonial service who rose to the pinnacle of being Chief Magistrate of Hobart, Van Diemen's Land; and Thomas (1817–65), early in his career an officer in the 60th Rifles, became in time the Lieutenant Governor of

Dominica and British Honduras.[49] Although three of the spinster sisters made a fruitless attempt to rescue Spring Garden by re-purchasing it from its trustees in 1838 for £4,999,[50] it was left to George Price (1812–90), the second-youngest son, to take up the burden of managing Worthy Park and to spend the majority of his life in unprofitable Jamaica, struggling with the debts of the encumbered estate and the problems of an island once wealthy though enslaved, but now impoverished though nominally free.

NOTES

[1] Davies Gilbert, *Parochial History of Cornwall*, I, 88.

[2] Pares, *West India Fortune*, 3–6; Boyd Alexander, *England's Wealthiest Son*, A *Study of William Beckford*, London, 1962.

[3] For an account of the sale of Trengwainton in 1839, see *Journal of the Statistical Society of London*, ii, 208. It was re-sold to the Bolitho family, the present owners, in 1866, for £33,000; *A Complete Parochial History of Cornwall*, Truro, William Lake, 1870, III, 219–20.

[4] That is, £6,000 against £2,500. In 1848, Thomas Price claimed that his father Rose Price had once received £13,000 a year.

[5] Davies Gilbert, I, 289.

[6] Edgar A. Rees, *Old Penzance*, Penzance, privately printed, 1956, 26–7.

[7] Sir Rose Price was the President of the Penzance Public Library from 1818 to 1824; Cyril Noall, *The Penzance Library, 1818–1968*, Penzance, 1968, 6–8. He became President of the Savings Bank in 1818 and of the S.P.C.K. branch in 1824. Both of the latter posts involved him in controversies, which can be traced in the Boase Papers, B.M. Add. MSS. 29281, ff. 133, 207, 218, 226. A letter written by Price to the Rev. C. V. Legrice (first Secretary of the Penzance Library) in January 1824, on a tedious religious issue, is of surpassing rudeness, in which attempted irony comes out as offensive sarcasm; *ibid.*, 207. The salt duties, a controversy in 1818, penalized the Cornish pilchard industry, which relied on exports to the West Indies as well as to southern Europe.

[8] Elizabeth Lambart's father Charles was married to Frances Dutton, sister of Ralph, Lord Sherborne, and her grandfather had been married to Thomasine Rochfort, sister of the first Earl of Belvedere. Rose's eldest son, Rose Lambart (1799–1826) married Catherine, the widow of the second Earl of Desart; his fifth son George (1812–90) married the Hon. Emily Plunkett, daughter of Lord Dunsany; and his daughter Jane married the Hon. Percy Moreton, son of the first Earl of Ducie. Elizabeth, the eldest daughter (1805–47) married John Basset in 1826; G. C. Boase, *Collecteana Cornubiensia*, Truro, Netherton and Worth, 1890. Portreath, just below Tehidy on the Atlantic coast of Cornwall, was the terminus for the first railway in Cornwall, begun in 1809, which served the mines around Redruth and St. Day; D. B. Barton, *The Redruth and Chacewater Railway, 1824–1915*, Truro, Barton, 1960, 14–15.

⁹ *Burke's Peerage, Baronetage and Knightage*, under 'Price of Trengwainton'.

¹⁰ These dealings are unravelled at great length in subsequent deeds, such as I.R.O. Deeds, 822/1 (1838), as well as in Rose Price's will (1831), I.R.O. Wills, 116/11. See also John Price to Thomas Smith, I.R.O. Deeds, 423/68 (1794). *Ibid.*, 481/81; 822/1.

¹¹ *Ibid.*, 481/81.

¹² *Ibid.*, 822/1.

¹³ Rose Price's will provides ample evidence of the importance he attached to his Jamaican estate records and their preservation. See Preface. The haphazard patterns of Thetford and Swansea when contrasted with Worthy Park are evident from the map of 1794, C.O. 441/4/4, 5. For the tumbledown condition of Mickleton in 1813 see *Worthy Park Plantation Book*, 1811–17, 84, compared with the frequent accounts of new buildings, repairs, and the good condition of buildings and plant at Worthy Park in subsequent books; for example, *ibid.*, 1821–4, 31 December 1821.

¹⁴ 'London, June 1, 1822: Shipped to Thomas Brailsford at Port Henderson on account and risk of Sir Rose Price—A Copper rum still to work off 680 gallons up to the manhole, shallow and in the improved plan to boil off quickly saving time and fuel, with brass manhole and cover ground steam tight with safety valves, copper loops to screw the head to same. Improved round waterway brass cock for discharging the same £23.4.4. A copper cone head with a large opening in the neck the same being well tinned with a square piece copper pipe to attach the same to the main worm on the estate, the arm and soldering to neck, so made to work with a condenser, £320.4.7.' *Worthy Park Plantation Book, 1821–4.* The cane-cutting mill was inserted with the date 1825 on the map of 1794, C.O. 441/4/4, 3.

¹⁵ I.R.O. Deeds, 679/206 (Russell and Derry Pens); 801/83 (Arthur's Seat slaves); 740/100–2 (Cocoree, 1826). The 127 slaves bought from Arthur's Seat cost £6,100, or an average of £48 each.

¹⁶ *Parliamentary Papers*, 1831–2, xx, quoted in W. L. Burn, 23.

¹⁷ These figures are nearly all derived from Ragatz's invaluable *Statistics*, including I, xxvi; V, v, vii; VI, i. The removal of the sugar drawbacks was by an Act of 59 Geo. III, c. 52. See also W. L. Burn, 23.

¹⁸ Computed by valuing sugar at £25 a hogshead and rum at £10 a puncheon. In 1811, Worthy Park produced 456 hogsheads of sugar and 147½ puncheons of rum, and in 1821, 479 hogsheads and 204 puncheons. Figures for the period 1815–34 are not regularly available, but Rose Price in 1834 reported that his estate was still expected to produce 500 hogsheads of sugar a year.

¹⁹ That is, from 33s. in 1821 to 24s. in 1831. Although Rose Price claimed an expected production of 500 hogsheads, the actual average was probably closer to 460 than to the average of 509 for 1795–1815.

²⁰ Mulgrave to Goderich, 17 April 1833, C.O. 137/188, quoted in W. L. Burn, 25.

²¹ L. J. Ragatz, *Guide for the Study of British Caribbean History, 1763–1834*, published as the Annual Report of the American Historical Association, Vol. III, Washington, 1930.

²² Published by T. Vigurs, Penzance, 1832.

²³ *Pledges*, 15. Rose Price castigated the authors of the abolition of the slave trade as self-advertising monomaniacs, who had been guilty 'of the greatest cruelty to ten thousands of the sons of Africa, whom they have driven into the

dreadful slavery of foreigners, and the destruction of many an opulent English family'.

24 *Pledges*, 8–9.

25 *Ibid.*, 10–11.

26 *Ibid.*, 11.

27 *Ibid.*, 1–2.

28 Rose Price cited Genesis c. 9, v. 25 in support of his case; *ibid.*, 32.

29 On 9 July 1821, 97 of Worthy Park's 503 slaves were sick with measles, with 162 listed as 'sickly' altogether; *Worthy Park Plantation Book, 1821–4*. The highest number of slaves manumitted in one year appears to have been nineteen, nearly all males, in 1834; *ibid.*, *1830–6*.

30 I.R.O. Deeds, 773/162. See accompanying table of slave population.

31 That is, 338:169 in 1817 and 295:40 in 1831; *Worthy Park Plantation Books*, 1811–17; 1830–6. In 1831, the youngest of the Africans was 50 years old.

32 For similar groups of working slaves in 1813, the average age of the males was 30 years, and of the women, 32; *ibid.*, 1811–17.

33 These figures all computed from the lists of slaves at Worthy Park on 1 January 1813, 9 July 1821, and 1 January 1831. The annual toll of deaths at Worthy Park fluctuated greatly, though the worst year of which we have record, 1830, still saw only 23 deaths. From the average of just under 13 out of 514 slaves between 1811 and 1817, the figures were: 1821, 10 out of 505; 1822, 17 of 494; 1823, 8 of 496; 1824, 18 of 484; 1830, 23 of 522; 1831, 21 of 517; 1832, 16 of 494; 1834, 7 of 467. In 1835, only five apprentices died, in 1836, 12, and a similar number in 1837. The ages of those who died were not given. This information was among the 'Increase and Decrease' data in the *Worthy Park Plantation Book*, 1811–17; 1821–4; 1830–6.

34 And even these figures may be exaggerated since the lists of slaves for 1821 and 1831 are obviously deficient.

35 She had also been the oldest slave in 1813, then 84. The records do not say whether she was African or Jamaican-born. The oldest slave in 1831 was Monimia, aged 85, who had been born in Jamaica in 1744.

36 The figures for Worthy Park re-computed into different age-groups to match summary of 1844 census returns in *Jamaica Almanack for 1845*, 84–5. Presumably, as in the burgeoning English towns during the Industrial Revolution, the young and able-bodied migrated to the towns, raising the birth-rate, while the older remained in the countryside, or retired there to die.

37 See Appendix II, 328.

38 That is, 301:219.

39 The chapel which was the fore-runner of the present Anglican Church in Lluidas Vale was begun by Rose Price in 1820s, and there were some instances of slave baptisms at Worthy Park as early as 1811; but these were tentative moves and may even have been regarded as 'inoculative' by Worthy Park's owner. See above, VI, note 111. For a general account of attitudes and actions in this period, see W. L. Burn, 90–8.

40 *Pledges*, 1.

41 Lloyd's, Juan de Bolas, Watermount and Mount Pleasant; *Jamaica Almanack for 1837*, 2.

42 Benjamin M'Mahon, *Jamaica Plantership*, Effingham, London, 1839, 59–63.

43 *Parliamentary Pocket Companion for 1833*, London, 1833, cited by W. L. Burn, 100, n. 1. The Cornish M.P. Sir Richard Vyvyan even stated that the Election had

completely eradicated the West India interest. The *Companion* calculated that 104 M.P.s, 47 of them new Members, were committed to immediate Emancipation.

⁴⁴ The process of drafting and passage is succintly described in W. L. Burn, 100–20. The British Act, drafted by James Stephen in a single week-end, was merely a guide for the colonial legislatures to follow, though the systems of Apprenticeship were practically identical in the end. Apprenticeship (which was not adopted at all in Antigua or Bermuda) was intended to last for eight years in the case of praedial workers, and six years for domestics, though in the event the Negroes became 'full free' on 1 August 1838. Slaves under the age of six were freed on 1 August 1834, provided they were maintained by their parents.

⁴⁵ He was legally, 'Owner in fee' of Spring Garden, 'Owner in fee, tenant in tail' of Worthy Park and Mickleton. Apprentices were, of course, tied to their estate, not to their owner.

⁴⁶ Archives, Inventories 151/210-13; I.R.O. Wills, 116/11. Rose Price was credited with 156 slaves at Worthy Park, valued at £6,279, or £42 each on the average; 11 being 'tradesmen' at £70 apiece, 61 in the Great Gang at £50, 29 in the Second Gang at £40, 14 in the Third at £30, and 5 in the Fourth at £55, with 36 invalids and children, valued at an average of £17 each. His 49 slaves at Mickleton were valued at £1,968, an average of £42 and ranging from £17 to £50; and his 69 at Spring Garden at a total of £3,018, averaging £44 and ranging from £30 to £70.

⁴⁷ 'Account of All Sums of Money Awarded by the Commissioners of Slavery Compensation', 21 December 1837, 11, 605, 606, Institute of Jamaica. All of Rose Price's slaves were at Spring Garden; those of the Talbots included 464 at Worthy Park (£3,579) and 79 at Mickleton Pen (£1,082).

⁴⁸ I.R.O. Wills, 116/11, enrolled 3 February 1835. Rose Price's other children were forbidden to have any dealings with Charles Dutton Price, on pain of similar treatment. The will oozes with religiosity to the point of the macabre. Rose Price's coffin was not to be nailed down for four days or until putrescence had set in, and he was to be buried with a locket of his wife's hair around his neck.

⁴⁹ *Burke's Peerage, Baronetage and Knightage.*

⁵⁰ I.R.O. Deeds, 819/228; Emily, Anna, and Julia Price to Earl Talbot, J. C. Talbot, and Lord Sherborne, 11 October 1838. Guanaboa was sold off by the sisters piecemeal, though Spring Garden was retained until 1869, when it was sold to L. F. Verley, I.R.O. Deeds, 950/103. See also *ibid.*, 861/200 (1844), 872/10 (1845), and 951/208 (1869) concerning Guanaboa, and 934/2 (1862), 947/89 (1867), and 949/19 (1868) concerning Spring Garden. Spring Garden in 1970 is still owned by the Verley family, and the Great House still stands, though in a sadly decrepit condition.

CHAPTER NINE

The Losing Struggle, 1834-1863

Apprenticeship was a pious fraud, a transitional expedient designed to convert the Negro work-force from the unwieldy coercion of slavery to a system, possibly more efficient but not necessarily more voluntary, of free wage labour. Apprenticeship failed in its operation because of structural faults and was brought to a premature conclusion in 1834; but its results were even less successful, since nothing could have induced the Negroes to continue working the estates save perhaps higher wages and more continuous employment than the estates were willing, or able, to provide. The predominant problem for the sugar industry during the later 1830s and early 1840s was therefore one of labour. A common solution throughout the West Indies was the importation of East Indian 'coolie' labourers; but rare estates, such as Worthy Park, which were able to draw upon fresh sources of capital, streamlined their operations by mechanization.

For a time, results at Worthy Park were promising. Production, which had slipped back 15 per cent during Apprenticeship and by 70 per cent on its sudden ending, picked up steadily until 1846 with the help of a moderate improvement in sugar prices. At this time, Worthy Park was the second-largest producer of sugar in Jamaica and was regarded as a model of improving management. To a large extent the estate seemed to have survived the loss of its guaranteed labour force. Yet in 1847 the equalization of duties coupled with the general depression brought a catastrophic fall in sugar prices which, but for a brief recovery in 1857, continued an inexorable slide until 1866. Despite the efforts of its enlightened resident owner–manager, Worthy Park staggered and fell beneath the weight of its debts, to which had been added the over-optimistic investment in mechanization amounting to at least £30,000.

Average Prices of Sugar in London with Worthy Park Production (where known)
1831–1866

	Price per h/h	Production (h/h)	Income Index (1834= 1,000)		Price per h/h	Production (h/h)	Income Index (1834= 1,000)
1831	23s. 8d.	471	774	1849	25s. 4d.		
1832	27s. 8d.	589	1130	1850	26s. 1d.		
1833	29s. 8d.	484	997	1851	25s. 6d.		
1834	29s. 5d.	489½	1000	1852	22s. 5d.		
1835	33s. 5d.	426½	988	1853	24s. 6d.		
1836	40s. 10d.	407	1154	1854	24s. 1d.		
1837	34s. 7d.	370	889	1855	26s. 4d.		
1838	33s. 8d.	406	949	1856	29s. 5d.	320	654
1839	39s. 2d.	342	928	1857	35s. 2d,	187¼	409
1840	49s. 1d.	139½	480	1858	27s. 4d.	261	496
1841	39s. 8d.	263	724	1859	25s. 11d.	260	472
1842	36s. 11d.	299	771	1860	26s. 10d.	350	689
1843	33s. 9d.	232	545	1861	23s. 5d.	345	561
1844	33s. 8d.	261	610	1862	22s. 1d.		
1845	32s. 11d.	309	706	1863	21s. 6d.		
1846	34s. 5d.	302¾	724	1864	26s. 9d.		
1847	28s. 3d.	266½	528	1865	22s. 1d.		
1848	23s. 8d.			1866	20s. 3d.		

Prices from D. G. Hall, 270; Production 1831–47 from Parliamentary Papers, 47; 1856–61 from Encumbered Estates material at P.R.O.

The sugar estates were comparatively fortunate in that their plight was brought before Parliament in England through the impassioned pleas of their owners and mortgagees, such as Thomas Price and Viscount Ingestre, who gave eloquent testimony concerning Worthy Park to the Select Committee on sugar and coffee of 1848. Parliament, already converted to free trade, did not reinstate protective duties, yet, with some reluctance, it partially rescued the beleaguered estates by the West Indies Encumbered Estates Act of 1854. The unfortunate Negroes had fewer advocates. Stereotyped as inherently idle for refusing to work for wages and made the scapegoats for the failure of the estates, they received only opposition in their often heroic efforts to establish peasant smallholdings, independent townships, and a separate social identity. Worthy Park was not the most unhappy of estates, for its natural advantages allowed it to survive when others failed, and between its proprietor–manager and his workers there was reciprocal respect. Yet, despite the warnings of George Price to Governor Eyre on resigning as Custos of St. Catherine in 1864, the general condition of Jamaica was allowed to deteriorate, until the tragic social upheaval of the following year became inevitable. Thereafter, despite the dissolution of the unrepresentative Assembly and the substitution of Crown Colony government, conditions did not generally improve and the later nineteenth century in Jamaica appears in retrospect a long dark valley, in which the Negroes suffered most of all.

Apprenticeship at Worthy Park, as in the rest of Jamaica, was almost bound to fail since it was neither full freedom nor coercion, and the Stipendiary Magistrates entrusted with carrying out its provisions were too distant, ignorant, or otherwise ineffectual either to protect the Negro or to compel him to work. The estates, while they still listed Apprentices as 'property' were eager to streamline their work-forces and to be relieved of non-productive hands. The ex-slaves, compelled by the Act to work $40\frac{1}{2}$ hours a week for their ex-masters, were eager to labour long hours for the first four days and have the rest of the week for their own pursuits, especially the cultivation of provision grounds.[1] The Magistrate and Police Constable stationed closest to Worthy Park were first at Spanish Town and then at Linstead, still a dozen miles across the mountains, and as official reports on Worthy Park were few and far between, it seems likely that Negroes and estate alike got as much as they could out of the transitional system, untrammelled by much outside interference.[2]

Whatever the reason, the Worthy Park work-force declined remarkably in the years before Apprenticeship ended in 1838. When the last return of slaves on the estate before the Emancipation Act came into effect was made in June 1834, there were 467 slaves registered; and yet on 31 December of the same year only 266 'laboureres belonging to Worthy Park' were listed. This fall was not quite so phenomenal as it appears at first, for the custom of accounting 'labourers' distinct from the total of slaves of all conditions had been in operation since the beginning of 1830. Yet in 1830 the total of 'labourers' had been 420[3] and this had declined somewhat irregularly in annual stages to the 266 of 1834. After 1834 the total declined further, though more slowly, to 260 in 1835, 248 in 1836, and 234 in the last full year of Apprenticeship, 93 of whom were men and 141 women. Over the same period of seven years, the registered Negro population of Spring Garden also fell from 83 to 65 and Mickleton from 86 to 19, representing a total decline on the three Price holdings from 589 to 350, or 59 per cent.

Although mortality figures were not given in the Worthy Park records during Apprenticeship as they had been during slavery, the general health of the 'labourers' had noticeably improved, and it is inconceivable that death accounted for the great decline in their numbers.[4] Manumission was a more likely reason, since in the last days of slavery and even during Apprenticeship Worthy Park, like most estates, capitalized on the willingness of Negroes who had somehow acquired means, to purchase their immediate freedom. In 1834 alone no less than 33 slaves were manumitted from Worthy Park and its associated 'pens', 14 being men, 18 women, and one a child. Yet, in accounting for the total decline it seems also likely that Worthy Park did not, or could not, detain or pursue Negroes who were eager to fend for themselves and went off to 'squat' in the hills.

During the entire Apprenticeship period, Worthy Park appears to have had enough workers to bring in the sugar crop, for as late as 1836 the estate was able to hire out apprentices both to other estates and to the parishes to work on roads, the going rate varying from £3 a year for domestics to £12 for first-class field labourers.[5] By 1837, however, the Worthy Park work-force of 234 was probably little larger than was strictly necessary, and there were signs in the gradual decrease in productivity since 1834 that it was difficult to get even moderate returns from quasi-slaves. In the first year of Apprenticeship at Worthy Park,

266 labourers produced 489 hogsheads of sugar, a ratio of 1·84 hogsheads per worker. This was not substantially lower than the 1·91 hogsheads per worker produced in 1832, though much below the figure of approximately 2·33 hogsheads per worker for the record year of 1812. In 1835 and 1836, however, productivity fell to 1·64 hogsheads per worker and in 1837, to 1·58.[6] After full freedom was granted in 1838, when Worthy Park only employed those workers she needed or could afford, productivity naturally rose once more, even though actual production continued to decline.[7]

Although the actual work achieved steadily fell below expectation, Worthy Park's management constantly attempted to rationalize the estate's work-force throughout the period of Apprenticeship, and even to humanize conditions where possible. In 1837, as a result of the Apprenticeship Act, the 248 labourers were more neatly divided into their occupational categories than ever before a categorization that would become important as the estate had to begin paying wages according to skills and usefulness. Only 17 were listed as craftsmen, six being carpenters, six coopers, two blacksmiths, and one each sawyer, mason, and boiler-man; and four were specialists in charge of the cattle, the hogs, the wagons, and the tallies used for piecework tasks. Nominally, the hated 'gangs' of slavery days has been disbanded, but the 173 manual labourers were still listed under four different 'classes', according to their ages, skills, and fitness, each being ruled by a 'superintendent' in the place of the former headman. In the First Class were 91 of the fittest workers, 82 of whom were under 40 years of age, while in the Second Class were 31 younger or less robust workers, 23 of whom were under 30 years old. The Third Class consisted of 36 of the youngest workers, none of whom was over 20, and the Fourth Class or Grass Cutter group was composed of 15 elderly or infirm workers still capable of manual toil. Of the remaining 50 'apprentices', nine were domestics and four 'nurses' in hospital and field (where they doubled as 'cooks'), ten were superannuated 'watchmen' and 27 listed as unemployed or unemployable.

Although they no longer worked directly under the threat of the lash, Worthy Park's workers doubtless found that the constraints of

Apprenticeship made the prospect of wage labour greatly preferable and the chance of working entirely for themselves the most attractive expectation of all. The hiring-out of apprentices, moreover, did give the Negroes wider experience of life outside the confines of their estate, and the shorter working hours far better chances of selling produce grown by themselves. Significantly, the Stipendiary Magistrate of St. Thomas-ye-Vale reported in April 1836 that the desire of Worthy Park's apprentices to work for wages was 'as strong now as it was once weak, and they labour for hire with more energy than during the estates time . . .',[8] while going on to praise the industry of the Negroes when working their own provision grounds. 'With a few exceptions of indolent characters,' reported the Magistrate, quoting Thomas W. Bullock, Worthy Park's overseer,

the apprentices on this property cultivate their grounds and gardens well . . . they are abundantly supplied with provisions and . . . they cultivate their grounds fully as well as previous to 1st August, 1834 . . . the indolent and idle characters [however] only partially work their grounds, depending a great measure on the different fruits and yams and occasional depredations in their master's cane-fields or in the grounds of their most industrious fellow-apprentices.[9]

Bearing in mind that industrious apprentices would want to work for themselves, and the idle not to work at all, it is not surprising that the sudden changeover to free wage labour on 1 August 1838 produced a labour crisis at Worthy Park, as elsewhere throughout the British West Indies. The crop of 1839 had been well planted in 1837 and 1838, and somehow 342 hogsheads were produced; but in 1840 the estate's production tumbled to $139\frac{1}{2}$ hogsheads, easily the lowest for more than a hundred years.

Worthy Park's co-proprietors and trustees were once more desperate, but with a last flurry of financial ingenuity they consolidated the complicated debts of the estate[10] and, early in 1841, sent out Thomas Price, Sir Rose's youngest son, to see what he could make of the estate. At 24, Thomas Price was just the age that the young Rose Price had been when sent out to Jamaica exactly fifty years before; but either he lacked his father's moral fibre or conditions were infinitely worse than they had been in 1791, for after only four months in Jamaica, Thomas Price returned to England in despair. The labour situation, he reported, was nothing short of disastrous, with only half of Worthy Park's fields in cultivation and the Negroes turning up only when they felt like working. Even though it was crop-time while Thomas Price was in Jamaica and wages were good, the Negroes could not be expected to work more than six hours in the day or $4\frac{1}{2}$ days in an average week. 'They generally went out at seven o'clock in the morning,' he recalled in 1848,

and they would work, with an hour's rest, till about 12, as far as I can remember, and they then turned out again at two or three o'clock and worked a couple of hours in the afternoon . . . and every other week they only worked four days; the usual days of work were Monday, Tuesday, Wednesday and Thursday, and every other week they worked on Friday; the Saturday they always took for themselves....[11]

Because none of the labourers cared to work at night, the Worthy Park factory was forced to close down every evening, and yet, according to Thomas Price, the estate was compelled to pay what workers it could get as much as 2s. a day, or 9s. for a 'week' of 27 hours' work.

To Thomas Price it seemed obvious that the Negroes preferred 'squatting' on the estate to working for wages. 'As a general rule,' he asserted,

the negro is not satisfied with his condition unless he has a horse, a blue tail-coat and a certain amount of land; he will do anything to obtain these; those are the things that he must have, and he can get those by working for a short time, he will then go away and make a holiday . . . they like the *otium cum dignitate*; they occupy their residences, and come down twice a week and work for a couple of days, and then return with a bottle of Bass's ale....[12]

Challenged that bottled ale was scarcely evidence of a champagne existence and that a couple of days' work would not provide a horse and blue tail-coat, Thomas Price had to admit that the independent Negroes made most of their income from growing provision crops for sale in the local markets. Moreover, unless the planters solved their labour problems or were given some form of aid by the imperial government, they would be forced to abandon their estates to the most ambitious and industrious of the Negro cultivators. This would spell ruin not only to the planters, but also to the innumerable mortgagors in England holding liens on West Indian property.[13]

This ultimate pessimism actually dates from 1848, when several remedies had already been tried, without sustained success. In 1843 George Price had gone out to Worthy Park, and he seems to have been at once more obdurate, more humane, and better endowed with financial resources than his younger brother. For another thing, he was already married and intended to make Jamaica his home. In 1839, at the age of 27, he had married the Hon. Emily Plunkett, daughter of the 14th Baron Dunsany, and, indeed, it was largely the financial backing provided by his father-in-law which enabled him to carry on his hopeless rearguard action, lasting twenty years, to save the affairs of Worthy Park.

Thomas Price had acknowledged that in regards to labour Worthy Park did enjoy two definite assets: unlike most estates it possessed a considerable 'old body of negroes' rooted by custom and the use of provision grounds to the estate itself; and because of the decay of the neighbouring estates it could also look forward to a monopoly of the available labour in the enclosed valley of Lluidas Vale.[14] George Price set himself the task of winning over the Negroes of Worthy Park and Lluidas Vale to more zealous and regular work, and in doing so he came to realize what Thomas Price had not grasped during his short sojourn in Jamaica and what the trustees, with their short-sighted concern for the total wage bill could not see: that the 'unreliability' of the Negro (like his 'promiscuity' under slavery) was a product of the system, not the reverse. Lord Bentinck's Select Committee of 1848 came very close to the truth when one of its members asked Thomas Price whether the lack of continuous labour in Jamaica of which the planters complained was not the fault of the planters themselves. 'I think that the negroes having set the example in the matter of not having given continuous labour, it is very possible that the planters may not have given them continuous work,' replied Thomas Price defensively, adding, 'but all the estates which are actually at work, I have reason to believe, would give as much continuous employment as they possibly could.' 'What you want is this,' Price was then asked, 'that at any moment when it suits your convenience you may be able to put your hand on the labourer?' 'Undoubtedly,' the planter flashed back, 'you could not have better expressed my meaning.' 'Can you expect to do that, unless you give continuous employment at continuous wages?' 'Certainly not; there are duties both on the one side and the other.'[15]

There is strong evidence in the wage-bills, as well as his widespread reputation as a fair employer,[16] that George Price during the 1840s did his best to pay fair wages, to iron out the irregular pattern of employment, and to provide better security for his workers. Although the work-force continued to be reduced, the total wage-bill rose; and although Worthy Park relied more heavily on piecework than on weekly rates, the workers probably worked rather more regularly throughout the year. In the first four years of George Price's régime the total wage-bill for non-white workers rose from £3,576 in 1844 to £4,013 in 1845, £4,982 in 1846, and £6,576 in 1847.[17] Compared with modern employment patterns, with very large numbers engaged during crop-time, moderate numbers during planting and the period of 'Christmas work', and very few indeed for the remainder of the year, Worthy Park's wage-bills for non-white workers during the 1840s showed no more than a 20 per cent variation above and below the mean during the crop and inter-crop periods. In a typical year, the average weekly wage-bill was about £95, with peaks of £115 and low points of £75.[18]

George Price's intention was that industry, skill, and loyalty would be rewarded by fair wages and security of employment, but despite his liberal views, a social hierarchy became entrenched at Worthy Park, the effects of which have lasted almost until the present day. At the top of the social scale were the salaried 'Staff', all white men, whose sense of 'apartness' was accentuated by the feeling that since 1834 only their colour and their official position distinguished them from the more ambitious Negroes. While George Price was at Worthy Park his modest salary of £200 a year was the highest paid, though previously the estate had paid £500 to an Attorney and £400 for an 'Attorney-Overseer'. George Price's Overseer, or under-manager, received £140, and the next in line were the 'Manufacturer' or factory-manager at £84 and the Distiller at £80. The six bookkeepers received salaries ranging from £70 down to £42, and even the two white ploughmen brought out from England under contract during the agricultural depression of the 1840s and paid only £35 and £20, regarded themselves as superior to the most talented and indispensable Negro.[19]

The permanently-employed Negroes were headed by a loyal élite consisting of the craftsmen and superintendents earning 2s. 6d. a day or about £28 a year, and ranging down to the watchmen, expected to work seven days and nights for 6s. and the humble rat-catcher paid 3s. a week. At the bottom of the socio-economic scale, however, were the ordinary labourers, whose wages ranged from the 9d. a day paid to female grasscutters and 10½d. for cane-weeders, to the 2s. which a cane-cutter normally made at piecework rates. Indeed, good cane-cutters sometimes earned 12s. a week, more than their superintendents, though their seasonal frenzy was no satisfactory alternative to year-round employment.

One expedient which was completely abandoned by 1844 was the levying of rents on Negro houses and grounds in order to reduce the wage-bills and to tax the Negroes who did not care to work for the estate. In 1839 as much as £342—more than 10 per cent of total wages—was deducted directly from Negroes' pay, and in the following year the total rent on homes was assessed at £257 and on provision grounds, £2,570. Attempts to collect this, however, proved vain and self-defeating. Those from whom rents were collected proved even less willing to work, and those who did not work had no money to pay. In 1842, the entire total of rent collected amounted to £49. 8s., and in 1848 Thomas Price reported that his brother had long since let the

Worthy Park Negroes live rent-free in the houses and on the grounds they had come to regard almost as their own.[20]

Despite paying fair wages and providing rent-free houses and gardens, Worthy Park still suffered from a shortage of labourers, which it sought to remedy by employing indentured immigrants. The first scheme, a misguided attempt in 1841 to renew the importation of white indentured 'servants', had failed even more decisively than its seventeenth-century equivalent. Of Worthy Park's only two recruits, the more ambitious one quickly graduated from the status of ploughman to that of book-keeper; the other, mistaking Jamaican rum for English ale, drank himself to death within eighteen months.[21] In 1841 a Parliamentary Sub-Committee had recommended the importation of 'free' African labourers, and from 1842 Worthy Park received a share of the trickle of 'new Africans' who went to Jamaica.[22] These Negro recruits—who continued to arrive until 1850 and even included escaped American slaves—however, were all too few to answer Worthy Park's needs, suffered from the same problems of training, acclimatization, and disease which had plagued the slaves, and, having identified with the creole Negroes, quickly acquired their distaste for labour on the estate. Much more was hoped for from the importation of Indian 'coolies' which began in 1845, under the sanction of the Colonial Secretary, Lord Stanley, and with the assistance of a Government loan.[23] These labourers, many of whom stayed after their contracts were up and who were reinforced at irregular intervals down to 1917, provided, in time, an important, and ethnically separate, element in Worthy Park's permanent work-force. But in 1848, Thomas Price and the other planters, who were arguing for Government sponsored labour at 2d. a day, were inclined to believe that the Indians did not warrant the cost of their transportation, which was as high as £25 compared with the Africans' £7.[24] Moreover, 'on the greater portion of the estates', asserted Thomas Price with typical exaggeration, 'they are able in a few weeks to earn sufficient money to buy an acre of land, and then they become squatters'.[25]

The most optimistic, visionary and controversial expedient used by George Price to reduce Worthy Park's dependence on casual labour and raise its profitability to compete with countries still employing slaves, was mechanization. From the beginning, George Price 'had to contend against the prejudices and ignorance, both of the negroes and the planters; the latter not only making his innovations the subject of their stupid ridicule, but of petty schemes to thwart them',[26] and in the depression year of 1848 his own brother publicly castigated him as an inexperienced English country gentleman whirled up in the enthusiasm for steam engines and railways which had transformed his native Cornwall.[27] Yet George Price's arguments for mechanization had been very carefully worked out. 'I felt convinced in the first place,' he told a Committee of the Jamaican Assembly in 1843,

that there would be a reduction in the protecting duties. I concluded that whatever amount of labour I was employing for any certain purpose, required the same amount of labour in a slave country. I calculated the expense that was incurred by the slave-owner, and I calculated that if I could accomplish the same purpose, by an investment, even to an equal amount in value of slaves, in simple machinery, subject to very trifling wear and tear, I should always be able to produce sugar cheaper than the slaveholder could. It was in consequence of the general complaint in the country of a want of labour, which could only be overcome by the introduction of machinery.[28]

From 1843 onwards, George Price ordered an increasing quantity of machinery from England, until credit ran out and his horrified trustees summoned him to England to account for his stewardship of Worthy Park. By that time, gross expenditure on the estate had risen from £5,542 in 1843 to £7,481 in 1844, £9,865 in 1845, £12,852 in 1846, and £18,856 in 1847, well over £3,000 having been spent on machinery in 1846 alone.[29] To raise productivity in the fields he purchased many new ploughs and 'clodcrushers' (harrows), aiming to reduce the normal team of oxen from twelve to six.[30] To take up the expected increase in production and bring the capacity of the factory up to thirty hogsheads a week, he bought new boilers and clarifiers, a new mill, a pump, a furnace, and, in April 1846, a magnificent new Boulton and Watt steam engine of 15 horsepower, which cost £1,777.[31] Yet George Price's most original investment was in a light railway several miles long, which was installed in stages between 1844 and 1846. This, the first estate railway in Jamaica, consisted of a main line running east and west with movable branch lines leading into each canefield and another branch to carry out the green trash from the factory. The carriage of canes and trash, which hitherto had employed 8 wains, 30 labourers, and 150 cattle, was now accomplished by eight persons and two dozen mules, with far greater dispatch. The only obvious drawback was that the reduction in the number of cattle meant a shorter supply of animal manure, all the more essential if productivity were to be raised to the maximum.[32]

At the same time as Worthy Park was experimenting with its tramway, the first Jamaican steam railway, which had been constructed between Kingston and Spanish Town in 1844, was being extended as far as the Rio Cobre gorge, in order to serve St. Thomas-ye-Vale and Lluidas Vale.[33] George Price himself was one of the planters behind the extension, having convinced the promoters that if they could carry out his sugar and bring in manure and supplies at low cost, he could double his production.[34] Indeed, when he testified before the Committee of the Jamaican Assembly in 1845, George Price went even further in his optimism. Worthy Park's sugar production, which he had raised from 190 hogsheads in 1843 and 200 hogsheads in 1844 to 400 hogsheads by 15 March 1845, he fully expected with mechanization to exceed the unprecedented total of 700 *tons* in 1846.[35]

Unfortunately, George Price greatly underestimated the difficulties to be overcome in mechanizing, as well as the effects of the loss of protection when coupled with a general economic slump. The machinery was ordered, if not paid for: it was quite another matter to get it to Worthy Park, erect it and have it running smoothly. Much of it was late arriving in Jamaica and then had to wait months on the wharf awaiting transport inland. The Jamaican Railway was less help than anticipated. The charges were high and from the inland terminus the 60 tons of machinery still had to be carted 15–16 miles over the mountains to Worthy Park in thirty wagons hauled by sixteen oxen each. In one year the estate lost no less than 100 draught animals, partly from a drought but mostly from the extra exertions laid upon them. Between 1846 and 1847 the expenditure on wharfage, railway charges and wagonage came to £1,518[36] and Worthy Park found itself unable to afford the railway charges to carry its sugar from Angels on to Kingston. It was therefore all the more discouraging that the opening of the railway had forced the closure of Port Henderson and added a dozen miles to the journey for the sugar wains.

Once up at Worthy Park, the machinery was often ineffectual, either through unsuitability or lack of skill in use. The tramway rails were too light (14 pounds to the yard where 25 pounds would have required half the number of shoes and cross-ties) and being of 'rolled iron' easily rusted in the Lluidas damp. Laid with insufficient ballast, they were hardly more passable than ordinary roadways in wet weather.[37] In the factory it was a tale of unmitigated misfortune, as George Price informed the House of Commons in February 1848:

Worthy Park: Sugar Sales and Income, 1841–1847
(according to Thomas Price, 1848)

	Produced hogsheads	Sold in London hh	Total received £	Average price per hh £ s.	Average per cwt (at 6½ cwt/hh) s. d.	'Official' average (see above, 209) s. d.
1841	263	216	5904	27 6	32 7	39 8
1842	299	273	7309	26 15	32 5	36 11
1843	232	190	4831	25 8	30 10	33 9
1844	261	321	7941	24 14	29 9	33 8
1845	309	214	5866	27 8	33 3	32 11
1846	302¾	352	8954	25 9	30 11	34 5
1847	266½	154	2566	16 12	20 2	28 3
1845 (est.)	468			16 0	19 6	23 8★

★ D. G. Hall, 270, otherwise P.P. 47, 4861; 52, 4915.

N.B. For gross income local sales and rum sales would have to be added. Thomas Price estimated that Worthy Park produced ½ puncheon of rum per hogshead of sugar and that a puncheon received generally about seven-eighths as much as a hogshead. The total in column 3 could therefore be raised by seven-sixteenths for London sales alone, making a total of (£43,371 + £18,975) £62,346 an average of rougly £8,907 for each year 1841–7 for London sales. The overall income must have averaged about £10,000.

... the merchants sent out a new mill in 1845, with ten serious defects in its construction, as pointed out by the engineer selected and sent out by themselves. This unfortunate mill broke, and caused the loss of about £8,000 worth of produce. In 1846 the water power went down to three horses, and there being no other power on the estate, half that crop was lost. In 1846 and 1847 an engine was erected with great labour and at great expense; the crop of 1847 was injured to the extent of at least 200 tons of sugar by the engine not having been sent for nine months after it was ordered. . . .[38]

The combined result was that the produce of Worthy Park in 1846, far from amounting to 700 tons (or 875 hogsheads) totalled 302¾ hogsheads, falling even further to 266½ in 1847.

Compounding the disappointing level of production was a disastrous fall in the price of sugar. In 1840, because of the very shortages caused by labour difficulties, the London price had risen to over 40s. per

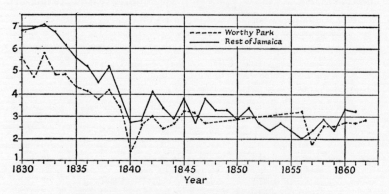

SUGAR PRODUCTION OF WORTHY PARK
AND JAMAICA, 1830–1862

hundredweight, and it had remained good until 1846, when the average London price was 34s. 5d. and Worthy Park received an average of 30s. 11d. For the six years from 1841 to 1846, Worthy Park received an average price of 31s. 8d. per hundredweight or £26. 10s. per hogshead for her sugar and about £14 per puncheon for her rum. Compared with a cost of production which was estimated at £25 for a hogshead of sugar and the half-puncheon of rum which was its by-product, this indicated that but for her huge investments and accumulated debts Worthy Park would have made a profit of up to £8 a hogshead between 1840 and 1846. At the beginning of 1847, however, the estate could only obtain 20s. 2d. per hundredweight, or £16. 12s. per hogshead for her sugars and was faced with a possible loss of up to £2 on each hogshead which she produced.[39]

The sudden slump in sugar prices was the result of the combination of waning protection and a fall in demand through the prolonged depression of 1846–9. In 1846 the new Whig Government of Lord Russell had forced through an Act equalizing the duty on all foreign sugars whether produced by slave or free labour and introducing a sliding scale by which the preference of 7s. per hundredweight enjoyed by colonial sugars would gradually be removed by 1851.[40] This gave a tremendous advantage to Cuba, Puerto Rico, and Brazil, which were said to be able to produce sugar for 4s. 2d. per hundredweight (£3. 10s. a hogshead) or even less.[41] At the same time, England was suffering one of the periodic economic crises which punctuated, and punctured, that expansive age. There were bad corn harvests in 1846 and 1847, the money market was stagnant and the first railway boom (in which more than a thousand companies had been floated) abruptly ended. In the summer and autumn of 1847 banks began to fail and the financial crisis spread to the West Indies like the ripples on a pond. Forty-eight sugar houses in England went bankrupt in eighteen months and, inevitably, with them tumbled the marginal estates. Private and public credit dried up altogether so that planters could not get advances even at usurious rates and colonial government loans at 6 per cent received no tenders whatsoever. Governors, planters, merchants appealed desperately to the imperial government, but free trade reigned. The House debated, the Select Committee presented its report, but all that the government did was to postpone the date when imperial preferences on sugar would be removed, from 1851 to 1854.

Late in 1847, George Price reluctantly joined the gloomy procession of West Indian managers returning to England, summarily recalled by Viscount Ingestre to answer for his 'extravagant mismanagement'.[42] Meanwhile, the trustees held up payment on every bill, redoubling the difficulties faced by Gilbert Shaw, the well-known pluralist Attorney appointed in George Price's place. 'I have been much and anxiously occupied endeavouring to keep things going and the estate from suffering in consequence of the noting of my bills by the trustees,' wrote Shaw to Thomas Price on 30 December 1847,

> The terrible scarcity of money, which as it exists to so great an extent in England, you may imagine is not less felt here; the alarm and apprehension at the banks, and in the mercantile, and indeed entire community, at, I may say, the numberless bills which have been protested in like manner, have brought about a crisis which seems to paralyze everyone. . . . On all sides, I hear of really good estates being abandoned by the proprietors, and there does not appear any one ready to come forward to carry them on either as lessees or purchasers. . . . It seems to me that little short of a miracle will save this country.[43]

As to Worthy Park, Gilbert Shaw had to admit that conditions were not quite so bad as elsewhere in Jamaica and that retrenchment and good fortune might save it from the fate of its neighbours. 'The estate is in really good order so far as the field is concerned,' he wrote,

> and we will begin the new year at a greatly reduced call for expense. What the general result will be at the end of the crop I cannot foretell, everything will depend on the price of produce. As you may understand from this letter, I have no faith in our ability to stand up against the slave grower of sugar. He will destroy us and then obtain a higher price for his produce than ever we did, and when Government wish to assist us we will be past all relief. Among the estates likely to go, I think [Swansea and Thetford] may be named; the former is, in fact, now for sale, and, of course, no one will buy. In happier times it would have been a splendid addition to Worthy Park; almost all the St. Dorothy estates are gone, I may say. Many in Vere will go, and eight or ten in Clarendon are decided on, and more will follow. Immigration is worse than useless now. . . .[44]

It was clear that if Jamaican estates and their proprietors were to suffer so, Gilbert Shaw could hold out little hope for their Negro labourers. Indeed, it was the Negroes' advance that had helped to retard Jamaica and the estates. 'There is no doubt,' he pontificated,

> that even as things have been, morality, religion, and all that tends to the increase of pure civilization, has been retrograding in this unfor-

tunate country among the lower classes. The sectarian influence, which was ever in reality a political and not a religious influence, is lost; their schools are deserted. The emancipated people being uneducated are incapable of appreciating the benefits of education, or of inculcating morality or social virtue; they are satisfied with having attained their freedom, and care for nothing more. . . . The question of educating the lower classes, and raising them in the scale of social beings, has attracted much attention of late years here, and considerable sums have been annually voted by the Assembly for this purpose, and I doubt not but in time much would have been accomplished; but I think it is plain a scheme of this kind can never be carried out or sustained, except the island is in a flourishing condition, her agriculture and her commerce in a prosperous state. . . .[45]

In England, George Price was fighting to save his reputation and his career, and doubtless also to preserve Worthy Park and its Negro inhabitants from the attentions of the moralizing Mr. Shaw. The Worthy Park trustees pointed out that before Emancipation the estate had enjoyed an income that 'averaged from £15,000 to £25,000' a year, and that even between 1841 and 1846 revenue had averaged at least £9,000, from which there should have been a clear profit of £3,000.[46] There was, indeed, the accumulated 'family' debt of £30,000 owed to the trustees, but the interest charges on this had quite easily been paid off out of income down to 1843, when George Price had started 'improving' the estate. As late as 1842 it had been possible to reduce the principal debt by £1,000 and to purchase three parcels of land for £200, and in 1842 and 1843 there were still a few hundred pounds left over as profits to the co-proprietors. Since 1843, however, the capital debt, secured by mortgages on the estate, had been boosted by £30,000 to £60,000, the annual charges at 5 per cent on which, amounting to £3,000, alone eradicated the average profit expected since 1841. Between 1843 and 1846 the interest on the mortgages was only paid out of money freshly borrowed, and in 1847 the trustees were not paid at all.

George Price claimed—and here for once he was supported by Thomas Price—that it was the standing 'family' debt which really crippled Worthy Park and that given time and fair sugar prices the investment in mechanization would pay off. Lord Dunsany at least had faith in George Price's arguments, and advanced £5,000 to settle the estate's most pressing commitments; but only on the understanding that his son-in-law would go back as manager to Worthy Park. Accordingly, George Price returned to Jamaica early in 1848, as determined as ever, though not so optimistic.

In Europe, the Hungry Forties were succeeded by the unprecedented prosperity of the 1850s and 1860s, and the demand for sugar by England's burgeoning population almost outstripped the world's ability to supply it. Even as protection waned, sugar prices made a moderate recovery from 1849, and only began to fall permanently below the level of 1848 in 1861. In fact, after plummeting to 21s. 1d. a hundredweight in the first year of fully equalized duties, the prices rose steadily for six years, averaging 28s. 6d. per hundredweight or £23. 10s. per hogshead between 1855 and 1860. Thomas Price's pessimistic forecast that the more Worthy Park produced, the more would be her loss was not fulfilled; and yet George Price was never able to fulfil his counter-plan of achieving prosperity by massive production.

Around the neck of the estate hung the burden of the standing debt, which steadily grew as it was found in many years impossible even to wipe off the interest on the mortgages. When this occurred the trustees naturally declined to honour bills drawn against their account. Economies were inevitable. No capital was available for improvements or even repairs, and the machinery never realized its sought potential. Wage bills were cut back to the level of 1842 and while for most employers this would have meant paying starvation wages, for George Price it implied employing fewer men. Consequently, even in the years of comparative prosperity from 1855 to 1860, Worthy Park only produced an average of 285 hogsheads of sugar a year and received an annual income of no more than £8,500. For the trustees and mercantile mortgagees, accustomed to a regular return from their other investments, Worthy Park was a constant reproach to their economy. From 1846 they were eager to dispose of the estate, if only they could find a buyer or cut through the Gordian knot of multiple 'incumbrances'; and after the passage of the Encumbered Estates Act of 1854 it was only a matter of time before Worthy Park was sold over the head of its resident manager.

The threat of losing his home and employment of nearly twenty years was depressing, but George Price's insecurity was as nothing compared with the plight of the emancipated Negroes, whose years of relative prosperity ended altogether in 1846.[47] Denied legal tenure of Crown Lands, agricultural assistance or education, they found the market for local produce greatly curtailed and that for export crops almost totally disappeared. Yet even if they swallowed their distaste for work on the estates, the chance of regular work at decent wages no longer existed. By 1860, half the estates of 1834 had folded up, and on the remaining properties most of the permanent labouring jobs were filled by the resident coolies, the responsible positions by that aspiring class of lighter-coloured Negroes who jealously adopted the modes and attitudes of the old white Staff. For the ordinary Negro, therefore, there was nothing but demoralizing poverty, casual labour, increasing frustration, and lasting alienation.

As he matured, George Price played an increasingly important part in Jamaica's public affairs, and it is to his undying credit that, almost alone among white politicians, he held a sincere respect for Jamaica's free Negro majority and had a realistic understanding of its problems. With something of his father's cantankerous assertiveness, he channelled his aggressions towards more disinterested ends, not hesitating to tell Assembly, Governor and Colonial Office, black man, coloured, or white, when he thought them wrong. A Member of the Legislative Council from 1854, he was soon in conflict with Governor Darling over the responsibility of the Legislative Council towards the elected Assembly. In 1863, when Worthy Park was finally sold, he moved his home to the seat of the Government in Spanish Town, and in the same year began his prolonged opposition to the oppressive Governor Eyre. The occasion was the 'Tramway Scandal' of 1862-5, which helped to convince the ordinary Jamaican of the cynical disregard for the proper welfare of the island held by its ruling class; but George Price's opposition had deeper roots, being based on a belief that Edward Eyre's arbitrary autocracy was not only unwise but also unjust. So well known was he for his independent and liberal views that it was to him that Andrew Ross and '39 other freeholders of Plantain Garden River' brought a petition in September 1865 alleging underpayment of wages and discrimination by planter magistrates.[48] Price later showed the petition to the Royal Commission, explaining that he had done nothing about it at the time because, like the petitioners themselves, his experience of the Governor and the Colonial Office had taught him that it was so much effort wasted. He had, however, resigned as Custos of St. Catherine's and Justice of the Peace in 1864 in protest against Governor Eyre's actions, forwarding two complaints for his father-in-law to bring up in the House of Lords.[49] These had little effect, but after the shambles of the Morant Bay massacre in 1865, George Price returned to England to carry on his campaign against the punitive Governor and the pusillanimous Colonial Office. Retiring to a very different island, the Isle of Wight, he contributed a devastating broadside to the controversy over Governor Eyre which split the whole of England in 1866.[50] This book, so markedly in contrast to his father's pamphlet of 1832, can serve as a fitting epigraph—or epitaph—for the 200-year régime of the Jamaican Prices.

By no means a rabid radical, George Price claimed, quite rightly, that his 22 years' experience of Jamaica gave him a more realistic appreciation of the problems of the island and its peoples than the prejudiced self-interest and impractical idealism which fired the antagonists in that celebrated dispute. 'I think it right to say,' he wrote,

that I am neither black nor brown, nor Baptist nor an Anti-Slavery or Exeter Hall man. I am not a philanthropist. . . . I am, therefore, not a friend of the black, but I desire to see him dealt justly by. I think him capable of improvement. . . .[51]

The real problems were not caused by the incapacity of the Negroes, but by the economic condition of Jamaica, its desertion by capitalists and skilled white workers, and the indifference and ignorance of government and English people. When he had gone out to Worthy Park in 1843, George Price had found:

In the district around (about 300 square miles) . . . nineteen sugar estates in full operation, having on them the usual white managers and people; other whites, attracted by the considerable amount of money then in circulation, being settled also in that district. In 1864, all these estates had long since ceased cultivation, except that with which I was connected; trees were growing out of the roofs and walls of nearly all the buildings; and all around was bush. With the exception of three or four, all the whites had vanished. . . .[52]

Into the gap had stepped the more able and ambitious of the coloured folk, who performed their tasks very creditably; but the loss in leadership and training was serious indeed. The ordinary Negro was no paragon. In fact, claimed Price, 'the lowest class of Negro is certainly *very* low, but in no way either in acts or words, lower than the lowest class of Englishmen, and in many respects very much above it . . .'.[53] The black Jamaican was no longer a very satisfactory labourer on estates; he tended to be an awful hypocrite in religion; and would lie without a blush if he thought the truth would be unpalatable to his hearers. Yet he was soberer than whites of all degrees, ate more temperately, and was 'as cleanly as the Englishmen of the lower classes, to whom clean water is unknown'.[54] For no good reason, the up-country Negro was intensely loyal,[55] and completely honest when it came to money. Many Negroes thought nothing of taking foodstuffs from George Price's fields, but 'during 22 years,' he wrote,

I sent weekly, and always at night, a distance of forty miles for silver, by boys; and I never lost a penny out of £80,000 so carried. Can this be done in England? . . .[56]

In fact, wrote Price with a whimsicality bound to endear him even less to Englishmen of Carlyle's persuasion, 'the negro in temper is very like the Irishman, and therefore very superior to the Englishman in that respect'.[57] Moreover, like the Irishman on his own potato-patch, the ordinary black countrymen of Jamaica, when working for himself, worked with a will. In this respect, George Price came close to the enlightened and percipient Sewell, who had written in 1860:

... the position of the Jamaican peasant ... is a standing rebuke to those who, wittingly or unwittingly, encourage the vulgar lie that the African can not possibly be elevated. ... The most ignorant work whenever they can get work. ... The whole people of Jamaica work; and if their work is often misdirected and wasteful, the blame does not surely rest with the unlettered classes.[58]

George Price believed that the Negroes still needed leadership and guidance as well as they needed education, but experience had forced him to the conclusion that all Negroes, black as well as brown, had excellent qualities when given the proper opportunities. In due course, he hoped, 'the black people will ultimately be able to assist materially in their own government', for already they had shown considerable ability. In his speech of resignation at Spanish Town in 1864 he had praised the coloured officials who had assisted him as Custos, Chairman of Boards, and magistrate. 'By these remarks,' he wrote later,

I meant to convey that the demeanour of the black members of those boards, their courtesy and orderly conduct, respect towards the chairman and each other, and manner of addressing the boards, and even the good sense and justice of their arguments, and willingness to be guided by those whom they knew to be able to guide and advise them rightly, were such as would have enabled them to pass muster in another assembly elsewhere.[59]

To hold these views in England in the 1860s was still unusual: to be an experienced Jamaican planter and hold them was almost unique.[60] In many ways, George Price was a man born out of his time, fated to strive for his very existence when the times were out of joint. Most of the other Prices of Worthy Park were able men, whose birth and abilities led them to the forefront of affairs; but all were men of their age. George Price's judgement of the potential of the Jamaican Negro, as of his estimate of the potential of mechanization in the sugar industry, was ridiculed in his day; but both were vindicated three-quarters of a century later. Perhaps it is therefore not too fanciful to suggest that George Price might be admitted as the only truly plantocratic member to the pantheon of Makers of Modern Jamaica.

NOTES

[1] W. L. Burn, 171—2.

[2] For schedule of tasks for St. John's see Appendix II, 328.

[3] Almost exactly the same as the total for all slaves, though in 1831 (after purchase and perhaps the transfer of 60 slaves from Mickleton) the total of slaves was up to 522 against 334 registered 'labourers'.

[4] Of the 248 apprentices on 1 January 1837, only 47 were ill or incapacitated in any way: 31 'weakly', 2 'sickly', 7 'invalids', 1 subject to fits, 1 scrofula, 1 yaws, and 4 with only one leg apiece; *Worthy Park Fragments, 1836–45.*

[5] Twenty-one first class at £12; 6 second at £9; 8 third at £7; 5 domestics for £15 total. Grand total £397 for 40 Negroes. *Mickleton Fragment, 1836–7.*

[6] 589 hogsheads produced by 309 labourers in 1832 and 705 hogsheads by 503 slaves (corrected to 317 using the same formula of 63 per cent labourers/total slaves as in 1832) in 1812.

[7] Precise statistics for the total number of workers employed by Worthy Park throughout the year are hard to come by after 1838, but it is unlikely that the average work-force in 1860 when 350 hogsheads were produced, was much more than 100 men, indicating a productivity as high as 3·5 hogsheads per man. It is worth pointing out here that in 1959, an average labour force of 290 men produced 7,000 tons of sugar, equivalent to 30·18 hogsheads per man.

[8] Parliamentary Papers, 1836, XV, Appendix X, 137, 153.

[9] *Ibid.*, Appendix 18, 214.

[10] By an instrument dated 15 December 1840, by which the estate was conveyed on trust to C. C. Talbot, Viscount Ingestre and T. C. Higgins, with certain commitments to Earl Dunsany; see below, X, 237.

[11] Parliamentary Papers, 4963–4, 1 March 1848, 56.

[12] *Ibid.*, 5130, 68.

[13] *Ibid.*, 5132–7.

[14] *Ibid.*, 5007, 60; 4972–3, 57.

[15] *Ibid.*, 5164–6, 70.

[16] S. Olivier, *The Myth of Governor Eyre*, London, 1933, 207.

[17] Parliamentary Papers, 48, 4879.

[18] These figures are derived from an average for 1845 and 1846; *Worthy Park Plantation Book, 1835–47.* If the salaries paid to white employees were added, the figures would be even more evenly distributed; roughly £125 mean, £145 high, £105 low.

[19] *Worthy Park Plantation Book,* 1835–7.

[20] Parliamentary Papers, 4966–9, 56; D. G. Hall, *Free Jamaica*, 20.

[21] George Price, *Jamaica and the Colonial Office*, London, 1866, 5.

[22] Parliamentary Papers, XXXIX, 379 *sqq.* See sugar sold to Immigrants in 'Crops and Proceeds, 1842', *Worthy Park Plantation Book,* 1835–47; George Price, *Jamaica and the Colonial Office*, 7; P.P. 1850–3, Part II, LXVII, 37.

[23] I. M. Cumpston, *Indians Overseas in British Territories*, London, O.U.P., 1953; D. G. Hall, 52–3.

[24] Donald Wood, *Trinidad in Transition*, London, O.U.P., 1968, 125.

[25] Parliamentary Papers, 60, 5006.

[26] Hall Pringle, *The Fall of the Sugar Planters of Jamaica*, London, 1869, 10 n.

[27] Parliamentary Papers, 64, 5075. Typical of the infection of railway and other

mechanical ideas which spread as far as Jamaica was, *Report on Mechanical Improvements in Tropical Agriculture and the Manufacture of Sugar* . . . . by James Anderson, F.R.S.E., Kingston, 1845, which George Price must have read since it was addressed to the Royal Agricultural Society of Jamaica.

28 Quoted by Sir C. Wood, Chancellor of the Exchequer in the Parliamentary debate on duties of 3 February 1848; *Hansard*, Third Series, XCVI, 1848, 69.

29 *Ibid.*, 99; Parliamentary Papers, 55, 4951.

30 *Ibid.*, 51–2, 4911; 62, 5038.

31 *Worthy Park Plantation Book*, 1835–47, 61. One radical new invention which George Price did not introduce was the vacuum pan, not brought into Jamaica till the 1860s or used by Worthy Park until 1906, although in use elsewhere since 1845.

32 *Hansard*, Third Series, XCVI (1848), 69.

33 It reached Angels in December 1845; W. Rodney Long, *Railways of Central America and the West Indies*, Washington, Government Printing Office, 1925, 326.

34 D. G. Hall, 36.

35 *Hansard*, Third Series, XCVI (1848), 69.

36 1846 wharfage £368, railway £280, wagonage £48; 1847 wharfage £187, railway £206, wagonage £429; Parliamentary Papers, 49, 4890–2.

37 *Ibid.*, 63, 5055–8; 64, 5062–3.

38 George Price to Mr. Hawes, quoted by H. Labouchere, M.P., *Hansard*, Third Series, XCVI (1848), 148–9. See also George Price, *Jamaica and the Colonial Office*, 139.

39 Parliamentary Papers, 53, 4916.

40 9/10 Vict., c. 97.

41 Lord Harris, the Governor of Trinidad, put it as low as half this figure; C.O. 295/160, Harris to Grey, 21 February 1848; D. Wood, 122.

42 At first he had refused paid leave, then challenged the suitability of the Attorney chosen to fill his place. It was only when Lord Ingestre, 'not being used to having one's orders so distinctly rebelled against', sent out the actual Power of Attorney replacing him that George Price agreed to sail to England; Parliamentary Papers, evidence of Lord Viscount Ingestre, M.P., 44.

43 *Ibid.*, 58–9, 4985.

44 *Ibid.*

45 *Ibid.*

46 *Ibid.*, 53–4, 4916–24. Thomas Price even nostalgically recalled his father in 1843 claiming that he was a ruined man, giving up his hounds and two of his liveried footmen, while he enjoyed £13,000 a year.

47 *Ibid.*, 57, 4980.

48 S. Olivier, *The Myth of Governor Eyre*, London, 1933, 200–1.

49 'Return To Addresses of House of Lords, June 3, July 26, 1864', *Papers on the Rebellion*, Vol. 1, Institute of Jamaica, 0972.9204.

50 *Jamaica and the Colonial Office*, London, 1866. George Price died in 1890.

51 *Ibid.*

52 *Ibid.*, 2.

53 *Ibid.*, 4.

54 *Ibid.*, 5.

55 'The name of the Queen and the slightest allusion to it . . . appears to act as a charm with these people', Price, underlining the blunder of the so-called Queen's Proclamation of 1865; *ibid.*, 4 n.

[56] *Ibid.*, 6.

[57] *Ibid.*, 5.

[58] Sewell, *The Ordeal of Free Labour in the British West Indies*, New York, 1861, 254.

[59] *Jamaica and the Colonial Office*, 3.

[60] One other exception was the Rev. Henry Clarke, the grandfather of the present owners of Worthy Park, who went out to Jamaica in 1846.

CHAPTER TEN

Nadir: Talbots and Calders, 1863-1918

The Encumbered Estates Act of 1854 can be seen as the last victory of the West India Interest in the English House of Commons, since it was passed out of tenderness for the holders of West Indian property; but, like slave compensation, Apprenticeship, and the delay in the removal of protective duties, it was merely a Parthian victory. Without the Act, encumbered estates could not have been sold; yet sale itself spelt defeat, prices were derisory, and, as with the compensations of 1834, it was found that the chief beneficiaries were not the planters but the merchants and mortgage-holders who had always been their creditors.

Worthy Park was typical of the estates sold under the terms of the Act of 1854. The long struggle of the Prices for survival was mercifully ended, and during the subsequent 65 years three fresh owners took up the hopeless task in turn. In retrospect, the period from 1863 to 1918 seems merely the gloomy trough of a long drawn-out depression between two summits of prosperity; but at the time it must have seemed an endless slide towards oblivion, with every expedient doomed to disappointment. Ironically, as the value of the estate declined, its area increased, until by 1880 it nominally possessed almost the whole of the Lluidas Vale, 12,000 acres in all. This was less an indi-

cation of Worthy Park's strength than of the utter decay of her neighbours, and the gradual change from intensive sugar cultivation to lax
diversification. Sugar continued to be grown—maintaining a continuous if tenuous thread to Worthy Park's economic history—but
this was almost by habit, in faint expectation of an upturn in world
sugar prices. Successively, coffee, cocoa and bananas were tried as
viable alternative and supplementary crops, only to be stifled after
initial promise by competition from other countries. It was fitting that
the last of the nineteenth-century owners of Worthy Park, J. V. Calder,
was chiefly known as a cattleman, for under his régime Worthy Park,
for all its splendid agricultural potential, became little more than a
straggly—and far from prosperous—cattle pen.

At the busiest of times in the best of years, Worthy Park employed
fewer than 250 men; yet within the compass of Lluidas Vale and in the
valleys around lived a hundred times that number. This rapidly growing population exerted constant pressure on Worthy Park. To eke out
a living, or avoid actual starvation, the Negroes frequently stole from
the fields of the estate, and many of them actually 'squatted' on the
marginal pockets in the Worthy Park hills. But the most obvious
problem of all was the independent existence of Lluidas Vale village,
which had grown from nothing to a slum of 2,000 people since
Emancipation, and now seemed to the owners of Worthy Park something like a canker close to the heart of the estate.

The discovery that most of the remaining West Indian estates were
so encumbered with complicated debts that it was impossible even for
insolvent proprietors to sell them, was one of the incidental results of
the sugar inquiry of 1848. The iron grip of the law of entail had already
been loosened by legal reform; what was now needed was a complete
overhaul of the laws concerning bankruptcy and liquidation. As the
law stood, there was no way of selling property while any mortgages
or debts remained unpaid, yet no way in which mortgagees or creditors could be paid in proportion to their shares of the overall debt. It
was these problems which the West Indian Encumbered Estates Act
of 1854 set out to solve: establishing the principle that creditors be paid
in proportion to the debts; setting up machinery in the form of a Court

of Commissioners to ascertain the authentic details of debts and to organise the sale of property; and compelling the acceptance of proportional settlements.[1]

The original Act passed through Parliament with little difficulty, but it was seven years before it came into operation. First, unforeseen technical problems arose, such as the claim of merchants holding liens on the agricultural produce of an estate to precedence in payment over mortgage holders, a principle based upon maritime law and West Indian custom which was not known in English common or statute law. Amendments were enacted, but before the Court could start operations the first Chief Commissioner died. Then there were delays in persuading the island assemblies to pass the required enabling Acts. Most of the legislatures were by now moribund; but there was also widespread local scepticism about the Act, which was seen as a measure which would drain rather than replenish the fund of cash in the British West Indies, and would benefit only the metropolitan merchants.

It was not until 1858 that the Encumbered Estates Commission came into being and the enabling Act was not passed by Jamaica until 1861. Then it was one thing to make the sale of encumbered estates technically feasible; quite another to effect satisfactory sales or any sales at all. After the slump of 1854, the value of West Indian estates had risen somewhat in the years of better prices between 1855 and 1860, but by the time the Commission had creaked into action the value of property had slumped once more. The first sales were of thirty-two Jamaican estates in 1861, but the prices received, varying from £100 for 100 acres to £4,500 for 2,388 acres, were hardly encouraging. Those who hoped that the Act would aid the distressed planters or even the long-suffering mortgage-holders, were bitterly disappointed, criticizing the expense and delays of litigation and the fact that by recognizing the 'consignee's lien' the Act impoverished all claimants save the merchants.[2] What they could not accept was that the sugar industry in its old form was practically dead and that the Act was a Draconian expedient to effect the retrenchment, consolidation, and diversification which the West Indian economy required. In this light the Encumbered Estates Commission was highly successful, and by the time its affairs were wound up between 1885 and 1892 it had achieved its purpose.[3]

Worthy Park was typical of the estates which passed through the slow and thorough mills of the Encumbered Estates Commission.[4] Its affairs were found to be complicated almost beyond hope of resolution; yet with archeological skill, the commissioners reconstructed the financial history of the estate since 1789 and simplified (if it could not greatly reduce) the commitments. Two helpful features emerged from their inquiries: that in 1834 Sir Rose Price had effectively disentailed the estate by the provisions of his will, and that by the consolidation of December 1840 the trustees had expunged or taken over many of the earlier debts. Moreover, by good management Worthy Park was much less committed than many other estates to merchant creditors for advances to keep on going. None the less, total commitments of no less than £68,000 remained, and there were well over twenty persons claiming a share of the estate. These included the heirs of William Cardale (one of John Price's creditors) all the descendants of Sir Rose Price and all the trustees on their own behalf. The executors of Lord Dunsany were particularly insistent, having already been to court on five occasions since 1849 to establish rights against the estate for money invested.

The respective shares were eventually resolved and Worthy Park was first advertised for sale by auction in June 1862. Notices were sent out to merchants and brokers in London, Liverpool, and Bristol, in which the estate's total acreage was given at 4,122, of which 230 were in canes and 620 in guinea grass. There was also a field of 50 allotments let out to the resident labourers at 8s. each per year. The average produce between 1856 and 1862 had been 235 hogsheads of sugar and 12,900 gallons of rum. The description of buildings listed many of those still found at Worthy Park a century later. The Great House was in good order, and in the main compound on its neighbouring hillock were the overseer's residence, a range of stables, sheds, and stores and a 'police station'. In the factory yard the steam engine and the main machinery for milling, boiling, and curing were now under one roof, though the water-mill, distillery, fuel house, and shops for carpenters, coopers, and smiths were separate. Elsewhere there were labourers' cottages and 'accommodation' for fifty immigrants and thirty to forty 'jobbers'. Mickleton was described as consisting of 623 acres of 'common grass and brushwood'.[5]

Although Worthy Park had been called the best sugar estate in Jamaica, the highest bid received at the first auction was one of £3,500, with £150 more for Mickleton. The estate was consequently withdrawn from the market. On 24 December 1862, however, it was decided to sell at auction the following summer at whatever price, though the 15th Lord Dunsany put in a pathetic plea that it 'should not be sold at a very inadequate price' in view of his father's large investments. The auction was held on 23 June 1863, and although 'there was a large attendance and considerable competition' Worthy Park was sold to the Earl of Shrewsbury and Talbot of Belgrave Square, exclusive of stock, for £8,550. Mickleton was sold to one Michael Solomon for £300. The price received represented little more than an eighth of Worthy Park's debts or a sixteenth of the value placed on the estate by Sir Rose Price in 1834; little more, in fact, than one year's gross income during the management of George Price. Yet so depressed was the market that The Times reported that 'The prices were considered good under the circumstances and showed a rise in the value of West Indian property.'[6]

All proceeds from the sale were handed over to the trustees for distribution to the beneficiaries according to their shares, presumably at the rate of 2s. 6d. in the pound, and by this action the connection of the Prices with Worthy Park was finally severed.[7] At first glance it might seem that since the Earl of Shrewsbury had purchased Worthy Park there had been some legal chicanery afoot by which the most powerful of the trustees had consolidated his hold upon an estate he already controlled. Not so. The new Earl of Shrewsbury was in a position to know Worthy Park well, but was not a trustee or even a close relative of the 17th Earl who had been Sir Rose Price's brother-in-law. This grandee had died, unmarried, in 1856, to be succeeded by his distant cousin, Henry John, the 3rd Earl of Talbot (1803–68) who had purchased Worthy Park to settle on his two younger sons.

Both of Worthy Park's new owners went on to careers that were as successful as the estate itself was undistinguished; and for the first time Worthy Park was at the very periphery of a family's interest. Indeed, only one of the owners ever visited Worthy Park, a brief visit in 1875. Walter Cecil Talbot (1834–1904), who changed his surname to Carpenter to accommodate the will of the Countess of Tyrconnell from whom he inherited Kiplin, Yorkshire, in 1868, had joined the Royal Navy in 1847 and served in the Crimea, eventually becoming an Admiral and A.D.C. to Queen Victoria. He was also Conservative M.P. for County Waterford between 1859 and 1865. His brother, Reginald Arthur Talbot (1841–1929) also sat as a Conservative M.P., for Stafford between 1869 and 1874, but chose a military career. He served in the Zulu War, the Egyptian campaigns of 1882–5 and, now a general, was Commander-in-Chief of British forces in Egypt between 1899 and 1903. He too was appointed A.D.C. to Queen Victoria, and between 1904 and 1908 was Governor of Victoria in Australia. It was he who visited Worthy Park in 1875.[8]

Carpenter and Talbot did not inherit Worthy Park until 1870, after their father died,[9] and Talbot's trip to Jamaica in 1875 was obviously intended as the almost traditional visitation by a new absentee proprietor at the earliest possible occasion to ginger up the overseer and set reform in motion. It was a most inauspicious time to take over a Jamaican plantation chiefly devoted to sugar production, since conditions for British colonial sugar were bad and gradually growing worse. It is true that all British import duties on sugar were removed in 1874 and lower consumer prices meant a stimulation of demand; but this merely tended to emphasize the advantages of cane-sugar producing areas, such as Cuba, which enjoyed an infusion of foreign capital, cheap labour, and large undeveloped fertile areas suitable for centralization; or those European countries which were prepared to subsidize the producers of beet for sugar, and even to 'dump' their excess production on the rest of the world. When Germany adopted this policy in 1884 it was castigated by British sugar producers as a calculated plan to harm the British Empire, though they might with equal justice have attacked the policy-makers of the British Board of

Trade who continued to adhere to the gospel of free trade, indifferent to its imperial implications.

After 1874, the huge expansion of the United States market gave the Jamaican producers some relief, particularly after the abolition of slavery in Cuba in 1885 and during that country's periodic civil disorders. In 1891, the U.S.A. adopted a policy of trade reciprocity which promised much for Jamaican sugar; but this was reversed under President McKinley only three years later, and the Jamaican sugar industry declined towards its lowest point of all.

Wholesale bankruptcies and the sales through the Encumbered Estates Commission had led to a great decline in the numbers of Jamaican estates. At the time of Emancipation there had been 600 estates producing sugar in Jamaica; but by 1866 this number had been halved. In 1875 there was still 244 sugar estates, but many were *in extremis*, and by the time of the Sugar Commission of 1896 the number had fallen to 140. This represented a 75 per cent fall in the total of estates in just over sixty years; yet aggregate sugar production, though it declined drastically, did not fall quite so far. In 1834, Jamaica produced some 63,000 tons of sugar and in 1866 only some 27,000; but in 1875 and 1896 alike the production was close to 22,000 tons. Moreover, the output of 1875 was produced from 244 estates averaging 197 acres of canes; that of 1896 from 140 estates with an average of 219 acres in cultivation.[10] Clearly there had been in Jamaica a considerable degree of consolidation, made possible by improved agronomy and factory technology and the introduction of some centralized factories. Yet in these essential developments Jamaica was far outstripped by competing countries, and the Report of the 1896 Commission advised that only in diversification could Jamaican estates avoid extinction. Looking at Jamaica as a whole, much had already been achieved in this direction, for as early as 1865 sugar only comprised 41·5 per cent of the value of Jamaican exports, and in 1875 the figure was closer to one-third.[11] Yet the alternative crops were merely those produced by a multitude of small farmers, and most estates found the problems of converting from sugar production almost insurmountable.

From the notes which Captain R. A. Talbot left behind for the instruction of the resident manager at Worthy Park in 1875[12] we can learn much of the sorry state into which the estate had fallen in the dozen years since George Price had left, and of the effect of the changes that had occurred in the general Jamaican economy. The Great House, which might never again be occupied by Worthy Park's owner, was in such disrepair that Talbot considered having it pulled down, before changing his mind (it fell down and was dismantled some twenty years later). The overseer's house and adjacent book-keepers' quarters were likewise dilapidated, and Talbot left orders for substantial repairs, as well as structural changes aimed at increasing the overseer's comfort and separating him socially from his often intemperate white underlings.[13]

The Negro labourers were not forgotten, for apparently Worthy Park still suffered from the difficulty of attracting and retaining reliable help. Several old cottages near the works and on the road to the village were to be repaired and a dozen new 'negro houses' built 'between the gutter and the road with a small piece of ground for a garden to be let to the labourers by the month'. In general, ordered Talbot, 'every inducement is to be made to increase the supply of labour by renting houses on the estate only to those who work upon it and by inducing fresh people to settle'.

Extremely serious for the running of the estate, the road from Shady Grove (as the village was generally called then) to Ewarton was 'in very bad order' and Talbot suggested that the Government be approached to increase the grant and raise its status once more to that of main road. A major work intended by Captain Talbot on the estate itself was the more efficient use of the aqueduct now that most of the factory's power was derived from steam. He ordered that the 'mill dam' be cleaned and deepened and the brickwork repointed at the end of the 1876 crop, and an estimate be called for of the cost of extending the 'gutter wall', from the factory across the road and towards the overseer's yard, 'with a view to irrigating the lower cane-pieces'. Meanwhile, a separate trench was to be cut for excess water past the Great House and through Well Piece, in order to irrigate Flower Piece, Cabbage Tree Piece, and Sorrell Hill. In addition, much greater attention was to be paid to manuring, the establishment of a plant nursery and the concentration of cane-pieces in only the most fertile and accessible areas.

In the factory, Captain Talbot was most concerned with the inefficient operation of the flues, which led to a great wastage of fuel. 'The amount of heat arriving at the multitubular boiler,' he wrote,

should be sufficient to keep up steam for the clarifiers and for the engine without any auxiliary fire with one set of coppers in use. . . . It appears however that when both sets of coppers are in use that the amount of heat arriving at the boiler is less than when only the left hand set is working. This should be remedied by altering the flues. The copper fire under the right hand set of coppers does not boil as well as the one on the left hand set. The oven is to be set back so that the fire may be more directly under the taches. . . .

Captain Talbot also left detailed instructions for the greater efficiency and more scrupulous upkeep of the apparatus in the distillery. The newest still had not worn at all well and the engineer had reported that this was due to lack of regular cleaning. Accordingly, the stillhouse book-keeper was ordered to have the stills thoroughly cleaned each Monday morning and to enter in the stillhouse report that this had been done.

From Talbot's report of 1875 it is obvious that Worthy Park's new owners did not have much money to invest in new machinery, only ordering repairs and maintenance that could be carried out on the estate itself. The only important innovations which the Talbots introduced into the factory were an Aspinall pan and centrifuges installed around 1887. Although the principle of the vacuum pan had long been known in 1875, Worthy Park did not adopt this much more efficient method of sugar production until 1906, under J. V. Calder.[14] Even the aqueduct extensions recommended by Captain Talbot were never carried out, and Worthy Park is still not irrigated.

The chief concern of Carpenter and Talbot was clearly to get the maximum out of the available machinery and land, and hope for better times. Yet sugar production and productivity were at least maintained throughout their régime and were actually increased whenever prices were somewhat better than average. In 1879, when annual returns were first given in the *Jamaica Almanack*, Worthy Park had 302 of its 8,368 acres in canes and produced 257 tons of sugar and 206 puncheons of rum. This was not significantly less than the 276 tons produced in 1861 and the acreage yield was actually better.[15] Although the average in canes increased steadily to 433 in 1895 with only one slight reduction in 1886, the factory production of sugar fluctuated more than ever before or since in response to the prices obtainable, varying from 420 tons in 1881 to only 112 tons in 1886. In 1896, however, the acreage was savagely reduced by almost a third to 300 acres and production, which had averaged 363 tons per year between 1894 and 1896 fell to an average of 295 tons between 1897 and 1899. Overall, Worthy Park's sugar production between 1879 and 1899 averaged 301 tons per year from 373 acres or approximately 1·52 per cent of the average total of Jamaican production.[16]

In the worst years, when it was scarcely worth producing sugar for export at all, there was a readier market for Jamaica's distinctive rums.[17] From being an almost accidental by-product of the sugar-making process, rum received much more care and attention. At Worthy Park throughout the Talbot and Calder régimes, as in the rest of Jamaica, relatively much more rum was produced than in earlier days. Between 1879 and 1899, the estate's rum production averaged no less than 309 puncheons a year against 301 tons of sugar, compared with a production during George Price's residence that was computed at approximately half a puncheon per hogshead. Since the price received for rum remained fairly steady at about 2s. 6d. a gallon, or £14 per puncheon, the income from rum represented an increasingly important share of Worthy Park's total revenue, and in some later years actually exceeded the income from sugar.

Though its position more than 25 miles inland remained a drawback, Worthy Park under the Talbots did have the advantages of being far less scattered than ever before and having almost unlimited opportunities for expansion within Lluidas Vale. The railway, which was extended, under great difficulties, from Angels through the Rio Cobre

Worthy Park Diversification, 1879–1917

	i	ii	iii	iv	v	vi	vii	viii	x
		Sugar	Pun-cheons rum	Sugar * Jamaica (th.tons)	W.P. total acreage	Cocoa acreage	Bananas acreage	Gross acreage	No. cattle
	Acres	Tons							
1879	302	257	206	25·7	8,368				
80	312	257	206	16·8	8,067				
1	334	420	450	30·7	6,830				
2	339	346	443	24·6	7,577				
4	372	300	483	20·0					
6	357	112	110	18·4	7,738				
7	406	347	295	19·6	8,008				
9	426	355	424	17·9	8,008				
90	426	234	364	16·8	6,200				
1	426	280	370	23·4	7,229				
3	426	240	350	21·9		121			
4	433	350	300	24·0	8,132	121			
5	433	350	280	23·4	8,032	121			
6	425	389	262	23·0	7,968	121			
7	300	289	244	16·4	7,049	127			
8	306	298	250	14·5	7,318	127			
9	312	298	209	18·3	8,454	127			
1900	294	353	289	19·8	10,151	149	20		
1	294	424	318	16·0	10,153	149	27		
2	280	425	284	20·3	11,762	***	***		
3	280	355	274	13·6	11,762	50	123		
4	303	363	280	9·9	11,262	300			
5	302	352	227	11·9	11,262	300		1267	661
6	302	314	180	21·8	10,282	300	50	1267	518
7	334	373	201	14·0	10,088	279	50	1497	657
8	334	275	213	24·0	10,003	279	65	1499	520
10	368	255	365	20·0	10,000	300	50	1719	540
11	368	410	265	19·4	10,000	300	100	1719	560
12	368	397	194	9·9	11,762	300	100	1719	560
13	368	380	250	4·9	11,762	300	100	1719	800
14	450	250	134	20·8	11,762	300**	100	1130	708
15	326	293	208	15·7	11,762	300	100	1497	650
16	326	347	307	25·2	11,762	300	115	1497	497
17	400	285	208	34·3	11,454	400	10	1497	730

From *Jamaica Almanacks;* * Noel Deerr, *History of Sugar.*
** W. P. third largest cocoa producer.
*** Serious hurricane damaged crops especially in St. Catherine's; *Jamaica Almanack*, 1902–3, 528.

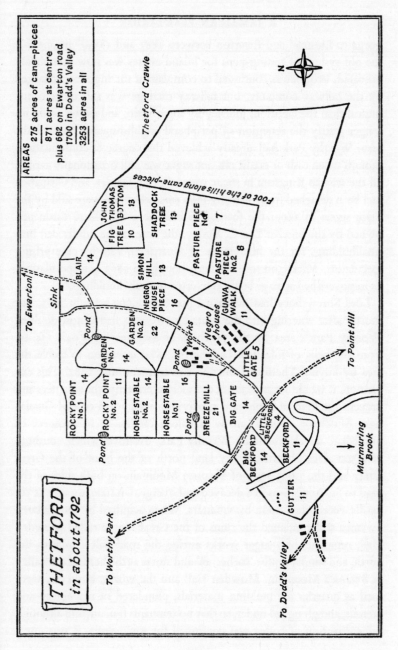

THETFORD
in about 1792

AREAS
275 acres of cane-pieces
871 acres at centre
plus 682 on Ewarton road
1700 in Dodd's Valley
3253 acres in all

N

To Ewarton

Thetford Crawle

Foot of the hills along cane-pieces

BLAIR
14

FIG
TREE
10

JOHN
THOMAS
BOTTOM
13

SHADDOCK
TREE
13

SIMON HILL
13

PASTURE PIECE
No. 1
7

Sink

Pond

GARDEN
No. 2
22

NEGRO
HOUSE
PIECE
16

GUAVA
WALK
11

PASTURE
PIECE
No. 2
8

ROCKY
POINT
No. 1
14

ROCKY
POINT
No. 2
11

GARDEN
No. 1
14

Pond

Works

Negro
houses

Pond

LITTLE
GATE
5

HORSE
STABLE
No. 2
14

HORSE
STABLE
No. 1
16

Pond

BREEZE MILL
21

BIG GATE
14

To Point Hill

To Worthy Park

BIG
BECKFORD
14

LITTLE
BECKFORD
4

BECKFORD
11

GUTTER
11

Murmuring Brook

To Dodd's Valley

I

245

gorge to Linstead and Ewarton between 1881 and 1885,[18] meant that the old system of resting-pens for inland estates was now completely outdated. Proprietors continued to complain at the high rates charged by the railway company, but railway carriage was still more economical than the laborious journey by sugar wain, and estates could no longer justify the retention of peripheral establishments. As we have seen, Worthy Park had already achieved this degree of consolidation, though when cash or credit ran out sugar was still occasionally carried all the way to Kingston in sugar wains. Spring Garden and Guanaboa had been detached from Worthy Park since 1834 and were sold by the Price sisters in 1869; the former to become a 1,000-acre cattle pen owned by the butcher Leo C. Verley, the latter to be subdivided into smallholdings for the inhabitants of Guanaboa Vale by enterprising speculators. Mickleton too had been bought in 1863 as a speculation, its impoverished acreage being converted into smallholdings.[19]

Lord Shrewsbury had purchased just over 4,000 acres in 1863, but shortly after entering into the estate his two sons had almost doubled Worthy Park's area by the purchase of Swansea for £641. 15s. 4d. from the heirs of Elizabeth Laugher in 1874, going on to treble the area by buying Thetford from the Government after 1881. This expansion, it would seem, was just as much to pre-empt the squatters and prevent the kind of haphazard subdivision which had eroded Guanaboa, Mickleton, and so many Jamaican estates, as in prospect of immediate development by Worthy Park. Swansea, which consisted of 2,500 acres of fertile valley land north of the bend of the Great Gully and the 1,075 acres of Swansea Mountain on both sides of the road to St. Ann's, was in a decayed and overgrown state, though as yet hardly encroached upon by squatters. When acquired by the Talbots, Swansea still contained the ruins of the Great House called Mowden Hall, remnants of a sugar works astride the road half a mile to the north, and sundry coffee 'barbecues' and stores at the head of the valley in Swansea Mountain. Mowden Hall and the works, however, were used as quarries for building materials, plundered of machinery and utensils, and ploughed under, so that no remnants remain; and although the cultivation of coffee was continued for some years, it was not a success, and the buildings on Swansea Mountain suffered the fate of those lower down. Captain Talbot ordered in 1875 that 110 acres of Swansea's best land should be planted in canes for the crop of 1877; but while the sugar slump continued the rest of Swansea remained as rough pasture and ruinates, or reverted to secondary underbrush almost like a jungle.[20]

Thetford was at once more attractive agriculturally yet more scattered, more sadly decayed and more extensively encroached upon than Swansea. Under the management of Peek Fuller it had been Lluidas Vale's most vigorous estate, had swallowed up Murmuring Brook in the 1780s and for a few years ran two factories. Its lands almost surrounded Worthy Park. The two chief blocks were the 871 acres centred on the works to the south-east of Worthy Park, and the huge tract of Dodd's Valley to the west, which were connected by the narrow bridge of land called Beckford's. Besides this, there were more than 750 acres along the Murmuring Brook and astride the Point Hill road (150 acres of which were 'undivided between Thetford and Worthy Park') and a further 682 acres of mountain land on the Ewarton road, called Thetford Crawle. At its best, however, Thetford's lands were hillier and less easily worked than Worthy Park's central areas, its factories were less efficient, and its transportation problems much more severe. The hilly nature and very dispersion of Thetford's cane-pieces, and the lack of well-paved intervals, made carrying canes and sugar difficult enough when the Point Hill road was the main exit from Lluidas Vale: when Old Harbour was closed up, Thetford's lack of easy access to the Ewarton road made it particularly vulnerable. Thetford survived the difficult years after 1805, but upon the emancipation of the slaves it suddenly collapsed, throwing its Negro inhabitants into a leaderless dislocation far more serious than on better-ordered estates such as Worthy Park. For a time Thetford's proprietorship was rested, confusingly, in Greenwich Hospital; but between 1867 and 1873 it reverted to the Jamaican Government for persistent non-payment of quit-rents, under the terms of the District Courts Land Law of 1867. By 1881 it was a ragged spectre of its former self, its sugar lands and savannas overgrown, and its mountain areas

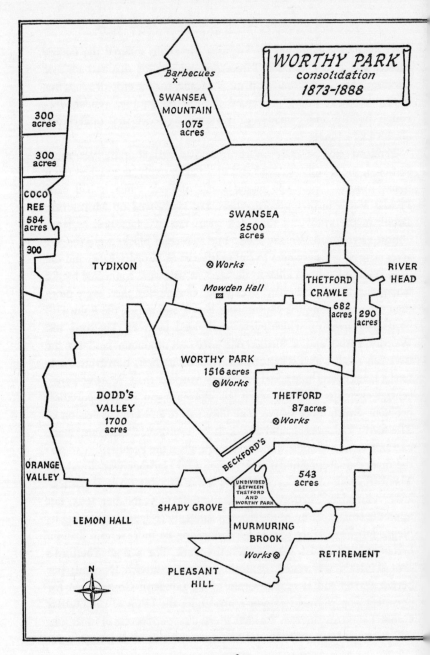

248

and much of the land adjacent to Shady Grove hopelessly encroached upon by 'small settlers' with little or no legal tenure.

In October 1881 the Jamaican Government put Thetford up for public auction, and Talbot and Carpenter, seizing their chance, purchased it for £1,300. Only then did they discover that the Government had already leased all but ninety-one of Thetford's 4,045 acres for seven years to two Kingston pen-keepers, R. B. Benjamin and R. G. Newman, and it was not until 1888 that the brothers obtained undivided title to the land.[21]

The Talbots realized the potential of the sugar lands south of their own and the value of the excellent grazing on the great savanna west of the Tydixon track. Yet they were unable to develop the lands fully and, indeed, for a long time were unable, or unwilling, to evict the squatters who swarmed over most of the marginal land, contenting themselves that they had at least achieved the preservation of a squatter-free belt completely surrounding the original Worthy Park. Except for Shady Grove itself, the only land in Lluidas Vale proper which Worthy Park's proprietors did not now control was Tydixon (which remained independent until 1953), which was difficult to cultivate, though not quite so inaccessible as the mountain-locked Cocoree.

Having consolidated the territory of Worthy Park, the chief concern of the Talbots, and therefore of their overseer, J. R. Scarlett, was to raise the income of the expanded estate. Greatly augmented sugar production was out of the question and diversification promised better prospects, at least in theory. It was not until the régime of J. V. Calder, however, that sugar became less than the major component of Worthy Park's economy. Worthy Park's owners and overseer were certainly ingenious in searching for new crops. Most of Jamaica's traditional minor cash crops such as indigo, pimento, and ginger were considered or tried without success, and for a brief period even tuberoses were grown for perfume essence, though with the same depressing results. Rather more hopeful were coffee and cocoa.

For a dozen years, coffee continued to be grown on Swansea Mountain, but the distance of the groves from the hub of the estate offset the advantage which an operation as large as Worthy Park should have had over the peasant smallholders, and when disease hit the trees and the international price of coffee tumbled as the result of hugely increased cultivation in other countries, particularly Brazil, production at Worthy Park ceased.

Cocoa, the demand for which had first been stimulated by the reduction of the English duty to 1*d.* a pound in 1853, was a more encouraging enterprise, largely because it was too sophisticated a crop for peasant farmers to cultivate. By 1893, 121 acres of cocoa trees had been planted which within a few years were bearing well. They could not, however, work the miracle of dissuading the Talbots from selling out during the depression of the later 1890s, and it was left to J. V. Calder to continue the expansion of cocoa cultivation.

John Vassal Calder, who purchased Worthy Park in July 1899 for £8,200,[22] was a pen-keeper from Westmoreland, completely disillusioned with sugar production yet determined to make what he could from his splendid new property. By 1902, 149 acres of cocoa were being grown when a disastrous hurricane swept central Jamaica and Worthy Park's trees were completely wiped out. Undaunted, Calder replanted and by 1910 Worthy Park was the third largest producer of cocoa in Jamaica, with 300 acres. Throughout the First World War prices continued to be good, and in 1917 Worthy Park reached a peak of production with 400 acres in cultivation (exactly the same as area in canes). By that time, however, West Africa had started to produce cocoa in huge quantities under the aegis of the British chocolate firms, and with the end of the war came the end of the modest Jamaican cocoa boom.

A third possibility for diversification was presented by banana cultivation, made profitable by the opening up of the American and British markets by fast steamboats in the later 1890s. Bananas were known to grow easily on most Jamaican soils, and J. V. Calder found them an excellent crop to plant in the spaces between the rows of cocoa trees. The first plantings shared the fate of the cocoa in 1902, but the establishment of Elders and Fyffes' trade between the Jamaican north shore and Avonmouth docks and the savage competition that ensued between Fyffes and the American United Fruit

Company, encouraged Calder to plant 123 acres in 1903. Thereafter, Worthy Park never grew less than 50 acres of bananas a year up to the First World War, though the gradual buying out of Elders, Fyffes by the United Fruit Company was a serious portent for independent growers.

Cattle remained important at Worthy Park throughout the Talbot period, but overtook sugar and all other crops combined in importance during the régime of J. V. Calder. Worthy Park's own reliance on working steers had long since declined through the replacement of cattle-drawn cane-carts by the tramway and the substantial replacement of sugar wains by the Jamaica Railway, but a heavy demand continued from other less fortunate estates. In 1898, J. V. Calder calculated that an estate producing 200 tons of sugar needed twenty new draft steers every year, and this demand was outstripped by the growing Jamaican market for beef. 'The best customer we have is the butcher,' declared Calder. 'The sugar planter comes next.'[23] A large cattle population also greatly benefited an estate by providing much-needed manure. Under the Talbots Worthy Park had kept between 200 and 300 cattle, but after 1899 these numbers were more than doubled, reaching a peak of 800 in 1913. The acreage of the estate was huge, but the grasslands had greatly deteriorated and each animal ideally needed several acres for grazing. Under J. V. Calder the lowland savannas became insufficient for Worthy Park's stock, and the rapacious herds were thrust up into the interlocking glades of the surrounding hills. It was this development more than any other which drove home to Worthy Park's management the continuing problem of the squatters in the hills.

Since 1838, the Government had been notoriously reluctant to allocate Crown Lands to smallholders, and after 1865 it was a definite policy to prevent illegal encroachment. In the latter year a Surveyor's Department was established and by an Act of 1867,[24] a procedure was set up by which estates or major leaseholders from the Government could serve notice and, by proceedings in the local courts, evict squatters from their lands. In all, the Government recovered 275,000 acres of alienated land;[25] but since the impetus generally came from the managers of large estates, and most of Worthy Park's squatters were on Thetford lands for which the estate had little use, very little was done around Lluidas Vale until the 1890s.

Not that the estate was completely unaware of the extent of encroachment, or of the advantages of establishing its rights against the squatters. Despite the general poverty, Worthy Park still suffered from labour shortages during crop-times, and rooting out the squatters would increase the floating labour force, and, by increasing competition, make lower wages possible. Besides this, squatters who would not work for wages and preferred not to move could be required to pay rent. In 1880, J. R. Scarlett requested the famous Crown Surveyor Thomas Harrison to draw up a survey of Thetford Crawle, and the map produced by Harrison showed that the narrow pockets, amounting to no more than a quarter of the Crawle's 667 acres, were being farmed by at least forty squatters. These 'settlers', three of whom were women, mostly lived in huts close to the main Ewarton road, and some of them even grew coffee and coconuts as well as ground provisions on their one or two acres of land.[26] The neighbouring areas belonging wholly to Worthy Park were also found to be heavily infiltrated, and some of these were cleared.

Ironically, Worthy Park's general concern for its legal tenure was exacerbated by the Small Holdings Law of 1895, by which the Government intended, at last, to encourage legal smallholdings of from five to 50 acres. Clearly, unless legal rights were established by the estate over all the lands to which it held title or which it might ever need, they might be alienated for ever. This, as much as the demands of his cattle for the mountain pastures, explains why J. V. Calder was moved to establish full control over Thetford lands in 1899 and to carry out a ruthless campaign of clearing the mountain tracts, which was practically completed by 1914.

Very few traces of the Worthy Park squatters remain, and today in the glades of Thetford Crawle it is difficult to imagine the bustling activity of peasant farming that was carried on there a century ago. Some of the dispossessed pushed even farther into the unprofitable hills, or took leases on government land in neighbouring parts of

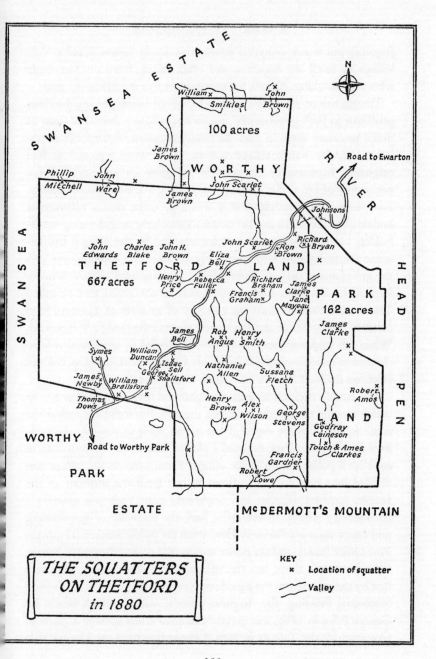

THE SQUATTERS
ON THETFORD
in 1880

KEY
× Location of squatter
⌇ Valley

253

Jamaica; but many crowded down into Shady Grove–Lluidas Vale village to swell the hopeless, and often sullen, force of 'free wage labourers' working, if at all, for only four or five months in the year.

The growth of 'free villages' close to the old estates presented serious problems to both government and estates, whose policies had done as much to create them as had the huge expansion of Jamaica's population. Lluidas Vale's village was in many ways typical.[27] It had originated haphazardly through the fortunate circumstances of the availability of Dr. Quier's Shady Grove for sale and subdivision. In the first phase after Emancipation it was little more than a picturesque huddle of houses and a market centre to which the neighbouring small-holders brought their provisions for sale; but by the 1880s it had become a teeming slum with absolutely no amenities, spilling over into the government land of Thetford and pressing hard against Worthy Park itself. By 1893, J. R. Scarlett was so concerned that he asked Thomas Harrison to draw up a survey of 21 acres of Thetford land between Shady Grove and Beckford's close to the Dodd's Valley road. When this land was found to be totally covered by small settlers who claimed to have purchased from Shady Grove, notices were served and evictions made of those who refused to pay rent.[28]

The estate's decision to press its rights and levy rents for the lots to which it could prove title, stemmed the tide. But it did not endear the estate to the villagers, especially as it was made at roughly the same time that Worthy Park donated a plot of land to the Government to establish a police station in the village. From 1880 on the village was divided into two distinct sections. In one lived the majority of the people, tumbled together and desperately poor, their sole amenity a rudimentary school. In the other half, the influence of government and estate were intertwined. Here were the public market (1875), the Post Office (1881), and the police station (1884); also the rented houses, the Chinamen's shops and the village's only water supply, provided free by the estate from the aqueduct. Nearby stood Lluidas Vale's most substantial building, the Anglican church, which though begun by George Price in 1829, was greatly extended when granted a glebe of five acres by the Talbots in 1884.[29] From that time on, Lluidas Vale

Lluidas Vale village, 1970, showing police station,
post office, and church.

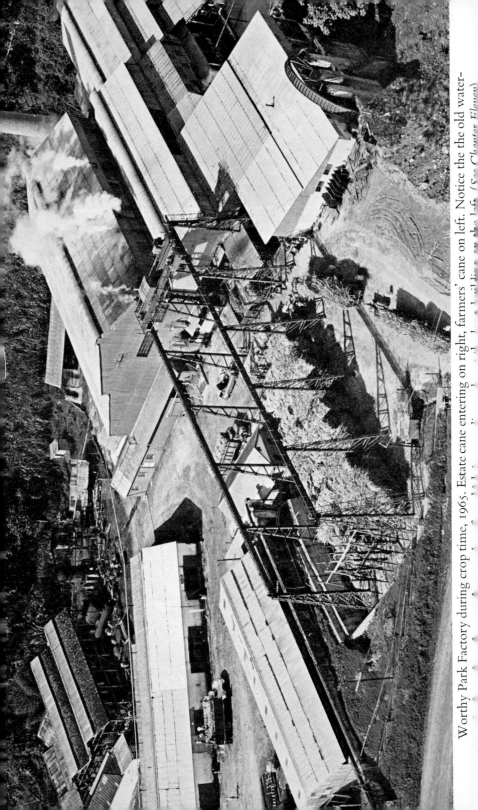

Worthy Park Factory during crop time, 1965. Estate cane entering on right, farmers' cane on left. Notice the the old water-wheel building on the left. (See Chapter Eleven)

became a separate cure with its own resident minister, often a dedicated social worker, but whose relationship to the Worthy Park Great House was not so different from that of an eighteenth-century rector to his squire.

With its severely limited facilities, the village of Lluidas Vale took over the functions for the valley once performed by Point Hill, as Point Hill itself had taken over from Guanaboa a century before. Yet it is not surprising that in the mind of the ordinary villager the estate, the Government, and the once-established church were as closely identified at the start of the twentieth century as they had been in previous centuries; nor that even today, as the corollary of economic dependence on the estate, the village has tended towards an independent attitude in both politics and religion.

The alienation which doubtless existed was all the more tragic in that the social divisions were not strictly between rich and poor. In the period before the First World War, everyone was poor; and in their degree the white planters suffered almost as much as the ordinary Negro. This was particularly true of J. V. Calder who, unlike the Talbots, was a native Jamaican without the consolations of the well-connected absentee or the rewards of a flourishing other career to fall back upon. In the sugar industry, the development of the Canadian market[30] and the removal in 1903, after long negotiations, of the bounties paid by many European countries to their beet producers, might have benefited Jamaica had not Cuba by now attained its full potential under direct American control. Although Worthy Park had reduced its costs to £8. 15s. per ton of sugar and the same for each puncheon of rum (largely by reducing its total wage bill to £3,100 a year)[31] the prices dipped below this in 1910. More and more Jamaican estates went under, until the total of 140 in 1896 was halved once more. In 1913, Jamaican production reached its lowest since 1711, with only 4,891 tons. Worthy Park continued to produce an average of 338 tons a year between 1910 and 1914, and in 1913 its 380 tons represented a record 6·9 per cent of Jamaican production; but this was probably merely multiplying her operational losses. A rum production which averaged 242 puncheons a year over the same period was little consolation since escalating imperial excise duties were increasingly pricing Jamaican rum out of the market. Cocoa and bananas were faring much better, but cattle, upon which J. V. Calder relied so heavily, suffered along with sugar, since the general depression priced beef out of the range of Jamaican consumers and the closure of estates reduced the demand for working steers to an unprofitable trickle.

The First World War, chiefly by halting European beet production and increasing the demand for rum to supply the British armed forces, brought a substantial revival to the Jamaican sugar industry, while wartime prosperity in the U.S.A. raised prices for bananas and cocoa as well as for sugar. These prospects, however, were largely illusory, since the Worthy Park, like many Jamaican estates, could not quickly increase production. Wartime employment elsewhere and high prices for ground provisions had led to a serious labour shortage, and necesary replacements for the factory were unobtainable. By now, moreover, J. V. Calder had had enough of Worthy Park and its problems. Worn out from overwork and isolation, his health broke down and, with three of his four sons off at the war he allowed the estate to slip into an even deeper state of dilapidation. In 1917, Calder was forced to go to New York for a serious operation and, sceptical of his own ability to carry on and of the chances of the wartime boom to survive the peace, he allowed the rumour to circulate that Worthy Park was up for sale. A younger, more resilient or resourceful man, or one with a greater emotional attachment to Worthy Park, would have gained heart from the conditions to carry on. But to J. V. Calder they merely presented an opportunity that might never be repeated, to sell out at a profit and enjoy a comfortable retirement.

NOTES

[1] Details of the Act and its effects are mostly from R. W. Beachey, *The Jamaican Sugar Industry in the Later Nineteenth Century*, Blackwell, Oxford, 1955.
[2] *Ibid.*, 28.
[3] *Ibid.*, 29.
[4] The thoroughness of which can be seen by examining C.O. 441/4/4.

5 This and subsequent information is from C.O. 441/4/4.

6 *The Times*, 27 June 1863, 12, i.

7 Though, as we have seen, Spring Garden and Guanaboa were not sold until 1863. The beneficiaries under the 1893 settlement included Dunsany and the other trustees, all the surviving Prices including Sir Charles Dutton Price (who had revived his interest in the estate in 1840); but not the Cardales, whose interest was held by the Court to have been expunged by time.

8 *Burke's Peerage*, 1967; *Who was Who*, 1897–1916 (1920); 1929–1940 (1941).

9 By a complicated deed in which the brothers nominally purchased Worthy Park from their father's estate for £12,000 in order to pay off a debt of £7,195 still owed by Lord Shrewsbury to T. C. Higgins, one of the old trustees.

10 The actual figures were: 1875, 244 estates totalling 48,246 acres; 1896, 140, totalling 30,711 acres; Beachey, 123–4.

11 *Ibid.*, 43.

12 At back of *Worthy Park Plantation Book*, 1836–47.

13 This may have achieved its purpose, for J. R. Scarlett remained as overseer at Worthy Park from 1879 to 1899, an unusually long tenure; *Jamaica Almanacks*, 1880–1900.

14 Talbot, *Jamaica Almanacks*, 1887–8; 1906–7. In 1930, Fred Clarke obtained and installed the famous original Jamaican vacuum pan from Albion Estate.

15 0·851 tons or 1·123 hogsheads per acre in 1879, against 0·803 tons or 1·060 hogsheads in 1861.

16 Compared with approximately 3 per cent today.

17 Beachey, 75.

18 And the cost of the loan of £65,000 for the Porus and Ewarton branches. The Ewarton spur was opened on 13 August 1885, the line being completed from Linstead to Port Antonio only in 1896; W. R. Long, *Railways of Central America and the West Indies*, 326–36.

19 As late as 1851, an accurate map of Jamaica did not show a township of Linstead, merely a courthouse and 'house of correction' close to the old Tavern rather to the north of Mickleton property. The town grew up only after this period around the famous Linstead Market, the natural focus of the trade of Thomas-ye-Vale.

20 Swansea had fallen into debt and decay long before 1861, when Moses Sanguinette the mortgage-holder of eleven-twelfths of the estate conveyed his share to James Davidson and H. F. Colthirst. Ironically, as the value of Swansea declined, its owners multiplied, so that Talbot and Carpenter purchased from five persons. Conveyance 9 June 1873, recorded 4 April 1874; I.R.O. Deeds, 963/250.

21 Conveyance by Jamaican Government to Talbot and Carpenter dated 6 December 1881, recorded 13 January 1882; I.R.O. Deeds, 14/36. The lease to R. B. Benjamin was for 3,300 acres, dated 22 October 1880; that to R. G. Newman for 654 acres of Thetford Mountain, dated 12 August 1881.

22 Indenture of sale by Talbot and Carpenter to J. V. Calder dated 28 March 1899, signed by Rear-Admiral W. C. Carpenter at Richmond, Yorkshire, and by Major-General R. A. J. Talbot at Cairo, Egypt. Worthy Park, alias 'Lluidas Plantation' with Cocoree was said to consist of 4,120 acres, Swansea, 'alias Mowden Hall', of 2,999 acres, and Thetford of 4,045 acres, a total of 11,164 acres, less the 5½ acres for the church glebe and the single acre for the police station in Lluidas Vale village.

[23] Jamaican Government Inquiry, 1898.

[24] No. 37 of 1867.

[25] Olivier, *Jamaica* (1933), 386.

[26] See Harrison sketch map of April 1880; Institute of Jamaica.

[27] Compare the report of the D.M.O. of nearby Linstead to the Commission of 1896–7 that 'Idleness, Pauperism and crime are on the increase'; Parliamentary Papers, 1898, LI, 281.

[28] See map of 22 November 1893, Institute of Jamaica.

[29] I.R.O. Deeds, 43/241. Conveyance dated 6 June 1884; recorded 29 December 1887.

[30] A beginning was made with Laurier's unilateral preference agreement in 1898, consolidated by the bilateral agreements between Canada and the British West Indies of 1912, 1920, and 1926. D. G. L. Fraser, *Canada's Role in the West Indies*, Toronto, Canadian Institute of International Affairs, 1964, 5–8.

[31] P.P., 1898, LI, 368.

CHAPTER ELEVEN

Renaissance: The Coming of the Clarkes, 1918-1945

The history of Worthy Park in the twentieth century is a classic success story, almost a triumph, but one in the tradition of Samuel Smiles or Horatio Alger rather than a fantasy of instant achievement. Progress switchbacked, but from the backwardness and despair of the period before the First World War, Worthy Park had been converted into one of the soundest of Jamaican plantations by the end of the Second: not by the fortuitous quirks of a smiling providence alone, but by a fortunate concatenation of good luck, good management, and sheer hard work.

The chief authors of this transformation, two generations of the Clarke family, were not products of the traditional Jamaican ruling class, which had almost departed the Jamaican scene, but comparative newcomers who determinedly rose from the second rank of island society by taking advantage of that limited social mobility which tends to occur in periods of economic dislocation. Yet once in command at Worthy Park they naturally assumed many of the formulae familiar to us from an earlier age. *Plus ça change plus c'est la même chose.* Modern technology has not radically changed the ancient mysteries of cane cultivation, animal husbandry, or plantation management; and despite the huge increases in population and the extension of liberal democracy, society in Lluidas Vale still revolves around the plantation and its ruling class. To most this seems entirely natural and no mere gratuitous subordination. As in the eighteenth century, the character and very success of Worthy Park depends not solely on the will of the owners, but on the marriage of capital and expertise, and on the harmonious partnership of management and workers, that most elusive of Jamaican relationships.

The patriarch of the Worthy Park Clarkes was Henry Clarke, who went out to Jamaica from England at the age of 18 in 1846. Conditions during that period would have blighted the ambitions of most young men, but from the testimony of his contemporaries and the evidence of the diary he kept for most of his adult life, Henry Clarke was no ordinary mortal. Although largely self taught, he became a schoolmaster at Savanna-la-Mar, being moved a few years later to take orders in the established Anglican church. For the remainder of his life he held sundry livings in western Jamaica, combining his pastoral duties with the welfare of the people of the island in general, the foundation of the Westmoreland Building Society (originally formed to provide loans for small farmers) and the raising of a vigorous family of eleven children. He was also for several years an active Member of the Jamaican Legislative Council, appearing before two Royal Commissions as a trenchant critic of the *status quo*. Widely respected, he was yet regarded as something of an eccentric, being both a philosopher of unconventional views and an inventor considerably in advance of his times. Affectionately paternalistic, he was so outspoken in the cause of the common Jamaican that Lord Olivier reckoned him 'one of the most sincere, courageous, and hard-working men he ever knew'.[1] Leonardo-like, he filled his notebooks with revolutionary new projects, most remarkably a hydroplane propeller that lacked but power for proof, and a rotary steam turbine intended to remedy this deficiency that anticipated the work of Samuel Parsons.[2] Henry Clarke also invented at least one process aimed at improving the manufacture of sugar,[3] for he dreamed of rescuing the derelict sugar industry and saving the economy of Jamaica while at the same time making his family's fortune. Instead, he whittled away much of his own hard-earned money, ignoring the fact that the sugar industry could not have raised capital even for machines that increased productivity a hundred-fold.

Sublimely impractical in many ways, the Rev. Henry Clarke did contrive to leave a small trust fund to provide each of his unmarried daughters with a modest independent income, while ensuring that each of his five sons enjoyed a practical livelihood. Four became involved in the management of sugar estates (of which there were 22 in Westmoreland alone at that time), combining this profitless occupation with some other. One followed in his father's footsteps and became an Anglican minister, one was a lawyer in Savanna-la-Mar, and a third son, Hugh, the family's best businessman, became an officer in the Westmoreland Building Society while also managing Henry Clarke's estate. Frederick Lister Clarke, the family's best and most fortunate farmer and the eventual purchaser of Worthy Park, was Henry Clarke's fourth son.

Fred Clarke's formal education was even sketchier than his father's. In 1883, after two years at Potsdam (rechristened Munro College during the First World War), he was apprenticed as boiling-house book-keeper at Barham Estate, Westmoreland, at the formative age of 15. To the end of his life in 1932 he remained more at home in the fields and factory than in the drawing room, his sober and determined character and somewhat ingenuous philosophy owing more to his father and his own experiences than to schoolbooks.

For almost thirty years Fred Clarke 'served others at a salary that about made both ends meet',[4] gaining an immense knowledge of sugar estate management while painfully building up his own small fund of capital. It was not until 1903, when he was 35, that he became the manager of an estate, Richmond in St. Ann's, and considered himself ready to marry, choosing a local girl just half his age. As his family grew rapidly from two to six, Fred Clarke gained a reputation as a rigorous improving manager, while at the same time travelling the length of Jamaica as an assessor for the Westmoreland Building Society.

After four years at Richmond, Fred Clarke began to manage Black-heath in Westmoreland on behalf of his brother Hugh, who had obtained the estate cheaply largely through his management of the Clarke Trust. In 1911, Fred Clarke netted £1,500 from Coolshade, a small sugar estate in Westmoreland which he had built up from dereliction, and two years later was entrusted with Meylersfield, a decayed property on the banks of the swampy Cabarita River, by its mortgage-holders, Messrs. Thompson, Hankey. By means of an ingenious drainage system and a radical reorganization of the estate's affairs, the tireless Fred Clarke was able to double Meylersfield's production and quadruple its profitability. Within three years, aided by the sugar boom that accompanied the First World War, the owners were able to sell what had been regarded as a worthless estate for £45,000.[5]

A less scrupulous man might have regarded efforts which brought profit to others and unemployment to himself as misdirected, but Fred Clarke's success at Meylersfield was not unrewarded. Thompson, Hankey donated an *ex gratia* commission of £2,500, and Hugh Clarke raised his brother's salary to £1,000 a year as he was able to turn his undivided attention towards Blackheath, itself once nearly as badly run down as Meylersfield but later regarded as 'the finest property in Westmoreland'.[6]

Although severe hurricanes scourged western Jamaica in 1916 and 1917, slowing down progress at Blackheath, Fred Clarke had good grounds for complacency by early 1918. Sugar prices were higher than they had been for a century and credit was once more readily available. With £6,000 in the bank, an excellent salary and a five-year contract, Fred Clarke at the age of 50 was a highly respected citizen, church-warden, director of the Building Society, and trustee of several estates. He was not yet quite a planter, however, being still a member of that inferior stratum of white West Indian society, the managerial class.

The vulnerability of Fred Clarke's position was dramatically emphasized by a bombshell which burst on 26 May 1918. On that day he read without warning in the *Daily Gleaner* that his brother was advertising Blackheath for sale. Fred Clarke reckoned that the estate was actually worth £20,000 and was prepared to go as high as £25,000 in order to stay on there, but Hugh, relying on the wartime inflation in real estate values, was hoping for at least £50,000. It was with considerable disappointment that Fred Clarke faced the prospect of climbing once more from a lower rung on the ladder of his success.[7]

At this bleak juncture fortune offered Fred Clarke his most splendid opportunity, which he seized with typical decisiveness. On Saturday, 8 July 1918, while negotiations with Hugh Clarke were breaking down, he heard the rumour that Worthy Park in distant St. Catherine's was up for sale. Apparently J. V. Calder, having gone to New York for an operation, had decided that with only one son available to work the estate he had better sell Worthy Park while there was still a market. Some ten years before, Fred Clarke had valued Worthy Park on behalf of the Westmoreland Building Society and was well aware of its potential worth. At the £40,000 which J. V. Calder was said to be asking, it 'would be an infinitely better bargain than Blackheath at £25,000'.[8]

In the greatest secrecy, Fred Clarke cabled to J. V. Calder in New York and received a ten-day option on Worthy Park at £50,000. Meanwhile, he was scouting around for money to add to his own meagre £6,000. For obvious reasons he was pretty sure of a sizeable mortgage from the Westmoreland Building Society, but a likely additional source was 'Laddie' James (S. B. Haughton-James), a wealthy young friend who had already shown an interest in a share of Blackheath and of whose family estate, the Saddler Trust, Fred Clarke was a trustee. Laddie James was enthusiastic, and together the two men went up on 16 July to look at Worthy Park, driving by Mandeville, May Pen, and the Spring Garden road in James's brand new motor car.

Once again Fred Clarke was struck by the tremendous area of Worthy Park's land and the wild beauty of its setting, but found that the estate had deteriorated even further in the previous decade. The canefields were straggly and the crop was expected to be small, the factory cluttered with antiquated machinery and the dwelling house, 'a rambling old thing with zinc sheets all over the original shingles', was shared by the owner with his book-keepers. Yet the cattle, though running almost wild, appeared to be flourishing, the 400 acres of cocoa and bananas were healthy, and over the lowlands the bush grew so densely that the whole area would obviously produce much more sugar 'under intelligent management'.[9] On returning to Westmoreland, Clarke and James decided to offer Calder 40,000 guineas and, two weeks later, Calder agreed to a price of £44,000.

After some hesitation, the Building Society advanced a first mortgage of £30,000, having received an independent valuation of £55,000;[10] but difficulties arose over Laddie James's share of the partnership. Originally it was decided that James would put up £10,000 to Clarke's £5,000, Clarke to pay back £2,500 as soon as possible, to equalize the shares. Fred Clarke and his fellow trustees on the Saddler Trust decided to advance Laddie James £10,000 on the security of the estate called Paradise,[11] but Cargill and Cargill, the Trust's solicitors, balked at the terms of the Worthy Park partnership. For a time it seemed that the whole transaction would fall to the ground, but Fred Clarke insisted that Laddie James was still obligated and eventually persuaded the Cargills to agree to an outright loan of the £10,000, on a second mortgage of Worthy Park.

As the price of the second mortgage, Fred Clarke—to his chagrin—was forced to resign from the Saddler Trust; but the net result was that instead of being a mere partner he was now the sole owner of Worthy Park. Moreover, he had only had to put up £4,000 of his own money and had a small balance in the bank for operating expenses, augmented by the sale of his personal stock at Blackheath. He had forfeited, however, the £1,000 severance pay agreed to in his contract with Hugh Clarke, and was unsuccessful in his application to the Colonial Bank for an agricultural lien of £5,000. The way ahead for Worthy Park did not promise to be a primrose path. 'There is no doubt about it that Worthy Park is a splendid property,' Fred Clarke wrote on 1 September 1918, 'but it has been very badly managed and is in bad order and the present cultivation will give a very poor crop for next year. I don't see how I can make anything off it between now and the end of next year, but I hope to pay my way and to get in a good field of canes for 1920 crop.'

Fred Clarke took up residence at Worthy Park before the Calders had finished packing, arriving with his Secretary/Accountant Stanley Richards on 2 September 1918, and spending the following week riding round counting, inspecting, and planning developments. It was a depressing duty. With only 240 acres in canes, the sugar acreage was the least it had been since the lifetime of Colonel Charles Price. As 'Bull' Lewis the pen manager (who went to Worthy Park in 1920) recalled fifty years later, three-quarters of the 1970 sugar land was then in 'pingwin and star-apple bush', and the majority of the cattle were so wild that they could not be accurately counted and had to be shot down like game when beef was needed. The estate roads and the all-important road to the railhead at Ewarton were in an appalling condition, even for the mule-wains which were the only means of shipping out produce. Miles of derelict tramway meandered uselessly through the fields, and the steam engines and vacuum pans in the factory were so dilapidated that it was all they could do to produce the 1919 crop of 280 tons of sugar, a total that would have given Sir Rose Price an apoplexy a century before.

One consolation to Fred Clarke was the discovery that in the sprawling 'Worthy Park' village was a well-kept Anglican church, presided over by a proper Englishman, the Rev. Brassington. From his first Sunday at Worthy Park, Fred Clarke was a diligent attender, invariably accompanied by his wife and family after their arrival in October 1918. To the present day, the Clarkes have remained pillars of the Anglican church in Lluidas Vale, despite the defection of most of the villagers to every shade of nonconformity. This pattern of patronage was one with which Fred Clarke had naturally been familiar in Westmoreland all his life.

Indeed, it was the importation of personnel and methods from a 'foreign' part of Jamaica which caused Fred Clarke his first problems at Worthy Park. The Clarkes brought with them from Blackheath some of their managerial staff, domestics, and senior workmen, and this must have caused a degree of dislocation in Lluidas Vale. Besides this, Fred Clarke resolutely introduced Westmoreland methods of cultivation (not all suited to Worthy Park's soil conditions) and western Jamaican piecework rates and wages, and thereby brought upon himself labour discontent. When the labourers struck for higher wages in Fred Clarke's very first week at Worthy Park he did 'not attach much importance to it', since it was 'generally the custom when a new manager takes charge',[12] and when the cane-cutters showed little enthusiasm to attack his first crop in January 1919, he attributed it to unfamiliarity with new conditions.[13] But as petty strikes constantly recurred, Fred Clarke was forced to regard his labour problems in a more serious light.

The attitude of Worthy Park's new master to his Negro labourers was much more akin to traditional paternalism than to modern industrial relations. To Fred Clarke's mind, it seems it was never the question of a living wage which was at stake, but what the estate could reasonably afford. When, for example, the workers almost rebelled at planting time in 1919, he did not defend the average daily rate of 2s. 9d., but pointed out that he was paying an aggregate wage-bill far in excess of that of J. V. Calder; and later, when wages were cut in times of low prices, he was quick to explain that the estate could not otherwise avoid complete collapse.[14] Yet even in prosperous times it was not wages which were increased so much as opportunities for work. Whenever he felt that conditions permitted it, Fred Clarke did his utmost to discover wage tasks for idle labourers around Christmas time, although in harder times the full extent of his benevolence was to provide land for labourers at very low rentals so that they could make some living during the slack season. At the end of exceptional crops such as that of 1920, however, he did sponsor a saturnalian 'crop-over', when two or three cows were butchered and there was a free issue of beef, rum, and sugar.

At other times, Fred Clarke appears to have been decidedly hazy about the actual living conditions of the men who toiled for him. When the Sugar Commission of 1929 asked about the diet of labourers living in the village, he 'almost had a softening of the brain' when looking over the questionnaire and was forced to ask his cook for the prices of staple items. When 'Cookie' replied that they were 'all different prices 'cording to season' he passed on the questionnaire to Arthur Clarke.[15] As to the labourers and their families living in the Worthy Park barracks, Fred Clarke was more concerned, especially when epidemics such as the Spanish 'flu of 1918 threatened to spread to the nearby home of the Clarkes. In 1927 and 1930 when there were cases of typhoid in the barracks he sent fresh milk and medicines and employed a woman to act as nurse. Although he always claimed that the estate could not afford to improve the barracks, he was angered at the lack of medical facilities provided by the Government. In December 1930, for example, he sent a girl from the barracks who was desperately ill with typhoid to Linstead in a hired car. She was refused entry at Linstead hospital and sent on to Spanish Town, where she died. 'Instead of stuffing education down these people's throat and unfitting them for the station in life in which it has pleased God to place them,' Fred Clarke wrote in his diary, 'they would be doing a greater service to them if they would provide more free hospital treatment and free medical attention.'[16]

Throughout the history of Jamaica the planters of Jamaica had relied upon the courts of the island to sustain the socio-economic *status quo*, and Fred Clarke was the unquestioning inheritor of this tradition. He prided himself on being stern but just, and relied upon the courts to uphold his somewhat austere conception of duty, as well as to protect his business contracts. Himself a J.P., he did not hesitate to prosecute strikers and malingerers under the archaic Masters and Servants Laws, as well as to use the courts to evict squatters or tenants who did not pay their rents.[17] These were matters of principle, however unpleasant or seemingly unimportant the rewards. Litigation was also regarded as necessary in order to protect Clarke interests against the operations of sharp-dealing merchants or even business associates. Before the formation of the Sugar Manufacturers' Association, Fred Clarke, like all planters in their traditional struggle with the merchant class, expected to go to court in arbitration of disputes over sugar shipments and payments. In his first tenuous year at Worthy Park, Fred Clarke also went so far as to sue J. V. Calder for £1,000 alleging short measure in cattle and house furniture, and even to allow his lawyers to press those of Laddie James to speed up the paying over of the crucial loan of £10,000.[18]

When Fred Clarke himself was threatened with court proceedings it was, quite naturally, something of a different story. When a neighbour (in Blackheath days) complained of stinking effluent from the factory, when J. V. Calder made a counter-claim alleging non-payment for seed and manure, when the Receiver-General of Jamaica demanded unpaid income tax, or when a government official asserted that Worthy Park's 'coolie barracks' were uninhabitable, Fred Clarke's diaries registered an entirely human, albeit private, yelp of anguish.

In more positive ways, his efforts during the first three years at Worthy Park were the finest achievements of Fred Clarke's busy life. Increasing efficiency and expanding production with tireless ingenuity, he did not allow the record sugar prices of 1920 to waylay him into a fool's paradise, but ploughed back income into improvements, so that Worthy Park was narrowly able to withstand later shocks.

Fred Clarke's first action was to tear up the five miles of tramway 75 years old and sell them to the United Fruit Company for £2,000. Deciding that the mule wains caused uneconomic delays, he invested in Worthy Park's first motor truck, a Federal costing £750, which reduced the journey to Ewarton railway station from a day to an hour. A second truck was added in 1920 to speed the collection of cane from the fields. In reorganizing the factory, Fred Clarke, with no mechanical training, faced an almost insuperable task. His first crop was laboriously ground by the water-mill dating from 1866, and then only after the Murmuring Brook dam-head and aqueduct had been cleaned and re-pointed. By taking the advice of a consulting engineer and employing more competent staff, however, he was able to revive one of the two old steam engines for the 1920 crop and the other in time for the crop of 1921. By that time, some money was available for vital replacements.

In the cultivation of sugar-cane Fred Clarke needed little counsel, but he did call in experts to advise him on cattle, cocoa, and bananas; and for the first time at Worthy Park, specialists were employed to look after each of these branches of the estate's economy. With the aim of diversifying still further and bringing in more casual income, Fred Clarke also invested in sheep, pigs, and barnyard fowls, the last of which were cared for by 'Mammie' Clarke and the children.[19] Until he had established himself, Fred Clarke was not too proud to sell mutton, pork, and chickens in the local markets, as well as small parcels of sugar and rum to local retailers. He also purchased very cheaply 'wet' sugar in 50-gallon oil drums from small farmers round about, most of which was processed into rum.

These petty dealings were always viewed as interim expedients, while Worthy Park's major cultivation was being expanded and made more efficient. Fred Clarke was not even very enthusiastic about cocoa and bananas, since they were susceptible to spoilage and damage from excessive rainfall such as that which occurred in June 1919. He was, above all, a sugar man, and turned his chief attentions to the expansion of sugar acreage and yields, with striking results. In the dozen years of active life which remained to him, he completely reshaped the map of Worthy Park, trebling the area of cane-pieces and reviving for the first time some of the ancient sugar lands of Thetford and Swansea. With the doubling of the yield of cane per acre and the 15 per cent increase of efficiency made in the factory, the overall production was raised eight-fold. Even in the first two years, sugar production soared from the 205 tons grown in 1918—Calder's last crop—to 510 in 1920.

Since the effect of changes could not become apparent during 1919, however, the period before the harvesting of the 1920 crop was one of desperate budgeting, and it was only by the last-minute aid of a loan of £3,000 from Thompson, Hankey that Worthy Park was able to survive. The sequel was dramatic. Thanks to the post-war demand, slow general recovery and world-wide speculation, sugar prices rose to unprecedented levels, reaching well over £100 per ton in May 1920, compared with what had been considered a good price of £26 in 1919. Unlike many planters, whose crops were disappointingly small or already committed at previous prices, Fred Clarke had a handsome crop which he was able to sell for a minimum of £70 and a maximum of £103 per ton. For most of his 300 puncheons of rum he also received 7s. 6d. a gallon and, to his pious amazement, he discovered that after only two years at Worthy Park, he had made a clear profit of no less than £30,000. 'How with only £6,000 I have purchased Worthy Park for £44,000,' he wrote in his diary in July 1920,

... how all the attempts to block me were upset and turned to my interest—how Laddie James and his advisers compelled him to withdraw and leave me sole owner. How I have struggled through the first year and how I have cleared £30,000 in one crop is as a dream to me. That it was all God's ordering I can have no doubt, but with what object I do not know. Anyway I am praying that his love and bounty towards us will make us all serve him better and love him more.

I have paid off Laddie James's loan of £10,000 today and am writing the Building Society to ask the Directors if they will take a repayment of £10,000. ...

For a few months, even the sober Fred Clarke was on top of the world, splurging on a handsome motor car and talking of sending his children to England for their education and retiring there himself in the not-too-distant future. Fortunately, however, his natural caution prevailed. While some Jamaican planters dissipated their sudden affluence in folly and others spent far more than their earnings in grandiose new factories,[20] Fred Clarke quietly invested as much as he could afford in new machinery for the factory. For, as his instinct correctly predicted, the 'dance of the millions' of 1920 was followed by a prolonged slump that was terrible in its contrast. It was as well that the Building Society had decided not to accept the repayment of £10,000, for it was twenty years before the Clarkes could renew the offer and thirty years before it was paid off completely, and as for the £3,000 supertax owed on the 1920 profits, it was many years too before that was finally paid.[21]

The fortunes made in 1920 led to world-wide over-production, which was exacerbated by the post-war revival of the sugar-beet-producing countries and the complete absence of effective international controls. Sugar prices zigzagged downwards to the levels reached in the later nineteenth century and then below those, until even the enemies of the sugar industry realized that sugar was selling below the cost of production. As time went on, Great Britain and Canada gave some preference to British colonial sugar, but this was offset by declining consumption brought on by the general depression. Priced out of the consumers' reach by excise duties, rum suffered even more, and became almost unsaleable at any price. In 1921, the prices received for sugar and rum were only a fifth of those obtained the year before, and although there were slight recoveries in 1923 and 1925, the planters cleared less than £12 per ton for sugar and 1s. 6d. a gallon for rum between 1927 and 1929. In 1930, the c.i.f. London price of sugar reached a record low of £4. 15s., and even with the preferential duty, Jamaican producers were receiving under £8 per ton, possibly half the cost of production and a twelfth of the price received a decade before.

It is against this background that the progress of Worthy Park during the second and final phase of Fred Clarke's ownership should be measured. His chief strategy was to produce as much sugar as possible as cheaply as possible, in the ever-fading hope of a rise in prices. By 1930, the estate was producing 1,800 tons of sugar from 820 acres of canes in a two-phase crop that continued with barely a break from January to December. But at this level, the factory was stretched beyond its proper capacity and without capital could not be extended, or even properly maintained. While sugar and rum prices were fair, Worthy Park could keep its head above water; but expanding production when prices were below costs simply multiplied deficits, since even with savage reductions and economies, wage and fuel bills and the cost of running repairs had to be met. Rum production, which Fred Clarke reckoned should account for a third of the income of a properly managed estate, ceased altogether at Worthy Park between 1926 and 1929 for lack of a profitable outlet, and had it not been possible to revive it in 1930, the estate might have foundered there and then.

As it was, the notions of an extravagant education for the children and a luxurious retirement like an eighteenth-century absentee were put aside. Of Fred Clarke's three sons, only Clement, the eldest, after a period at Munro, was sent to school in England, and he returned to help his father in 1922 instead of going on to university. The other two boys, Owen and George, were given a technical education designed to make them independent of Worthy Park, and worked their way through McGill University in Canada to engineering degrees. Fred Clarke himself was never able to retire.[22] Instead, his only indulgences were trips to sanitoria in the United States in 1922, 1923, 1930, and 1932 to recoup his deteriorating health, on the last of which he died.

What battered and finally broke Fred Clarke was the constant struggle for existence at Worthy Park. Running the huge estate was burden enough, but to this was added the incessant struggle to obtain the best market prices for sugar and rum, and the humiliating quest for money to carry on from crop to crop. In those long past days before co-operation and controls, it was left entirely to the planter as to what and how much he should grow, when and to whom he should sell; and the mastery of market strategy and tactics were essential for the very existence of estates.

Health, prices, credit: these were the preoccupations which ran ceaselessly through the 2,000 pages of Fred Clarke's diaries; but their convolution can best be conveyed by the quotation of two detailed examples from periods of contrasted fortune:

Friday, April 9, 1920. . . . Fred L. Myers of Kingston offered me £72 per ton for my sugar, and as the controlled price in England for April was fixed at £67 I considered this a good offer. I however was a bit suspicious about it and went up to Kingston yesterday to enquire of Mr. Rose, who is Thompson, Hankey's agent, if he had had any news from them of the rising prices. He said no, so I went to Myers and told him that I would not accept £72 but that I would be prepared to accept £75. Rather to my surprise, he accepted my offer and I sold 100 tons. Today I have been offered £80 per ton, so I dropped £500 on the sale of 100 tons yesterday. Anyway, the price is a splendid one and I have been very fortunate in my sales of sugar this year as I did not sell beforehand as some other planters did. Several of them sold their crops, or the greater part of them, at prices ranging from £30 to £45. So far I have sold none below £70 save the 8% for island consumption which the Food Controller has commandeered at £35. 10. 0. . . .

Wednesday, April 28, 1920. . . . The price of sugar has now reached £100 per ton and everybody is holding, expecting it to go higher. . . .

Sunday, May 8, 1920. . . . I was offered £100 a ton for the Worthy Park sugar by Fred L. Myers and Son, and £103 by Mr. Vernon Alexander for June delivery of Grocery is equivalent to about £109, I have decided not to sell. . . .

Thursday, June 17, 1920. . . . On my way to Kingston on Tuesday am., I received a cable from the Hankeys in reply to one from me as to whether Worthy Park sugar did not pass as Grocery by the Grading Committee what price it was likely to fetch. They called back that as Refining it would net about £83 a ton. This is rather a blow to me as I have over 200 tons unsold. At the controlled price for Grocery in England it ought to have netted about £105 per ton. The cable really meant that if the sugar did not come up to the Grocery standard it would probably net about £83 per ton, on a loss to me of about £22 per ton, which would aggregate about £4,400 on the 200 tons. I went round to all the sugar people in Kingston and tried to get what information I could with respect to the sugar market. I understand that there has been a drop of about £25 per ton on sugar, but that the price fixed by the Food Controller in England for June sales was practically £105 per ton and for July £109, and Messrs Myers inform me that the sugar I had sold them passed as Grocery and they seemed to think my sugars arriving in June ought to net over £100 per ton. I then went to see Mr. Vernon Alexander, who is buying for some firm in America and offered him a 100 tons of the sugar which I had not yet shipped, and was very much relieved when he offered me £100 per ton. He added that he had just called his firm about some other sugars and that if they authorised him to pay more, he would make me a better offer. I then went to Fred L. Myers and told them that I had 132 tons of sugar shipped to London, but that the Hankeys were doubtful whether the quality would pass as Grocery (judging from the small samples I sent them) and if they, Fred L. Myers, were prepared to buy the sugar, I would be inclined to sell to them at £105 per ton, provided that the Hankeys had not committed themselves to any sale or contract. They said they would wire me their reply today. So far I have had no news from Mr. Alexander, but a while ago I received a telegram from Myers, to say that they would take the sugar I had on the wharf at a £100 per ton, and asking me to quote my lowest price for the 132 tons I had unsold in London. I have arranged to go to see them in Kingston in the a.m. before deciding anything definite, but it is some relief to me to know that there is some prospect of my receiving the £100 per ton, instead of having to sell at £83. There is undoubtedly a slump in the sugar market at present, but everyone seems to think that there will be a big rise later on. . . .

Saturday, June 19, 1920. . . . Went to Kingston yesterday and saw Mr Rose and Mr Henderson. They tell me they have heard nothing in regard to the sugar market. Went on to Mr Vernon Alexander and told him that I would not accept his offer of £100 a ton for the sugar but that I would take £105. He said he was sorry he could make no better offer than £100 per ton. I then went on to Fred L. Myers and accepted their offer for the balance of the crop which will probably be anything between 80/90 tons (at £100 per ton). This is the first sugar that I have sold at that price. So far I have sold in Jamaica at £70 and £75 and my first shipment to England fetched about £84. I have shipped to the Hankeys the unsold 132 tons. It is quite uncertain what this will fetch. According to the Hankeys if this is graded by the Sugar Committee as Grocery it will fetch about £109. . . . I have cabled them not to sell at less than £100 per ton and I believe that if they cannot get that I may be able to sell the sugar in London to Myers at the £100. . . .

★ ★ ★ ★ ★ ★ ★ ★ ★

Wednesday, March 29, 1922. . . . I have now exhausted my credit at the bank, and as I have 300 tons of sugar unsold I went up with the ideas of trying to sell 200 tons. I went to Hendersons' and Mr. James Henderson told me that sugars had been sold as high as £15. 10. 0 the week before but there had since been a drop in prices. I went down to Morrison and Morrison [his solicitors] and asked them to try and find out from the Loan Board what they were selling at. They replied that the week before last they had sold at £15. 10. 0; last week they sold none, and this week they are asking £16. I then went to Myers. Myers was not there but his clerk took an option from me at £15. 10. 0 delivered at their wharf, the option to expire at 2 o'clock. At that hour I went round to them and Mr. Morris told me that Mr. Myers said he could not take up the offer. I then went round to Lascelles de Mercado, and their manager took an option on the 200 tons until Saturday April 1, at £15. 10. 0, which means that they have until that date to decide. I then went round to the Canadian Bank of Commerce and told them what I had done, and they agreed to allow me to overdraw my account £500 until I could carry through the sale of the sugar.

June 26, 1922 [from a letter to Stainton Clarke, Sweet River, Savanna-la-Mar]. . . . I am in rather an awkward position just now. I held the greater part of my sugar as I told you. Friday June 16 I decided to offer it to Myers at £16. 10. 0, in the railway stores, which is equivalent to about £17. f.o.b. Jamaica. I did not, as people were pressing me for money, and the Canadian Bank of Commerce, from whom I had had advances, said they could not let the matter lie over indefinitely. Myers had telegraphed, asking me to give him an option on the sugar until the following Monday or Tuesday. I telegraphed

from Ewarton at 7 o'clock on Saturday morning offering him my
sugars at £16. 10. 0 subject to prompt reply by wire. He got the
telegram at 8 o'clock on Saturday a.m. and I did not receive his reply
until midday on the following Monday a.m., in which he accepted
the sugars. By that time the price had risen considerably. I wired him
back to say that a reply received 48 hours after my wire asking for
prompt reply by wire could not be considered a prompt reply and I
refused to deliver the sugar. His defence is that he is a Jew, that his
business is closed on Saturday and that Monday was his first opportunity of getting a telegram through. But according to the telegraph
regulations, messages can be sent at any hour of the day or night, on
Sundays or weekdays and the penalty for out of ordinary hours is a
double rate on the message plus 2/– to the clerk handling the message.
I contend that in making the offer, I had not got to consider Myers'
religious principles, and if these prevented him giving me a prompt
reply then he was not in a position to accept my offer, and further, if
his Jewish sabbath terminated on Saturday evening he could have sent
a telegram accepting it, either on Saturday evening, Saturday night or
Sunday.

I have seen Charlie Morrison on the matter, also Bagot Gray.
Morrison is doubtful, but Gray says that I have a strong case and I
should refuse to deliver. I had an interview with Myers on Thursday
and he said if I would accept the position he would give me £100
additional. I refused this and we arranged to submit the matter to
arbitration. . . . It is a matter of £1,000 to me and is worth the fighting
for. On the other hand, if I lose it I have the satisfaction of knowing
that I did not sell at £14 as I might have done.

I have got the catalogue and prices for Clifton Springs Sanitorium.
The rates seem to be very much more than you stated. A single room
without lavatory is £49 per month, which is about £12 per week,
and that is without any of the other charges. I figure that it will cost
me about £20 per week. . . .[23]

Fred Clarke's chief concern in skittering from firm to firm was to
avoid the thralldom to rapacious merchants suffered by his eighteenth-
century predecessors. To his advantage he enjoyed the use of the
telegraph and much more sophisticated banking techniques; but as
conditions deteriorated, his efforts to retain economic independence
gradually failed. In July 1929, despite a crop of almost 1,500 tons of
sugar, the Canadian Bank of Commerce refused to advance the short-

term loan of £5,000 to see the estate through to the beginning of the subsequent crop which they had provided for the previous eight years. Consequently, Fred Clarke was forced to grant the handling of his entire crop to Messrs. Lascelles de Mercado, in return for a loan of £5,000 at 6 per cent. In this way he was liable to the payment of a commission of $2\frac{1}{2}$ per cent on foreign sales and 5 per cent on island sales, a total of between £400 and £500, which he had hitherto saved by handling the sales himself. Lascelles renewed the loan in 1930, but in 1931 conditions had become so desperate that they would only advance £5,000 on the security of a second mortgage on Worthy Park and all its stock, as well as having the absolute control of all sales of sugar and rum.

By the last year of his life, Fred Clarke was a deeply disappointed man. In his diary, the earlier ebullience and later resilience was succeeded by a tone of pessimistic fatalism. On several occasions he would have sold out altogether had there been any sort of market for Worthy Park, and when the younger boys approached graduation in 1931, that worst of years, he felt fearful for their future.

Wednesday, May 6, 1931. . . . The boys write in great spirits about coming out for their vacation. Things are in such a depressed condition that they have not yet been able to secure any jobs in Canada. . . . I hope they will not be disappointed but life is, more or less made up of disappointments, and one's expectations of the future are very seldom realised. . . .

Wednesday, May 27, 1931. . . . Poor Ed Morris writes in great concern. . . . The Westmoreland Building Society is allowing him only £20 per week on Shrewsbury, a place that should be spending £150 per week.

I don't know how it is all going to end, but things look pretty desperate.

We have received a cable from the boys at McGill today reading "Both graduated". . . .

Monday June 15, 1931. . . . I still have a little money left which I am trying to hold on to until we start crop again at the end of July. Under the agricultural lien, Lascelles de Mercado and Co. will advance me on the unreaped portion of the crop. This will take us to the end of September. Then the question will be whether I will be able to get them to give me a further credit to carry on until I start reaping the 1932 crop in January.

I have decided that it will be quite impossible to carry on under present circumstances and to pay the same rates of wages and most reluctantly I have notified all the employees today that there will be a reduction of $12\frac{1}{2}\%$ on their wages and salaries. This is going to cause quite a lot of dissatisfaction and resentment, as in most cases they are not intelligent enough to realise the position, but I have no alternative and feel that I must make some effort to save the situation. . . .

Fred L. Clarke died suddenly in August 1932 after an operation, and Owen Clarke came from Canada to help his brother Clement at Worthy Park. Living conditions on the family estate were not going to be any easier than those in depression-racked Canada, but Owen Clarke proceeded on the principle that if times were going to be hard it would be far better to endure them in a place he knew and loved. The third brother, George Clarke, although he remained on in Canada as an engineer until after the Second World War, kept closely in touch with Worthy Park and was always consulted about important developments.

Although it was not immediately obvious, a corner had been turned by 1932, and since that time Worthy Park has made steady progress with few serious setbacks. While this has been due to a gradual improvement in general conditions, especially since 1939, coupled with the enlightened energies of the three younger Clarkes, it has also owed much to the work of their father. Far from being swamped by succeeding crises, he had laid a sound basis for expansion in field and factory at Worthy Park and had also relieved his sons of much of the worry about fluctuating prices which had bedevilled his own existence. It was not until sugar prices were standardized by the British Ministry of Food in 1939 that the responsibility for 'playing the market' was taken entirely out of the hands of the growers, but by placing his entire production in the hands of a single reliable factor in 1929 Fred Clarke had greatly simplified selling operations. Moreover, in 1934, Clement Clarke was able to transfer the Worthy Park business from Lascelles in Kingston to the ever-faithful Hankeys in London, and thus save the estate the $2\frac{1}{2}$ per cent commission on sales which had seemed such a waste to his father. These developments in selling technique, however, were overshadowed by the creation of the Sugar and Rum Pools and Sugar Manufacturers' Association of Jamaica between 1929 and 1932, in which Fred Clarke had played a vital part.

In 1929, at the time that the Olivier Commission had been making its searching examination of the sugar industry, Fred Clarke had been among the most vocal members of the planters' lobby which met at the Imperial Association Rooms in Kingston, and which persuaded the Jamaican Government to provide a subsidy of £2 a ton for sugar in 1930, and a further subsidy of £60,000 in 1931.[24] More important, Fred Clarke was one of the seven original members of the Sugar Board set up by the Government out of the infant S.M.A., which in 1930 persuaded all planters to co-operate in fixing sugar prices for local consumption. By raising consumer prices to between 2d. and 3d. a pound while fixing commission for wholesalers and retailers at $7\frac{1}{2}$ per cent and 10 per cent respectively (with $\frac{1}{2}$ per cent to the managing broker), the Sugar Manufacturers assured the planters of between £14. 10s. and £22 per ton for the 20 per cent of their sugar destined for local consumption, at a time when the U.K. price was well under £10 per ton.[25] Owing to the critical tone of the report of the Olivier Commission and the opposition of the Elected Members of the Jamaican Legislative Council, the local subsidy was never renewed; but the Sugar Pool did tide over many of the planters, not only until 1932, when the British and Canadian Governments greatly increased the scale of imperial preference, but to 1939, when the Second World War raised export sugar prices to highly profitable levels once again. Indeed, after 1940 the situation regarding island sales was reversed, and planters were forced to sell some of their sugar locally at prices well below those obtainable abroad, a situation that had already occurred in 1920.

Once a measure of co-operation in the production and sale of sugar had been achieved, Fred Clarke campaigned strongly for similar co-operation in the sale of rum, and for a reduction in the scale of imperial excise duties. Progress here was slower, but a Rum Pool was created under the auspices of the S.M.A. in 1932 which was given statutory authority under the Spirits Control Law 11 of 1934.[26] As a result, in years of low demand such as 1934-9 and since 1950, Worthy Park, along with other estates has actually been paid a 'cess' for not producing rum, provided that the price obtainable for molasses does not rise above a predetermined level. In contrast, in 1928 Fred Clarke had been unable to produce rum for lack of demand, and was forced to sell molasses at 6d. a gallon for industrial purposes.

After 1932 then, Worthy Park operated under a new covenant. Instead of one isolated and overworked owner, operations were carried out under the benevolent aegis of the S.M.A. by two, and later three, of his sons, with Arthur Clarke as a link between the old and new régimes. Worthy Park was owned equally by each of Fred Clarke's children, but Clement Clarke, as oldest son and one of his father's executors, always remained the senior partner. Gradually, however, first Owen and then George assumed more equal responsibility, while the influence of Arthur Clarke declined as he approached retirement. At first the organization was loosely structured, but in October 1936 duties were clearly demarcated for the first time and the functions of factory, farm, and pen were separated. Thereafter, management meetings were regularly held, with formal minutes being sent to absent co-proprietors. In the later 1930s the services of a professional accountant began to be used and in 1949, after several years of discussion, the family partnership was made into a limited liability company, being divided into Worthy Park Factory Ltd. and Worthy Park Farms Ltd. for accountancy and taxation convenience some years later.

Although Arthur Clarke continued to hold special responsibility for the cane and other crops and Stanley Richards ran the office until after the Second World War, while 'Bull' Lewis continued to manage the Pen, the restless quest of the younger Clarkes for business efficiency and greater professionalism sometimes grated with the older hands. Justification, however, lay with the results. Although as Fred Clarke's children grew to adulthood and began to marry the calls upon capital multiplied, the estate began to make a modest profit, which increased steadily year by year. The vast majority of this, however, was ploughed back into the business, particularly the factory, which for years had been severely overworked. Here the engineering training of Owen Clarke (while not directed specifically towards sugar technology) was invaluable; not only in getting the best out of existing machinery, but in buying at knockdown prices and expertly installing secondhand machinery from the dozens of less fortunate estates which had been forced to suspend operations. Between 1935 and 1940 Worthy Park made nearly £38,000 in gross profits, but during this period £10,000 was repaid to the Westmoreland Building Society and no less than £24,000 was spent upon the factory. It was only these improvements that enabled the factory to satisfy the tremendous increase in the demands made upon it between 1940 and 1945.

	Gross profits £	Rum pool proceeds £	Total 'Additions to Assets' £	Factory improvements £
1933	3,718	1007	248	248
1934	5,091	2224	4212	
1935	2,474	1814	1189	467
1936	3,625	2228	7233	6853
1937	7,131	2445	7264	6427
1938	4,419	2882	1983	1723
1939	6,566	3049	4408	3663
1940	13,504	3435	7206	4897[27]

The formation of the S.M.A. had in fact been followed by the further and final consolidation of the sugar factories which was one of the most constructive of the recommendations of the Olivier Report. From a total of 134 sugar estates with factories in 1897 and 59 in 1920, the number fell to 35 in 1930 and 20 in 1945, though the actual production of sugar in Jamaica rose from 16,000 tons in 1897, to 40,000 tons in 1920 and 68,000 tons in 1930, to 152,000 tons in 1945. This production was greatly augmented after 1939 by the purchase of canes from small farmers, the proportion of farmers' canes rising to almost 50 per cent by the end of the war. These developments were clearly reflected at Worthy Park, one of the smallest of the surviving factory estates, though the expansion of the fields and the increase in the intake of farmers' canes were determined by the rather limited speed at which capital became available to expand the factory and to introduce motor vehicles to help speed the crops. Production was aided, however, by technical improvements in cane cultivation and sugar boiling which followed Owen Clarke's completion of a short course in sugar technology at Louisiana State University in 1934[28] and the creation of a Research Department by the S.M.A. in 1942. As a result, the acreage yield at Worthy Park has increased from under one ton of sugar in 1918 and just over three tons in 1945 to the present level of almost five tons, and the number of tons of cane needed to produce a ton of sugar fell from 12·8 in 1930 to 7·4 in 1938, a level that has scarcely been bettered since. Total sugar production at Worthy Park rose from 510

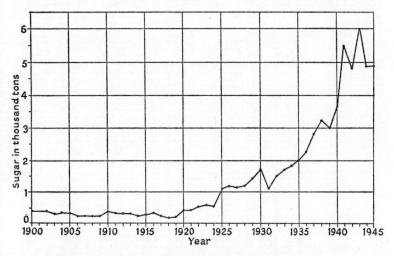

WORTHY PARK SUGAR PRODUCTION, 1900–1945

tons from 340 acres in 1920 to 1,755 tons from 819 acres in 1930, and 4,844 tons from 1,023 estate acres (with 30 per cent of the cane purchased from small farmers) in 1945. The Worthy Park share of the Jamaica total, as little as 0·5 per cent in 1918 and 1·3 per cent in 1920, rose to 2·6 per cent in 1930 and 3·2 per cent in 1945, a proportion that would have been even higher had the estate been able to use the present ratio of seven tons of farmers' canes to five tons of estate canes rather than only 30 per cent farmers' cane.[29]

Sugar Crops on Worthy Park Estate, 1920–1936

Year	Acres in cane	Estate cane tons	Farmers' canes tons	Total cane tons	Tons sugar	Tons cane per acre	Sugar per acre	Tons cane per ton sugar	Rainfall inches	Cost per ton sugar £ s. d.	Selling price per ton £ s. d.	Loss per ton £ s. d.	Gain per ton £ s. d.
1920	340	8,644	60	8,704	510	25·4	1·5	17·1	48·16				
1921	364	8,745	77	8,822	538	24·0	1·49	16·4	70·44				
1922	427	8,554	176	8,730	700	20·1	1·61	12·4	30·36				
1923	485	7,633	77	7,710	686	15·5	1·38	11·2	46·94				
1924	472	6,510	35	6,545	641	13·8	1·35	10·2	60·15				
1925	525	13,500	140	13,640	1033	25·7	1·95	13·2	42·93				
1926	571	14,478	436	14,914	1203	25·3	2·04	12·4	62·64				
1927	648	14,959	316	15,275	1165	23·0	1·76	13·1	57·70				
1928	626	13,553	91	13,644	1206	21·6	1·91	11·3	45·15	14 17 4	14 4 0	13 4	
1929	759	17,249	4	17,253	1465	22·7	1·92	11·8	54·71	12 8 9	11 3 3	1 5 6	
(1920–9)	5217	113,825	1412	115,237	9147	21·8	1·73	12·6	51·91				
1930	819	21,797	28	21,825	1755	26·6	2·06	12·4	39·55 ⎫	10 12 8	11 2 7		9 11
1931	779	15,196	8	15,204	1252	19·9	1·64	12·1	62·02 ⎪				
1932	670	16,646	47	16,693	1509	24·8	2·25	11·0	59·27 ⎬	8 18 11	11 10 0		2 11 1
1933	893	19,810	27	19,837	1765	22·2	1·98	11·2	119·74 ⎪	8 14 2	11 5 0		2 10 1
1934	907	20,858	32	20,890	1850	23·0	2·03	11·3	69·85 ⎭	8 10 0	10 17 7		1 11 7
1935	863	18,359	199	18,558	1979	21·3	2·26	9·4	55·88	8 10 0			
1936	938	21,838	236	22,074	2326	23·3	2·45	9·5	88·5	7 17 5	9 10 5		1 13 0

Sugar Crops on Worthy Park Estate, 1930–1945

Year	Acres in cane	Estate cane tons	Farmers' canes tons	Total cane tons	Tons sugar	Tons cane per acre	Sugar per acre	Tons cane per ton sugar	Rainfall inches	Cost per ton sugar £ s. d.	Selling price per ton £ s. d.	Gain per ton sugar £ s. d.
1930	819	21,797	28	21,825	1755	26·6	2·06	12·4	39·55 ⎱	10 12 8	11 2 7	9 11
1931	779	15,196	8	15,204	1252	19·9	1·64	12·1	62·02 ⎰			
1932	670	16,646	47	16,693	1509	24·8	2·25	11·0	59·27			
1933	893	19,810	27	19,837	1765	22·2	1·98	11·2	119·74	8 18 11	11 10 0	2 11 1
1934	907	20,858	32	20,890	1850	23·0	2·03	11·3	69·85	8 14 2	11 5 0	2 10 10
1935	863	18,359	199	18,558	1979	21·3	2·26	9·4	55·88	8 10 0	10 1 7	1 11 7
1936	938	21,838	236	22,074	2326	23·3	2·45	9·5	88·5	7 17 5	9 10 5	1 13 0
1937	868	22,472	368	22,840	2815	24·21	3·00	8·11	56·71	7 10 0	10 2 1	2 12 1
1938	895	22,940	1,893	24,832	3238	25·63	3·34	7·66	38·60	7 18 3	9 9 4	1 11 1
1939	940	20,285	1,836	22,121	2999	21·50	2·91	7·37	59·12	8 19 1	10 18 7	1 19 6
1940	1019	27,559	1,371	28,930	3715	27·02	3·48	7·76	47·81	8 9 1	12 10 1	4 0 3
1941	1162	37,363	10,373	47,736	5501	32·15	3·71	8·68	44·43			
1942	1224	23,783	13,924	37,707	4785	19·20	2·44	7·88	74·17			
1943	1159	30,806	17,484	48,290	5946	26·5	3·20	8·12	56·45			
1944	948	21,570	14,801	36,371	4881	23·7	3·18	7·45	60·19			
1945	1023	26,971	10,961	37,932	4844	26·3	3·36	7·83	67·72			

In 1929, when Worthy Park made 1,465 tons of sugar from its own canes and still made a loss, Fred Clarke showed Mr. Anderson, a visiting engineer, around his works. Anderson praised the layout and operations, but told Clarke he should make extensions and improvements which would enable him to take off 2,000 tons of sugar every year. Knowing better than the engineer of the non-availability of capital, Fred Clarke laughingly remarked that he would have to leave such visionary developments to his heirs. Had he known that the 2,000 tons would be doubled within eight years of his death and multiplied eight times within twenty years, he would doubtless have been incredulous. For their part, however, the two sons surviving in 1970 attribute the present success very largely to the basis laid by their father, both in the *annus mirabilis* of 1920 and in the long years of endurance which followed.

NOTES

[1] S. Olivier, *The Myth of Governor Eyre*, op. cit., 128–30, 242–4.
[2] British Patents, 1943 (1867), 1958 (1867), 2226 (1857).
[3] *Ibid.*, 1600 (1857).
[4] Fred Clarke's Diary, 1920, p. 40.
[5] Sold to the Charleys, it became part of Frome eventually in the 1950s.
[6] Advertisement in *Daily Gleaner*, 26 May 1918, inserted in Diary, 28 May 1918.
[7] Diary, 2 July 1918. Blackheath was in fact sold for £65,000 in December 1919. Later, like Meylersfield, it was swallowed by Tate and Lyle's property at Frome.
[8] Diary, 9 July 1918.
[9] *Ibid.*, 20 July 1918.
[10] Made up of Pen, £12,000; Commons, £10,000; Sugar, £33,000 (Factory only, £10,000).
[11] Diary, 14 August 1918.
[12] *Ibid.*, 8 September 1918.
[13] *Ibid.*, 1 January 1919.
[14] *Ibid.*, 3 September 1919.
[15] *Ibid.*, 23 October 1929.
[16] *Ibid.*, 24 July 1930.
[17] For example, Diary, 28 April 1928; 29 May 1930; 11 July 1931.
[18] Calder counter-claimed, but his plea was not accepted by the court. The original claim was settled out of court. The 'threatening noises' to James's lawyers produced the desired effect without a court case. All these transactions occurred

with surprisingly little loss of amicability all round. Litigation was a universal fact of life in old Jamaica.

19 Mrs. Clarke also 'mothered' the younger staff, who continued to live in a wing of the owner's house.

20 For example, the Pringle family; Diary, 17 March 1923.

21 As late as 1931, £143 remained unpaid.

22 Or even to accept the nomination to the Legislative Council or the post of Custos of St. Catherine's offered him in 1924, despite his contentions that 'agricultural interests' should be better represented in the Jamaican Government.

23 The Myers arbitration, on which hinged Fred Clarke's trip to America, was decided in Clarke's favour on 22 July 1922.

24 Law 22 of 1929 and Law 13 of 1931. The payment of the £60,000 was made possible by the redemption of the loan of that amount made by Jamaica to the United Kingdom during the First World War.

25 This was enacted by the Sugar Industry Aid Law, No. 26 of 1929. The planters were still to grow as much cane as they wished, but the amount of sugar allocated for island sales was determined on 1929 totals.

26 C. 365, Revised Edition of Laws of Jamaica.

27 Figures given in private letter from C. K. Clarke to G. F. Clarke in 1941.

28 The most important by-product of Owen Clarke's Louisiana interlude was the discovery that since Worthy Park's cane was naturally of a quality as high as any in Jamaica, productivity could most easily be aided by improvements in the factory rather than the fields.

29 The proportion in 1964, however, was still only 3 per cent (14,000 to 474,000, with 14:9 Farmers' canes).

CHAPTER TWELVE

Present and Future

Throughout the long history of Worthy Park certain themes have constantly recurred or provided a continuous thread for the narrative: the planters, the labourers, sugar itself. Yet since the Second World War and the achievement of Jamaican independence, change has so accelerated that the scale of operations, their very nature and their context have altered almost beyond recognition. Modern company management and advanced technology have almost entirely replaced the time-worn methods and attitudes of the old plantocracy. Sugar—more carefully controlled than ever before—still dominates but does not enslave the economy, for cattle and citrus production provide diversified income and employment. Labour is organized—though imperfectly—and receives a somewhat fuller share of the fruits of its toil and better welfare services. Moreover, by providing factory facilities for hundreds of farmers round about, Worthy Park has given far more small producers a chance of sharing in its economic good fortune than would once have been thought possible.

In 1970 it is true to say that Worthy Park has accommodated itself to modern conditions with remarkable flexibility and economic success, and the contribution it has made to the general economy have been the soundest arguments for its continued existence. Yet Jamaica remains disastrously overpopulated and desperately poor, and is consequently beset by pressures for radical reform. Sugar employment, as always, is seasonal and the mechanization necessary to make the estates yet more efficient is bound to reduce the labour force further. Lluidas Vale, moreover, contains far more people than Worthy Park could ever employ and in the valley, as in the rest of Jamaica, there is a growing hunger for land. Political radicals therefore tend to claim that sugar has ever been Jamaica's 'sweet malefactor' and that sugar estates—especially those privately owned—are 'caterpillars of the commonwealth'. To the perennial uncertainty that bedevils the production of sugar is added the more sinister spectre of political distemper. In predicting Worthy Park's future it will be necessary to estimate whether more or less traditional forms and values will continue to be enough to deflect, contain, or adapt the forces of change, or whether any degree of flexibility will be sufficient to continue the estate in a recognizable form for a further three centuries or even three decades.

As a benefit of the consolidation of the sugar factories, the efficient organization of the Sugar Manufacturers' Association and the ever-widening system of controls, the Jamaican sugar industry did not undergo the violent fluctuations of fortune after the Second World War that had followed the Armistice in 1918. Indeed, in mere production Jamaican sugar has expanded even more rapidly since 1945 than between 1939 and 1945; and in this quantitative expansion Worthy Park has more than maintained its place.

A world-wide shortage of sugar continued long after 1945, and for six years the British Ministry of Food continued the wartime quota arrangements that provided producers with a guaranteed outlet and stable high prices. By 1951, however, world production had soared once more and prices were falling towards a dangerous level, and when the British Labour Government—dedicated to low consumer prices—negotiated the 'Black Pact' with Cuba whereby cheap Cuban sugar was allowed to undercut British West Indian produce, a crisis impended. The situation was saved, largely through the lobbying of the British West Indies Sugar Association (formed in 1942), by the signing of the first Commonwealth Sugar Agreement in December 1951, shortly after the Conservative Government of Winston Churchill returned to power in Britain. This Agreement, which came into operation in 1953 and has been renewed continuously since, theoretically limited British West Indian sugar exports for the first time, but in fact enabled production to continue at a more viable level than would have been possible with untrammelled free trade. A basic quota of exports to the U.K. was established at an annually negotiated price, designed to be 'reasonably remunerative to efficient producers'.[1] In addition there is a much smaller 'Free Quota' of exports from the British West Indies to Canada and the U.K. at a price determined by the current world free market price of sugar, plus the scale of imperial preferences.[2] The Commonwealth Agreement quotas for Jamaica total 270,000 tons a year, of which some 218,000 tons are on the Negotiated Price Quota.

Attempts to set up an advantageous International Sugar Agreement have been much less successful, though the brake applied to all non-Communist sugar exporting areas undoubtedly did prevent runaway overproduction. A first Agreement signed in 1937 was inoperative because of the war, but others were negotiated in 1953 and 1958. These allocated quotas of up to almost a million tons for the British West Indies; but since the Commonwealth quotas already granted were deducted from this total, the islands were only permitted to export a few thousand tons into the general world market. Jamaica's share was nil until 1956 and an average of only about 22,000 tons a year between 1956 and 1961, at prices that barely paid for the cost of production.

Local Jamaican sales have continued to be controlled by the Jamaican Government 'on the recommendation of the Sugar Control Board, acting on the advice of the Sugar Manufacturers' Association', as they have since 1930. An annual quota is fixed, ranging from 31,000 tons in 1945 to 76,000 tons in 1965, and a scale of prices for the six grades of sugar, designed to provide a 'reasonable margin of profit' to manufacturers, wholesalers, and retailers, as well as a substantial excise duty for the Jamaican Government.[3] Consequently, sugar prices to the Jamaican consumer are not substantially lower than to the British or Canadian, though local processers are allocated sugar at preferential rates geared to the very low world free market price.

As a result of the post-war allocations and controls, Jamaican sugar production, which had averaged about 150,000 tons a year during the war and 250,000 tons between 1945 and 1951, stabilized at around 350,000 tons in the later 1950s, and the prices received by Jamaican manufacturers averaged around £40 a ton, at a time when free market world prices fell as low as £15. In 1958, however, occurred a further windfall with Castro's *coup* in Cuba and the subsequent nationalization of the Cuban sugar industry. As the result of Cuba's intransigence, the International Sugar Agreement broke down in 1962, and with the U.S. embargo on Cuban exports the free market

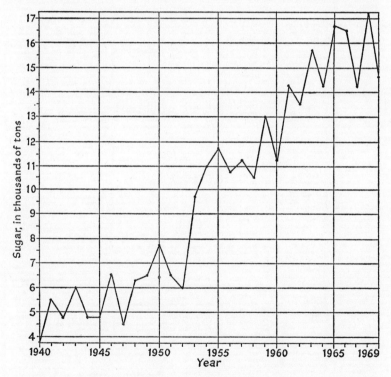

WORTHY PARK ESTATE: SUGAR PRODUCTION, 1940–1969

Worthy Park: Quality of Canes Delivered, 1950–1969

Year	Estate cane Tons	TC/TS (96°)	TC/TS theoretical	% Difference	Farmers' cane Tons	TC/TS (96°)	Total cane Tons	Average TC/TS (96°)
1950	39,298·00	8·25			27,559·00	8·49	66,857·00	8·35
1951	26,333·59	7·74	7·61	3·18	24,793·00	7·82	51,126·59	7·78
1952	26,639·00	7·86	7·47	4·23	21,491·00	8·26	48,130·00	7·95
1953	42,980·913	7·80	7·59	4·41	33,938·66	8·10	76,919·573	7·92
1954	47,859·74	7·94	7·01	6·66	39,500·85	8·00	87,360·59	7·96
1955	46,882·98	7·51	7·22	5·62	42,029·25	7·50	88,912·23	7·50
1956	46,093·60	7·65	7·26	3·71	35,456·20	7·68	81,549·80	7·58
1957	44,796·125	7·54	7·32	4·44	42,935·95	8·05	87,732·075	7·67
1958	44,510·35	7·66	7·50	5·90	38,643·738	7·97	83,154·088	7·80
1959	50,167·65	7·974	7·37	5·27	59,956·17	8·587	110,123·82	8·300
1960	47,624·38	7·775	7·10	6·21	43,618·50	8·021	91,242·88	7·891
1961	45,845·55	7·571	7·17	5·03	67,214·40	7·887	113,059·95	7·756
1962	45,112·31	7·545	7·14	5·31	61,973·86	7·960	107,086·17	7·780
1963	47,000·41	7·544	7·41	2·88	77,419·88	8·025	124,420·29	7·837
1964	44,067·51	7·632	7·31	4·94	70,084·73	8·093	114,152·24	7·909
1965	46,307·93	7·690	7·40	5·13	86,920·13	7·883	133,228·05	7·81
1966	49,014·36	7·802	7·36	4·91	85,137·78	8·129	134,152·14	8·006
1967	43,411·90	7·735	7·35	4·97	71,256·65	8·002	114,668·55	7·899
1968	52,001·38	7·239	6·88	5·26	77,464·30	7·571	129,465·67	7·435
1969	48,213·18	7·991	7·57		70,836·77	8·214	119,049·95	8·122

world price for sugar soared to £93 per ton in 1963. In addition, a sugar-starved U.S.A. began to admit non-quota allocations of Jamaican sugar that averaged 91,000 tons a year between 1961 and 1965, at prices that averaged a highly lucrative £65 per ton.[4] In 1965, Jamaica achieved an all-time record production of 506,348 tons of sugar, more than five times the level of 1940 (or 1805), one half of the cane being produced on the eighteen great estates and the other half by the 22,000 small farmers scattered throughout the island. This scale of production was not severely affected by the negotiation of a new International Sugar Agreement in 1968, though the results of the threatened adherence of the United Kingdom to the European Common Market might be far more serious.

The graph of Worthy Park's sugar production, geared to the island's quotas, has, of course, closely followed that of Jamaica, varied only by the more jagged appearance caused by small local seasonal fluctuations. Worthy Park's share of the total Jamaican production has remained steadily at about 3 per cent since 1945, averaging 6,112 tons of sugar a year between 1945 and 1951 and 10,590 tons between 1952 and 1960. Since 1960 there has been a further surge, and over the last decade

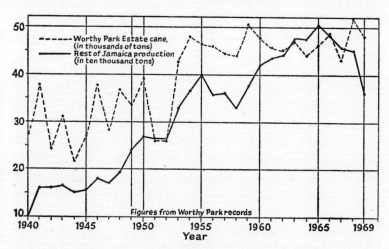

WORTHY PARK AND JAMAICAN PRODUCTION, 1940–1969

291

Worthy Park's factory has produced an annual average of 15,350 tons of sugar, with a peak production of 17,225 tons in 1968. These figures represent an average daily production during crop time of over 134 tons of sugar, from 1,000 tons of cane. Worthy Park's increased production has largely been made possible by huge increases in the purchase of cane from small farmers. These amounted to 10,961 tons in 1945, but had risen to 24,793 tons in 1951 and 86,920 tons in 1965, the proportion of farmers' canes in the total consumed by the factory rising from 28·9 per cent in 1945 to 48·6 per cent in 1951 and 65·4 per cent in 1965, compared with 50·8 per cent for the whole of Jamaica.[5] Even without the help of the small cane farmers, Worthy Park's own production of canes rose from an average of about 30,500 tons a year between 1940 and 1952, to 45,000 tons between 1953 and 1968.

Very largely as a result of the sixfold increase in sugar production and guaranteed fair prices, Worthy Park has been transformed over the last thirty years from a small family business into a major enterprise with an annual turnover of almost a million pounds. It is worth remembering that in the year Fred Clarke died the entire revenue of the estate was £22,656, and this had not reached £40,000 a year by the outbreak of the Second World War. By 1946, however, revenue had reached £150,000, and ten years later, £423,000. By 1966, receipts totalled more than three-quarters of a million pounds, and in the record year of 1968 this figure was exceeded by the income from sugar alone, and total revenue for factory and farms topped £1,000,000 for the first time.[6] Yet gross revenue, it need hardly be said, is no index of profitability, and the descent of several larger Jamaican estates towards bankruptcy and closure in recent years has shown that Worthy Park's success has not been entirely fortuitous. Indeed, the quantitative increase in turnover has not diminished but multiplied Worthy Park's problems, and it is only by a constant quest for greater efficiency and diversification that the estate has managed to survive and prosper.

In increasing the capability of the Worthy Park factory large capital investments have ungrudgingly been made, especially since the end of the Second World War. Between 1939 and 1945 some £25,700 was spent, mostly on secondhand machinery, in raising capacity from 3,000 to 6,000 tons; but in the twenty years after 1945 ten times this amount was spent, much of it on brand-new equipment, in order to expand production towards 18,000 tons a year.[7] While by no means ultra-modern, Worthy Park factory works so close to capacity that to increase its production by 50 per cent would require further expenditure of at least a quarter million pounds.

The sugar lands in Lluidas Vale have also been brought almost to capacity. Since 1940 some 300 acres of grassland, chiefly in Swansea and Tydixon, have been turned over to canes, increasing the acreage by some 30 per cent. Yet during the same period the estate's production of canes has risen by almost 50 per cent, and this has been achieved by remarkable improvements in acreage yields. After the creation of the Research Department by the S.M.A. in 1942 and particularly after the return of George Clarke to Jamaica in 1946, field experiments were ceaselessly carried out, so that Arthur Clarke just before he retired wryly complained that he did not know where the 'experiments' ended and the serious planting began.[8] Just as the factory employs laboratory staff constantly to analyse cane and processed sugar, so the field division of Worthy Park employed a full-time agronomist until 1965 to keep meteorological records, to analyse soils and to supervise the never-ending quest to find better-yielding varieties of cane, as well as those resistant to disease or to solve the problem of 'cow-itch' which complicates the cane-cutters' task.[9] Huge investments have been made in chemical fertilizers, both to improve newly opened cane-pieces and to increase the yield of fields in ratoons, and in sprays against pests and weeds. Since 1960 sprays and even fertilizers have increasingly been applied by 'crop-dusting' planes rather than laboriously by hand. In this way, tasks that normally take thousands of man-hours are performed in a single day when climatic conditions are exactly right.[10]

Between 1940 and 1942 the average yield at Worthy Park was a highly satisfactory 26·73 tons of cane per acre; but this was raised to 33·93 tons between 1953 and 1968. Ratooning to fifth and even further ratoons is employed, but thanks to scientific fertilizing the yield of ratoons has increased proportionately even more than that of plant canes, especially since modern practice is to harvest plants after a year, not eighteen months as in the past. Coupled with the steady improvement in the efficiency of the factory, the improved quality of all canes led to a reduction in the number of tons of cane needed to produce a ton of sugar (at 96° sucrose) from an average of 8·23 between 1940 and 1952, to 7·74 between 1953 and 1968. Moreover, in the eighteen years before 1968, the estate canes averaged 7·69 tons cane/ton sugar compared with 8 tons cane/ton sugar for cane purchased from farmers.[11]

All in all, Worthy Park, which between 1928 and 1939 produced an average of 2·313 tons of sugar per acre per year and between 1940 and 1952 3·238 tons per acre, produced a highly creditable average of 4·608 tons per acre in the period from 1953 to 1968. In overall efficiency, Worthy Park, for long one of the best of Jamaican estates, reached a position of absolute primacy in 1968, when the Research Department of the S.M.A. also reported that the estate's record of producing sugar at a rate of 7·76 hundredweights per acre per month was 'comparable with the best cane growing areas in the world'.[12]

Jamaican Sugar Estates, Table of Overall Index of Efficiency, 1966–1968

	1966		1967		1968	
	Index	Place	Index	Place	Index	Place
Monymusk	73·03	2	71·76	5	70·21	8
New Yarmouth	74·70	1	71·98	4	72·18	2
Caymanas	65·36	17	66·68	17	67·18	17
Appleton	71·71	6	72·99	1	71·52	3
Richmond–Llandovery	71·84	5	69·80	9	69·03	10
Duckenfield (J.S.E.)	68·95	12	68·20	14	68·44	12
Bernard Lodge	67·16	15	70·86	7	70·38	6
Frome	71·36	8	70·96	6	71·35	4
Worthy Park	72·69	3	72·08	3	73·47	1
Barnett	71·36	7	70·51	8	68·59	11
Gray's Inn	67·08	16	68·17	15	70·25	7
Sevens	72·64	4	68·56	12	69·68	9
Long Pond (T.E. Ltd.)	70·79	10	69·34	10	67·81	13
Innswood	68·59	13	69·28	11	67·51	15
Hampden	69·18	11	68·26	13	67·71	14
Serge Island	68·11	14	67·34	16	67·26	16
Bybrook	71·32	9	72·64	2	70·45	5
Holland	64·22	18	63·18	18	64·97	18
Arithmetical average	70·00	–	69·59	–	69·33	–

Extract from C. R. D. Shannon's Report to Sugar Research Department, 1968.

Frederick Lister Clarke (1868–1932), the modern
founder of Worthy Park. (*See Chapter Eleven*)

Worthy Park cattle, 1969, with some of their trophies. On the left, 'Bull' Lewis, Pen Manager, at Worthy Park since 1930. In the background, 'Thide's Blue Mountain', otherwise Mount Diabolo.

The transport of cane to the factory and sugar to the ports have been facilitated by a tremendous increase in the number of motor vehicles operated or contracted by Worthy Park. As late as 1948 the entire motor vehicle pool on the estate consisted of four new three-ton Bedford trucks, four old Federals dating from Fred Clarke's days, four war surplus Ford army trucks and two caterpillar-tracked ex-army bren-gun carriers.[13] In the twenty years after 1948, however, more than £200,000 was spent on new tractors, trucks, and bulk sugar carriers, and Worthy Park's perennial transportation problem has been solved in the most economical way possible. One of Clement Clarke's economies in the 1930s had been the trucking of sugar direct to Kingston to avoid the high railway freights from Ewarton; but high sugar prices and the lowering of railway tariffs during the Second World War made it economic to use the Ewarton branch line once again. This change was shortlived, however, for in 1950 the Linstead–Ewarton line was closed to general traffic and Worthy Park reverted to road transport, gradually converting to bulk carriage in specially designed ten-ton trucks. From 1952 an increasing proportion of the estate's sugar was shipped not from the south coast but from St. Ann's Bay, and in 1962 the entire shipment of Worthy Park's sugar was switched to Ocho Rios, where the bulk-loading facilities are run in close conjunction with the Reynolds Aluminium bauxite operations.

To any visitor, especially between January and June, it is apparent that Worthy Park remains predominantly a sugar estate. But canefields take up only some 1,500 of its 12,000 acres, and without the other operations it might be in no better economic plight than many struggling Jamaican sugar estates. In fact, of Worthy Park's total revenue of £917,000 in 1968, £49,000 came from the cattle pen and £54,000 from citrus growing, both of which, after years of subsidy by the sugar operations, had begun to contribute a modest share to the general profit of Worthy Park plantation. Cattle, of course, have always flourished in Lluidas Vale, even in the period before sugar was grown, but Francis or Rose Price would stare in amazement at Worthy Park's waving pangola grasses and sleek herds of Brahman and Cross beef cattle. For 200 years the chief purpose of keeping cattle was to turn the mills and haul the wains, but as the result of mechanization Worthy Park's herd of 'working steers' has gradually disappeared.[14] Instead there are now over 1,500 cattle grown for beef or as pedigree breeding stock. Jamaica has always been desperately short of protein foods, and the Government, especially since Independence, actively encourages beef production. Unfortunately, in its intention to bring fresh beef within the range of the ordinary people, the Government also attempts to impose price controls which make the economic raising of beef virtually impossible. Cheap beef for all Jamaicans must await cheaper production through much more generous government subsidies, though even now Worthy Park's workers do receive the traditional sale of beef at bargain prices every Friday afternoon.

Worthy Park Pen, though it cannot yet bring sirloin to the masses, has performed priceless services to the Jamaican cattle industry in raising the quality of island-bred stock. The pedigree breeding operation, which some of Worthy Park's Directors as late as 1955 regarded as an unjustifiable hobby of Owen Clarke's,[15] has since brought fame to the estate through an almost monotonous series of First Prizes at the Frome, Denbigh and Hague Agricultural Shows. As a result, bulls and breeding cows bearing the Worthy Park 'W.P.' brand have been sold not only in Jamaica but also throughout Central and tropical South America. It is perhaps significant that one of the portraits which adorn the boardroom at Worthy Park is that of Sugar Baron, the grandsire of the Worthy Park Brahman champion bulls, whose proud visage confronts those of Fred and Clement Clarke.

Citrus growing, the most recent of Worthy Park's major operations, has taken over the position once occupied by cocoa and bananas, both of which were squeezed out of existence at the beginning of the Second World War. Citrus is ideally suited to the climate of the Jamaican uplands and will grow well on marginal lands and slopes which are not economic for sugar cane. But it is a difficult crop, susceptible to flood and wind damage and requiring much attention when grown on acid soils such as those in Lluidas Vale. Again it is true to say that only a large estate such as Worthy Park, prepared to lavish capital, patience, and technical expertise, could make citrus pay at all. Cultivation was begun with 65 acres planted between 1943 and 1944, which were extended as the result of a trip by Clement Clarke to examine citrus growing in Trinidad, in 1945. In October 1949 a special Management Meeting was held to determine the future of citrus cultivation, at which it was reported that in the first ten years each acre planted was expected to have cost £255 and yet bring in a revenue of only £170.[16] Yet after a lengthy and fairly heated debate it was decided that the longer term prospects were encouraging, and a large extension of the citrus groves was authorized.[17] In the event, production rose to 18,000 boxes of fruit in 1953 from 300 acres, and to 90,000 boxes from 375 acres in 1965, 74 per cent being oranges, 18 per cent grapefruit, and 8 per cent ortaniques.

Worthy Park's citrus crops have suffered at different times from disease, drought, and flood, but the most serious setbacks have been the result of unpredictable fluctuations in the market. In this respect, Jamaican citrus growers are in much the same predicament as the sugar producers before 1930, except that citrus fruit cannot be kept on the trees or stored for long after ripening, and the citrus market is therefore even more subject that sugar once was to glut and famine. In 1967, for example, prices were exceptionally good, with sales as high as 30s. a box (to 'new higglers'), whereas in other years boxes have been sold to processors for as little as 2s. 6d. apiece. Until Jamaican citrus growers are as well organized as the sugar manufacturers and the citrus market is as well controlled as the international sugar market, growing citrus in Jamaica is bound to be an adventurous and worrisome business.

As an estate dedicated to the principle of diversification, Worthy Park is naturally always on the lookout for profitable new crops to plant on its less productive acreages; but so far no crop has offered the agricultural equivalent of the philosopher's stone. In 1950 several stands of mahoe, a cabinet-makers' wood, were planted on the slopes of Lluidas Blue Mountain, but though mahoe is a relatively fast-growing tree this was obviously a very long-term investment. The same applied to the planting of trees in the same area in 1966 to produce kola nuts—used in soft drinks—some time in the 1980s. With somewhat less originality, tobacco was tried, without success, in 1953, and in 1967, with the encouragement of the Government, a serious effort was made to grow Jamaican coffee once more. An experimental field was prepared beside the Ewarton road, but the first planting was made hurriedly in expectation of a visit from the Minister of Agriculture and most of the seedlings died of drought. Replanted, they appeared to be flourishing three years later, but at the very earliest the Worthy Park brand of Blue Mountain coffee could not be expected on the market before 1971.

Coffee was once the most lucrative cash crop for the smallholders in the mountainous interior of Jamaica, and in the post-Emancipation period the hills around Lluidas Vale were dotted with 'barbecues' and aromatic with the ripening beans. Competition from Brazil and Central America, however, gradually consigned the trees to bush and the 'settlers' to that level of bare subsistence as described in the settlement of 'Yacca' by the anthropologist Edith Clarke. The small farmers were always willing to grow sugar-cane, but transportation was expensive and the factories were rarely able to buy farmers' canes, however low the price. In 1937 a law was passed setting up machinery for the registration of cane farmers to factories for the supply of canes,[18] but this was a dead letter until the demand generated by the Second World War outran the cane-producing capacity of the factory estates.

For the first two years of the war Worthy Park continued to produce well over 90 per cent of the canes used in its factory, but by 1941 the small farmers—already producing a third of all Jamaican canes—were strong enough to encourage the Government to pass the law setting up the All Island Cane Farmers' Association. By this law[19] factories were compelled to accept all canes offered by farmers registered to them by the Sugar Control Board. Cane prices were standardized by a formula which took into account the average price received from all processed sugar and 'blackstrap' (exhausted) molasses, with variations according to sucrose content. Consequently, the proportion of Worthy Park's canes received from farmers rose to 41 per cent by the end of the war and, after a slight recession in the later 1940s, to over 60 per cent with the subsequent expansion of demand. The total paid for farmers' canes rose from £16,000 in 1940 to £31,000 in 1945 and a peak of almost

£260,000 in 1965, when 2,800 farmers were supplying canes from sixteen different areas within an approximate radius of ten miles.[20]

Progress, however, was not entirely smooth. Above all a factory requires a supply of canes that is predictable from year to year and

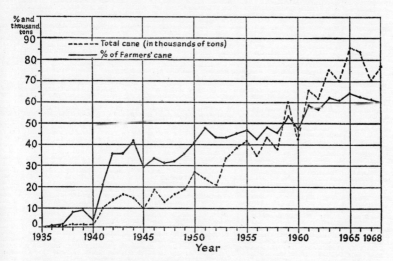

WORTHY PARK: PERCENTAGE OF FARMERS' CANE AND TOTAL CANE, 1935–1968.

arrives steadily throughout the time of crop. The manifold difficulties faced by the cane farmers make these desiderata hard to achieve and tend to support the contention that canes can only be grown with maximum efficiency on centralized estates. Sugar cane will grow like a weed on fertile tropical lowlands, but in pockets in the hills it is subject to soil deficiencies and climatic extremes, is difficult to reap and often almost impossible to transport. Generations of improvident cropping have denuded many areas of the Jamaican backlands. Years of shrivelling drought may be followed by floods which rot and wash out the cane, and make the mountain tracks impassible despite the heroic efforts of the independent hauliers with their battered trucks. The mountain men, while among the hardiest are the most independent of Jamaicans, and naturally it is difficult to convince them of the value

WORTHY PARK CANE FARMERS

Worthy Park Cane Farmers, 1951–1968

Payment points	Areas	Farmers 1968	Tons cane Av. 1951–5	Tons cane 1968	Per cent Total 1951–4	Per cent Total 1968	Relative prices (2nd payment 1967) per ton s.	d.
A. Lluidas Vale (Pay Office)	Lluidas Vale	234	2,213	4,149	6·3	5·4	22	3½
	Tydixon	82	669	1,400	1·9	1·9	20	8½
	Tydixon Farmers							
B. Point Hill (Loan Bank)	Garden Hill	163	2,057	2,429	5·7	3·1	20	8
	Pusey	326	2,420	5,550	6·8	7·1	21	5
	Point Hill		1,375		3·9		21	5
C. Croft's Hill (Oscar Johnson's)	Croft's Hill 'A'	216	5,710	9,042	13·3	11·7	24	1½
	'B'	209		8,761		11·3	22	5
	Top Hill	95	736	2,433	2·1	3·1	21	9
	St. John		695		2·0		21	9
	Burn's		936		2·6		22	11½
	Seven Grounds	97	684	4,914	1·9	6·4	22	11½
D. Kellit's (Community Centre)	Sinks	124	2,930	5,010	8·3	6·5	22	7
	Kellit's	87	1,999	2,635	5·7	3·5	23	7½
	Brandon Hill	237	1,709	6,467	4·3	8·3	24	9½
	Rhoden Hall	178	1,544	5,522	4·4	7·1	23	6
	Sandy River	116	1,134	2,474	3·2	3·2	25	4½
	Jericho	102	1,596	3,191	4·4	4·1	23	7
	Good Hope		987		2·8		22	5½
	Pedro's	287	2,128	6,102	6·0	7·9	22	5½
E. Others	Macknie (& Tate's)	265	1,494	7,386	4·2	9·5	22	2½
	Turtle Pond		400		1·1			
	Worthy Park		1,817		5·1			
		2,818	35,530	77,465	100·0	100·0		

N.B. Of the three payments for farmers' canes, the first is according to weight after delivery, the second according to sugar content after process and analysis, the third according to prices received after sale of sugar. Currently the farmers receive an arbitrary £2 per ton in the first payment, 95 per cent of the estimated final price (less the £2 per ton paid) at the second payment, and the remainder at the third payment. The average total price received by farmers in 1968 was £3. 16s. per ton of cane.

of any expenditure which eats into their already meagre incomes. Prices paid for cane rarely rise much above £3 a ton, and yet out of this must come the farmers' contributions to the A.I.J.C.F.A., the cost of fertilizers bought on their behalf, and transportation charges as high as 14s. a ton from distant areas.

Worthy Park, like the other members of the S.M.A., does what it can to instruct the farmers in better husbandry and to organize cane deliveries and payments as equitably and efficiently as possible. But cane farming operations are bewilderingly fragmented. Worthy Park's 2,800 farmers produce an annual average of only 28 tons of cane and receive only about £85 in an average year; but the actual situation is even worse. Of Worthy Park's suppliers, some 25 per cent produce 75 per cent of the total cane, the remaining 75 per cent producing a pitiful average of only 11 tons of cane a year, worth maybe £35.[21] It is not surprising then that the smallholders of Point Hill, Croft's Hill, and Kellit's sometimes regard cane production as a hopeless enterprise. In bad years they are discouraged into letting their canefields lapse and are easily beguiled into other cultivations which promise better returns, such as ginger, which enjoyed a minor boom just after the Second World War.[22] Often the cane farmers feel that the sugar estates pay them less than they should for their cane; yet for their part the estates cannot pay much more for the farmers' canes than the cost of estate-produced canes and still hope to make a profit. Usually they are grateful for the smallholders' canes and are determined to do what they can to ease the farmers' lot; but for their pains they suffer from the dilemma of being deprived of canes when times are bad and prices low and yet accused of refusing new registrations when times are good and prices high.[23]

Despite occasional differences, the cane farmers have at least one element, labour relations, in common with the estates. Many of the more substantial farmers are themselves employers of labour and therefore tend to identify with the estates in their labour negotiations. In addition, the cane farmers all need the factories in continuous operation during crop time and are not often in sympathy with labour tactics which place pressure on the estates by closing down the factories. There have even been examples of cane farmers providing 'blackleg' labour to cut Worthy Park's canes and keep the factory operating.[24]

The partial identification of the cane farmers with the planters rather than the proletariat, although many of the independent farmers are far poorer than labourers earning steady wages, is one of the peculiarities of Jamaican industrial relations. Another is the close association of Jamaican trade unions with political parties, which has existed since both trade unions and parties began. In the early days this identification was essential and it contributed largely to the successive achievement of full representative government, internal self-government and Independence; but once parties proliferated, each with its distinctive trade union, a rivalry and confusion followed from which both Jamaican politics and industrial relations have suffered since. Even today, collective bargaining in the true sense hardly exists in the Jamaican sugar industry. The admixture of purely political issues with matters solely concerning industrial relations, the tendency of workers to bargain their votes for industrial action, and the dangerous custom of striking before calling in the unions and then having to rely upon arbitration, have damaged the sugar estates and yet weakened the sugar workers' cause without greatly strengthening any one political party.[25] In this situation, management would be quite easily able to play off one union (or political party) against another to their own advantage; but there is no evidence that they do so. It is not necessary.

Although Worthy Park was among the most conservative of estates, it did not suffer directly in the labour disturbances which culminated in the Frome riots of 1938 and led to the creation of the Bustamente Industrial Trade Union. This was less because conditions in Lluidas Vale were any better than in Westmoreland than that Alexander Bustamente saw the huge impersonal, corporation-owned estates as being more easily unionized and more vulnerable than small estates that were family-owned and managed. In the early 1940s, however, strike action during crop time, characterized by picketing, coercion, and even arson, spread to all estates, including Worthy Park. The Clarke brothers, in their own bailiwick, were quite prepared to fight the unions even if it meant the closure of the estate, though in the long run large concessions were made on their behalf by the S.M.A. These began with the pioneer settlements negotiated by Norman Manley on behalf of the B.I.T.U. in March and December 1941 and January 1942 (while Bustamente was in jail), concerning hours, wages, and the procedure for the arbitration of disputes under the Trades Disputes Law of 1939. Since that time, negotiations at the top level have progressively improved workers' wages, hours, and conditions, so that wages are now graded strictly to function and task and are tied, albeit loosely, to the cost of living and the price of sugar, a 48-hour week is standard, and fully employed workers enjoy holidays and sick leave with pay, and modest pension benefits.[26] Since 1963, moreover, Worthy Park, along with all Jamaican estates, has accepted the principle of the 'union shop' for sugar workers (that is, that all workers in canefields and factory should be members of one of the various unions), an acceptance that was, perhaps, not entirely unrelated to the fragmentation of the unions which had reached a peak by then.

At the local level there has, unfortunately, been intermittent discord over details, so that Worthy Park has suffered strikes of varying severity during no less than thirteen of the twenty-eight crop periods between 1944 and 1970. Nominally these have concerned such matters as the right of dismissal, the technical methods of operation, and the allocation of categories to workers; but they have been exacerbated by the largely unsuccessful attempts by the various unions to gain a monopoly at Worthy Park.

During the wartime years, the disputes were often in the nature of personal confrontations between the somewhat autocratic Clarkes and the charismatic Bustamente. In March 1944, for example, just about the time that he had broken away from the People's National Party to form the Jamaica Labour Party as the political arm of the B.I.T.U., 'Busta' wrote concerning the dismissal of two draymen (one of whom was a B.I.T.U. delegate) who had been 'impertinent' to Owen Clarke:

March 24, 1944

To Clement Clarke Esq.,
Worthy Park Estate,
Lluidas Vale Post Office.

Dear Sir,

It has been reported to me that you said when you fire a man he stays fired. The reply to that is when I stop your sugar estate it stops too. . . . So don't talk too much Mr. Clarke, for as long as you have a sugar estate and there is work to be done you need my co-operation. I have the workers and if it were not for me your canes would rot, and trouble is brewing on your property. . . .

I understand that you have refused to employ some of the workers because they did not start your work. This being the case you have victimised them and have violated the terms of the Agreement, and once you violate it I can take reprisals against your sugar estate. Some people today depend upon Defence Regulations until they get burnt. Look how much you people cried when you could not get your estate started and instead of co-operating you have done a lot of loud talk and high-handed actions to the workers. . . .

I am told that your estate is on the verge of being closed down, and if that should happen don't call me. I would not move from here. I would laugh at you and say it serves you right. You think it is perhaps one crop which you have to take off or that you have more laws in your hands than we have. You telegraphed to say that you have police statement. I don't believe in the police unless I get them under cross-examination and I have good reason not to believe.

. . . You need me more than I will ever need you. I heard that you were tough and I was not inclined to have the workers start your mills, so as to bring you to your senses. But for the good of your Sugar Association I lost money and energy to have it done. My advice to you is that you had better co-operate or I am going to compel co-operation. . . .

I have sent a copy of this letter to the Sugar Manufacturers' Association so that they can see that there is smoke. And where there is smoke there may be fire.

Yours faithfully,
Alexander Bustamente,
President.[27]

As time went on, the principal antagonists mellowed, or at least the management of Worthy Park came to realize that the influence of

'Busta' (who, since he was first named Clarke, it has jokingly been suggested was perhaps a relation of the owners of Worthy Park) was far more benign than that of some other labour organizers, particularly those on the left wing of the P.N.P.'s Trades Union Council. The recognition, in January 1945, of the B.I.T.U. by the sugar manufacturers as the sole bargaining agents for the sugar workers, and the concurrent pledge by the S.M.A. that, 'all things being equal', B.I.T.U. members would be given preference in employment, encouraged the T.U.C. to increase the vigour of its operations. In 1946 a serious strike at Worthy Park was virtually broken by 'blackleg' labour brought down from the hills and the power of the B.I.T.U. was obviously on the wane. Subsequent strikes were characterized by inter-union strife, personal violence and property damage, to the degree that some planters labelled the organizers 'professional agitators' or even 'Communists'.

As a result of its tactical successes in the prolonged strikes of 1950 and 1951, the T.U.C. claimed the right to be a bargaining agent for sugar workers, and by a workers' poll organized by the Labour Department in June 1951, it carried two estates, including Worthy Park.[28] For a time it seemed that a union held the whip hand over the management of Worthy Park and relations reached a peak of acrimony and distrust. In 1954, however, a further ideological rift within the P.N.P. almost destroyed the T.U.C. As a result of a 'purge' of the radical wing of the party, which was then in power, the National Workers' Union was formed by the more moderate P.N.P. unionists, under the leadership of Michael Manley, the Prime Minister's son. The N.W.U. gained immediate recognition, carried out an intensive recruiting campaign with the aid of the A.F.L./C.I.O. and the Cuban Sugar Workers' Union throughout the later 1950s and actually ousted the T.U.C. as a bargaining agent for sugar workers in 1961. It was the J.L.P. and the B.I.T.U., however, which led Jamaica into independence in 1962, under the leadership of the ageing hero, Bustamente.

As we have seen, political fragmentation has decisively weakened trade unionism in Jamaica, and it has been the generalized threat of disruption and the persuasiveness of the party in power rather than trade union strength *per se* which have encouraged the S.M.A. to bring about many of the important changes that have occurred in recent years. On the local scene, trade unions are now even less evident than they are in the Jamaican capital. Worthy Park, for example, is still not completely unionized. 'Staff' are not unionized, being under contract (with increases on merit); citrus and pen workers are not unionized either, being able to negotiate collectively more satisfactorily directly with the management. Lluidas Vale as a whole is strongly P.N.P. and most of the sugar workers are nominally members of the N.W.U.; but since Independence the management of Worthy Park, like that of most estates, has become more and more favourably disposed towards the J.L.P. and the B.I.T.U., particularly since the P.N.P. in opposition has drafted what the planters regard as a cynically radical platform of land reforms that include the nationalization and subdivision of sugar estates. The J.L.P., moreover, stands squarely for the American alliance which means so much for Jamaican security as well as Jamaican sugar exports, tied as it is to a policy of isolating Cuba economically as well as politically.

Whatever the motives, Worthy Park and the other estates under the aegis of the S.M.A. have brought distinct improvements to the lot of their workers over the recent years of prosperity. Thanks to the structure of work tasks and the crop bonuses varying between 8 per cent and 17 per cent, average wages are higher than the statutory minima laid down in 1960 and 1965. Since 1958 there has been a system of severance pay in cases of redundancy, and in 1960 a sugar workers' pension scheme was introduced, made possible by the initial contribution of £1,250,000 by the sugar manufacturers and cane farmers from the Sugar Price Stabilization Fund and subsequent contributions from a cess on the price of export sugar.[29] Worthy Park in fact anticipated the national scheme by many years in bringing in a system of small weekly payments to aged workers 'in deserving cases' in 1944.[30] In 1948 the estate provided a large playing field and pavilion for use in inter-estate contests such as the Crum-Ewing cricket competition, and in 1951 a 'Lock-up Store' for the sale of groceries at reasonable prices, the moderate profits of which went into a welfare fund for the Staff.

Far more important for the general well-being of Worthy Park have been the improvements made in health services in the last two decades. As late as 1950 the incidence of yaws and venereal disease in Lluidas Vale was far higher than it had been in slavery days, when many estates could boast a resident doctor of some kind.[31] The nearest government clinic was at Point Hill, and although Worthy Park offered premises to the Government at a nominal rent in 1943 and the Sugar Industry Labour Welfare Board was established in 1948 by a statutory levy of 10s. per ton on sugar, it was not until 1951 that a clinic was set up at Worthy Park (as on 16 of the 23 Jamaican sugar estates) with a resident nurse and weekly visits from a doctor. At first the statistics were horrifying. In the first year, no less than 331 cases of yaws, 250 of syphilis, and 28 of gonorrhea were treated. Within a very short time, however, yaws was practically eradicated and syphilis reduced below the national average; only gonorrhea, as in the whole of Jamaica, remaining a recurrent social problem. Once medical conditions at Worthy Park were stabilized, services were expanded to include dental, ante-natal and birth control clinics, as well as regular visits from the government anti-tuberculosis units. Setting the seal on the new medical régime was the creation of a baby-care clinic in 1953, which held annual competitions for the bonniest baby on the estate.

The inhabitants of the Vale of Lluidas rely upon Worthy Park for most of their medical services and their water supply, the estate is the only notable employer of labour and source of circulating cash in the valley, and the pattern of life is determined by the tempo of the sugar year. Yet Lluidas Vale village is in no other senses a 'company town'. Worthy Park estate owns some of the freeholds in the area of well-spaced shops and decent houses near the church, police station, post office, and 'village square'; but the most densely populated area, a congeries of family 'yards' with houses almost piggy-back upon them, is the subdivided residue of Shady Grove, once owned by Dr. Quier. Indeed, there is still a sociological rift between the estate and the village, which dates back to the foundation of the latter by displaced Negroes after Emancipation. On the estate live the privileged Staff in their comfortable rent-free bungalows, and the full-time workers in small wooden houses with gardens, most of which are rent-free. The village is the home of the casual worker and the workless. Stagnant during the *tempo moto*, or slow time between crops, it is crammed, lively and disorderly in crop-time; a disjunctive pattern of life bound to contribute to the social dislocation of village life.

As Edith Clarke has movingly described the village under the thin disguise of 'Sugar Town' in *My Mother Who Fathered Me*, Lluidas Vale is more like Kingston itself than a typical cohesive inland village. Its population is 'too large, too mixed, and too mobile for the development of any strong community sense. What associations there are tend to be sectional and do not provide a relational system which involves continuous mutual co-operation and inter-dependence.'[32] The only community sense is found on the estate itself, a feeling of coherence, contribution, belonging. On the estate the wages of loyalty is reasonable security; while the village remains the home of the restless, rootless underemployed.

The unfortunate dichotomy between Worthy Park and Lluidas Vale, which is not assuaged completely by such company largesse as Christmas work and the annual Christmas treat for village children, is based on a dilemma common to all sugar estates: that at present employment must be seasonal for the majority of workers. For the workers themselves the disadvantages of this situation are painfully obvious; yet for the estates too it provides the perennial worry that there will not be sufficient labour when crop-time comes around. At different periods, migration of workers to Cuba, the U.S.A., and the United Kingdom, as well as 'irresponsible' strikes, have deprived the estates of workers to cut the ripening cane. The estates, as usual, have a solution to their problem which they are eager to employ; but this is no general panacea. Full mechanization, besides increasing productivity, would end the dependence on seasonal workers and provide a continuity of employment for those working on sugar estates. But this permanent labour force would inevitably be reduced in size, and the seasonal workers, at present underemployed, would join the smouldering ranks of the Jamaican unemployed.

Worthy Park: Cane-Cutting Data, 1951–5 and 1967–8

Table I

	1951	1952	1953	1954	1955	1967	1968
Crop period (weeks)	15	14	19	20	21	16	21
Cutters	142	121	113	106	108	234*	224*
Man-weeks worked	1,374	1,436	1,922	1,980	1,878		
Cane cut (tons)	25,254	25,740	41,222	46,769	45,783	42,694	50,993
Cane per acre	22·8	23·0	35·5	37·5	36·7		
Average cutters p.w.	91	103	101	99	89		
Cane cut p.w.	1,684	1,839	2,170	2,338	2,180		
Cane per cutter	18·5	17·9	21·5	23·6	24·4		
Av. weeks per cutter	9·7	12·0	17·0	18·7	17·4	9·0	9·8
As % of crop	64·7	85·7	90·0	93·5	82·9	56·5	46·8
Rate per ton	4s. 2½d.	4s. 10d.	4s. 10d.	4s. 10d.	4s. 10d.	5s. 3½d.–7s. 6d.†	5s. 3½d.–7s. 6d.†
Including Sundays	4s. 8d.	5s. 3½d.	5s. 3½d.	5s. 3½d.	5s. 3½d.		
Av. weekly wages	£4. 6s. 4d.	£4. 4s. 9d.	£5. 3s. 9d.	£6. 4s. 11d.	£6. 9s. 8d.	£7. 1s. 5d.‡	£7. 18s. 7d.‡
With bonus			£6. 3s. 6d.	£6. 15s. 5d.	£7. 0s. 6d.		

* Mechanical and Cut and Carry Gangs' Total.
† First figure, Mechanical; second, Cut and Carry.
‡ Converted from figures in Table III, 312.

Sudden switches to mechanization accompanied by a wholesale lay-off of workers, such as that attempted by the West Indies Sugar Company at Monymusk in 1958, have understandably been followed by some social dislocation and considerable concern in the labour movement. Yet the present labour situation, even without full mechanization, is highly unsatisfactory to workers as well as estates. This is

Table II: Gangs separated, 1955

	A. Rhoden's	B. Clarke's	C. Gordon's	Totals
Cane cut	15,890	14,461	15,432	45,783
Sundays	3,172	2,702	2,842	8,716
Cutters	36	35	37	108
Man-weeks	637	607	634	1,878
Sundays %	20	18·7	18·4	19·0
Crop totals per cutter	441	413	417	424
Per cutter per week	24·9	23·8	24·3	24·4

Tables I and II in Minute Book of Management Meetings, 1954–5, by Meeting of February 1955.

N.B. In 1962 of over 200 cutters only 103 completed 100 days' work and only 49 qualified for 2½ per cent Holiday Bonus for working five-sevenths of crop.

particularly true of field workers. Comparison of tables of employment by Worthy Park Farms Limited in 1959 and 1966 shows that already the mean employment level had fallen from 290 to 205; yet the unhealthy seasonal imbalance remained. Of the field workers tabulated, only some twenty to thirty were 'general workers' employed throughout the year. The number of 'cultivation workers' rose to peaks above the mean levels during crop and planting times and during the period of Christmas work, but fell to nil after Christmas, during the August holidays and during strikes. The final category, 'harvesting workers' raised the total workers employed to almost 650 at the height of the 1959 crop and to 430 in 1966, but fell away entirely during the six-week strike of 1959 and outside the crop periods of twenty weeks in 1959 and nineteen weeks in 1966. Average weekly earnings of cane-cutters, barely £1 in 1938, had risen to £4. 5s. 0d. in 1952 and, with bonuses, to £7 in 1955 and over £10 in 1969. Yet in 1962, of the 200 cane-cutters listed on the wage-rolls, only 103 completed 100 days' work in the year, and a mere 49 qualified for the 2½ per cent holiday

Table III: 1967 and 1968

Duration of crop	1967 23 January–17 May Mechanical	Cut and carry		1968 22 January–21 June Mechanical	Cut and carry
Days worked	107	109		116	122
Not required	7	5		9	4
Strike	0	0		26	26
Carting at end	1	1		1	1
Total	115	115		152	153
Five-sevenths of crop	82	82		108	109
Attendance: 82–109 days	53	33	109–122 days	10	4
70–81 days	11	24	100–108 days	21	9
50–69 days	14	38	80–99 days	41	20
1–49 days	13	48	50–79 days	26	26
			1–49 days	35	32
	91	143		133	91
Total man days	7,132	8,145		9,684	5,752
Production tons	26,666	16,028		40,098	10,895
Man days worked	7,132	8,145		9,684	5,752
Basic rate per ton	5s. 3½d.	7s. 6d.		5s. 3½d.	7s. 6d.
Production per man day	3·738	1·967		4·140	1·894
Gross earnings	£8,198	£6,685		£12,665	£1,894
Earnings per man day	23s.	16s. 5d.		26s. 1d.	16s. 6d.
Less tops, clean rows, cow itch, etc.	5¾d.	3½d.		10½d.	3d.
Actual earnings per man day	22s. 6¼d.	16s. 1½d.		25s. 2½d.	16s. 3d.
Sunday/holiday % above basic	8·50	7·77		11·25	11·88
Actual days worked	107	109		116	122
Av. production per day	247	147		350	100
Man days lost (based on daily attendance, using theoretical requirements men per day)	101				
% man days lost (as % total man days worked)	0·66				

bonus for working a minimum of five-sevenths of the total period of the crop.

When the 45 permanent members of senior and junior Staff, the workers in the factory, the citrus groves, and the Pen are added to the totals of sugar field-workers, the seasonal imbalance is not nearly so marked. Moreover, the estate constantly seeks ways—such as the custom borrowed from slavery days of staggering maintenance work wherever possible and in diversifying into crops such as citrus, coffee,

and kola nuts which bear fruit out of the time of the sugar harvest—
in which to ameliorate the situation. Nonetheless, in 1968, for example, when the average number of persons employed by Worthy
Park throughout the year was 569, the total number employed in any
one week varied from 236 in the first week in January to 848 in the
first week in June. Except for the last week in the year when only nine
were employed, the total of citrus workers varied only from 67 in
mid-October to 125 in mid-July and Pen workers from an average of
22 in March and April to 47 in August and September; yet in the factory the work-force fluctuated from 25 in the first week of the New
Year to 217 at the height of the crop.

Worthy Park, as a business operation and not a philanthropic venture, has always been more concerned with its total wage-bill than with
the earnings of individual workers. Yet—again in purely business
terms—the estate could afford a similar total wage-bill for a smaller,
more cohesive, work-force, as long as productivity were raised. For
their part, the workers fortunate enough to gain permanent employment would enjoy greater job security and a greatly improved standard
of living. In this situation, the estate might discover to be artificial the
hard-and-fast socio-economic distinction made between privileged
Staff and unprivileged proletariat, which seems to be a paradoxical
survival from the ancient days when black men laboured and white
men ruled.[33]

As long ago as 1960, George Clarke pointed out to the biennial
meeting of the British West Indies Sugar Technologists' Association
that while in Jamaica it took 20 man-days to produce a ton of sugar,
the figures for Puerto Rico were 11·5, for Louisiana 7·7, and for
Hawaii, the most mechanized of all sugar areas, only 2·6. Clearly
Jamaican management, labour, and government would have to learn
from these competing countries if they wished Jamaican sugar to survive. For the estates it would mean fresh capitalization, with the
acceptance of a financial structure in which depreciation costs of
machinery alone would be higher than the labour cost of operating
and servicing the machines. Control of operations would pass from the
field overseer to the garage technician, with much greater emphasis on

technical training and specialist skills. Government, which readily subsidized new industries, should be persuaded to support Jamaica's oldest industry by providing capital loans and training schemes, so that rich foreign operators like the aluminium companies could not, or did not have to, poach the technicians trained on the sugar estates.[34]

In 1960 George Clarke advocated the gradual expansion of mechanization in five progressive stages: in the preparation of land for canes, the chemical control of weeds and disease, better mechanical loading, aerial fertilization and mechanical harvesting. By 1970 large strides have been made in the first four of these; the gradual switch to mechanical loading after 1962, for example, almost outmoding the traditional system of cut-and-carry gangs.[35] Worthy Park's productivity figures are down to under 12 man-days per ton of sugar.[36] As yet, however, there does not exist a cane harvesting machine suitable for Jamaican conditions, and even the most up-to-date machine would mean the abandonment of hilly cane-pieces, the installation of expensive cleaning machines in the factory to remove excess soil and trash, and the cessation of operations during very wet conditions. Besides this, the problems of capitalization and technical skills, and—most delicate of all—the question of government and union support, remain to be solved.

In winning over the political parties and the unions which provide the basis of the parties' support, the sugar estates are involved in the confrontation of two rival economic philosophies. The estates naturally argue that sugar always has been, is and always should be the backbone of the Jamaican economy, providing, directly by wages and indirectly by levies and other means, great benefits for the general population. Moreover, they argue, the present system of factories served by large estates and small farmers in almost equal parts is the most equitable, if not quite the most efficient, method of production. Yet so great is the cost of production that even now estates, including those in fertile lowland areas close to the coast, are yearly faced with closure,[37] and even with excellent sugar export prices the Jamaican government is unable to cream off more than a small fraction of sugar income for the general welfare. Accordingly, such progressive inland estates as Worthy

Park argue that in order to survive and to contribute to Jamaica as a whole, the estates must raise their productivity by ruthless efficiency, mechanization, and in diversification, and in all of these processes the Jamaican Government has a duty to give what support and encouragement it can.

Against the estates' philosophy is ranged that expressed in its most extreme form by the New World group centred at the University of the West Indies, which while it is not affiliated with an established political party has a powerful influence on opposition doctrines. This philosophy maintains that Jamaica is essentially a country of small producers, who are deprived of their equivalent of 'five acres and a cow' by the monopolization of the best lands by the selfish and uneconomic producers of sugar, heirs of the old plantocracy. Worthy Park, they argue, hardly needs 12,000 acres to produce 1,500 acres of canes, even if sugar is regarded as a salutary contribution to the general Jamaican economy. Far better, they maintain, to subdivide the land for the benefit of the land-starved small producer, even if this were to lead to the collapse of the sugar industry in its present form.[38]

The socio-economic philosophy of the New World group, though it is based on a deep-rooted hatred for any system which dates back to slavery days, as well as on a well-justified admiration of the achievements of the independent Negro smallholders since 1838, is strongly contested. The population of Jamaica has expanded so rapidly that the peasant smallholder is no longer the standard or realizable type of Jamaican. All the estates could be swallowed by those who hunger for five acres of land without making more than a temporary pause in the waxing tide of unemployment in Jamaican towns. There seems to be, moreover, a tendency in the ambitious to aspire towards the most profitable means of production, and the tendency for producers to consolidate holdings (a process apparent among the cane farmers since 1939 as with the larger sugar estates since their very beginning) might merely be repeated all over again. Even if the land were subdivided into limited holdings and the factories nationalized, it is difficult to believe that crops suitable for export could be produced even as efficiently and cheaply as at present. The Jamaican Government, instead of receiving increased revenue from sugar, would likely be forced to subsidize agriculture from such exhaustible and fickle industries as bauxite mining and tourism. The aluminium companies, though they have contributed many benefits to Jamaica, would soon switch their bauxite operations to alternative sources in other countries if punitively taxed, and tourism would quickly evaporate if political and social unrest in Jamaica increased. The examples of Haiti and Cuba are warnings for Jamaica of the results of the removal of foreign capital, an almost exclusive dependence on peasant smallholdings, and nationalization.

As recently as 1938, Clement Clarke considered the selling-off of Worthy Park land as an antidote to social unrest, as long as the factory could be guaranteed its supply of canes.[39] The increase in prices which followed the beginning of the Second World War, however, made Clement and his brothers as adamantly opposed to alienating the estate as they were dedicated to efficiency and diversification. The 'radical' new Tenancy Law of 1946, aimed at giving tenant smallholders greater security on their lands, was actually used to regularize tenancies that had grown lax, to delineate boundaries more exactly and to evict squatters and encroachers.[40] Similarly, the new Land Tax Law brought in by the P.N.P. in 1959, by quadrupling Worthy Park's assessment,[41] made the management more than ever keen to insist that value was derived from every acre and every tenement. We have already seen how the flat bottom land was utilized for sugar, fertile hills for citrus, savanna land and forest glades for grazing cattle; but now even the forest cover on the mountainsides was regarded as essential for the estate in cooling the air and bringing down extra rainfall.[42] In 1966, Worthy Park, besides having 500 acres let out to tenants at 36s. per acre per year, donated 278 acres of land in Dodd's Valley to the Government for a 'low cost' housing scheme, on the agreement that the estate's workers be given preference on the housing lists;[43] but this small loss of land had been much more than offset by the buying of Tydixon from Dr. McCulloch in 1955. This purchase, represented the culmination of the 300-year process of Worthy Park's territorial consolidation.

The year 1970, besides being the tercentenary of Francis Price's first patent for 840 acres in Lluidas Vale, is a decisive landmark in Worthy Park's history since it marks the transfer of management to another generation of the Clarkes. Clement Clarke died in 1967, having retired from active management in 1964 after more than forty years' involvement, and Owen and George Clarke intend to retire soon after the tercentenary celebrations, leaving the management to their sons and nephews.

A tremendous responsibility rests on the shoulders of these young men, and they, like the rest of Jamaica, might do well to ponder on the history of their inheritance. In many ways it would be a tragedy if an estate such as Worthy Park, which has survived so many vicissitudes over three hundred years, were to perish now. But its survival must be justified not on romantic and sentimental but on cold hard economic grounds. Outworn modes and attitudes will not serve Jamaica's future, which will contain enough pitfalls without inviting more bitterness and recriminations about the worst of the past. Besides national stability, a government favourably disposed, and continuing fair prices for its sugar and other produce, Worthy Park needs a management not only continuing to dedicate itself to the affairs of the estate and the welfare of those who work upon it, but also a readiness continually to move with the times; looking to Jamaica's future with hope and flexibility, but with pride and respect for the best of the past.

NOTES

[1] Negotiated annually in October or November until 1966, after which it was fixed three years at a time. Jamaica's N.P.Q. prices have varied between £40. 15s. per ton c.i.f. in 1955-6 to £47. 10s. f.o.b. in 1966-9.

[2] Averaging £1 per ton.

[3] Ranging from £2. 6s. 8d. per ton from 'D' grade sugar to £9. 6s. 8d. for refined; C. A. Bloomfield, *Sugar in Jamaica*, n.d. (1965). Currently, the price fixed for local sales is regarded as uneconomic by the producers.

[4] I.e., at 7 c. per pound c.i.f. These prices, however, were lower than the free market world price in 1963 and in 1964. In the later 1960s, however, when the free market world price fell once more to half the cost of production, U.S. quota prices remained 'good', compared with the British N.P.Q. price, which Jamaican planters regarded as 'fair'.

[5] There has been a slight reduction since, and the level is currently at about 60 per cent for Worthy Park.

[6] Factory £803,000; farms £294,000.

[7] The actual figure is approximately £259,000.

[8] *Management Meeting Minutes*, 1948.

[9] Since 1965 the records have been kept by a senior member of the Field Staff and the samples have been sent away to the Sugar Research Station in Mandeville.

[10] Fertilizer, for example, is best applied after rain. Field workers are very reluctant to work in rain but to the crop-dusters working around squalls is just one more hazard in their normal day's work. The present air-strip, only 2,000 feet long, was completed in 1965.

[11] Figures of ratios of cane to sugar used by manufacturers and farmers are confusing to the layman, who would probably tend simply to divide tons of cane consumed by tons of sugar produced. Since sugar produced varies in sucrose (Worthy Park's being commonly 97°), the figures, as here, are normally corrected for 96° sucrose. A third type of figure called the 'theoretical average', in which comparative factory efficiency is discounted, is also used as an accurate gauge of 'farm' efficiency. Yet since thinly grown and even diseased cane sometimes has a high sucrose content, better indices of farm efficiency are tons cane/acre, tons sugar/acre, or, best of all, hundredweights sugar/acre per month.

[12] *S.M.A. Research Department Report*, 30 September 1968.

[13] Half-yearly Report on Transport, 31 December 1948.

[14] As late as 1955 there were still seventy-two 'working stock' of 1,540 animals in the Pen, though this included horses and mules and only twenty-four were steers.

[15] Management Meeting, 20 February 1955.

[16] Planting and maintenance, £145; fertilizer, £60; overheads, £50; production rising from one-half box per tree or fifty boxes per acre in the fifth year, to two boxes per tree and 200 per acre in the tenth year.

[17] Management Meeting of 11 October 1949. Owen Clarke argued strongly for increased capitalization in the factory which would guarantee a 4 per cent return.

[18] Sugar Industry Control Law 43 of 1937 (now Chapter 302 of Revised Edition). Its main intention was to restrict the scale of factory production following the projected International Sugar Agreement of 1957.

[19] The Sugar Cane Farmers (Incorporation and Cess) Law 75 of 1941 (now Chapter 371 of the Revised Edition).

[20] See accompanying tables and map.

[21] The figures for the whole of Jamaica are 22 per cent farmers producing 85 per cent of the cane; Bloomfield, 21.

[22] Doubtless they would all grow 'ganja' (*cannabis resin*), save for the savage government repression.

[23] For example, in 1963 when sugar prices were at their highest since the war Cedric Titus of the A.I.J.C.F.A. demanded that Worthy Park register more farmers, whereas in 1967 canefields were being abandoned and Worthy Park had great difficulty in finding new farmers prepared to plant cane.

[24] For example, during the 1946 strike.

[25] William H. Knowles, *Trade Union Development and Industrial Relations in the British West Indies*, Berkeley, University of California Press, 1959.

[26] Bloomfield, 23–30.

[27] Interleaved in Management Meeting Minutes for 1944.

[28] The other was Barnett. Worthy Park figures: workers 929; voted 813 (87·5 per cent); T.U.C. 599; B.I.T.U. 192; spoiled 22.

[29] Bloomfield, 28–30.

[30] Management Meeting of 17 July 1944. The sum was only 3s. 9d. per week but in addition the recipients were given the chance of task work within their reduced capabilities.

[31] See H. S. Burns, 'When Every Estate had its Doctor', *Daily Gleaner*, 28 April 1951. In 1833 there were 200 doctors for 350,000; in 1861, 50 for 440,000; and in 1951, 240 for 1,300,000.

[32] Clarke, 24. Edith Clarke, the daughter of Hugh Clarke the owner of Black-heath, has inherited more of the social consciousness of her grandfather the Rev. Henry Clarke than an identification with plantocratic ideas.

[33] The management of Worthy Park Farms has already predicted that with complete mechanization, the total work-force during crop time could be reduced to 160 by 1976, compared with an out-of-crop average of 90. These figures compare with approximately 350 and 125 in 1966, and 520 and 150 in 1959.

[34] 'Some of the hurdles to be cleared by those proposing changes in the sugar industry', *Farmer's Weekly*, Saturday, 19 November 1960.

[35] Though not without endless troubles with the unions.

[36] Approximately 85,000 man days for 7,000 tons of sugar. Cf. with 7·76 hundredweights sugar acre per month; see above, 9.

[37] Caymanas, for example, stopped production in 1968, Richmond, Barnett, and Serge Island in 1969.

[38] Contrasting sugar land with total estate acreage is particularly misleading since only 26·7 per cent of the area is arable in any sense, and much of that marginal. The Worthy Park Estate Land Use Analysis produced by the Sugar Research Department in their 30 September 1966 Report listed land use as follows:

	Acres
Cane	1,550
Citrus	375
Improved pasture	1,612
Common pasture	1,161
Woodland	6,507
Tenants	559
Non-agricultural land	500
Land recently given Jamaican Government	278
Total	12,542

For an articulate debate on the land question see, for example, 'Sugar and Change; a symposium', *New World* (Jamaica), V, 1–2, 1969, 32–57.

[39] C. K. Clarke to G. F. Clarke, 6 September 1938. Clement Clarke made the offer in writing to Colonial Secretary—offering to sell all land but the factory, a small piece surrounding it and the water supply—but received no official reply.

[40] About the same time, estate workers were deprived of the custom whereby they could cultivate small areas of estate land privately for growing canes; 15 July 1944.

[41] From £1,572 to £3,686.

[42] A concept difficult to convey to the squatter who would like to burn off an acre or two of forest and cultivate his 'ganja' safe from police interference.

[43] Completed in 1969 the units at £1,130 each, payable at the rate of £100 down and a mortgage of 6 per cent or £7. 10s. a month were too expensive and none have as yet been occupied.

Appendix One

Worthy Park: A Year's Total Supplies during the Eighteenth Century (1789).

A.
AN ACCOUNT of Stores imported by the Betsey Captṇ Laurie, from London, for the year 1789. and when received from Spring Garden ....

Mark No.		QUANTITY and QUALITY of the Goods	When received
LP No. 1 a 3	3	Puncheons with 17 pieces Ozna-burghs, Check Musquito Nett Lawn & Thread .... }	28ᵗʰ February
No. 4	1	300 gallon Copper Boiler	
— 5	1	Cask with 4 brass Strainers............	13ᵗʰ February
— 6	–	a case with 3 Copper Ladles, Clamps, & 2 potting Basons	20ᵗʰ Do,,—
7.	–	a Case w:ᵗʰ 2 plantation saddles & furniture	
8.		a Chest w: a Glaziers Diamond & 42 Squares best NC......................	20ᵗʰ February
9.		a Puncheon w:ᵗʰ 20 Dozen Negro Hatts.....................................	12ᵗʰ March
		a Hogshead of fine Porter	Great House July 18: 1 Lot
	4	Hogsheads of Coals	
	3	Puncheons of Marble lime .... {	1 reced 13ᵗʰ March / 1 Do— 15 May / 1 Do 26 ozs 1750
10 a 13	4	Puncheons with 45 pieces white frized Negro blanketting .... {	3 reced the 3 March / 1 Do— 12th Do.
21 a 22	2	Jugs of Linseed Oil .... {	5ᵗʰ May 1 jug rec / 13 May 1 —Do—
— 23	1	Jug of Neat foot Oil	7ᵗʰ May
— 25	1	Rundlet of Red Paint .... Rundlet of Ground white lead ... }	13ᵗʰ May.
— 27	1	Box with 12 bottles Mustard & Oil,	

Mark No.		QUANTITY and QUALITY of the Goods	When received
		Pepper Gunpowder etc. 26	26th February
28	1	Cask with 6 gross of Corks	Great House
18 a 20	3	Casks with Lamp Oil	⌈1 reced 13 Febry ⎨1 Do— 26 —Do ⌊1 Do— 12 March
	5	barrells of fine flour 　　　　1 Bll—26th Febry 　　　　1 Do—13 March	2 blls flour 30 March 1 Do, Do—31 Do
	6	Kegs contg: 4 bushells of Split pease and 2 bushells of Oatmeal	⌈4 kegs peas 30th March ⎨2 Do oatmeal 31 Do
	2	Sheets of mill'd Lead	⌊Nov. 6 1 sheet
		Deliv'd ac Mt. River in lieu one barow'd 　　　　　　　　1 sheet	
	4	Pieces Lead	3 pieces del. ....
No. 30	–	A Case of Stationary	17th February
31	–	a Cask of 40 m 6 dz. Coopers Nails...	13th March
32	–	A Cask with 30 m 8 dz. —Do.	13th February
33	–	A Cask with 21 m 10 dz. —Nails ...	⎫
34	–	A cask with 4 m 30 dz.—Do	⎬20th April
35	–	A Cask with 6 m 30 dz. —Do	13th May
36	–	A Cask with 20 m —6 dz. Shingling Nails, Net Brass boxes, Lince Pins & Workers & 1 doz. cattle Chains	⎫ ⎬17th February ⎭
37	–	A Cask with Hoes & Bills & Mill- wrights Tools —etc.	11th March
38	–	A Cask with Smiths Coopers & Carpenters Tools etc.	11th March
39	–	brass wired Strainers	17 February
40	1	Farriers Anvil	
	2	Iron Axle trees & 21 bundles of Puncheon Hoops	2 bun. 20th April 90 5 Do 9 June 2 Do 7 July
40	–	A Box w:th Tick & Sheeting & other necessarys for the House ...	37 Hoops 11 Aug 11 17 February
—	–	A Box w:th Garden Seeds	Great House
41	–	A Box with a Cheshire Cheese	26th February
42	–	A Box with Doctor's Medicines ...	28th February
—	1	Treble 1 Dub Block of 12 Inch. & 2 Dub of 10 In: w:th $\frac{e}{y}$ furniture ...	26th February
—	–	161¼ Yards of cutt and tar'd Tar- poling	26^{ht} Do.......
—	–	120 fathom of white Rope & 4 pounds of twine	
—	1	Coil of Tarr'd Rope	26th February

AN ACCOUNT of STORES imported by the
B.   EDWARD, Capt. James Drew from Bristol for the
year 1789. and when received from Spring Garden......

Mark & NO.		QUANTITY and QUALITY of the Goods	When received
LP	–	120 Half bundles of Puncheon ... Hoops	Expended on making the sugar hogsheads
		120 ... Do. ...... Pipe ... Do.	1 set 29 Dec.
		3 Setts of Truss Hoops ...	
		3 Dozen of Best Ox Bows	1 doz. 4th July
			1 dz. 23 Feb. 90

AN ACCOUNT of STORES imported by the
C.   HENNIKER Captn: Thomas Harrison from London
for the year 1789. and when received from Spring
Garden ....

LP—	3	Mill Cases.................................	
	2	Side Gudgeons...........................	
NO: 1—	–	A Case with Sundry materials for the mill...............................	
2—	–	A Ditto — with ... DO″	1790
	–	Ditto.........................	July 4th:-
4.	–	Ditto.........................	
5.	–	Ditto.........................	
		.... SPARE WORK.............	
	1	Mill Case	
	1	Side Gudgeon	
NO. 6.	–	A Case with Sundry materials for Do.	
7.	–	A Do. — wth:... Do. ... for Do.	1790
8.	–	A Bottle & Basket wth: Oil	July 4th:

322

AN ACCOUNT OF STORES imported by the DIANA
D. CAPT^{n}: Thomas Seaward from Cork ...... for the year
1789. and when received from SPRING GARDEN............

When Received		Bbls Beef 15.	Pork 2.	½ Bbls of Tongue 4.	Firkins of Butter 4.	Boxes Candles 3.	D° Soap 2.	Kegs of Tallow 6.	Bbls. of Herrings 70.	
LP.										
1789.										
March	10th	–	–	–	1	–	–	–	2	
„	16	2	–	–	–	–	–	–	4	
„	17	–	–	–	–	–	–	–	2	
„	23	2	1	–	–	1	1	–	3	The Candles & Soap left at the Great House
„	27	–	–	–	–	–	–	–	2	
April	4	–	–	–	1	–	–	–	–	
„	27	–	–	–	–	–	–	–	4	
„	30	–	–	–	–	–	–	–	2	
May	2	–	–	1	–	–	–	–	–	
„	11	–	–	–	–	1	1	2	–	The Candles & Soap left at Great House
„	23	–	–	1	1	–	–	–	–	Left at Great House
„	28	–	–	–	1	–	–	–	–	
June	19	1	–	–	–	–	–	–	–	
„	24	2	–	–	–	–	–	–	4	
„	26	–	–	–	–	–	–	–	4	
„	30	–	–	–	–	–	–	–	8	
Sept.	4	4	–	–	–	–	–	–	6	
„	10	2	–	–	–	–	–	–	4	
Octo^{r}:	9.	–	–	–	–	–	–	–	4	
„	20	2	–	–	–	–	–	1	2	
Nov^{r}:—	6	–	–	–	–	–	–	–	2	
„	18	1	1	1	–	–	–	–	10	
Decem^{r},,	4	–	–	–	–	–	–	–	7	
Omitted										
July	8	1	–	–	–	–	–	–	–	
„	27	1	–	–	–	–	–	–	–	
Omitt^{d}										
May	12	–	–	–	–	–	–	1	–	
1790										
January	1	–	–	1	–	–	–	1	–	At the Great House......"
Feb.^{ry}	12	–	–	–	–	1	–	–	–	D°
			1 at Gr. House			–		1 omit^{d}.		
		15	2	4	4	3	2	6	70	

AN ACCOUNT of Sundry ARTICLES
received for the use of WORTHY PARK for the year
1789 exclusive of the supplies from England & Ireland

E.

When Received	Quality of the Goods	From whence received	When open'd or delivered	When expended
1789. January				
10th	1 Sheet of lead for 9 coppers	Borrow'd from Mountain River	25th: January 1789	28th: January 1789
1	1 Barrell of Flour	Kingston	13: February	15th March
26	1 Barrell of fine flour	Kingston	13 Feb'ry	March 15th
,,	1 Do. ... of coarse Do.	Kingston	15th February. 89	April 3rd
			1 half brl of beef	
28th.	2 half brl of bee		29 Jany—March 1.	
,,	1 Barrell of Lamp Oil	Kingston	October 9th	
,,	1 Do. ... of Tar			
,,	1 Keg of Tallow		4 February	April 8th
30.	1 Hhd. of salt		30th: January 1789.	March 25th
,,	1 Do. of Coals	B. Cradock	Do.	
31	1 Keg of Tallow	Kingston	April 8th	July 5th
22:	1 Firkin of Butter	Kingston		
13th.	½ Barrell of Beef	Do.		
17.	1 Do. Common flour		3rd April	May 5th
Omitted ẹ̄ February	A Firkin of Butter		Left at the Great House	
,,	1 Cask rodz. Nails	Kingston	March 16th:	April 7th
,,	1 Do. of Cod-fish		18th: February	July 30th:
,,	1 Sett of Hhd Truss Hoops			
March				
26	1 Barrell of Beef	Capt: Fairclough	March 1	23rd March
3.	1 Hhd of salt	Capt: Powell	March 25th	16th April
5.	500 red oak Staves	Kingston		

		Article	Shipped by	Date	Date
omitted Jan'ry	16 }	13 Bundles of Hoops	Do		
"		½ Cask of 6 dz. Nails	Do	March 16th	April 13
		1 m ... of 30 dz. Do	Do		18th August
omitted Janry	30.	11 Bundles of long Hoops			
"		10 ... Do ... short Do	Capt Powell		
February	17th.	10½ bundles of long Hoops	Do		
	26th.	10 Do ...... Short Do.	Kingston		
March	7.	8 Do ...... wood Do	Do		
	11.	600 red Oak staves	Capt Powell		
"		50 White Do Staves	Capt Jump		
	13.	50 pieces of Heading	Do		
	24th.	6 bundles of wood Hoops	Kingston		
"		6 ... Do ... DO ... 12 ft. long	Capt Powell		
		2 ... DO ... Do ... 10 ... DO	Kingston	March 26th	
"	25th	½ Hhd of Coals	Do		
	26	200 red Oak Staves	Kingston		
March	26.	2 Brls of Coals	Capt Powell		
		100 Red Oak staves	Kingston		
April	27th.	Do Do Do	Do	April 15	May 17.
	11th.	1 punchn. Salt	Capt. Jump		
"		10 bunds. of long Hoops	Fame.		
	14	200 red Oak staves	Kingston		
	20	6 bundles of short wood Hoops	Fame		
	25th	100 red oak staves	Kingston		
May	11	2 Kegs of Mill Grease	Kingston	May 20th:	July 12th.
	12th	1 Do ... Do	Do	June 19:	July rd
	13th	¾ of a Puncheon of Salt	Kingston	July 3th:	July 27.–
	19.	1 Barrell of flour	Do	July—11th	July 11th
June	24.	1 Do ...... Do & 1 Firk: butter GH	Do		
July —	4.	4 barrells of American Herrings	Capt Jump		
	18.	1 Hhd of Salt	Capt Laurie	July 18th	
"		1 Do ... of Coals			

When Received	Quality of the Goods	From whence received	When open'd or delivered	When expended
Aug^st: 27.th	3 barrells of flour	Kingston	July 28 1 O.H. 1 sent to G.H.	August 17th.
11.th	1 barrell of coarse flour	Do	1 Bt July 28	August 4th
19.	1 Do ... of fine Do	Do	Aug^st 11th	August 17th.
21.	6 Barrells of Indian Meal	Do	Aug^st: 19th.	Sept^r: 4.
	5 DO ... of flour	Kingston		
	2 firkins of Buter			
	1 Keg of Peas		22nd August	Sept. 14th
Omitted 15.	1 Barrell of Coals remaind: of a Hhd	Capt. Laurie		
26.	1 Punch^n: Corn	Kingston	August 15	Sept: 15
	½ Do ... Do	Do	Sept: 15th	...... 22nd
Sept: 10.	20 pieces of Heading	Do		
18.	½ punch^n: Corn	Do		
	⅔ of a tierce of Cod fish		Sept: 18	Nov^r: 5th
	50 White oak staves			
	20 pieces of Heading			
October 20th	12 bush^s: of seed Corn	Cash	Sept: 23rd	Octo 9th
9.th	1 tierce of Rice	Kingston	Octo^r: 12th	Nov^r: 12th
20.	1 Hhd of Coals	D^a. McDonald		
Nov: 6	2 bls of Indian Meal	Kingston	Nov. 8 Dec. 23	October 22nd Janry 20.
18.	2 Do ... of flour		Nov. 19 Decem. 3	Decem. 2 Decem. 13th

Nov: 19th　Decem. 1st

	Item	Destination	Notes
23	½ tierce of rice	Do......	
	350 red Oak Staves	Kingston	Novr. 30th — Us'd in making Hh'ds — us'd at Overseers House
28	1 barrele of Tarr		
	150 red oak Staves	Kingston	
	1 Firkin butter		
Decem^a: 4	200 red oak Staves	Do	Us'd in making Hh'ds
7th	300 red oak Do		
	50 White Oak Do	Kingston	Decem^r. 13　Janry 7, 1790 — 1 pB.. 13 Janry ... Janry 22 — 1 d°. 23 d°. ...... Do ... 31th
	1 barrele of Superfine flour		
9	2½ Bb'ls Beef	d°	
,,	8 Bundles Wood Hoops		
,,	300 R.O. Staves		Us'd in making Hh'ds
14	300 d°	d°	
,,	12 Bundles Hoops		
17	1 Tierce Rice		1 Sent to Great House — 1 ope'd 8. Jan^y ... 19 Janry
,,	2 Bbls Flour		Us'd in making Hhds
21	300 R.O. Staves	d°	
29	400 d° d°		
,,	300 d° d°	d°	Janry 20 ...... Febry 11
,,	1 Bbl. Flour	d°	
31	1 Firkin Butter	d°	Us'd in making Hhds — consum'd at Smith's Shop.
	350 R.O. Staves		
	2 Bbls Coals pt. of attchd	Old Harb^r	

Appendix Two

Work load of Apprentices in St. John's Parish, 1837.

ST. JOHN'S.

CULTIVATION OF THE SUGAR CANE

Chopping up and heaping cattle pens, 11 able hands for each heap of 55 wain loads.

Stocking up or hoeing off the usual description of fallow cane lands preparatory to re-opening, 10 to 12 per acre.

Digging cane holes on particularly stiff land, dimensions, four feet by four, and depth six to eight inches, 55 holes per day each able hand.

Ditto ditto on all other descriptions of land, dimensions four and a half feet by four, and depth eight to 10 inches, 60 holes per day each able hand.

Cross-holing, 15 able hands per acre.

Distributing dung from heaps, each heap being in the centre of an acre, giving as above stated, 19 ditto ditto.

Trimming cane tops in the intervals, carrying and planting the same, and moderately trenching the land, 10 ditto ditto.

Weeding and supplying young plant canes, 10 to 12 ditto ditto.

Root trashing and full banking plant canes, 14 to 16 ditto ditto.

First and second trashing of plant canes, six to eight ditto ditto.

Subsequent trashings, bedding the lodged canes, eight to 10 ditto ditto.

Turning trash and digging corn holes through ratoons, six ditto ditto.

Subsequent hoeings and mouldings of ratoons, 10 ditto ditto.

Trashing ratoons, seven ditto ditto.

Cutting and tying plant canes, nine ditto ditto.

Ditto ditto ratoons, 12 ditto ditto.

An able hand to dig and load wains, with dung or mould, at the rate of one load per hour.

COFFEE CULTIVATION

Cleaning and suckering well-established coffee, 15 able hands per acre.

Ditto ditto old coffee pieces, 16 ditto ditto.

Field picking (carrying home one bushel to barbicues) from well established pruned and full bearing coffee, each able hand three bushels per diem.

Hand picking and sorting for market well cured fair average coffee, each ditto ditto two ditto per diem.

PIMENTO CULTIVATION

One breaker being allowed to four pickers, each able picker one and a half bushel per diem.

Hand picking, fanning, sorting, and bagging for market, each able hand five bags per ditto.

CLEANING PASTURES, ERECTING FENCES, ETC., ETC.

Cleaning Guinea grass pieces, once per annum, five able hands per acre.

Ditto common pastures ditto ditto, six ditto ditto.

Digging post holes, each hole to be two feet deep, 120 holes each able hand per diem.

Making good four eye mortice posts and heaping the same in one spot, six posts for ditto ditto.

Ditto ditto three ditto ditto ditto ditto, eight posts for ditto ditto.

Cutting and heaping in one spot fence rails 16 feet long in ditto, 65 rails for ditto ditto.

Ditto ditto ditto bundles of wattles seven feet long, 25 wattles each bundle, 20 bundles for ditto ditto.

Ditto ditto ditto bamboos, 80 bamboos, ditto ditto.

One able hand to cut and heap one cord of wood per diem.

Two able hands to complete 200 feet of mortice post and rail fence per diem, post holes being dug, and materials on the spot.

One able hand to dig eight feet of ditch four feet deep, four and a half wide at top, and two and a half at bottom, and throw up bank therefrom per diem.

One ditto ditto to plant penguins along 100 feet of such bank per diem.

One ditto ditto to dig 60 good yam hills per diem.

Building dry walls four and a half feet high, all materials being placed convenient, two builders to complete 33 feet per diem.

Breaking lime stones for kilns very small, each able hand to break two and a half barrels per diem.

Number of bricks to be moulded per diem by one moulder, having the customary assistants, 1500.

COOPER'S WORK

Each cooper to make complete three puncheons per week from white oak staves, and four ditto from puncheon packs each cooper to complete six tierces per week. Each cooper to complete four and a half sugar hogsheads from red oak, or four from country staves per week. Each cooper to head up seven hogsheads per diem. Each two able hands sent to the woods to split 1800 shingles or 900 staves including all work per week. Each cooper to hew 675 staves or 1350 shingles, per week.

(Signed) THOMAS BOWDEN,
JNO. BOORRA,   }   Planters
E. W. BOURKE,
JOHN PRICE NASH,   Millwright

June 16, 1837.

Bibliography

MANUSCRIPT MATERIAL

Worthy Park Manuscripts

Worthy Park Plantation Books, 1783–7; 1787–91; 1791–1811; 1811–17; 1821–4; 1830–6; 1836–45.
Mickleton Plantation Book, 1836–7.
Thetford Plantation Book, 1798–1808.
Worthy Park Wage Records, 1846–1970.
Worthy Park Management Minutes, 1936–70.
Worthy Park Financial Statements, 1926–70.
Statistical Data from Research Dept., Sugar Manufacturers' Association.
Meteorological Reports.
Miscellaneous Deeds and Map Fragments.
Fred Clarke's Diaries, 1915–32.
Interview Tapes.

Island Record Office

Deeds: Old Series, 1673–1878; New Series, 1879–99.
Wills: 1689–1835, Libers 1–116.
Parish Registers, Births, Marriages, Deaths,
   St. Catherine, 1665–
   St. John,   1665–

Jamaica Archives

Chancery Records, 1788–1805.
Crop Accounts, Vols. 1–50.
Inventories, 1729–1836, Nos. 15–151.
Manumission Records, 1779–1829, Nos. 13–64.

Land Patents, 1665–1808, Vols. 2–38.
Parish Records, St. Thomas In the Vale, Minutes, 1789–1802.
Port Henderson Journals, 1795–1804; 1805–12.
St. John's Plat Books, 1665–82.

Institute of Jamaica

Dawkins Manuscripts.
Young Collection.
Index to Long's History of Jamaica.
Returns of the Commissioners of Slavery Compensation, 1837.
Maps, of Jamaica.
   of Parish of St. Catherine.
   of Parish of St. John.
   of Worthy Park (uncatalogued).

Public Record Office

Colonial Office Series
   C.O. 1, 32. Muster of General Venables' Regiment.
   C.O. 137, 61–191.
   C.O. 441/4/4. Encumbered Estates Series.
   P.R.O. 30/8/153. Chatham Papers.

British Museum

Edward Long Papers, Add. MSS. 12, 402–12, 440.
Boase Papers, Add. MSS. 29,281, ff. 133, 207, 218, 226.
Gashry Papers, Add. MSS. 19,038, f. 8.

PRINTED PRIMARY

Hansard, Third Series, XCVI, 1848.
Jamaica Almanacks, 1751–1914, Kingston.
The Jamaica Gazette, 1745–75.
Jamaica Handbooks, 1881–, Kingston.
Journals of the Assembly of Jamaica, 1663–1826, 14 vols., Jamaica, 1795–1829.
Parliamentary Papers 1789, Inquiry into the State of the Sugar Colonies.
   1836, XV, Report from the Committee on Negro Apprenticeship.
   1848, XXIII, I, Select Committee on Sugar and Coffee Planting.
   1852–3, LXVII, Part II, Accounts and Papers.
   1866, XXXI, I. Report of the Jamaica Royal Commission.
   1866, LI, II. Report of the Jamaica Royal Commission.
   1884, XLVI, I, Report of the Royal Commission to Inquire into the Public Revenue of the West Indies.
   1898, LI, Report of the West India Royal Commission.
The Laws of Jamaica, 1681–1793, 7 vols., St. Jago de la Vega, Jamaica, 1802–24.
Calendar of State Papers, Colonial Series, America and the West Indies, 1574–1737, (Noel Sainsbury and others eds.), 43 vols., London, Longmans and H.M.S.O., 1860–1963.

BIBLIOGRAPHIES

F. Cundall, *Bibliographia Jamaicensis*, New York, 1902.
Elsa V. Goveia, *A Study of the Historiography of the British West Indies to the end of the Nineteenth Century*, Mexico, 1956.
L. J. Ragatz, *A Guide for the Study of British Caribbean History, 1763–1834*, Washington, 1930.
E. Williams, *British Historians and the West Indies*, New York, 1967.
W. Rodney, *Bibliography of the Caribbean*, University of the West Indies, Jamaica (n.d.).

CONTEMPORARY PRINTED

Rev. G. W. Bridges, *The Annals of Jamaica*, 2 vols., London, 1828.
William Beckford, *A Descriptive Account of the Island of Jamaica*, 2 vols., London, 1790.
R. C. Dallas, *The History of the Maroons*, 2 vols., London, 1803.
Bryan Edwards, *The History, Civil and Commercial, of the West Indies*, 2 vols., London, 1793.
Charles Leslie, *A New History of Jamaica*, London, 1740.
Matthew Gregory Lewis, *A Journal of a West Indian Proprietor*, London, 1834.
Edward Long, *The History of Jamaica*, 3 vols., London, 1774.
B. M'Mahon, *Jamaican Plantership*, London, 1839.
Hall Pringle, *The Fall of the Sugar Planters of Jamaica*, London, 1869.
George Price, *Jamaica and the Colonial Office*, London, 1869.
Rose Price, *Pledges on Colonial Slavery*, Penzance, 1832.
J. Quier, J. Hume, and others, *Letters and Essays . . . on the West Indies by different practitioners*, London, 1778.
W. G. Sewell, *The Ordeal of Free Labour in the British West Indies*, New York, 1861.
Sir Hans Sloane, *A Voyage to the Islands Madera, Barbados, Nieves, S. Christophers, and Jamaica, with the Natural History of the last of those Islands*, 2 vols., London, 1702.
C. R. Williams, *A Journey through Jamaica . . . 1823*, London, 1827.
Lady Nugent's Journal, 1801–1805, P. Wright (ed.), Institute of Jamaica, Kingston, Jamaica, 1966.
The Jamaica Association Developed, Jamaica, 1757.
Interesting Tracts Relating to the Island of Jamaica, St. Jago de la Vega, 1800.

PRINTED SECONDARY

B. Alexander, *England's Wealthiest Son, A Study of William Beckford*, London, 1962.
F. Armytage, *The Free Port System in the British West Indies*, London, Royal Empire Society's Imperial Studies, Longmans, 1953.
R. W. Beachey, *The Jamaican Sugar Industry in the later Nineteenth Century*, Blackwell, Oxford, 1955.
Clinton V. Black, *History of Jamaica*, London, Collins, 1958.
W. L. Burn, *Emancipation and Apprenticeship in the British West Indies*, London, Cape, 1937.

I. M. Cumpston, *Indians Overseas in British Territories, 1834–1854*, London, 1953.

F. Cundall, *Historic Jamaica*, London, for the Institute of Jamaica by the West India Committee, 1915.

——, *The Governors of Jamaica in the First Half of the Eighteenth Century*, London, 1937.

F. Cundall and J. L. Pietersz, *Jamaica under the Spaniards*, Kingston, Institute of Jamaica, 1919.

P. D. Curtin, *Two Jamaicas: The Role of Ideas in a Tropical Colony*, Harvard University Press, 1955.

Noel Deerr, *History of Sugar*, 2 vols., London, 1949–50.

G. Eisner, *Jamaica, 1830–1930. A Study in Economic Growth*, Manchester University Press, 1961.

W. A. Feurtado, *Official and Other Personages of Jamaica, 1660–1790*, Jamaica, 1896.

C. H. Firth (ed.), *The Narrative of General Venables*, London, Longmans for the Royal Historical Society, 1900.

D. G. L. Fraser, *Canada's Role in the West Indies*, Toronto, Canadian Institute of International Affairs, 1964.

Mary Gaunt, *Where the Twain Meet*, London, 1922.

Elsa V. Goveia, *Slave Society in the British Leeward Islands at the end of the Eighteenth Century*, Yale University Press, 1965.

D. G. Hall, *Free Jamaica, 1838–1865; An Economic History*, Yale University Press, 1959.

——, *Ideas and Illustrations in Economic History*, New York, 1964.

James Harrington, *Oceana*, (edited by S. B. Liljegren), Heidelberg, 1924.

V. T. Harlow, *The Foundation of the Second British Empire, 1763–1793*, 2 vols., Oxford, 1952–65.

W. H. Knowles, *Trade Union Development and Industrial Relations in the British West Indies*, Berkeley, University of California Press, 1959.

N. B. Livingston, *Sketch Pedigrees of Some of the Early Settlers in Jamaica*, Kingston, 1909.

A. F. Madden and V. T. Harlow, *British Colonial Developments, 1774–1834*, select documents, Oxford, Clarendon Press, 1953.

W. L. Mathieson, *British Slavery and its Abolition, 1823–1828*, London, Longmans, 1926.

——, *British Slave Emancipation, 1838–1849*, London, 1932.

George Metcalfe, *Royal Government and Political Conflict in Jamaica*, London, Longmans for Royal Commonwealth Society, Imperial Studies, No. XXVII, 1965.

A. P. Newton, *The European Nations in the West Indies, 1492–1688*, London, 1933.

S. Olivier, *The Myth of Governor Eyre*, London, Hogarth Press, 1933.

——, *Jamaica, the Blessed Island*, London, Faber, 1936.

R. Pares, *War and Trade in the West Indies*, Oxford, 1936.

——, *A West India Fortune*, London, 1950.

——, *Yankees and Creoles*, London, 1956.

——, *Merchants and Planters*, Cambridge, 1960.

Orlando H. Patterson, *The Sociology of Slavery*, London, McGibbon and Kee, 1967.

L. M. Penson, *The Colonial Agents of the British West Indies*, London, 1924.

F. W. Pitman, *The Development of the British West Indies, 1700–1763*, Yale University Press, 1917.

335

L. J. Ragatz, *The Fall of the Planter Class in the British Caribbean, 1763–1833*, London, 1928.
——, *Statistics for the Study of British Caribbean Economic History, 1763–1833*, London, 1927.
G. W. Roberts, *The Population of Jamaica*, Cambridge, 1957.
Carey Robinson, *The Fighting Maroons of Jamaica*, Jamaica, Collins, 1969.
S. A. G. Taylor, *The Western Design, An Account of Cromwell's Expedition to the Caribbean*, Kingston, Institute of Jamaica for the Jamaica Historical Society, 1965.
A. P. Thornton, *West India Policy Under the Restoration*, Oxford, 1950.
Agnes M. Whitson, *The Constitutional History of Jamaica, 1660–1729*, London, 1929.
E. Williams, *Capitalism and Slavery*, University of North Carolina Press, 1944.
D. Wood, *Trinidad in Transition: The Years after Slavery*, Oxford University Press, 1968.
P. Wright (ed.), *Monumental Inscriptions of Jamaica*, Society of Genealogists, London, 1966.

ARTICLES

W. Barrett, 'Caribbean Sugar Production Standards in the Seventeenth and Eighteenth Centuries', in J. Parker (ed.) *Merchants and Scholars*, Minnesota, 1967, 147–70.
J. H. Bennett, 'Carey Helyar, Merchant and Planter of Seventeenth-Century Jamaica', *William and Mary Quarterly*, June 1969, 53–76.
J. E. Duerden, 'Aboriginal Indian Remains in Jamaica', *Journal of the Institute of Jamaica*, Vol. 2, 4, July 1897.
Richard S. Dunn, 'The Barbados Census of 1680: Profile of the Richest Colony in English America', *William and Mary Quarterly*, January 1969.
D. G. Hall, 'Incalculability as a Feature of Sugar Production during the Eighteenth Century', *Social and Economic Studies*, Vol. 10, No. 3, September 1961.
——, 'Slaves and Slavery in the British West Indies', *Social and Economic Studies*, Vol. II, No. 4, December 1962.
R. R. Howard, 'Introduction to the Archeology of Jamaica', *American Antiquity*, Vol. 31, No. 2, 1966.
U. B. Phillips, 'A Jamaican Slave Plantation', *American Historical Review*, Vol. XIV, No. 3, April 1914.
F. W. Pitman, 'The West Indian absentee planter as a British Colonial type', *Proceedings of the American Historical Association*, 1927.
R. B. Sheridan, 'The Wealth of Jamaica in the Eighteenth Century', *Economic History Review*, Second Series, XVIII, 2, 1965.
——, 'The Wealth of Jamaica in the Eighteenth Century: A Rejoinder', *Economic History Review*, Second Series, XXI, April 1968.
R. P. Thomas, 'The Sugar Colonies of the Old Empire: Profit or Loss for Great Britain?', *Economic History Review*, Second Series, XXI, April 1968.

Index

Increase of the Negroes on Worthy Park, Estate from 1st Janry 1787 to the 1st Janry 1788

Months	date		Males	Females	Total
January	1	To number of Negroes as Wm Genl List taken this day	165	141	3..
	14	Helen deliverd of a Girl Named Kitty	"	1	
	18	Brot from Spa Town Goal a Negroe man named Athol	1	"	
February	11	Baddy deliverd of a Boy named Petit ...	1	"	
March	8	Bought of Edwd Brailsford 30 Negroes ..	15	15	
	17	Dolly deliverd of a Mollatto Girl nama Kitty .	"	1	
April	10	Prue deliverd of a Boy Named Cyrus ...	1	"	
	20	Joany deliverd of a Girl Named Molly ...	"	1	
Sepr	24	Betsy deliverd of a Girl Nama Lucy	"	1	
Octor	22	Sigilly deliverd of a Girl named Violet	"	1	
		Litte Bess deliverd of a Boy Named Swash	1	"	
Decr	20	Emma deliverd of a Girl named Peggy	"	1	
	27	Succaba deliverd of a Boy named Rodney	1	"	1
			185	162	31

born — 10
6 dt —— 15 men ⎫ of Brailsford
0o —— 15 women ⎭